BOOKS BY
RICHMOND LATTIMORE

POETRY
Poems 1957
Sestina for a Far-off Summer
The Stride of Time
Poems from Three Decades

LITERARY HISTORY AND CRITICISM
Themes in Greek and Latin Epitaphs
The Poetry of Greek Tragedy
Story Patterns in Greek Tragedy

TRANSLATIONS
The Odes of Pindar
The Iliad of Homer
The Odyssey of Homer
Greek Lyrics
Aeschylus, Oresteia
Euripides, The Trojan Women
Euripides, Alcestis
Euripides, Helen
Euripides, Rhesus
Euripides, Iphigeneia in Tauris
Aristophanes, The Frogs
Hesiod
The Revelation of John
The Four Gospels and the Revelation
Acts and Letters of the Apostles

THE NEW
TESTAMENT

THE NEW TESTAMENT

Translated by
Richmond Lattimore

North Point Press

Farrar · Straus · Giroux

New York

North Point Press
A division of Farrar, Straus and Giroux
18 West 18th Street, New York 10011

Printed in the United States of America
First published in 1996 by North Point Press
First paperback edition, 1997

Originally published by Farrar, Straus and Giroux in two volumes as
The Four Gospels and the Revelation, copyright © 1962, 1979 by
Richmond Lattimore, and *Acts and Letters of the Apostles*, copyright
© 1982 by Richmond Lattimore

The Library of Congress has catalogued the hardcover edition as follows:
Bible. N.T. English. Lattimore. 1996.
    The New Testament / translated by Richmond Lattimore. —
1st ed.
        p.   cm.
    Originally published in 2 v. c1979–c1982.

    Paperback ISBN-13: 978-0-86547-524-3
    Paperback ISBN-10: 0-86547-524-5

    I. Lattimore, Richmond Alexander, 1906–   . II. Title.
BS2095.L26   1996
225.5'209—DC20   96-23825

PUBLISHER'S NOTE: The prefaces to each of the original volumes have
been combined in this edition, and amended slightly, for readability.

17 19 21 23 22 20 18

Contents

Preface

¶ IT WAS WHILE I WAS TEACHING VARious Greek texts to beginning students that I was struck by the natural ease with which *Revelation* turned itself into English. I undertook the translation, and *The Revelation of John* appeared as a separate volume in 1962. I continued with the Four Gospels, but with many interruptions for other tasks.

I have held throughout to the principle of keeping as close to the Greek as possible, not only for sense and for individual words, but in the belief that fidelity to the original word order and syntax may yield an English prose that to some extent reflects the style of the original. The aim of at least some other contemporary translators has been, avowedly, just the opposite: to be faithful to the sense but to render it in contemporary idiom. This is, of course, a perfectly legitimate aim, and is part of the reason why there is room for a number of modern translations.

Let me illustrate. I have translated *Mark* 10.27: "For men it is impossible, but not for God, since for God all things are possible." I could have written: "Men cannot do it, but God can do anything." That says the same thing, but does not reflect the way Mark wrote. At *John* 11.21 and 32, first Martha, then Mary says: "Lord, if you had been here, my brother would not have died." So I translated, and cannot claim originality, for the words are identical with those of the Revised Standard Version. I had thought that so simple a statement could be translated *only* in this one way. But I have not found it in any other translation that I have consulted.

Consider a more extended passage. For *Mark* 7.1–5 I have written: "Then the Pharisees gathered to him, and some of the scribes who had come from Jerusalem, seeing that some of the disciples were eating their bread with profane, that is, unwashed, hands: for the Pharisees, and all the Jews, will not eat unless they have washed hand against fist, thus keeping the tradition of their elders; and when they come from the marketplace they will not eat unless they have purified themselves, and there are many other observances that are traditional with them, the washing of cups and vessels both wooden and bronze: the Pharisees and the scribes asked him: Why do your disciples not walk according to the tradition of our elders, but eat their bread with profane hands?" Let me try to put this into what is more like a contemporary idiom: "The Pharisees, with some of the scribes, went out from Jerusalem to visit him. They noticed that some of his disciples ate without first washing their hands, which made their hands profane. The Pharisees and the Jews in general observe a tradition handed down from their ancestors not to eat without first washing their hands thoroughly. When they come in from the marketplace they will not eat until they have purified themselves. They have many other such traditions, like washing their cups, whether these are made of wood or bronze. Because of all this the

Pharisees and the scribes asked Jesus: Why do your disciples disobey our ancestral tradition by eating with profane hands?"

Now, other modern translators have modernized this passage much more successfully than I have. My heart is not in this kind of rearrangement of the syntax. Still, all the essential meaning is there. But to me it reads much less like Mark than the version which stands in my translation.

It will follow, or should, that since each of the Gospels, and *Revelation*, is the work of a different author with a different style, they should read differently in English. I noted that *Revelation* seemed to translate itself, and my aim has been to let all of my texts translate themselves with as little interference as possible. But it is not always so easy. To go from *Revelation* to *Matthew* is like going from Ruskin to Carlyle. *Mark* in particular offers problems. Since Mark is, by general if not universal consent, the earliest evangelist, we start with his gospel. Matthew and Luke drew on him extensively, but constantly saw fit to rewrite him after their own manners. He can, as illustrated above, be abrupt and crabbed. Also, the nature of the language itself produces difficulties. There are some terms, such as the various forms of *skandalon* (see note on *Matthew* 5.29, page 572), which cannot always be translated in the same way, which really cannot be translated at all, but for which the translator will have to devise some kind of paraphrase which will convey the essential sense.

¶ THE FOUR GOSPELS ARE FOLLOWED IN the New Testament by the *Acts of the Apostles*, which, though far from being a complete account, is the earliest consecutive story of early Christianity that we have. It can be regarded as a continuation of *The Gospel According to Luke*. This is implied in the opening sentence, addressed, as is the Gospel, to Theophilus; and there is little or no doubt among scholars that the author is the Luke of the Gospel.

Acts begins with the ascension of Jesus Christ to heaven and the formation of the church in Jerusalem. From there, Christianity is preached abroad by various ministers. In the early part of the story the dominant figure is Saint Peter. The second half of the work, however, becomes almost exclusively the tale of Saint Paul: his missions to the Greek cities of the Roman Empire (the Gentiles), the oppositions he encountered, his arrest in Jerusalem, and his arrival in Rome. Not long after that arrival, Luke somewhat abruptly (as it seems to me) ends his story. Paul spent some time as a prisoner in Rome. He is usually thought to have been martyred during the persecutions of Christians when Nero was Emperor, perhaps in A.D. 64, or on an individual charge before that, but the evidence is not conclusive.

Acts is usually dated with and immediately after *Luke*, about A.D. 85. That would put it considerably later than Paul's own writings. Still, it is useful to read it first, so as to have a more or less continuous background for Paul's letters.

These, the Epistles of Paul as they are canonically called, are his letters to various Christian communities or churches. They sometimes address themselves to particular problems, but also set forth, again and again, Paul's own theological doctrines and his principles for Christian behavior. There are also four letters to individuals.

For the letters of Paul I have followed a traditional order, but a better sense of time would be gained by reading them in some such order as this: First, letters written before the journey to Rome: *First* and *Second Thessalonians, Galatians, First* and *Second Corinthians, Romans*; and then the letters from Rome: *Colossians* (with *Philemon*, to a member of that community), *Ephesians*, and *Philippians*.

The two letters to Timothy and the one to Titus are commonly grouped together and known as the *Pastoral Letters*. Timothy and Titus are well known as associates of Paul, and the letters bear his characteristic self-identification at the beginning. But their authenticity has been seriously questioned. The style and language differ in places from what is characteristic of Paul's other writing, while the three do resemble one another in those respects. *First Timothy* and *Titus* speak of the institution of bishops and elders, which seems to point to a later stage in the development of the Church.

The Letter to the Hebrews is included with the letters of Paul, but the name of Paul does not appear in the text. There have been many speculations about date and authorship, but no final answer (except, perhaps, that it is not by Paul).

Next comes the group known as *The General Letters* (or *Catholic Epistles, Epistoloi Katholikoi*). The name signifies that they are addressed (most of them at least) to the whole Christian community rather than to separate churches, as Paul's letters were. *The Letter of James* is believed by some to be the work of James the brother of Jesus Christ, one of the chief men in the original church in Jerusalem. *The First Letter of Peter* is often credited to the great apostle himself. Not so *The Second Letter of Peter*, which has close affinities with *The Letter of Jude*.

This, in turn, may just possibly be from the hand of the Jude (Judah, Judas) who was also a brother of Jesus Christ. As for the three letters ascribed to John, the second two are brief real letters apparently by the same writer. *The First Letter of John*, though it, too, may be by the same author, is quite different. It is a tract or homily, which shows strong resemblances to the Fourth Gospel, and is thought by some to be the work of the same John. Not one of these attributions can be called certain.

In general, I have translated *Acts and Letters* as a companion piece to *The Four Gospels*, following the same principle of trying to let the authors of the Greek speak for themselves in English. In the case of Saint Paul, that has not always been so easy.

I have written some simple notes, to explain my translations or give alternative interpretations. Without competence to comment on the manuscript tradition, I have simply followed the text of Westcott and Hort, *The New Testament in Greek* (New York: Macmillan, 1957). The rare exceptions have been noted. Words enclosed in square brackets are of doubtful authenticity. I have also regularly consulted *The Pelican Gospel Commentaries*, namely, D. E. Nineham, *Saint Mark*; J. C. Fenton, *Saint Matthew*; G. B. Caird, *Saint Luke*; and John Marsh, *Saint John*.

I have also made far greater use of the great dictionary which can be cited, briefly, as W. F. Arndt and F. W. Gingrich (and now F. W. Danker), *A Greek-English Lexicon of the New Testament and Other Early Christian Literature*, 2nd edition (Chicago and London: University of Chicago Press, 1958).

It is a pleasure to record my obligations and thanks: to my publishers; to Alice Lattimore for help in preparing the manuscript; to Frederick Morgan for recommending publication, and to the memory of Fred Wieck, the earliest editor of my poems and translations.

MARK

Mark is believed to have written his gospel after Peter's death in Rome, which is presumed to have been around A.D. 64. It is generally agreed that Mark's is the earliest of the four gospels.

⟨ THE BEGINNING OF THE GOSPEL OF Jesus Christ. As it is written in Isaiah the prophet: Behold, I send forth my messenger before your face, who will make ready your way. The voice of one crying in the desert: prepare the way of the Lord, make straight the roads before him. John the Baptist was in the desert preaching the baptism of repentance for the remission of sins. And all the land of Judaea came out to him and all the people of Jerusalem, and they were baptized by him in the river Jordan, confessing their sins. John was clothed in camel's hair, and a belt of hide around his waist, and he ate locusts and wild honey. And he preached, saying: He who is stronger than I is coming after me, and I am not fit to stoop down and untie the thong of his shoes. I baptized you with water, but he will baptize you with the Holy Spirit.

And it happened in those days that Jesus came from Nazareth in Galilee and was baptized in the Jordan by John. And as soon as he came out of the water he saw the skies split and the Spirit like a dove descending upon him; and there came a voice from the skies, saying: You are my son whom I love, with you I am well pleased. And immediately the Spirit drove him out into the desert. And he was in the desert forty days, being tested by Satan, and he lived with the wild animals, and the angels served him.

After John was betrayed Jesus came into Galilee preaching the gospel of God, saying: The time is fulfilled and the Kingdom of God is near. Repent and believe in the gospel. And as he went along past the Sea of Galilee, he saw Simon and Andrew the brother of Simon casting their nets in the sea, for they were fishermen. And Jesus said to them: Come, follow me, and I will make you fishers of men. And at once they left their nets and followed him. And going on a little farther he saw James the son of Zebedee and John his brother, these also in their boat mending their nets. And at once he called them. And leaving their father Zebedee in the boat with the hired workers they went away, and followed him.

They came into Capernaum. And at once on the sabbath he went into the synagogue and taught; and they were astonished at his teaching, for he taught them as one who has authority and not like the scribes. And immediately in their synagogue there was a man possessed by an unclean spirit, and he cried out, saying: What is there between us and you, Jesus of Nazareth? Did you come to destroy us? I know you, who you are, God's holy one. Jesus reproved him, saying: Be silent and go out from him. And convulsing him and crying out in a great voice the unclean spirit went out of the man. All were amazed, so that they took counsel together, saying: What is this thing: a new kind of teaching? By his authority he gives orders even to unclean spirits, and they obey him. And immediately the rumor of him spread into the whole region about Galilee.

When they came out of the synagogue, they went immediately to the house of Simon and Andrew, along with James and John. And Simon's mother-in-law was lying in a fever, and they told him about her forthwith. He went over and took her by the hand and raised her; and the fever left her, and she served them. When it was evening, after the sun set, they brought to him all those who were ill, and those afflicted with demons, and the whole city was assembled before his door. And he healed many who were ill with various diseases, and he cast out many demons, and would not let them speak, because they knew him. Then very early in the morning he got up and went out to a lonely place, and there he prayed. Simon and his companions went in search of him, and found him, and said to him: All are looking for you. He said to them: Let us go elsewhere, to the neighboring communities, so that I may preach there also; for that is what I set out to do. And he went into all of Galilee preaching in the synagogues and casting out demons.

A leper came to him and entreated him, saying: If you wish, you can make me clean. He took pity on him, and stretched out his hand and touched him, saying: I wish it; be clean. And at once the leprosy went from him, and he was made clean. Then he sent him away at once with a stern order, saying: See that you tell no one, but go and show yourself to the priest, and bring him the gift for your purification that Moses ordained, as a proof to them. But the man went out and began to talk about it at length and spread the story about, so that Jesus could no longer come openly into the city, but must remain outside in unfrequented places. And they came to him from every direction.

¶ When he returned to Capernaum, it became known, after a few days, that he was in a house there; and so many gathered that there was no space before the door and he preached the word to them. They came bringing him a paralytic who was carried aloft by four men. When they could not reach him because of the crowd, they took away the roof from over the place where Jesus was, and when they had made an opening they lowered the bed where the paralytic lay. Jesus seeing their faith said to the paralytic: My child, your sins are forgiven. There were some of the scribes sitting by, and they said to themselves in their hearts: Why does this man talk this way? He blasphemes. Who can forgive sins, except God alone? Jesus knew at once in his mind what they were saying to themselves, and said: Why do you have such thoughts in your hearts? Which is easier, to say to the paralytic: Your sins are forgiven, or to say: Arise, take up your bed and walk about? But so that you may know that the son of man has authority to forgive sins upon earth—he said to the paralytic: I tell you, rise, take up your bed, and go to your house. And the man arose and took up his bed and went out, in the sight of all; so that all were astonished and glorified God, saying: We have never seen the like.

He went back to the seaside; and all the multitude came to him, and he taught them. As he went by, he saw Levi the son of Alphaeus sitting in the tollhouse, and said to him: Follow me. And he stood up and followed him. And it happened that he dined in his house, and many tax collectors and sinners dined with Jesus and his disciples;

for there were many of them, and they followed him. The scribes of the Pharisees, seeing that he ate with sinners and tax collectors, said to his disciples: Why does he eat with tax collectors and sinners? Jesus heard them, and said to them: The strong do not need a physician, but those who are in poor health. I did not come to summon the just, but the sinners.

The disciples of John, and the Pharisees, were fasting. And they came and said to him: Why do the disciples of John and the disciples of the Pharisees fast, but your disciples do not fast? Jesus said to them: Surely the members of the wedding party cannot fast while the bridegroom is with them? For as long a time as they have the bridegroom with them they cannot fast. The days will come when the bridegroom is taken away from them; then on that day they will fast. No one sews a patch of unfulled cloth on an old coat; if he does, the new filling pulls from the old and makes the tear worse. And no one puts new wine into old skins; if he does, the wine will break the skins, and both wine and skins are lost.

It came about that on the sabbath he went walking through the sown fields, and his disciples began to pick the ears of grain as they went. And the Pharisees said to him: Why are your disciples doing what is forbidden on the sabbath? He said to them: Have you never read what David did when he was in need, and hungry, he himself and those with him? He went into the house of God when Abiathar was high priest, and ate the show bread, which none but the priests are permitted to eat, and gave it also to those who were with him. And he said to them: The sabbath was made for the sake of man, not man for the sake of the sabbath. Thus the son of man is lord even of the sabbath.

❡ Once again he entered the synagogue, and there was a man there with an arm that was withered. They were watching him to see if he would heal him on the sabbath, so that they might bring a charge against him. Jesus said to the man with the withered arm: Come out into our midst. Then he said to them: Is it permitted to do good or evil on the sabbath, to save a life or destroy it? They were silent. He looked around at them in anger, exasperated at the hardness of their hearts, and said to the man: Stretch out your arm. And he stretched it out, and it became sound again. Then the Pharisees went out and immediately began plotting against him, together with the Herodians, to destroy him.

Then Jesus with his disciples withdrew to the seashores, and a great multitude followed from Galilee, and from Judaea and from Jerusalem and from Idumaea and from beyond the Jordan and the region of Tyre and Sidon; a great multitude came to him when they heard what he was doing. And he told his disciples that they should secure a boat for him, because of the crowd, so that they should not crush him; for he healed many, so that they thrust in upon him, to have those who were in torment touch him. And the unclean spirits when they saw him fell down before him and cried out, saying: You are the son of God. And he charged them many times not to divulge what he was doing.

Then he went up on the mountain and summoned to him those whom he had chosen; and they went forth and joined him. He made the number twelve, whom he named apostles, so that they might be with him, and so that he might send them forth to preach and to have authority to cast out demons. He established the twelve, Peter, the name he gave to Simon, and James the son of Zebedee and John the brother of James (and he gave them the name Boanerges, which means sons of thunder), and Andrew and Philip and Bartholomew and Matthew and Thomas and James the son of Alphaeus and Thaddeus and Simon the Cananaean and Judas Iscariot, who in fact betrayed him.

Then he went into a house; and the crowd gathered again, so that they could not even eat their bread. When his own people heard of this, they went forth to get control of him, for they said that he was out of his mind. And the scribes who had come down from Jerusalem said that Beelzebub had hold of him, and that it was through the prince of the demons that he drove out demons. He called them to him and said to them through parables: How can Satan drive out Satan? And if a kingdom is divided against itself, that kingdom cannot stand. And if a house is divided against itself, that house will not be able to stand. And if Satan rises up against himself and is divided, he cannot stand but comes to an end. But no one can go into the house of the strong man and seize his goods, unless first he binds the strong man; then he can plunder his house. Truly I tell you, all shall be forgiven the sons of men, their sins and such blasphemies as they may speak; but if one blasphemes against the Holy Spirit, he shall have no forgiveness ever, but shall be guilty of everlasting sin. This was because they said he had an unclean spirit. Then his mother and his brothers came and stood outside and sent one in to summon him. The crowd was seated around him, and they said to him: See, your mother and your brothers are outside looking for you. He answered and said to them: Who is my mother and who are my brothers? And looking about at those who were sitting in a circle around him, he said: Here is my mother, here are my brothers; whoever does the will of God is my brother and sister and mother.

¶ Once again he began to teach beside the seashore. And the greatest multitude gathered to hear him, so that he went aboard the ship and was seated out to sea, and all the multitude was on shore facing the sea. He taught them a great deal in parables, and said to them in his discourse: Listen. Behold, a sower went out to sow. And it happened as he sowed that some of the grain fell beside the way, and birds came and ate it. Some fell on stony ground where there was not much soil, and it shot up quickly because there was no depth of soil; and when the sun came up it was parched and because it had no roots it dried away. Some fell among thorns, and the thorns grew up and stifled it, and it bore no fruit. But some fell upon the good soil, and it bore fruit, and shot up and increased, and yielded thirtyfold and sixtyfold and a hundredfold. And he said: He who has ears, let him hear. When they were alone, his followers along with the twelve asked him about the parables. He said to them: To you are given the secrets of the Kingdom of God; but to those who are outside all comes through parables, so that they may have sight but not see, and hear but not understand, lest they be converted and forgiven. And he said to them: You did not read this parable? Then how shall you understand all the parables? The sower sows the word. And these are the ones beside the way where the word is sown, and as soon as they hear it Satan comes and snatches the word that has been sown among them. And there are some who are as if sown on stony ground, who when they hear the word accept it with joy; and they have no roots in themselves but are men of the moment, and when there comes affliction and persecution, because of the word, they do not stand fast. And others are those who were sown among thorns; these are the ones who hear the word, and concern for the world and the beguilement of riches and desires for other things come upon them and stifle the word, and it bears no fruit. And the others are those who were sown upon the good soil, who hear the word and accept it and bear fruit thirtyfold and sixtyfold and a hundredfold. Then he said to them: Surely the lamp is not brought in so as to be set under a basket or under the bed rather than to be set on a stand; for there is nothing hidden except to be shown, nor anything concealed except to be brought to light. He who has ears to hear, let him hear. And he said to them: Consider what you hear. Your measure will be made by the measure by which you measure, and more shall be added for you. When a man has, he shall be given; when one has not, even what he has shall be taken away from him. And he said: The Kingdom of God is as when a man sows his seed in the ground, and sleeps and wakes night and day, and the seed grows and increases without his knowing it; for of itself the earth bears fruit, first the blade, then the ear, then the full grain in the ear. But when the grain gives its yield, he puts forth the sickle, for the time of harvesting is come. And he said: To what shall we liken the Kingdom of God, and in what parable shall we place it? It is like the seed of mustard, which when it is sown in the ground is smaller than all the seeds on earth, but when it has been sown, it shoots up and becomes greater than all the other greens, and puts forth great branches, so that the birds of the air may nest in its shadow. With many such parables he spoke the word to them, according to what they could comprehend; but he did not talk with them except in parables; but privately with his own disciples he expounded all.

That same day when it was evening he said to them: Let us cross over to the other side. They sent away the multitude and took him along on the ship just as he was, and there were other ships with him. There came a sudden great storm of wind, and waves dashed against the ship so that it was beginning to fill. He was in the stern asleep with his head on his pillow; and they woke him and said: Master, do you not care whether we perish? He woke and scolded the wind and said to the sea: Silence, be still. And the sea subsided and there was a great calm. Then he said to them: Why are you frightened? Do you not yet have faith? And they were seized with a great fear and said to each other: Who is this, that the wind and sea obey him?

◀ They reached the other side of the sea and the land of the Gerasenes. As Jesus stepped from the ship, a man possessed by an unclean spirit came out of the tombs and met him. He had made his dwelling among the tombs, and nobody could now bind him with chains; because he had often been bound with chains and fetters, and the chains had been torn apart by him and the fetters pounded to pieces, and no one was strong enough to subdue him. Day long and night long he was among the tombs and the hills, crying aloud and beating himself with stones. Seeing Jesus from afar he ran to him and bowed down before him and cried out in a great voice, saying: What have I to do with you, Jesus, son of the most high God? I adjure you before God, do not torment me. For Jesus had been saying to him: Go forth, unclean spirit, from the man. And he asked him: What is your name? He answered: My name is Legion, because we are many. And he implored him at length not to send them out of the country. By the hillside there was a great herd of swine feeding; and the spirits implored him, saying: Send us into the swine, so we may enter into them. He consented. And the unclean spirits came forth and entered into the swine, and the herd rushed over the cliff into the sea, as many as two thousand, and were drowned in the sea. Those who had been herding them fled and carried the news to the city and the countryside; and people came to see what had happened. Then they came up to Jesus, and they saw the man who had been possessed by demons sitting clothed and in his right mind, the man who had had the legion, and they were frightened. Those who had seen told them how it had happened with the man possessed by demons, and about the swine. And they began to entreat him to leave their territory. As he boarded the ship, the man who had been afflicted by demons asked if he could go along with him. Jesus refused him and said: Go home to your people and tell them what your lord did for you and how he took pity on you. And he went, and began to report in the Decapolis what Jesus had done for him. And all marveled.

After Jesus had crossed with his ship back to the other side, a great crowd gathered about him; and he was by the sea. And there came to him one of the leaders of the synagogue, Jairus by name, and when he saw him he fell at his feet and implored him at length, saying: My little daughter is at the point of death; so come and lay your hands upon her, so that she may recover and live. He went with him; and a great throng followed, and they were crowding against him. There was a woman who had been bleeding for twelve years, and had been treated in many ways by many physicians, and had spent all that she had, and got no benefit but rather got worse; she had heard about Jesus, and she came up behind him in the crowd and touched his mantle; for she said to herself: If I touch only his mantle I shall be healed. And immediately the source of her flow of blood dried up, and she knew in her body that she had been healed of her affliction. Immediately Jesus felt in himself that power had gone forth from him, and he turned about and said: Who touched my mantle? His disciples said to him: Do you see the throng that is crowding upon you, and yet do you ask: Who touched me? And he looked around to see who had done it. And the woman, in fear and trembling, knowing what had happened to her, threw herself down before him and told him the whole truth. He said to her: My daughter, your faith has saved you; go in peace and be healed of your affliction. While he was still talking, they came from the house of the leader of the synagogue saying: Your daughter has died; why do you continue to trouble the master? Jesus disregarded the talk that was going on and said to the leader of the synagogue: Have no fear, only have faith. And he would not let anyone follow him except Peter and James and John the brother of James. They entered the house of the leader of the synagogue, and he was aware of a great tumult, and people weeping and lamenting greatly, and going in he said to them: Why this tumult and weeping? The child has not died, she is asleep. They laughed at him. He drove out all the others, and took with him the father and mother of the child and those who were with him, and went in where the child was; and he

took the child's hand, and said to her: Talitha cum; which
is, translated: Little girl, I say to you: Awake. At once the
little girl got up and walked about, for she was twelve
years old. They were seized with great amazement. And
he charged them at length that no one should be told
about this; and he said she should be given something to
eat.

¶ He left that place and went to his own country, and his
disciples followed him. When it was the sabbath he began
to teach in the synagogue; and most of those who heard
him were astonished and said: From where does the man
derive all this, and what is this wisdom that has been
given to him, and what are these powers that are fulfilled
by his hands? Is not this the carpenter, the son of Mary
and the brother of James and Joseph and Judas and Simon?
And are not his sisters here among us? And they made it
difficult for him. Jesus said to them: No prophet is rejected except in his own country, and among his own
kinsmen, and in his own house. And he could not exercise
any power there, except that he laid his hands on a few
who were sick and healed them; and he marveled at
their lack of faith.

He circulated among the villages, teaching. And he
summoned the twelve and began to send them out two by
two, and he gave them power over unclean spirits, and he
instructed them not to take anything with them for the
journey, except only a staff, no bread, no bag, no coppers
for the money belt, with sandals on their feet, and no
extra tunic. And he said to them: Once you enter a house,
remain there until you leave the district. And when a
place will not receive you and people will not listen to

you, as you leave it shake the dust from the soles of your feet in witness against them. And they went forth and preached the message of repentance, and drove out many demons, and anointed with oil many who were sick, and healed them.

Now King Herod heard of this, for the name of Jesus had become well known to him; and they were saying that John the Baptist had risen from the dead, and for that reason the powers were working in him. But others said that it was Elijah, and others that it was a prophet, like one of the Prophets. But when Herod heard of it, he said: This is John whom I beheaded. He has arisen. For Herod himself had sent men out and seized John and confined him in prison, on account of Herodias the wife of Philip his brother and his marriage to her. For John had said to Herod: It is not lawful for you to take the wife of your brother. Herodias held a grudge against him and wished to kill him, but she was not able to; for Herod was afraid of John, knowing that he was a just and holy man, and he kept him safe; and when he listened to him he was much perplexed, and yet he listened with pleasure. Then her opportunity came when Herod on his birthday gave a banquet for the nobles and captains and foremost people of Galilee; and the daughter of Herodias came before them and danced, and she pleased Herod and his guests. And the king said to the girl: Ask me what you wish and I will give it to you. And he swore to her: Whatever you ask me for I will give you, up to half of my kingdom. She went out and said to her mother: What shall I ask for? She said: The head of John the Baptist. So she hastened back to the king and made her request, saying: I wish you to give me forthwith the head of John the Baptist, on a platter. Though the king was grieved, because of the oaths and the guests he was unwilling to deny her; and immediately he sent a guardsman with orders to bring back his head. And the man went and beheaded him in the prison and brought his head on a platter and gave it to the girl, and the girl gave it to her mother. When his disciples heard of it they came and took up the body and laid it in a tomb.

The apostles rejoined Jesus and reported all they had done and all their teaching. He said to them: Come with me, you only, to a private place and rest a while. For there were many coming and going and they had no opportunity even to eat. And they went away on their ship, privately, to a deserted place. But many saw them going and were aware of them, and from all the cities they ran together on foot to that place, and arrived there before them. When he came ashore, he saw a great multitude, and he was sorry for them because they were like sheep without a shepherd, and he began to teach them at length. As it was growing very late, his disciples came to him and said: This is a lonely place and the time is late. Send them away so they may go to the farms and the villages round about and buy themselves something to eat. He answered and said to them: You give them something to eat. They said to him: Shall we go and buy two hundred denarii worth of loaves and give them to them to eat? But he said to them: How many loaves do you have? Go and see. When they had found out, they said: Five, and two fish. He gave them orders that all should be set down party by party on the green grass; and they took their places group by group, fifty and a hundred at a time. Then he took the five loaves and the two fish, and looked up into the sky, and gave a blessing, and broke the loaves and gave them to his disciples to set before them; and he divided the two fish among all. And all ate, and were fed; and they took up enough broken pieces of bread and fish to fill twelve baskets. Those who ate the loaves were five thousand men.

Immediately then he made his disciples board the ship and go on before him to the other side, to Bethsaida, while he was dismissing the multitude. When he had taken leave of them, he went off to the mountain to pray. When it was evening the ship was in the middle of the sea, and he was alone on the land. And seeing that they had to struggle to row, for the wind was against them, about the fourth watch of the night he came to them walking on the sea. He meant to pass by them. But when they saw him walking on the sea, they thought he was a phantom, and cried out; for they all saw him and they were shaken. At once he talked with them and said: Take heart, it is I. Do not fear. He went aboard the ship and was among them, and the wind fell. But they were still all too much disturbed, for they had not understood about the loaves, but their hearts had become impenetrable.

They crossed over to the other shore and came to Gennesaret and moored there. And when they disembarked, people at once recognized him, and overran that whole country and began to bring their afflicted out on litters wherever they heard that he was. And wherever he went, into villages and cities and farms, and in the public places, they set down their sick, and begged that these might only touch the hem of his mantle. And those who touched it were healed.

❡ Then the Pharisees gathered to him, and some of the scribes who had come from Jerusalem, seeing that some of the disciples were eating their bread with profane, that is, unwashed, hands: for the Pharisees, and all the Jews, will not eat unless they have washed hand against fist, thus keeping the tradition of their elders; and when they come from the marketplace they will not eat unless they have purified themselves, and there are many other observances that are traditional with them, the washing of cups and vessels both wooden and bronze: the Pharisees and the scribes asked him: Why do your disciples not walk according to the tradition of our elders, but eat their bread with profane hands? He said to them: Well did Isaiah prophesy concerning you hypocrites, as it is written: This people honors me with the lips, but their heart is far away from me; they worship me vainly, teaching doctrines which are the precepts of men: relinquishing the commandment of God you cling to the tradition of men. And he said to them: You do well to reject the commandment of God so that you may keep your own tradition. For Moses said: Give due right to your father and mother; and: Let him who speaks rudely to his father or mother be put to death. But you say: If a man says to his father or his mother: Whatever I owe you is Corban, which means "gift to God," then you no longer let him do anything for his father or mother, making void the word of God through that tradition which you hand down. And you do many other things of such a nature as this.

Then he summoned the multitude once again and said to them: Listen to me and understand. There is nothing which can go into a man from the outside and defile him; but it is what comes out of a man that defiles him. And when he went indoors, away from the multitude, his disciples asked him about the parable. He said to them: Are even you so unable to understand? Do you not see that anything that goes into a man from the outside cannot defile him, because it passes not into the heart but into the belly, and thence goes into the privy? Thus he made all food clean. Then he said: What comes out of a man, that is what defiles him; for from inside the hearts of men proceed the vile thoughts, fornications, thefts, murders, adulteries, greedy dealings, vices, trickery, laxity, the vicious eye, blasphemy, pride, wildness. All these vicious things come from inside, and they defile a man.

He removed from there and went to the region around Tyre. There he entered a house and wished that no one should know him, but he could not remain hidden. Immediately a woman whose little daughter was possessed by an unclean spirit heard about him, and she came and threw herself at his feet. This was a Greek woman, by birth a Phoenician from Syria; and she asked him to drive out the demon from her daughter. He said to her: First let the children be fed; for it is not good to take the bread of the children and throw it to the dogs. But she answered him and said: Yes, Lord, even the dogs under the table eat of the children's crumbs. He said to her: Because of this saying, go; the demon has left your daughter. And she went back to her house and found the child lying on her bed, and the demon was gone.

Returning again from the region of Tyre, he went by way of Sidon to the Sea of Galilee through the middle of the Decapolis territory. They brought him a man who was deaf and could barely speak, and entreated him to lay his hand upon him. Then taking him away from the throng by himself, he put his fingers into the man's ears, and spat, and touched his tongue, and looked up into the sky and groaned and said to him: Ephphatha, which means: Be opened. And his ears were opened, and the binding of his tongue was dissolved, and he spoke normally. He charged them to tell no one but the more he charged them the more they spread the news. And they were very much astonished, saying: He has done everything well, and he makes the deaf hear and the speechless speak.

❡ In those days, when there was once again a great multitude and they did not have anything to eat, Jesus called his disciples to him and said to them: I have pity for the multitude, because it is now three days they have stayed with me, and they have nothing to eat; and if I send them home hungry they will give out on the way. And some of them come from far away. His disciples answered him, saying: How shall we have enough bread in the desert to be able to feed these people? He asked them: How many loaves do you have? They said: Seven. Then he gave the word to the people to settle on the ground, and he took the seven loaves and gave thanks and broke them and gave them to his disciples to set before the people; and they set them before the multitude. And they had a few small fish; and he blessed them and told them to serve these also. And they ate and were fed, and they picked up what was left over from the broken pieces, seven baskets full. There were about four thousand people. Then he sent them away; and immediately embarking on the ship with his disciples he made for Dalmanutha and those parts.

Then the Pharisees came forth and began to argue with him, demanding that he give them a sign from the sky, making trial of him. He groaned in his spirit and said: Why does this generation ask for a sign? Truly I tell you, no sign shall be given to this generation. Then he left them, and going on board once more he crossed over to the other side. They had forgotten to take bread and except for one loaf they had nothing with them on the ship. He enjoined them, saying: Look to it, beware of the leaven of the Pharisees and the leaven of Herod. They were talking among themselves about not having bread. And he was aware of it and said to them: Why do you talk about not having bread? Do you not yet see, do you not understand? Are your hearts impenetrable? Do you have eyes, but do not see, and ears, but do not hear? And do you not remember when I broke the five loaves for the five thousand, how many baskets full of fragments you picked up? And they told him: Twelve. And when it was seven for the four thousand, how many basketfuls of fragments did you pick up? And they told him: Seven. And he said to them: Do you still not understand?

They came to Bethsaida. And they brought him a blind man and entreated him to touch him. And he took the blind man's hand and brought him away outside the village, and spat in his eyes, and laid his hands on him, and asked him: Do you see anything? He looked again and said: I see people, like seeing trees walking about. Then again he put his hands over his eyes, and the man looked hard, and recovered, and saw all things clearly. And Jesus sent him home, saying: Do not even go into the village.

Then Jesus and his disciples went forth to the villages of Caesarea Philippi; and on the way he questioned his disciples, asking them: Who do people say that I am? They answered and said: John the Baptist; and others say Elijah, and others one of the prophets. Then he asked them: And you, who do you say I am? Peter answered and said to him: You are the Christ. Then he warned them to tell no one about him.

Then he began to explain to them that the son of man must suffer much and be rejected by the elders and the high priests and the scribes, and be killed, and rise up after three days. He was telling them frankly. And Peter laid his hand upon him and tried to warn him, and he turned about and looked at his disciples and reproved Peter and said: Go behind me, Satan; because you do not think the thoughts of God, but of men.

Then summoning the multitude together with his disciples, he said to them: If anyone wishes to go after me, let him deny himself and take up his cross and follow me. For he who wishes to save his life shall lose it; and he who loses his life for the sake of me and the gospel shall save it. For what does it advantage a man to gain the whole world and pay for it with his life? What can a man give that is worth as much as his life? He who is ashamed of me and my words in this adulterous and sinful generation, of him will the son of man be ashamed when he comes in the glory of his father with the holy angels.

¶ And he said to them: Truly I tell you that there are some of those who stand here who will not taste of death until they see the Kingdom of God arrived in power.

Then after six days Jesus took with him Peter and James and John, and led them up on a high mountain, alone, by themselves. And he was transfigured before them, and his clothing turned very white, gleaming with a whiteness no fuller on earth could give. And Elijah was seen by them, with Moses, and they were talking with Jesus. And Peter spoke forth and said to Jesus: Master, it is good for us to be here; and let us make three shelters, one for you and one for Moses and one for Elijah. For he did not know what to say, for they were very frightened. And there came a cloud that covered them, and there came a voice from the cloud: This is my son whom I love; listen to him. And suddenly looking around they could no longer see anyone with them, except Jesus alone. As they came down from the mountain he charged them that they should tell no one what they had seen, except when the son of man should rise up from the dead. And they kept his commandment, while questioning among themselves what it might mean to rise from the dead. And they questioned him, saying: What do the scribes mean that first Elijah must come? He said to them: Elijah shall come first and restore all things. And how is it written about the son of man, that he must suffer much and be set at nought? But I say to you that Elijah came and they did with him as they wished, as it is written about him.

As they returned to the disciples, they saw a great crowd about them, and scribes arguing with them. And as soon as they saw him all the multitude were greatly amazed, and at once they ran up to him and greeted him. And he asked them: What are you discussing with them? A man in the crowd answered him: Master, I have brought my son to you. He has a speechless spirit. And when this seizes upon him, it batters him, and he foams and his teeth chatter, and he wastes away. I told your disciples to drive it out, and they were not able to. He answered and said to them: O generation without faith, how long shall I be with you? How long shall I endure you? Bring him to me. And they brought him to him. When he saw Jesus, the spirit at once convulsed the boy, and he fell on the ground and rolled about, foaming. Then Jesus asked the father: How long has this been happening to him? He said: Since he was little; and many times it has thrown him into fire and into water, to destroy him. But if you can, take pity on us and help us. Jesus said to

him: If you can? All things are possible to him who believes. At once the father of the boy cried out and said: I
believe. Help my unbelief. Jesus seeing that the crowd
was growing around him admonished the unclean spirit,
saying to it: You speechless deaf spirit, I command you, go
forth from him, and never enter him again. And the spirit,
with much screaming and struggling, went out of the boy;
and he became like a corpse, so that most of the people
said he had died. But Jesus took him by the hand and
raised him up, and he stood. When he had gone indoors,
his disciples asked him privately: Why were we not able
to drive it out? He said to them: This kind cannot be
made to go forth except by prayer.

Going from there they proceeded through Galilee, and
he did not want anyone to be aware of them; for he was
teaching his disciples, and telling them: The son of man
will be turned over into the hands of men, and they will
kill him; and three days after being killed he will rise up.
But they did not understand what he said, and they were
afraid to ask him.

They came to Capernaum; and when he was indoors,
he asked them: What were you talking about on the way?
They were silent, for they had been talking on the way
about who was the greatest. He sat down and called the
twelve and said to them: Whoever wishes to be first must
be last of all and servant of all. And taking a child he set
him in the midst of them, and embraced him, and said:
Whoever accepts a child like one of these in my name,
accepts me; and he who accepts me accepts not me but
him who sent me.

John said to him: Master, we saw a man driving out
demons in your name, and we tried to stop him, because
he was not one of our following. But Jesus said: Do not

stop him; for there is no one who will exercise power in my name and then will be able to speak ill of me. For he who is not against us is for us. For if anyone gives you a cup of water to drink because you are named as being Christ's, truly I tell you he shall not lose his reward. And if anyone misleads one of these little ones who have faith, it were better for him to have a millstone hung about his neck and be thrown into the sea. And if your hand makes you go amiss, cut it off; it is better for you to go into life one-handed than with both hands to wander off into Gehenna, into the quenchless fire. And if your foot makes you go amiss, cut it off; it is better for you to go into life lame than with both feet to be thrown into Gehenna. And if your eye makes you go amiss, pluck it out; it is better for you to go one-eyed into the Kingdom of God than with both eyes to be thrown into Gehenna, where their worm does not die and the fire is not quenched. For everyone will be salted with fire. Salt is good; but if the salt is salt no more, with what will you season it? Keep the salt in yourselves, and be at peace with each other.

❦ Removing from there, he went into the territory of Judea and beyond the Jordan, and again crowds gathered about him, and again he taught them as he was accustomed to do. And Pharisees came to him and asked him whether it were lawful for a man to divorce his wife, making trial of him. He answered and said to them: What did Moses decree for you? They said: Moses permitted a man to write a note of divorce, and so divorce her. But Jesus said to them: It was for your hardness of heart that he wrote you this commandment. But from the beginning of creation God made them male and female. Because of this a man will leave his father and his mother, and they will be two in one flesh. So that they are no longer two but one flesh. Then what God has joined together let man not separate. At the house his disciples questioned him again about this. And he told them: He who divorces his wife and marries another is committing adultery against her, and if she has divorced her husband and marries another she is committing adultery.

And they brought children to him, so that he might lay his hands on them. And his disciples scolded them. But seeing this, Jesus was vexed and said to them: Let the children come to me and do not prevent them; for of such is the Kingdom of God. Truly I tell you, he who does not receive the Kingdom of God like a child may not enter into it. And he embraced them and blessed them, laying his hands upon them.

As he set forth on his way, a man ran up and knelt before him and asked him: Good master, what must I do to inherit life everlasting? Jesus answered: Why do you call me good? No one is good but God alone. You know the commandments: Do not murder, do not commit adultery, do not steal, do not bear false witness, do not defraud; honor your father and your mother. He said to him: Master, I have kept all these commandments from my youth. Jesus looked at him with affection and said: One thing you lack: go sell all you have and give it to the poor, and you shall have a treasury in heaven; and come and follow me. He was downcast at that saying and went sadly away; for he was one who had many possessions. Jesus looked around at his disciples and said: How hard it will be for those with money to enter the Kingdom of God. His disciples were astonished at his words. But Jesus spoke forth again and said to them: My children, how hard it is to enter the Kingdom of God; it is easier for a camel to pass through the eye of a needle than for a rich man to enter the Kingdom of God. They were very much astonished and asked him: Who then can be saved? Jesus looked at them and said: For men it is impossible, but not for God, since for God all things are possible. Peter began to say to him: See, we have given up everything and followed you. And Jesus said: Truly I tell you, there is no one who has given up house or brothers or sisters or mother or father or children or lands for the sake of me and the gospel who will not receive a hundredfold [now in this time, houses and brothers and sisters and mothers and children and lands, with persecutions], and in the time to come life everlasting. And many who are first shall be last, and many who are last shall be first.

They were on the road going up to Jerusalem, and Jesus was leading the way, and they were amazed, and those who followed were afraid. And taking the twelve again, he began to tell them what was going to happen to him: Behold, we are going up to Jerusalem, and the son of man will be given over to the high priests and the scribes, and they will condemn him to death, and give him over to the Gentiles, and they will mock him and spit upon him and flog him, and kill him, and after three days he will rise.

Then James and John, the sons of Zebedee, came up to him and said: Master, we wish you to do for us whatever we ask you to. He said to them: What do you wish me to do for you? They said to him: Grant us that in your glory we may sit one on your right and one on your left. Jesus said to them: You do not know what you are asking. Can you drink the cup which I drink, or be baptized with the baptism with which I am baptized? They said to him: We can. Jesus said to them: You shall drink the cup which I drink, and be baptized with the baptism with which I am baptized; but to sit on my right or on my left, that is not mine to give, but it is theirs for whom it has been made ready. When the other ten heard about it, they began to be indignant over James and John. And Jesus called them to him and said: You know that those who are supposed to rule over the Gentiles act as lords over them and their great men exercise power over them. It is not thus with you; but he who wishes to be great among you shall be your servant, and he who wishes to be first among you shall be the slave of all; for the son of man came not to be served but to serve, and to give his own life for the redemption of many.

And they came to Jericho. And as he was on his way out of Jericho with his disciples and a considerable multitude, Bartimaeus the son of Timaeus, a blind beggar, was sitting by the road. And hearing that it was Jesus of Nazareth, he began to cry aloud and say: Jesus, son of David, have pity on me. And many people told him angrily to be quiet, but he cried out all the more: Son of David, have pity on me. And Jesus stopped and said: Call him. And they called the blind man, saying to him: Take heart, rise up, he is calling you. He threw off his mantle and sprang to his feet and went to Jesus. Jesus spoke forth and said: What do you wish me to do for you? The blind man said to him: Master, let me see again. And Jesus said to him: Go; your faith has healed you. And at once he could see again, and he followed him on his way.

⁌ When they came near Jerusalem, to Bethphage and Bethany, at the Mount of Olives, he sent two of his disciples ahead and told them: Go into the village that lies before you, and presently as you go in you will find a colt, tethered, on which no man has ever ridden. Untie him and bring him. And if anyone says to you: Why are you doing this? say: His master needs him; and he will return him to this place at once. And they went and found a colt tethered by the door, outside in the street, and they untied him. And some of those who were standing there said to them: What are you doing, untying the colt? They answered as Jesus had told them; and they let them be. And they brought the colt to Jesus, and they piled their clothing upon the colt, and he sat on him. And many strewed their clothing in the road, and others strewed branches they had cut in the countryside. And those who went before him and who came after him cried aloud: Hosanna. Blessed is he who comes in the name of the Lord. Blessed is the kingdom of our father David that is coming. Hosanna in the highest! And he entered into Jerusalem, into the temple; and after looking about at everything, since the time was now late, he went out to Bethany with the twelve.

On the next day as they went out from Bethany, he was hungry; and seeing in the distance a fig tree which had leaves, he went to see if he could find anything on it; and when he reached it he found nothing but the leaves, for it was not the season for figs. Then he spoke forth and said to it: May no one eat fruit from you any more, forever. And his disciples heard him.

They came to Jerusalem. And he went into the temple and began to drive out those who sold and bought in the temple, and he overturned the tables of the money changers and the stalls of the sellers of doves, and he would not let anyone carry any vessel through the temple, and he taught them and said: Is it not written that: My house shall be called a house of prayer for all the nations? But you have made it into a den of robbers. And the high priests and the scribes heard him, and looked for a way to destroy him; for they feared him, for all the populace was smitten with his teaching.

When it was late, they went forth from the city.

As they passed by in the morning they saw the fig tree dried up, from the roots; and Peter remembered and said to him: Master, see, the fig tree which you cursed is dried up. Jesus answered and said to them: Have faith in God. Truly I tell you, if one says to this mountain: Rise up and throw yourself into the sea, and does not deliberate in his heart but believes that what he talks about is happening, it shall be his. Therefore I tell you, all that you pray for and ask for, believe that you get it, and it shall be yours. And when you stand praying, forget anything you have against anyone, so that your father in heaven may forgive your transgressions.

They returned to Jerusalem. And as he walked about in the temple, the high priests and the scribes and the elders came to him and said: By what authority do you do this? Or who gave you this authority, to do these things? Jesus said to them: I will ask you one thing, and you answer me, and I will tell you by what authority I do this. Was the baptism of John from heaven or from men? Answer me. They discussed this among themselves, saying: If we say: From heaven, he will say: Then why did you not believe him? But if we say: From men— They were afraid of the people, for these all held John to be truly a prophet. And they answered Jesus and said: We do not know. And Jesus said to them: Neither will I tell you by what authority I do these things.

◖ Then he began to talk to them in parables: A man planted a vineyard and ran a fence about it and dug a pit for the wine press and built a tower, and let it out to farmers and left the country. And when the time came, he sent a slave to the farmers to receive from the farmers some of the fruits of the vineyard. And they took him and lashed him and sent him away empty-handed. And again he sent them another slave; and they broke the head of that one and outraged him. And he sent another; and that one they killed; and many others, lashing some, killing some. He had one more, a beloved son; he was the last he sent them, saying: They will respect my son. But they, the farmers, said among themselves: This is the heir. Come, let us kill him and the inheritance will be ours. And they took him and killed him, and threw him out of the vineyard. What will the lord of the vineyard do? He will come and destroy the farmers, and give the vineyard to others. Have you not read this scripture: The stone that the builders rejected has come to be at the head of the corner. It was made by the Lord, and is wonderful in our sight? They were looking for a way to seize him; also they were afraid of the people. They knew that the parable he told was directed against them. They let him be and went away.

Then they sent him some of the Pharisees and Herodians to try to catch him up in what he said. And they came, and said to him: Master, we know that you are truthful and care for no man, for you are no respecter of persons but teach the way of God truthfully. Is it lawful to pay the assessment to Caesar or not? Shall we give or not give? He knew their hypocrisy and said to them: Why do you tempt me? Bring me a denarius so I may look at it. They brought him one. He said to them: Whose is the image and whose name is inscribed? They said: Caesar's. And Jesus said: Give Caesar what is Caesar's and God what is God's. And they wondered at him.

Sadducees also came to him, who say that there is no resurrection, and they questioned him, saying: Master, Moses wrote for us: If a man's brother dies and leaves a wife, but has no children, the brother should take the wife and raise up issue for his brother. There were seven brothers. The first took a wife, and died and left no issue. And the second took her, and died without leaving issue, and the third likewise. All seven left no issue. Last of all the woman also died. In the resurrection, whose wife shall she be, of these men? For all seven had her as wife. Jesus said to them: Is this not why you go astray, through knowing neither the scriptures nor the power of God? For when they rise from the dead they do not marry nor are they married but are as the angels in heaven. And as for the dead, that they waken, have you not read in the book of Moses, at the bush, how God spoke to him saying: I am the God of Abraham and the God of Isaac and the God of Jacob? God is not God of the dead but of the living. You are far astray.

Then one of the scribes, who had listened to their discussion and knew that he had answered them well, came to him and asked him: Which is the first commandment of all? Jesus answered: The first is: Hear, Israel, the Lord our God the Lord is one; and you shall love the Lord your God with all your heart and all your spirit and all your mind and all your strength. This is the second: You shall love your neighbor as yourself. There is no other commandment greater than these. The scribe said to him: Well said, master; what you said is true, that he is one and there is no other but he; and to love him with all the heart and all the understanding and all strength, and to love one's neighbor as oneself, is worth more than all the burnt offerings and the sacrifices. And Jesus, perceiving that he had answered intelligently, said: You are not far from the Kingdom of God. And no one dared question him after that.

And Jesus spoke forth and said, as he taught in the temple: How is it that the scribes say that the Christ is the son of David? David himself said, under the Holy Spirit: The Lord said to my lord: Sit on my right so that I may put your enemies beneath your feet. David himself calls him lord. Then how can he be his son?

And the masses heard him with pleasure. And in his teaching he said: Turn away from the scribes who desire to walk about in their robes, who desire the salutations in the public places and the first seats in the synagogues and the foremost couches at the dinners, who eat up the houses of the widows, and pray long as an excuse. The greater the condemnation these will receive.

Then he sat down across from the treasury and watched how the multitude put coins into the treasury. And many rich people put in many coins. And there came a poor widow who put in two half pennies, that is, one penny. Calling his disciples to him, he said to them: Truly I tell you, this widow, who is poor, has put in more than all who have put money into the treasury. For they all put in out of their surplus, but out of her deficit she gave all that she had, her whole livelihood.

❧ As he was leaving the temple, one of his disciples said to him: See, master, what stones, what buildings! And Jesus said to him: Are you looking at the great buildings?

Nothing here will escape destruction and no stone will be left on another. Then he sat down on the Mount of Olives opposite the temple, and Peter and James and John and Andrew asked him privately: Tell us when this shall be, and what will be the sign when all these things are to be accomplished. And Jesus began to tell them: See to it that no one leads you astray. For many will come in my name, saying: I am he. And they will lead many astray. And when you hear of wars and the rumors of wars, do not be frightened. This must be, but the end is not yet. For nation shall rise up against nation and kingdom against kingdom, there will be earthquakes in the lands, there will be famines. This is the beginning of the agony. And look to yourselves. They will turn you over to the councils and you will be lashed in the synagogues, and you will be set before leaders and kings because of me, to testify to them. And first the gospel must be preached to all the peoples. And when they turn you over and bring you to trial, do not take any forethought for what you will say, but whatever is given to you in that hour, say it, for it will not be you who speak but the Holy Spirit. And brother will betray brother to death, and the father his child, and children will rise up against their parents and work their death; and you will be hated by all because of my name. But he who endures to the end will be saved. But when you see the abomination of desolation standing where it should not—and let him who reads this take note of it—then let those who are in Judaea flee to the mountains, and let him who is on his housetop not come down or go inside to take up anything from his house, and let him who is in the field not turn back to pick up his coat. Woe to the women who are with child and the women who are nursing in those days. Pray that it will not come in the wintertime; for those days will be an affliction such as there has not been from the beginning of creation, which God created, until now, and may not be again. And if the Lord had not cut short the days, no flesh would be saved; but for the sake of the chosen, whom he chose, he did cut short the days. And then, if someone says to you: See, here is the Christ; see, he is there, do not believe him. For false Christs and false prophets will rise up, and they will present signs and portents to mislead the chosen, if that may be done. Be watchful; I have foretold all to you. But in those days after that affliction, the sun will be darkened and the moon will not give her light, and the stars will be falling out of the sky, and the powers in the skies will be shaken. And then they will see the son of man coming in the clouds with great power and glory; and then he will send out his angels and gather his chosen together from the four winds, from the end of the earth to the end of the sky. From the fig tree learn its parable. When its branch is tender and it puts forth leaves, you know that the summer is near; so also you, when you see these things happening, know that he is near, at your doors. Truly I tell you that this generation will not pass by before all these things are done. The sky and the earth will pass away but my words will not pass away. But concerning that day and the hour none knows, not the angels in heaven or the son, only the father. Be watchful and wakeful; you do not know when the time will come; as when a man has gone on a journey and left his house and given his slaves charge over it, to each his task, and told the doorkeeper he must be watchful. Be watchful then, you do not know when the lord of the house is coming, in the evening or at midnight or at cock-crow or in the morning; lest he come suddenly and find you sleeping. What I say to you I say to all: be watchful.

¶ After two days, it would be the Passover and the feast of Unleavened Bread. And the high priests and the scribes were looking for a way to capture him by treachery and kill him; for they said: Not during the festival, for so there will be rioting among the people.

And when he was in Bethany in the house of Simon the leper, and at dinner, a woman came with an alabaster vessel full of ointment of nard, pure and precious; and she broke open the jar and poured the ointment over his head. But there were some who grumbled among themselves: Why was there this waste of ointment? The ointment could have been sold for upward of three hundred denarii and the money given to the poor. And they scolded her. But Jesus said: Let her be. Why are you hard on her? She has done a good thing for me. For always you have the poor with you, and you can do them good whenever you will, but you do not always have me. She did what she could, she took the opportunity to anoint my body in advance for my burial. Truly I tell you, wherever the gospel is preached through all the world, what she did will also be spoken of, in memory of her.

And Judas Iscariot, he who was one of the twelve, went off to the high priests, so as to betray him to them. And they were pleased when they heard him and promised to give him money. And he looked for an easy opportunity to betray him.

Now on the first day of Unleavened Bread, when they used to sacrifice the paschal lamb, his disciples said to him: Where do you wish us to go and make preparations for you to eat the feast of the Passover? He sent forth two of his disciples, and told them: Go into the city, and a man carrying a pot of water will meet you. Follow him, and wherever he enters, say to the master of the house: The master says: Where is my guest chamber where I can eat the Passover dinner with my disciples? And he will show you a large upper room, furnished and ready. There prepare for us. And the disciples went forth, and went into the city, and found all as he had told them, and made ready the Passover. When it was evening, he arrived with the twelve. And as they were at table and eating, Jesus said: Truly I tell you that one of you will betray me, the one who is eating with me. They began to be bitterly hurt, and to say, one by one: Surely, not I? He said to them: One of the twelve, the one who dips into the dish with me; because the son of man goes his way as it has been written concerning him, but woe to that man through whom the son of man is betrayed. It were well for that man if he had never been born. And as they ate, he took a loaf of bread and blessed it and broke it and gave it to them and said: Take it; this is my body. And he took a cup and gave thanks and gave it to them, and they all drank from it. And he said to them: This is my blood, of the covenant, which is shed for the sake of many. Truly I tell you that I will not again drink of the produce of the vine, until I drink it, new wine, in the Kingdom of God.

And they sang the hymn and went out to the Mount of Olives. And Jesus said to them: You will all be made to fail me; for it is written: I will strike the shepherd, and the sheep will be scattered; but after my resurrection I will lead the way for you into Galilee. But Peter said to him: Even if all fail you, yet I will not. Jesus said to him:

Truly I tell you that in this very night, before the cock crows twice, you will disown me three times. But he said very forcefully: Even if I must die with you, I will never disown you. And so said they all.

They came to a place whose name is Gethsemane, and he said to his disciples: Sit down here while I pray. And he took with him Peter and James and John; and then he began to be shaken and distressed, and he said to them: My soul is in anguish to the point of death. Stay here and keep watch. And going forward a little he threw himself on the ground, and prayed that, if it were possible, the hour might pass him by. And he said: Abba, father, for you all things are possible. Remove this cup from me. But not what I wish, but what you wish. He went back and found them sleeping, and said to Peter: Simon, are you sleeping? Were you not strong enough to keep watch for a single hour? Be wakeful, and pray, that you may not be brought to the test. The spirit is eager, but the flesh is weak. And going back again he prayed, in the same words. And coming back again he found them sleeping, for their eyes were heavy, and they did not know how to answer him. And he came a third time and said to them: So you are still asleep and resting. It is enough. The hour has come; behold, the son of man is betrayed into the hands of sinners. Rise up, let us go; see, my betrayer is near.

Immediately, while he was still speaking, Judas came, one of the twelve, and with him a crowd, with swords and clubs, from the high priests and the scribes and the elders. He who betrayed him had told them the sign to watch for, saying to them: The one I kiss will be the man. Seize him, and take him away, carefully. And right upon his arrival he came up to him and said: Master; and kissed him. And they laid hands on him and bound him. But one of his supporters drew his sword and struck the slave of the high priest and took off his ear. Then Jesus spoke forth and said to them: You come out with swords and clubs to arrest me as if I were a highwayman? Day by day I was near you in the temple, teaching, and you did not seize me. But let the scriptures be fulfilled.

And all left him and fled away.

And there was a certain young man who had been following him, wearing a linen garment over his bare skin. And they seized him, and he fled naked, leaving the linen garment behind.

They took Jesus away to the high priest, and all the high priests and the elders and the scribes assembled. And Peter had followed him from a distance, into the courtyard of the high priest, and he was sitting there with the servingmen and warming himself at the fire. And the high priests and the entire council were looking for some evidence against Jesus so that they could have him killed, and they could find none; for many brought false witness against him, and their testimony did not agree. And some stood up and testified falsely against him, saying: We have heard him say: I will tear down this temple which was made with hands, and in three days I will build another, not made with hands. But not even so did their testimony agree. Then the high priest stood up among them and questioned Jesus, saying: Have you no answer? What is this testimony that they bring against you? But he was silent and did not answer. Again the high priest questioned him and said: Are you the Christ, the son of the Blessed One? Jesus said: I am he, and you will see the son of man sitting on the right of the power and coming with the clouds of the sky. The high priest tore his clothing and said: Why do we still need witnesses? Did you hear the blasphemy? What is your view? They all judged that he deserved death. Then some began to spit upon him, and to cover his face and then beat him with their fists and say to him: Prophesy. And the servingmen took him over and beat him.

And while Peter was below in the courtyard there came one of the serving girls of the high priest, and seeing Peter warming himself, she looked at him and said: You also were with the Nazarene, with Jesus. But he denied it, saying: I neither know nor understand what you mean. And he went out into the forecourt. But the girl saw him and began saying once more to those who were standing by: This is one of them. Once more he denied it. And after a little while those who were standing by said to Peter: Truly you are one of them, since you are a Galilaean. Then he began to swear and to say on oath: I do not know the man of whom you speak. And thereupon the cock crowed for the second time. And Peter remembered what Jesus had told him: Before the cock crows twice you will disown me three times. And he threw himself down and wept.

◀ Early the next day the high priests with the elders and the scribes and the entire council held a meeting: and they bound Jesus and took him away and gave him over to Pilate. And Pilate asked him: Are you the King of the Jews? He answered him and said: It is you who say it. And the high priests brought many charges against him. And Pilate again asked him: Have you no answer? See how much they charge you with. But Jesus gave no further answer, so that Pilate was amazed.

For the festival, he used to release to them one prisoner,

whichever one they asked for. The man called Barabbas
was imprisoned among the insurgents who had done
murder during the uprising. And the crowd came up and
began to demand that he do by them according to his
custom. Pilate answered them, saying: Do you wish me
to release your King of the Jews? For he perceived that
they had handed him over for spite. But the high priests
stirred up the crowd, so that he might rather give them
Barabbas. Pilate once again spoke to them and said: What
then shall I do with the man you call the King of the Jews?
And they cried out once more: Crucify him. Pilate said to
them: Why? What harm has he done? But they screamed
all the more, saying: Crucify him. So Pilate wishing to
satisfy the crowd released Barabbas to them, and had
Jesus scourged and gave him over to be crucified.

The soldiers led him inside the court, that is, the residence, and they called up their whole battalion. They
clothed him in purple and wove a wreath of thorns and
put it on him. And they began to acclaim him with: Hail,
King of the Jews. And they beat him about the head with a
reed, and spat upon him, and going down on their knees
they did obeisance to him. And after they had mocked
him, they took off the purple and put his own clothes on
him. And they led him out, to crucify him. And a certain
Simon of Cyrene, the father of Alexander and Rufus, was
passing by on his way in from the country, and they impressed him for carrying the cross. And they took him to
the place Golgotha, which translated is the Place of the
Skull. And they offered him wine mixed with myrrh,
which he would not take. And they crucified him, and
divided up his clothes, casting lots for them, for who
would take which. It was the third hour and they
crucified him. And the charge against him was inscribed:

The King of the Jews. And with him they crucified two robbers, one on his right and one on his left. And those who
passed by blasphemed against him, wagging their heads
and saying: Ha, you would tear down the temple and rebuild it in three days, save yourself by coming down from
the cross. So likewise the high priests, mocking him together, along with the scribes, said: He saved others, he
cannot save himself. Let the anointed, the King of Israel,
come down now from the cross, so that we may see and
believe. And those who were crucified with him also
spoke abusively to him.

  And when it was the sixth hour, there was darkness
over all the earth until the ninth hour. In the ninth hour
Jesus cried out in a great voice: Elōi elōi lama
sabachthanei? Which translated is: My God, my God, why
have you forsaken me? Then some of those who were
standing there said: See, he calls to Elijah. And someone
ran up with a sponge soaked in vinegar and put on the end
of a reed and offered it to him to drink, saying: Come, let us
see if Elijah will come to bring him down. But Jesus uttered a great cry and breathed his last. And the veil of the
temple was split in two from top to bottom. And when he
saw that he thus breathed his last, the centurion who was
posted across from him said: In truth this man was the
Son of God. And there were women watching from a distance, among them Mary the Magdalene, and Mary the
mother of James the lesser and Joses, and Salome, who
when he was in Galilee had followed him and served him,
and many others who had come up with him to
Jerusalem.

  By nightfall, when it was the Day of Preparation, which
is the day before the sabbath, there arrived Joseph of
Arimathaea, a reputable member of the council who him-

self was also looking for the Kingdom of God; and he took courage and went into the presence of Pilate and asked for the body of Jesus. But Pilate thought it very strange if he were already dead, and summoning the centurion he asked if he had died yet; and when he learned from the centurion that he had, he presented the corpse to Joseph. And Joseph bought linen, and took him down and wrapped him in the linen, and laid him in a tomb which had been cut in the rock, and rolled a stone against the door of the tomb. And Mary the Magdalene and Mary the mother of Joses were watching where he was laid.

◀ And when the sabbath was over, Mary the Magdalene and Mary the mother of James and Salome bought spices so that they might go and anoint him. And very early on the first day of the week they went to the tomb, where the sun had risen. And they were saying to each other: Who will roll away the stone for us, out of the door of the tomb? Then looking again they saw that the stone, which was very large, had been rolled away. And going into the tomb they saw a young man sitting in the right-hand part, wearing a white robe. And they were startled into amazement. But he said to them: Do not be thus amazed. You are looking for Jesus the Nazarene, who was crucified. He has risen, he is not here. See the place where they laid him. But go and tell his disciples, and Peter: He goes before you into Galilee. There you will see him, as he told you. And they went out and fled from the tomb, for trembling and panic had hold of them. And they said nothing to anyone, for they were afraid.

[Then after he had arisen early on the first day of the week, he appeared first to Mary the Magdalene, from whom he had cast out seven demons. She went and told the news to those who had been with him, who were mourning and weeping; and they, when they heard that he was alive and had been seen by her, did not believe her. After that he appeared to two of them as they were walking. It was in another form and they were on their way into the country. And they too went back and told the news to the others; but neither did they believe them. Later he appeared to the eleven themselves as they were at dinner, and he had blame for their lack of faith and the insensitivity of their hearts, because they had not believed those who had seen him risen from the dead. And he said to them: Go out into the whole world and preach the gospel to all creation. He who believes and is baptized shall be saved, but he who does not believe shall be condemned. And here are the signs that will go with the believers: In my name they will cast out demons, speak with tongues, hold snakes, and if they drink something lethal it cannot harm them, and they will lay their hands on the sick and these will be well.

After talking with them the Lord was taken up into heaven and sat down on the right of God. And they went forth and preached everywhere, the Lord working with them and confirming their message through the signs that accompanied them.]

[They reported briefly to Peter and his companions all that they had been told. And after that Jesus himself sent forth through them, from east to west, the holy and imperishable proclamation of everlasting salvation.]

MATTHEW

Matthew is believed to date from A.D. 75 at the latest,
but incorporating written accounts from an earlier date.

◀ THE BOOK OF THE ORIGIN OF JESUS
Christ the son of David the son of Abraham.

Abraham was the father of Isaac, and Isaac of Jacob,
Jacob of Judah and his brothers, and Judah of Perez and
Zarah by Tamar, and Perez of Hezron, and Hezron of Ram,
and Ram of Aminadab, and Aminadab of Nahshon, and
Nahshon of Salmon, and Salmon of Boaz by Rahab, and
Boaz of Obed by Ruth, and Obed of Jesse, and Jesse of
David the King. David was the father of Solomon by the
wife of Uriah, Solomon of Rehoboam, Rehoboam of
Abijah, and Abijah of Asa, and Asa of Jehosaphat, and
Jehosaphat of Joram, and Joram of Uzziah, and Uzziah of
Jotham, and Jotham of Ahaz, and Ahaz of Hezekiah,
Hezekiah of Manasseh, Manasseh of Amos, and Amos of
Josiah, and Josiah of Jechoniah and his brothers, at the
time of the Babylonian migration. After the Babylonian
migration Jechoniah was the father of Salathiel, Salathiel
of Zerubbabel, Zerubbabel of Abiud, and Abiud of
Eliakim, Eliakim of Azor, and Azor of Zadok, and Zadok
of Achim, Achim of Eliud, Eliud of Eleazar, Eleazar of
Matthan, and Matthan of Jacob, and Jacob of Joseph the

husband of Mary, from whom was born Jesus who is called the Christ.

Thus all the generations from Abraham to David are fourteen, and from David until the Babylonian migration fourteen generations, and from the Babylonian migration until Christ fourteen generations.

The birth of Jesus Christ came in this way: Mary his mother was engaged to Joseph, but before they came together she was found to be with child, by the Holy Spirit. And Joseph her husband, being a righteous man and not desiring to make her notorious, wished to put her away secretly. But as he was considering this, behold, the angel of the Lord appeared to him in a dream, saying: Joseph son of David, do not fear to accept Mary your wife, for what is conceived in her is of the Holy Spirit. And she will bear a son, and you shall call his name Jesus; for he shall save his people from their sins. All this was done in order that the word of the Lord might be fulfilled which was spoken through his prophet, saying: Behold, the maiden shall conceive in her womb, and she shall bear a son, and they shall call his name Emmanuel; which translated means, God is with us. And Joseph wakening from his sleep did as the angel of the Lord had told him, and he accepted his wife, and did not know her as a wife until she had borne a son. And he called his name, Jesus.

¶ When Jesus was born in Bethlehem in Judaea in the days of Herod the King, behold, Magians from the east came to Jerusalem, saying: Where is he who is born King of the Jews? For we saw his star in the east and have come to worship him. And hearing this King Herod was disturbed, and all Jerusalem with him, and calling together all the high priests and the scribes of the people he asked them where the Christ was born. And they said to him: In Bethlehem of Judaea; for thus it is written by the prophet: You also, Bethlehem, in the land of Judah, are by no means the least among the leaders of Judah; for out of you will come a leader who will be a shepherd of my people, Israel.

Then Herod called in the Magians secretly and found from them the exact time when the star had appeared, and sent them to Bethlehem, saying: Go and learn exactly about the child, and when you find him, bring back the news to me, so that I too may go and worship him. And they after hearing the King went on their way, and behold, the star, which they had seen in the east, led them until it came and stood above the place where the child was. And when they saw the star they were filled with a very great joy. Then going into the house they saw the child with Mary his mother, and they threw themselves down and worshipped him, and opening their strongboxes they proffered him gifts, gold and frankincense and myrrh. Then having been warned in a dream not to turn back to Herod, they went away by another road to their own country.

When they had gone, behold, an angel of the Lord appeared to Joseph in a dream, saying: Awake, take the child and his mother, and escape into Egypt, and remain there until I tell you. For Herod means to seek out the child to destroy him. Then he woke and took the child and his mother by night and went away into Egypt, and was there until the death of Herod; so that there might be fulfilled the word spoken by the Lord through his prophet, saying: Out of Egypt I have called my son.

Then Herod, seeing that he had been outwitted by the

Magians, was very angry, and sending out his men, he killed all the boy children in Bethlehem and all its outlying regions, those two years old or less, according to the time he had reckoned from the Magians. Then was fulfilled the word spoken by Jeremiah the prophet, saying: A voice was heard in Rama, weeping and much lamentation, Rachel weeping for her children, and she would not be comforted because they are gone.

Now when Herod died, behold, an angel of the Lord appeared in a dream to Joseph in Egypt, saying: Awake, take the child and his mother and go to the land of Israel; for those who sought the life of the child are dead. And he wakening took the child and his mother and went to the land of Israel. But hearing that Archelaus was King in Judaea in the place of his father Herod, he was afraid to go back there, and being warned in a dream, he withdrew to the region of Galilee, and reaching there settled in a city called Nazareth; so as to fulfill the word spoken by the prophets: He shall be called a Nazarene.

◀ In those days came John the Baptist preaching in the desert of Judaea, saying: Repent; for the Kingdom of Heaven is near. He was the one who was mentioned by Isaiah the prophet, saying: The voice of one crying in the desert: prepare the way of the Lord, straighten the roads before him. This John wore clothing made of camel's hair, and a belt of hide around his waist, and his food was locusts and wild honey. At that time Jerusalem came to him, and all Judaea and all the country about Jordan, and they were baptized by him in the river Jordan, confessing their sins. And seeing many of the Pharisees and Sadducees coming to baptism, he said to them: You viper's brood, who warned you to flee from the anger to come? Then produce fruit which is worthy of your repentance; and do not think to say among yourselves: We have Abraham for our father. For I say to you that out of these stones God can raise up children to Abraham. And by now the ax is set against the root of the trees; so that every tree that does not bear good fruit is cut out and thrown into the fire. I baptize you in water for repentance, but he who is coming after me is stronger than I, and I am not fit to carry his shoes; he will baptize you in the Holy Spirit and fire; his winnowing fan is in his hand, and he will clear his threshing floor and gather his grain into his storehouse and burn the chaff in quenchless fire.

Then came Jesus from Galilee to the Jordan and to John to be baptized by him. But he tried to prevent this, saying: I need to be baptized by you. And you come to me? But Jesus answered and said to him: Bear with me now; for so it is right for us to fulfill our whole duty. Then he consented. And when Jesus was baptized, at once he came out of the water, and behold, the skies opened, and he saw the Spirit of God coming down like a dove, descending upon him, and behold, a voice from the skies was heard saying: This is my son whom I love, in whom I am well pleased.

⟨ Then Jesus was led out into the desert by the Spirit, to be tested by the devil. And he fasted forty days and forty nights, and after that he was hungry. And coming up to him the tempter said: If you are the son of God, speak and make these stones become loaves of bread. But he answered, saying: It is written: not by bread alone shall man live, but in every word that issues through the mouth of God. Then the devil took him to the holy city and set him on the gable of the temple and said to him: If you are the son of God, throw yourself down; for it is written: He will charge his angels concerning you, and on their hands they will support you, so that never may you strike your foot against the stone. Jesus said to him: Again, it is written: You shall not tempt the Lord your God. Once more the devil led him to a very high mountain, and showed him all the kingdoms of the world and their glory, and said to him: All this I will give you if you will throw yourself down and worship me. But Jesus said to him: Go, Satan; for it is written: You shall worship the Lord your God, and shall serve him only. Then the devil let him be; and behold, angels came and served him.

When he heard that John had been betrayed, he withdrew into Galilee, and leaving Nazareth he came and settled in Capernaum by the sea, in the districts of Zebulun and Naphthali; so as to fulfill the word spoken by Isaiah the prophet, saying: Land of Zebulun and land of Naphthali, way to the sea, beyond Jordan, Galilee of the Gentiles, the people who were sitting in darkness saw a great light, they were sitting in the land of the shadow of death, and the light dawned on them.

From that time Jesus began to preach and to say: Repent; for the Kingdom of Heaven is near.

And as he walked by the Sea of Galilee he saw two brothers, Simon who was called Peter and Andrew his brother, casting their net into the sea, for they were fishermen. And he said to them: Come now and follow me, and I will make you fishers of men. And at once they left their nets and followed him. And as he went on from there he saw two more brothers, James the son of Zebedee and John his brother, in the boat with Zebedee their father, mending their nets. And he called them. And at once leaving the boat and their father they followed him.

And he went all over Galilee teaching in their synagogues and preaching the gospel of the kingdom and treating every sickness and every infirmity among the people. And the fame of him went into all Syria; and they brought him all who were in bad condition with complicated diseases and seized with pains, those afflicted with demons, and epilepsy, and paralytics, and he healed them. And many multitudes followed him from Galilee and the Decapolis and Jerusalem and Judaea and beyond the Jordan.

❡ And seeing the multitudes he went up onto the mountain, and when he was seated, his disciples came to him, and he opened his mouth and taught them, saying:

Blessed are the poor in spirit, because theirs is the Kingdom of Heaven.

Blessed are they who sorrow, because they shall be comforted.

Blessed are the gentle, because they shall inherit the earth.

Blessed are they who are hungry and thirsty for righteousness, because they shall be fed.

Blessed are they who have pity, because they shall be pitied.

Blessed are the pure in heart, because they shall see God.

Blessed are the peacemakers, because they shall be called the sons of God.

Blessed are they who are persecuted for their righteousness, because theirs is the Kingdom of Heaven.

Blessed are you when they shall revile you and persecute you and speak every evil thing of you, lying, because of me. Rejoice and be glad, because your reward in heaven is great; for thus did they persecute the prophets before you.

You are the salt of the earth; but if the salt loses its power, with what shall it be salted? It is good for nothing but to be thrown away and trampled by men. You are the light of the world. A city cannot be hidden when it is set on top of a hill. Nor do men light a lamp and set it under a basket, but they set it on a stand, and it gives its light to all in the house. So let your light shine before men, so that they may see your good works and glorify your father in heaven.

Do not think that I have come to destroy the law and the prophets. I have not come to destroy but to complete. Indeed, I say to you, until the sky and the earth are gone, not one iota or one end of a letter must go from the law, until all is done. He who breaks one of the least of these commandments and teaches men accordingly shall be called the least in the Kingdom of Heaven; he who performs and teaches these commandments shall be called great in the Kingdom of Heaven. For I tell you, if your righteousness is not more abundant than that of the scribes and the Pharisees, you may not enter the Kingdom of Heaven.

You have heard that it was said to the ancients: You shall not murder. He who murders shall be liable to judgment. I say to you that any man who is angry with his brother shall be liable to judgment; and he who says to his brother, fool, shall be liable before the council; and he who says to his brother, sinner, shall be liable to Gehenna. If then you bring your gift to the altar, and there remember that your brother has some grievance against you, leave your gift before the altar, and go first and be reconciled with your brother, and then go and offer your gift. Be quick to be conciliatory with your adversary at law when you are in the street with him, for fear your adversary may turn you over to the judge, and the judge to the officer, and you be thrown into prison. Truly I tell you, you cannot come out of there until you pay the last penny.

You have heard that it has been said: You shall not commit adultery. I tell you that any man who looks at a woman so as to desire her has already committed adultery with her in his heart. If your right eye makes you go amiss, take it out and cast it from you; it is better that one part of you should be lost instead of your whole body being cast into Gehenna. And if your right hand makes you go amiss, cut it off and cast it from you; it is better that one part of you should be lost instead of your whole body going to Gehenna. It has been said: If a man puts away his wife, let him give her a contract of divorce. I tell you that any man who puts away his wife, except for the reason of harlotry, is making her the victim of adultery; and any man who marries a wife who has been divorced is committing adultery. Again, you have heard that it has been said to the ancients: You shall not swear falsely, but you shall make good your oaths to the Lord. I tell you not to swear at all: not by heaven, because it is the throne of God; not by the earth, because it is the footstool for his feet; not by Jerusalem, because it is the city of the great king; not by your own head, because you cannot make one hair of it white or black. Let your speech be yes yes, no no; more than that comes from the evil one.

You have heard that it has been said: An eye for an eye and a tooth for a tooth. I tell you not to resist the wicked man; but if one strikes you on the right cheek, turn the other one to him also; and if a man wishes to go to law with you and take your tunic, give him your cloak also, and if one makes you his porter for a mile, go with him for two. Give to him who asks, and do not turn away one who wishes to borrow from you. You have heard that it has been said: You shall love your neighbor and hate your enemy. I tell you, love your enemies and pray for those who persecute you, so that you may be sons of your father who is in heaven, because he makes his sun rise on the evil and the good, and rains on the just and the unjust. For if you love those who love you, what reward do you have? Do not even the tax collectors do the same? And if you greet only your brothers, what do you do that is more than others do? Do not even the pagans do the same? Be perfect as your father in heaven is perfect.

◀ Take care not to practice your righteousness publicly before men so as to be seen by them; if you do, you shall have no recompense from your father in heaven. Then when you do charity, do not have a trumpet blown before you, as the hypocrites do in the synagogues and the streets, so that men may think well of them. Truly I tell you, they have their due reward. But when you do charity, let your left hand not know what your right hand is doing, so that your charity may be in secret; and your father, who sees what is secret, will reward you. And when you pray, you must not be like the hypocrites, who love to stand up in the synagogues and the corners of the squares to pray, so that they may be seen by men. Truly I tell you, they have their due reward. But when you pray, go into your inner room and close the door and pray to your father, who is in secret; and your father, who sees what is secret, will reward you. When you pray, do not babble as the pagans do; for they think that by saying much they will be heard. Do not then be like them; for your father knows what you need before you ask him. Pray thus, then: Our father in heaven, may your name be hallowed, may your kingdom come, may your will be done, as in heaven, so upon earth. Give us today our sufficient bread, and forgive us our debts, as we also have forgiven our debtors. And do not bring us into temptation, but deliver us from evil. For if you forgive men their offenses, your heavenly father will forgive you; but if you do not forgive men, neither will your father forgive you your offenses. And when you fast, do not scowl like the hypocrites; for they make ugly faces so that men can see that they are fasting. Truly I tell you, they have their due reward. But when you fast, anoint your head and wash your face, so that you may not show as fasting to men, but to your father, in secret; and your father, who sees what is secret, will reward you.

Do not store up your treasures on earth, where the moth and rust destroy them, and where burglars dig through and steal them; but store up your treasures in heaven, where neither moth nor rust destroys them, and where burglars do not dig through or steal; for where your treasure is, there also will be your heart. The lamp of the body is the eye. Thus if your eye is clear, your whole body is full of light; but if your eye is soiled, your whole body is dark. If the light in you is darkness, how dark it is. No man can serve two masters. For either he will hate the one and love the other, or he will cling to one and despise the other; you cannot serve God and mammon. Therefore I tell you, do not take thought for your life, what you will eat, or for your body, what you will wear. Is not your life more than its food and your body more than its clothing? Consider the birds of the sky, that they do not sow or harvest or collect for their granaries, and your heavenly father feeds them. Are you not preferred above them? Which of you by taking thought can add one cubit to his growth? And why do you take thought about clothing? Study the lilies in the field, how they grow. They do not toil or spin; yet I tell you, not even Solomon in all his glory was clothed like one of these. But if God so clothes the grass of the field, which grows today and tomorrow is thrown in the oven, will he not much more clothe you, you men of little faith? Do not then worry and say: What shall we eat? Or: What shall we drink? Or : What shall we wear? For all this the Gentiles study. Your father in heaven knows that you need all these things. But seek out first his kingdom and his justice, and all these things shall be given to you. Do not then take thought of tomorrow; tomorrow will take care of itself, sufficient to the day is its own evil.

◀ Do not judge, so you may not be judged. You shall be judged by that judgment by which you judge, and your measure will be made by the measure by which you measure. Why do you look at the straw which is in the eye of your brother, and not see the log which is in your eye? Or how will you say to your brother: Let me take the straw out of your eye, and behold, the log is in your eye. You hypocrite, first take the log out of your eye, and then you will see to take the straw out of the eye of your brother. Do not give what is sacred to the dogs, and do not cast your pearls before swine, lest they trample them under their feet and turn and rend you. Ask, and it shall be given you; seek, and you shall find; knock, and the door will be opened for you. Everyone who asks receives, and he who seeks finds, and for him who knocks the door will be opened. Or what man is there among you, whose son shall ask him for bread, that will give him a stone? Or ask him for fish, that will give him a snake? If then you, who are corrupt, know how to give good gifts to your children, by how much more your father who is in heaven will give good things to those who ask him. Whatever you wish men to do to you, so do to them. For this is the law and the prophets.

Go in through the narrow gate; because wide and spacious is the road that leads to destruction, and there are many who go in through it; because narrow is the gate and cramped the road that leads to life, and few are they who find it. Beware of the false prophets, who come to you in sheep's clothing, but inside they are ravening wolves. From their fruits you will know them. Do men gather grapes from thorns or figs from thistles? Thus every good tree produces good fruits, but the rotten tree produces bad fruits. A good tree cannot bear bad fruits, and a rotten tree cannot bear good fruits. Every tree that does not produce good fruit is cut out and thrown in the fire. So from their fruits you will know them. Not everyone who says to me Lord Lord will come into the Kingdom of Heaven, but he who does the will of my father in heaven. Many will say to me on that day: Lord,

Lord, did we not prophesy in your name, and in your name did we not cast out demons, and in your name did we not assume great powers? And then I shall admit to them: I never knew you. Go from me, for you do what is against the law.

Every man who hears what I say and does what I say shall be like the prudent man who built his house upon the rock. And the rain fell and the rivers came and the winds blew and dashed against that house, and it did not fall, for it was founded upon the rock. And every man who hears what I say and does not do what I say will be like the reckless man who built his house on the sand. And the rain fell and the rivers came and the winds blew and battered that house, and it fell, and that was a great fall.

And it happened that when Jesus had ended these words, the multitudes were astonished at his teaching, for he taught them as one who has authority, and not like their own scribes.

❡ When he came down from the mountain many multitudes followed him. And behold, a leper came and bowed before him, saying: Lord, if you wish, you can make me clean. And he stretched out his hand and touched him, saying: I wish it; be clean. And at once his leprosy was cleansed. And Jesus said to him: Be sure to tell no one, but go and show yourself to the priest and bring him the gift that Moses has ordained, as a proof to them.

When he came into Capernaum there came to him a centurion with a request, saying: Lord, my son is lying paralyzed in my house, in terrible pain. He said to him: I will go and treat him. But the centurion answered and said: Lord, I am not worthy that you should come under my roof; but only say it in a word, and my son will be healed. For I myself am a man under orders, and I have soldiers under me, and I say to this man: Go, and he goes, and to another: Come, and he comes, and to my slave: Do this, and he does it. Jesus hearing him was amazed and said to his followers: Truly I tell you, I have not found such faith in anyone in Israel. I tell you that many from the east and the west will come and feast with Abraham and Isaac and Jacob in the Kingdom of Heaven; but the sons of the kingdom shall be thrown into the outer darkness; and there will be weeping and gnashing of teeth. And Jesus said to the centurion: Go, as you have trusted, so let it befall you. And his son was healed in that hour.

Then Jesus, going into the house of Peter, saw his mother-in-law, who was lying in a fever, and he took her by the hand, and the fever left her; and she got up and served him. And when evening came, they brought him many who were afflicted with demons, and he cast out the spirits by a word, and healed all those who were suffering; so as to fulfill what had been said by the prophet Isaiah, saying: He took up our sicknesses and carried off our diseases.

Then Jesus, seeing a great multitude about him, gave the word to go to the other side. And one scribe came to him and said: Master, I will follow you wherever you go. And Jesus said to him: Foxes have holes, and the birds of the sky have nests, but the son of man has no place to lay his head. And another, one of his disciples, said to him: Lord, give me leave first to go and bury my father. But Jesus said to him: Follow me, and leave the dead to bury their own dead.

When he went aboard the ship, his disciples followed

him. And behold, there was a great upheaval on the sea, so that the ship was hidden by the waves; but he himself was asleep. And they came and waked him, saying: Lord, save us, we are perishing. And he said to them: Why are you frightened, you men of little faith? Then he rose up and admonished the winds and the sea, and there was a great calm. But the people wondered, saying: What sort of man is this, that the winds and the sea obey him? And when he crossed over into the country of the Gadarenes there met him two men possessed by demons, coming out of the tombs, very wild, so that none could force a way past on that road. And behold, they cried out, saying: What have we to do with you, son of God? Have you come thus before your time to torment us? A long way from them was a herd of many swine, feeding. And the demons entreated him, saying: If you throw us out, send us into the herd of swine. And he said to them: Go. And they came out and went into the herd of swine; and behold, the whole herd rushed over the cliff into the sea and died in the waters. Then the swineherds fled and when they came to their city told all the story of those who had been possessed by demons. And behold, all the city came out to meet Jesus, and when they saw him they begged him to go away from their territory.

⁋ Then he went aboard a ship and crossed over and came to his own city. And behold, they brought him a paralytic who was laid on a bed. And Jesus, seeing their faith, said to the paralytic: Take heart, my child, your sins are forgiven. And behold, some of the scribes said among themselves: This man blasphemes. Then Jesus, knowing their thoughts, said: Why do you think evil in your hearts?

Which then is easier: to say, Your sins are forgiven, or to say, Rise up and walk? But so that you may know that the son of man has authority on earth to forgive sins . . . Then he said to the paralytic: Rise up, take your bed and go to your house. And he rose up and went to his house. And the multitude seeing this were frightened and glorified God, who gave such authority to men.

And Jesus, going on from there, saw a man sitting in the tollhouse, named Matthew, and said to him: Follow me. And he stood up and followed him. And it happened as he dined in the house, behold, many tax collectors and sinners came and dined with Jesus and his disciples. And when they saw this the Pharisees said to his disciples: Why does your teacher eat with tax collectors and sinners? He heard them and said: The strong do not need a physician, but those who are in poor health. Go and learn the meaning of: I want mercy, not sacrifice; for I did not come to summon the righteous, but the sinners. Then the disciples of John came to him and said: Why do we and the Pharisees fast, but your disciples do not fast? And Jesus said to them: Surely the members of the wedding party cannot mourn while the bridegroom is with them? The days will come when the bridegroom is taken away from them, and then they will fast. No one sews a patch of unfulled cloth on an old coat; for the filling pulls from the coat and makes the tear worse. Nor do they put new wine in old skins; if they do, the skins break, and the wine spills, and the skins are destroyed; but they put new wine in new skins, and both are kept whole.

As he said this, behold, an official came and bowed down before him and said: My daughter died just now. But come and put your hand on her, and she will live. Jesus rose up and followed him, and his disciples followed. And behold, a woman who had been bleeding for twelve years came from behind and touched the border of his mantle; for she said to herself: If I only touch his mantle, I shall be healed. But Jesus turned and saw her and said: Take heart, my daughter; your faith has healed you. And the woman was well from that hour. Then Jesus went into the house of the official and saw the flute players and the noisy crowd, and said: Go away; for the girl has not died, but she is asleep. And they laughed at him. But when the crowd had been put out, he went in and took her hand, and the girl woke. And the story of this went out to the whole of that country.

Then as Jesus went on from there, two blind men followed him, crying out and saying: Pity us, son of David. As he went into the house, the blind men came up with him, and Jesus said to them: Do you believe that I can do this? They said to him: Yes, Lord. Then he touched their eyes and said: As you have faith, so let it be with you. And their eyes were opened. Then Jesus spoke severely to them, saying: See that nobody hears of this. But they went out and spread the news of him to the whole of that country. As they went out, behold, men brought him a deaf-mute who was possessed by a demon. And when the demon was driven out, the deaf-mute talked. Then the multitude wondered, saying: Never was anything seen like this in Israel. But the Pharisees said: He drives out demons through the prince of demons.

Now Jesus went about through all the cities and the villages, teaching in their synagogues and preaching the gospel of the kingdom and healing every sickness and every infirmity. And when he saw the multitudes he was moved with pity for them, because they had been distracted and turned loose like sheep without a shepherd.

Then he said to his disciples: The harvest is abundant, but the laborers few. Beg the master of the harvest to send out laborers to his harvest.

¶ Then calling to him his twelve disciples, he gave them authority over unclean spirits, to cast them out, and to treat every sickness and every infirmity. And these are the names of the twelve apostles: First, Simon, who was called Peter, and Andrew his brother, and James the son of Zebedee, and John his brother, Philip and Bartholomew, Thomas and Matthew the tax collector, James the son of Alphaeus and Thaddeus, Simon the Cananaean and Judas the Iscariot, even he who betrayed him. These twelve Jesus sent forth and gave them instructions, saying:

Do not go on the road to the Gentiles, and do not go into any city of the Samaritans. Make your way rather to the lost sheep of the house of Israel. As you go, preach and say that the Kingdom of Heaven is near. Heal the infirm, raise up the dead, make lepers clean, cast out demons. You have taken a free gift; give a free gift. Do not keep gold or silver or bronze in your money belts, or a bag for the journey or two garments or shoes or a staff. The laborer is worthy of food and clothing. Whatever city or village you enter, find out who within it is worthy; stay with him until you go on. As you enter his house, greet it; and if the house is worthy, let your peace be upon it; and if it is not worthy, let your peace return upon yourselves. And when one does not receive you or listen to your words, as you go out of that house or that city, shake the dust of it from your feet. Truly I tell you, it will be more tolerable for the land of Sodom and Gomorrah on the day of judgment than for that city. See, I send you out like

sheep into the midst of wolves; be then crafty like snakes
and innocent like doves. Beware of people; for they will
hand you over to the council boards, and they will flog
you in their synagogues, and you will be brought before
the leaders and the kings, because of me, to bear witness
before them and the Gentiles. But when they hand you
over, do not think about how you will speak; that will be
given to you at the time when you speak; for it will not be
you who speak but the spirit of your father speaking
through you. Brother will hand brother over to death,
father will hand over child, and children will stand up
against their parents and cause their death. You will be
hated by all because of my name; and he who endures it
to the end will be saved. When they persecute you in one
city, flee to the next one; for truly I tell you, you will not
be through with the cities of Israel before the son of man
comes. The disciple is not above the teacher, or the slave
above his master; it is enough for the disciple that he be as
his teacher and for the slave that he be as his master. If
then they call the head of the house Beelzebub, how
much more will they so call his domestics. Then do not
be afraid of them; for there is nothing concealed that shall
not be revealed, and nothing secret that shall not be
known. What I say to you in the dark, say in the light;
what is said in your ear, proclaim on the housetops. And
have no fear of those who kill the body but cannot kill the
soul; fear rather him who can destroy both soul and body
in Gehenna. Are not two sparrows sold for a penny? And
one of them will not fall to the ground without the
knowledge of your father. Also, the very hairs of your
head are all numbered. Then do not fear; you are worth
many sparrows. If any man shall acknowledge me before
men, I shall acknowledge him before my father in heaven;

if any shall deny me before men, I shall deny him before my father in heaven. Do not think that I have come to bring peace upon the earth. I have not come to bring peace, but a sword. I have come to set a man against his father, and a daughter against her mother, and a bride against her mother-in-law, and the household of a man will be his enemies. He who loves father or mother more than me is not worthy of me; and he who loves son or daughter more than me is not worthy of me; and he who does not take his cross and come along behind me is not worthy of me. He who finds his life shall lose it, and he who loses his life because of me shall find it. He who receives you receives me, and he who receives me receives him who sent me forth. He who receives a prophet in the name of a prophet shall have the reward of a prophet, and he who receives a just man in the name of a just man shall have the reward of a just man. And he who gives one of these small ones a cup of cold water to drink, if only in the name of a disciple, truly I tell you, he shall not lose his reward.

¶ Then it came about that when Jesus had finished instructing his twelve disciples, he went away from there to teach and preach in their cities. But John in his prison heard of the works of the Christ, and sent his disciples to him, and through them asked him: Are you the one who is to come, or shall we look for another? Jesus answered and said to them: Go and tell John what you are seeing and hearing. The blind see again and the lame walk, lepers are made clean and deaf-mutes hear, and the dead rise up and beggars are told good news. And blessed is he who does not go astray where I am concerned. As these went away

Jesus began to speak about John to the multitudes: What did you come out into the desert to see? A reed shaken by the wind? But what did you come out to see? A man wrapped in soft clothing? Behold, those who wear soft clothing are in the houses of the kings. But why did you come out? To see a prophet? Yes, I tell you, and more than a prophet. This is he about whom it was written: Behold, I send forth my messenger before your face, who will make your way ready before you. Truly I tell you, among men born of women there has not risen a greater one than John the Baptist; but one who is only a lesser one in the Kingdom of Heaven is greater than he. From the days of John the Baptist until now the Kingdom of Heaven has been forced and the violent have seized it. For all the prophets, and the law, prophesied until John; and if you wish to accept it, he himself is Elijah, who was to come. He who has ears, let him listen. To what shall I liken this generation? It is like children sitting in the public places who call out to others and say: We played the flute, but you did not dance; we lamented and you did not beat yourselves. For John came neither eating nor drinking and they say: He has a demon. The son of man came eating and drinking and they say: See, the man is an eater and wine drinker, a friend of tax collectors and sinners. And wisdom is justified by what it has done.

Then he began to blame the cities in which his greatest powers had been shown, because they had not repented: Woe to you, Chorazin. Woe to you, Bethsaida. For if there had been shown in Tyre and Sidon the powers that have been shown among you, long since they would have repented in sackcloth and ashes. But I tell you, it will be more tolerable for Tyre and Sidon on the day of judgment than it will be for you. And you, Capernaum, will you be exalted to heaven? You will go down to Hades. For if in Sodom there had been shown the powers that have been shown among you, Sodom would have remained until today. But I tell you that it will be more tolerable for the land of Sodom on the day of judgment than it will be for you.

At that time Jesus spoke and said: I thank you, father, lord of heaven and earth, because you have hidden these things from the clever and the understanding, and revealed them to the simple; yes, father, that thus it has been your pleasure in your sight. All was given to me by my father, and no one knows the son except the father, and no one knows the father except the son, and anyone to whom the son wishes to reveal it. Come to me, all who toil and are burdened, and I will give you rest. Take my yoke upon you and learn from me, because I am gentle and humble at heart, and you will find rest for your souls; for my yoke is good and my burden is light.

❡ At that time Jesus walked on the sabbath through the sown fields; and his disciples were hungry, and began to pick the ears of grain and eat them. But the Pharisees saw it and said to him: See, your disciples are doing what it is forbidden to do on the sabbath. But he said to them: Have you not read what David did when he was hungry, and those with him? How he went into the house of God, and they ate the show bread, which he was not permitted to eat, nor those with him, but only the priests? Or have you not read in the law that on sabbath days the priests in the temple profane the sabbath, and are not guilty? I tell you that here is a thing greater than the temple. But if you knew what this means: I wish mercy, not a sacrifice; then you would not have condemned the guiltless. For the son of man is lord of the sabbath. And passing on from there he went into their synagogue, and behold, there was a man with a withered arm. And they questioned him, saying: Is it lawful to heal on the sabbath? They meant to bring a charge against him. But he said to them: Will there be one of you who owns one sheep, and if it falls down a hole on the sabbath, will not take hold of it and pull it out? How much better a man is than a sheep. Thus it is permitted to do good on the sabbath. Then he said to the man: Stretch out your arm. And he stretched it, and it became sound, like the other arm. But the Pharisees went outside and began plotting against him to destroy him.

Jesus seeing this went away from them, and many followed him, and he healed them all, and charged them not to divulge what he was doing; so as to fulfill the word spoken by the prophet Isaiah, saying: Behold, my son, whom I have chosen, whom I love, and my soul is well pleased with him. I will put my spirit into him, and he will announce the judgment to the nations. He will not fight or cry out, nor will any hear his voice in the public places. He will not break the reed that is bent or quench the flax that is smoking, until he issues his judgment in triumph. And in his name the nations shall have hope.

Then there was brought to him a man possessed by a demon, blind and a deaf-mute, and he healed him, so that the deaf-mute talked and saw. Then all the multitudes were astonished and said: Is this not the son of David? But the Pharisees heard them and said: This man does not drive out demons except through Beelzebub, the prince of demons. He knew their thoughts and said to them: Every kingdom that is divided against itself is made desolate, and every city or house that is divided against itself will not stand. And if Satan drives out Satan, he is divided against himself. How then shall his kingdom stand? If through Beelzebub I drive out demons, through whom do your sons drive them out? Therefore they shall be your judges. But if I drive out demons by the spirit of God, then the Kingdom of God has come to you. Or how can one enter the house of the strong man and seize his goods, unless he first binds the strong man and then plunders his house? He who is not with me is against me, and he who does not join my meetings dispels them. Therefore, I tell you this, every sin and blasphemy shall be forgiven to men, but the blasphemy of the Spirit shall not be forgiven. And if one speaks a word against the son of man, it shall be forgiven him; but if one speaks against the Holy Spirit, it shall not be forgiven him, neither in this age nor the next. Either make the tree good and its fruit good, or make the tree bad and its fruit bad; for from the fruit the tree is known. You viper's brood, how can you say what is good when you are bad? For from what overflows the heart the mouth speaks. The good man issues good from his good storehouse, and the bad man issues bad from his bad storehouse. I tell you, every idle word men speak they shall account for on the day of judgment; for from your words you shall be justified, and from your words judgment shall be given against you.

Then some of the scribes and Pharisees answered him and said: Master, we wish to see a sign from you. He answered and said to them: A corrupt and adulterous generation asks for a sign, and no sign shall be given to it unless it be the sign of Jonah the prophet. For as Jonah was in the belly of the whale three days and three nights, so the son of man shall be in the heart of the earth three days and three nights. The men of Nineveh shall stand up on the day of judgment with this generation and condemn it; because they repented upon the proclamation of Jonah, and behold, there is more than Jonah here. The Queen of the South shall rise up on the day of judgment with this generation and condemn it; because she came from the ends of the earth to listen to the wisdom of Solomon, and behold, there is more than Solomon here. But when the unclean spirit goes out of a man, it wanders through waterless regions looking for a place to rest, and finds none. Then it says: I will return to my house that I came out from; and it comes and finds it free and swept and furnished. Then it goes and picks up seven more spirits worse than itself, and they go and settle there; and the end for that man is worse than the beginning. Thus it will be also with this evil generation.

While he was still talking with the multitudes, behold, his mother and his brothers stood outside, desiring to speak with him. And someone said to him: See, your mother and your brothers are standing outside and desire to speak with you. But he answered and said to the man who reported this: Who is my mother, and who are my brothers? And pointing his hand toward his disciples, he said: These are my mother and my brothers. For whoever does the will of my father in heaven is my brother and sister and mother.

❡ On that day Jesus went out of the house and sat beside the sea; and a great multitude gathered before him, so that he went aboard a ship and sat there, and all the multitude stood on the shore. And he talked to them, speaking mostly in parables: Behold, a sower went out to sow. And as he sowed, some of the grain fell beside the way, and birds came and ate it. Some fell on stony ground where there was not much soil, and it shot up quickly because there was no depth of soil, but when the sun came up it was parched, and because it had no roots it dried away. Some fell among thorns, and the thorns grew up and stifled it. But some fell upon the good soil and bore fruit, some a hundredfold, some sixtyfold, some thirty-fold. He who has ears, let him hear. Then his disciples came to him and said: Why do you talk to them in para-bles? He answered them and said: Because it is given to you to understand the secrets of the Kingdom of Heaven, but to them it is not given. When a man has, he shall be given, and it will be more than he needs; but when he has not, even what he has shall be taken away from him. Therefore I talk to them in parables, because they have sight but do not see, and hearing but do not hear or under-stand. And for them is fulfilled the prophecy of Isaiah, saying: With your hearing you shall hear and not under-stand, and you shall use your sight and look but not see. For the heart of this people is stiffened, and they hear with difficulty, and they have closed their eyes; so that they may never see with their eyes, or hear with their ears and with their hearts understand and turn back, so that I can heal them.

Blessed are your eyes because they see, and your ears because they hear. Truly I tell you that many prophets and good men have longed to see what you see, and not seen it, and to hear what you hear, and not heard it. Hear, then, the parable of the sower. To every man who hears the word of the Kingdom and does not understand it, the evil one comes and seizes what has been sown in his heart. This is the seed sown by the way. The seed sown on the stony ground is the man who hears the word and immediately accepts it with joy; but he has no root in himself, and he is a man of the moment, and when there comes affliction and persecution, because of the word, he does not stand fast. The seed sown among thorns is the man who hears the word, and concern for the world and the beguilement of riches stifle the word, and he bears no fruit. And the seed sown on the good soil is the man who hears the word and understands it, who bears fruit and makes it, one a hundredfold, one sixtyfold, and one thirtyfold.

He set before them another parable, saying: The Kingdom of Heaven is like a man who sowed good seed in his field. And while the people were asleep, his enemy came and sowed darnel in with the grain, and went away. When the plants grew and produced a crop, the darnel was seen. Then the slaves of the master came to him and said: Master, did you not sow good grain in your field? Where does the darnel come from? He said to them: A man who is my enemy did it. His slaves said: Do you wish us to go out and gather it? But he said: No, for fear that when you gather the darnel you may pull up the grain with it. Let them both grow until harvest time, and in the time of harvest I shall say to the harvesters: First gather the darnel, and bind it in sheaves for burning, but store the grain in my granary.

He set before them another parable, saying: The Kingdom of Heaven is like a grain of mustard, which a man took and sowed in his field; which is the smallest of all seeds, but when it grows, it is the largest of the greens and grows into a tree, so that the birds of the air come and nest in its branches.

He told them another parable: The Kingdom of Heaven

is like leaven, which a woman took and buried in three measures of dough, so that it all rose.

All this Jesus told the multitudes in parables, and he did not talk to them except in parables; so as to fulfill the word spoken by the prophet, saying: I will open my mouth in parables, and pour out what has been hidden since the creation. Then he sent away the multitudes and went to the house. And his disciples came to him and said: Make plain to us the parable of the darnel in the field. He answered them and said: The sower of the good seed is the son of man; the field is the world; the good seed is the sons of the Kingdom; the darnel is the sons of the evil one, and the enemy who sowed it is the devil; the harvest time is the end of the world, and the harvesters are angels. Then as the darnel is gathered and burned in the fire, so it is at the end of the world. The son of man will send out his angels, and they will gather from his Kingdom all that misleads, and the people who do what is not lawful, and cast them in the furnace of fire; and there will be weeping and gnashing of teeth. Then the righteous men will shine forth like the sun in the Kingdom of their father. He who has ears, let him hear. The Kingdom of Heaven is like a treasure hidden in the field, which a man found and hid, and for joy of it he goes and sells all he has and buys that field. Again, the Kingdom of Heaven is like a trader looking for fine pearls; he found one of great value, and went and sold all he had and bought it. Again, the Kingdom of Heaven is like a dragnet cast into the sea and netting every kind of fish; and when it is full they draw it out and sit on the beach and gather the good ones in baskets, but the bad they throw away. So will it be at the end of the world. The angels will go out and separate the bad from the midst of the righteous, and cast them in the furnace of fire; and there will be weeping and gnashing of teeth. Do you understand all this? They said to him: Yes. And he said to them: Therefore every scribe who is learned in the Kingdom of Heaven is like a man who is master of a house, who issues from his storehouse what is new and what is old.

Then it happened that when Jesus was through with these parables, he went away from there, and went to his own country and taught them in their synagogue, so that they were astonished, and said: Where has this man found this wisdom and these powers? Is not this the son of the carpenter? Is not his mother called Mary, and his brothers James and Joseph and Simon and Judas? And are not all his sisters with us? From where does this man derive all these powers? And they made it difficult for him. Jesus said to them: No prophet is rejected except in his own country and his own house. And he did not show his powers much there because of their lack of faith.

◀ At this time Herod the tetrarch heard the rumors about Jesus, and said to his children: This is John the Baptist. He has risen from the dead, and therefore powers are at work in him. For Herod had seized John and bound him and put him in prison, because of Herodias, the wife of Philip his brother. For John said to him: It is not lawful for you to have her. And Herod wished to kill him, but he was afraid of the people, because they held him as a prophet. But when it was Herod's birthday, the daughter of Herodias danced before them and pleased Herod, and he agreed with an oath to give her whatever she asked. And she, guided by her mother, said: Give me, here on a platter, the head of John the Baptist. The king was grieved, but because of his oath, and the guests at dinner, he ordered that it should be granted, and sent word and had John beheaded in the prison. Then the head was brought on a platter and given to the girl, and she took it to her mother. Then John's disciples came and took away his body and buried it, and went and told the news to Jesus.

When Jesus heard, he withdrew from there on a ship to a deserted place, privately; and the multitudes heard and followed him on foot from the cities. When he came ashore, he saw a great crowd, and was sorry for them, and healed those among them who were afflicted. Then when it was evening his disciples came to him, saying: This is a lonely place and the time is late; then send the people away so that they can go back to their villages and buy food. But Jesus said to them: There is no need for them to go. Give them something to eat yourselves. They said to him: We have nothing here but five loaves and two fish. He said: Bring them here to me. Then he told the people to take their places on the grass, and took the five loaves and the two fish, and looked up into the sky and gave a blessing, and broke the loaves and gave them to his disciples, and the disciples gave them to the people. And they all ate and were fed, and they picked up what was left over from the broken pieces, twelve baskets full. Those who ate were perhaps five thousand men, not counting women and children.

Then he made the disciples board the ship and precede him to the other side while he dismissed the multitude. And when he had dismissed the multitude, he went up on the mountain, by himself, to pray. When it was evening he was alone there. The ship was now many furlongs out from the land, battered by the waves, for the wind was against them. And in the fourth watch of the night he came toward them, walking on the sea. The disciples saw him walking on the sea and were shaken, saying it was a phantom, and from this fear they cried out. But at once Jesus talked to them, saying: Take heart, it is I; do not fear. Peter answered him and said: Lord, if it is you, bid me go to you on the water. He said: Come. Peter stepped down from the ship and walked on the water and went toward Jesus. But when he saw the storm he was frightened, and began to sink, and cried out, saying: Lord, save me. At once Jesus reached out his hand and took hold of him, and said: You have little faith. Why did you hesitate? And when they went aboard the ship, the wind fell. They who were on the ship worshipped him and said: Truly you are the son of God.

Then they crossed over and went to the country of Gennesaret, and the people of that region recognized him and sent word to all the country about, and brought to him all those who were afflicted, and begged of him that they might touch just the border of his mantle. And those who touched it were healed.

◀ Then Pharisees and scribes came to Jesus from Jerusalem, saying: Why do your disciples go against the tradition of our elders? For they do not wash their hands when they eat bread. And he answered them and said: Why do you also go against the commandment of God because of your own tradition? For God said: Give due right to your father and mother; and: Let him who speaks rudely to his father or mother be put to death. But you say: If one says to his father or mother: Whatever profit you might have had from me is a gift to God; then such a one will not have to give due right to his father or mother. And you have made void the word of God, because of your tradition. Hypocrites, Isaiah prophesied well concerning you, saying: This people honors me with the lips, but their heart is far away from me; they worship me vainly, teaching doctrines which are the precepts of men.

Then summoning the multitude he said to them: Hear and understand. It is not what goes into the mouth that defiles a man but what comes out of the mouth; that defiles a man. Then his disciples came to him and said: Do you know that the Pharisees who heard this word objected to it? He answered and said: Every plant which was not planted by my father in heaven shall be uprooted. Let them go. They are blind guides of blind men; when blind man guides blind man, both will fall into the pit. Peter answered him and said: Explain the parable to us. He said: Are even you still unable to understand? Do you not see that everything that goes into the mouth passes to the belly and is voided into the privy, but what comes out of the mouth comes from the heart, and that defiles a man. For from the heart come vile thoughts, murders, adulteries, fornications, thefts, false testimonies, blasphemies. These are what defile a man. To eat with unwashed hands does not defile a man.

Then Jesus left there and went away to the regions of Tyre and Sidon. And behold, a Canaanite woman from those parts came out and cried to him, saying: Pity me, son of David. My daughter is sadly vexed with a demon. But he said not a word in answer. Then his disciples came up to him and pressed him, saying: Send her away, for she follows us crying. He answered and said: I was not sent forth except after the lost sheep of the house of Israel. But she came and bowed before him, saying: Lord, help me.

He answered and said: It is not well to take the bread of the children and throw it to the dogs. But she said: Yes, Lord, for even the dogs eat from the crumbs that fall from the table of their masters. Then Jesus answered and said to her: Woman, your faith is great. Let it be as you wish. And her daughter was healed from that hour.

Then Jesus went from there and came beside the Sea of Galilee, and going up on the mountain he sat there. And there came to him great multitudes, having with them their lame, crippled, blind, deaf and dumb, and many others; and they flung them at his feet; and he healed them, so that the multitude were astonished when they saw deaf-mutes speaking, cripples made sound, and lame men walking about, and blind men seeing; and they glorified the God of Israel. But Jesus summoned his disciples to him and said: I have pity for the multitude, because it is now three days they have stayed with me, and they have nothing to eat; and I do not wish to send them away hungry, for fear they give out on the way. The disciples said: How shall we come by enough bread in the desert to feed such a multitude? And Jesus said to them: How many loaves do you have? They said: Seven, and a few little fish. Then he gave the word to the people to take their places on the ground, and took the loaves and the fish, and gave thanks, and broke them up and gave them to his disciples, and his disciples gave them to the people. And all ate and were fed, and they picked up what was left over from the broken pieces, seven baskets full. Those who ate were four thousand men, not counting women and children. Then he sent away the people and went aboard the ship, and came to the regions of Magadan.

¶ Then Pharisees and Sadducees came to him and made trial of him and asked him to show them a sign from the sky. He answered them and said: When it is sunset, you say: Fair weather, for the sky is red. And when it is dawn: Stormy today, for the sky is red and threatening. Do you know how to judge the face of the sky, and can you not judge the signs of the times? A corrupt and adulterous generation asks for a sign, and no sign shall be given to it, unless it be the sign of Jonah. Then he left them and went away.

When the disciples crossed to the other side they forgot to take bread. And Jesus said to them: Be watchful and beware of the leaven of the Pharisees and Sadducees. Then they talked among themselves, saying: We did not bring bread. Jesus perceived it and said: Why do you talk among yourselves, you men of little faith, about having no bread. Do you not yet see, do you not remember the five loaves of the five thousand and all the baskets you gathered? Or the seven loaves of the four thousand and all the baskets you gathered. How can you not see that I was not talking to you about bread? But beware of the leaven of the Pharisees and Sadducees. Then they understood that he had not told them to beware of the leaven of bread, but of the teaching of the Pharisees and Sadducees.

When Jesus came to the regions of Caesarea Philippi, he questioned his disciples, saying: Who do men say the son of man is? They said: Some say John the Baptist, some Elijah, and others say Jeremiah or one of the prophets. He said to them: And you, who do you say I am? And Simon Peter said: You are the Christ, the son of the living God. Jesus answered him and said: Blessed are you, Simon Bariona; for it was not flesh and blood that revealed this to you but my father who is in heaven. And I tell you, you are Peter, the Rock, and upon this rock I will build my church, and the gates of Hades shall have no power against it. I shall give you the keys of the Kingdom of Heaven, and what you close upon earth shall be closed in heaven, and what you open on earth shall be open in heaven.

Then he warned his disciples to tell no one that he was the Christ.

From that time, Jesus began to show his disciples that he must go to Jerusalem, and suffer much from the elders and the high priests and the scribes, and be killed, and rise up on the third day. But Peter laid his hand upon him and tried to warn him, and said: Lord, be of good cheer; this shall not happen to you. He turned to Peter and said: Go behind me, Satan; you would put me off my way, because you do not think the thoughts of God but the thoughts of men. Then Jesus said to his disciples: If anyone wishes to go after me, let him deny himself and take up his cross and follow me. For he who wishes to save his life will lose it; and he who loses his life for my sake shall find it. For what will it advantage a man if he gains the whole world but must pay with his life? Or what will a man give that is worth as much as his life? The son of man is to come in the glory of his father among his angels, and then he will give to each according to what each has done. Truly I tell you that there are some of those who stand here who will not taste of death until they see the son of man coming in his Kingdom.

❡ Then after six days Jesus took with him Peter and James and John the brother of James, and led them up on a high mountain, by themselves. And he was transfigured before them, and his face blazed like the sun, and his clothing became white as light. And behold, Moses and Elijah were seen talking with him. But Peter spoke forth and said to Jesus: Lord, it is good for us to be here. If you wish, I will make three shelters here, one for you and one for Moses and one for Elijah. While he was still speaking, behold, a shining cloud covered them, and behold, a voice from the cloud saying: This is my son whom I love, in whom I am well pleased. Listen to him. When the disciples heard, they threw themselves upon their faces and were greatly afraid. And Jesus came to them and laid his hands upon them and said: Rise up and do not fear. And lifting their eyes they saw no one except Jesus himself alone.

Then as they were coming down from the mountain Jesus enjoined them and said: Do not speak of the vision until the son of man is raised from the dead. And his disciples asked him and said: Why then do the scribes say that Elijah must come first. He answered and said: Elijah will come and will set all right again. But I tell you that Elijah has already come, and they did not know him, and did with him what they wished; thus also is the son of man to suffer at their hands. Then the disciples understood that he spoke to them about John the Baptist.

Then as they came to the multitude there came a man who knelt to him and said: Lord, have pity on my son, for he is epileptic and in evil case; for often he falls into the fire, and often into the water. And I brought him to your disciples, and they were not able to heal him. Jesus answered and said: O generation without faith and perverse, how long shall I be with you? How long shall I endure you? Bring him here to me. And Jesus scolded him, and the demon went out of him, and the boy was healed from that hour. Then his disciples came to Jesus privately and said: Why were we not able to cast it out? He said to them: Because of your little faith. Truly I tell you, if you have faith as large as a grain of mustard, you will say to this mountain: Move from here to there; and it will move, and nothing will be impossible to you.

Now as they gathered in Galilee, Jesus said to them: The son of man is to be given over into the hands of men, and they will kill him, and on the third day he will rise. And they were greatly saddened.

Then when they came to Capernaum, those who took up the two-drachma tax came up to Peter and said: Does not your teacher pay the two drachmas? He said: Yes. And as he was going into the house, Jesus intercepted him and said: What do you think, Simon? From whom do the kings of the earth take their taxes and their assessment? From their sons or from strangers? When he said: From strangers, Jesus said to him: Thus their sons go free. But so that we may cause them no trouble, go to the sea and let down your hook, and take the first fish that comes up, and open its mouth and you will find a stater. Take it and give it to them, for you and me.

◀ In that time, his disciples came to Jesus and said: Who is greater in the Kingdom of Heaven? Then he called a child to him and set him in the midst of them, and said: Truly I tell you, if you do not turn about and become as children are, you shall not enter the Kingdom of Heaven. He then who makes himself small as this child is, he shall be the greater in the Kingdom of Heaven. And if one accepts one child like this in my name, he accepts me. But if one leads astray one of these little ones who have faith in me, it is better for him to have a millstone hung about his

neck and be drowned in the sea. Woe to the world from
the troubles which shall be caused. For it is necessary for
the troubles to come, but woe to him through whom the
trouble comes. If your hand or foot makes you go amiss,
cut it off and throw it from you; for it is better to go into
life one-handed or lame than with both hands and both
feet to be thrown into everlasting fire. And if your eye
makes you go amiss, take it out and throw it from you; for
it is better for you to go into life with one eye than with
both eyes to be thrown into Gehenna. Take care that you
do not despise one of these little ones; for I tell you that
their angels in heaven forever look upon the face of my
father in heaven. What do you think? If a man has a hundred sheep, and one of them strays, will he not let the
ninety-nine go on the mountain, and go and look for the
one that has strayed? And if it befalls him to find it, truly I
tell you, he takes more joy over it than over the ninety-
nine that did not stray. Thus there is no intention on the
part of your father, who is in heaven, that one of these
little ones should be lost.

If your brother does you wrong, go and charge him with
it between you and him alone. If he listens to you, you
have won your brother over. But if he does not listen to
you, take along with you one or two more, so that everything said may be on the lips of two or three witnesses.
And if he will not listen to them, tell it to the congregation. And if he will not listen even to the congregation, let
him be to you as the Gentile and the tax collector. Truly I
tell you, all that you close on earth shall be closed in
heaven, and all that you open on earth shall be open in
heaven. Again I tell you, if two of you agree on earth
concerning everything they ask for, it shall be granted
them by my father in heaven. For where there are two or

three gathered together in my name, there I am in their midst.

Then Peter came to him and said: Lord, how many times shall my brother do me wrong, and I forgive him? As many as seven times? Jesus said to him: I tell you, not as many as seven times, but as many as seventy times seven. Thus the Kingdom of Heaven has been likened to a man who is a king, who wished to settle accounts with his slaves, and as he began to cast up accounts, there was brought to him one who was in his debt for ten thousand talents. When he could not pay it, the master said he must be sold, and his wife and children and all he had, and payment made. Then the slave threw himself down and worshipped him, saying: Delay your anger against me, and I will pay you back all. And the master took pity on his slave and let him go and forgave him his debt. That slave went out and found a fellow slave who owed him a hundred denarii, and seized him and choked him and said: Pay me back what you owe me. His fellow slave threw himself down before him and begged him, saying: Delay your anger against me and I will pay you back. But he would not, but went and threw him into prison until he should pay his debt. When his fellow slaves saw this they were much grieved and went and explained to their master all that had happened. Then the master called the man before him and said to him: Wicked slave, I forgave you all that other debt, since you begged me to. Should you not then have had pity on your fellow slave, as I myself pitied you? And the master in anger handed him over to the torturers until he could pay back all that he owed him. Thus also will my father in heaven do to you, unless each of you forgives his brother, from your heart.

❡ Then it came about that when Jesus had done with these sayings, he removed from Galilee and went into the border districts of Judaea, across Jordan. And many multitudes followed him, and he treated them.

Then Pharisees came to him, making trial of him and saying: Is it lawful for a man to divorce his wife, for any cause? He answered and said: Have you not read that from the beginning the creator made them male and female, and said: Because of this, a man will leave his father and mother and cling to his wife, and they will be two in one flesh. So that they are no longer two, but one flesh. Then what God has joined together, let man not separate. They said to him: Why then did Moses decree that one might give a note of divorce, and divorce her. He said to them: Moses, looking toward the hardness of your hearts, permitted you to divorce your wives; but it was not so from the beginning. And I tell you that he who divorces his wife, except for harlotry, and marries another, is committing adultery. His disciples said to him: If this is the case with man and wife, it is better not to marry. He said to them: Not all can accept this saying, but those to whom it is given. For there are sexless men who have been so from their mother's womb, and there are sexless men who have been made sexless by other men, and there are sexless men who have made themselves sexless for the sake of the Kingdom of Heaven. Let him who can accept, accept.

Then children were brought to him, so that he could lay his hands on them and pray for them. But his disciples scolded them. But Jesus said: Let the children be and do not prevent them from coming to me. For of such is the Kingdom of Heaven. And he laid his hands on them, and went away from there.

Then, behold, there was one who came to him and said:
Master, what shall I do that is good, so that I may have life
forever? He said to him: Why do you ask me about good?
One only is good. But if you wish to enter life, keep the
commandments. He said to him: Which commandments? Jesus said: That you shall not murder, or commit
adultery, or steal, or bear false witness; honor your father
and your mother, and love your neighbor as you love
yourself. The young man said to him: I have kept all these
commandments. What more must I do? Jesus said to him:
If you wish to be perfect, go sell what belongs to you and
give it to the poor, and you shall have a treasury in
heaven. And come and follow me. When the young man
heard what he said, he went sadly away; for he was one
who had many possessions. But Jesus said to his disciples:
Truly I tell you that it will be hard for a rich man to enter
the Kingdom of Heaven. And again I tell you that it is
easier for a camel to enter the eye of a needle than for a
rich man to enter the Kingdom of God. When his disciples
heard this, they were greatly astonished, and said: Who
then can be saved? Jesus looked at them and said: For men
it is impossible, but for God all things are possible. Then
Peter took him up and said: See, we have given up everything and followed you. What then will there be for us?
Jesus said to them: Truly I tell you, in the next life, when
the son of man is seated on the throne of his glory, you
who have followed me shall be seated, you also, upon
twelve thrones, and judge the twelve tribes of Israel. And
everyone who has given up houses or brothers or sisters or
father or mother or children or lands for the sake of my
name, shall have them back many times over and inherit
life everlasting. And many who are first shall be last, and
many who are last shall be first.

⁋ For the Kingdom of Heaven is like a man, the master of a house, who went out in the early morning to hire laborers for his vineyard. He agreed with the laborers for a denarius a day and sent them off to his vineyard. Then going out about the third hour he saw others standing idle in the marketplace, and said to them: Go on, you also, into my vineyard, and I will pay you whatever is fair. And they went. And going out again about the sixth and the ninth hour he did likewise. And about the eleventh hour he went out and found more men standing there, and said to them: Why are you standing thus idle all day? They said to him: Because nobody hired us. He said to them: Go on, you also, into my vineyard. Then when it was twilight the master of the vineyard said to his overseer: Call the laborers and pay them their wages, beginning with the last to come and going on to the first. And those who had come at the eleventh hour came and were paid a denarius each. And those who had been hired first came and thought they would receive more; and they also were paid a denarius each. But when they were paid they murmured against the master of the house, saying: Those who came last did one hour's work, and you have made them the equals of us, who bore the heaviness of the day and the heat. But he answered one of them and said: Friend, I do you no wrong. Did you not agree with me on one denarius? Take your wages and go. But I desire to give this last man the same as I gave you. Can I not do as I wish with what is my own? Or does your eye hurt because I am kind?

Thus they who are last shall be first and they who are first shall be last.

Then as Jesus set out to go up to Jerusalem he took the twelve with him, alone, and on the way he said to them: Behold, we are going to Jerusalem, and the son of man will be given over into the hands of the high priests and the scribes and they will condemn him to death, and give him over to the Gentiles to mock and flog and crucify; and on the third day he will rise.

At that time there came to him the mother of the sons of Zebedee with her sons, and bowed before him and had something to ask of him. He said to her: What do you wish? She said: Tell me that these, my two sons, shall sit on your right and on your left in your Kingdom. Jesus answered and said: You do not know what you are asking. Can you drink the cup that I am to drink? They said: We can. He said to them: You shall drink my cup; but for you to sit on my right and on my left, that is not mine to give, but it is for those who have been appointed by my father. Hearing this, the other ten were indignant over the two brothers. But Jesus called them to him and said: You know that the leaders of the Gentiles are lords over them, and their great men exercise power over them. It is not thus with you; but he who wishes to be great among you shall be your servant, and he who wishes to be first among you shall be your slave; as the son of man came not to be served but to serve, and to give his own life for the redemption of many.

Now as they were going out from Jericho a great crowd followed him. And behold, two blind men sitting by the road, hearing that Jesus was going by, cried aloud and said: Lord, have pity on us, son of David. But the people told them angrily to be quiet, but they cried the louder, saying: Lord, have pity on us, son of David. Jesus stopped and spoke to them and said: What do you wish me to do for you? They told him: Lord, let our eyes be opened. Jesus pitied them, and laid his hands on their eyes, and at once they saw, and followed him.

◀ Then as they came near Jerusalem and arrived at Bethphage, at the Mount of Olives, Jesus sent two of his disciples ahead, saying to them: Go on into the village that lies before you, and presently you will find a donkey, tethered, and a foal with her. Untie them and bring them to me. And if anyone says anything to you, say that their master needs them, and he will send them at once. This was done so as to fulfill the word spoken by the prophet, saying: Say to the daughter of Zion: Behold, your king comes to you, modest and riding on a donkey and with a foal, the son of a beast of burden. His disciples went and did as Jesus told them, and brought the donkey and the foal, and piled clothing on them, and he sat on this. And most of the crowd strewed clothing of their own in the road, and others cut branches from the trees and strewed them in the road. And the crowds who went before him and who came after him cried aloud, saying: Hosanna to the son of David. Blessed is he who comes in the name of the Lord. Hosanna in the highest. And when he entered Jerusalem, all the city was disturbed, and said: Who is this? And the multitude answered: This is the prophet Jesus of Nazareth in Galilee.

And Jesus went into the temple and drove out all who bought and sold in the temple, and overturned the tables of the money changers and the stalls of the sellers of doves, and said to them: It is written: My house shall be called a house of prayer, and you are making it a den of robbers. And the blind and the lame came to him in the temple, and he healed them. When the high priests and the scribes saw the wonders he performed, and that the boys cried out in the temple and said: Hosanna to the son of David, they were angry and said to him: Do you hear what they are saying? But Jesus said to them: Yes. Have you never read that from the mouths of children and babies you have composed praise?

Then he left them and went out of the city, into Bethany, and spent the night there. Early in the morning he came back to the city, and he was hungry. And seeing a single fig tree beside the road, he went to it, and found nothing on it except only leaves, and said to it: Let there be no more fruit from you, forevermore. And at once the fig tree dried up. His disciples seeing it were astonished and said: How did the fig tree suddenly dry up? Jesus answered them and said: Truly I tell you, if you have faith and do not deliberate, you can not only do what was done to the fig tree but you can even say to this mountain: Rise up and throw yourself into the sea, and it will happen; and all that you ask for by prayer, if you have faith, you shall receive.

Now when he had gone into the temple and was teaching there, the high priests and the elders of the people came to him, saying: By what authority do you do this, and who gave you this authority? Jesus answered and said to them: I too will ask you to tell me one thing, and if you tell me, I will tell you by what authority I do this. Whence came the baptism of John? From heaven or from men? They discussed this among themselves, saying: If we tell him: From heaven, he will say to us: Then why did you not believe him? But if we tell him: From men, then we have the people to fear, for they all hold John to be a prophet. And they answered Jesus and said: We do not know. He answered them in turn: Neither will I tell you by what authority I do this. What do you think? A man had two sons. He went to the first and said: My son, go out today and work in the vineyard. He answered and said: So I will, master; and did not go. He went to the second and spoke likewise; and he answered and said: I do not wish to; but later he repented and did go. Which of the two did his father's will? They said: The second. Jesus said to them: Truly I tell you that the tax collectors and the harlots shall go before you into the Kingdom of God. For John came to you in the way of righteousness, and you did not believe him; but the tax collectors and the harlots believed him; and when you saw it you did not repent, so as to believe him.

Hear one more parable. There was a man who was lord of a manor, and he planted a vineyard, and ran a fence about it and dug a pit for the wine press in it, and built a tower, and let it out to farmers, and left the country. When the time of the harvest was near, he sent his slaves to the farmers to take the harvest. And the farmers took his slaves, and one they lashed, and one they killed, and one they stoned. Again he sent slaves, more than the first ones, and they dealt with them in the same way. After this he sent his son, saying: They will respect my son. But when the farmers saw the son, they said among themselves: This is the heir. Come, let us kill him and take his inheritance. And they took him and cast him out of the vineyard and killed him. Now, when the lord of the vineyard comes, what will he do to those farmers? They said: He will destroy them evilly, as they are evil, and let the vineyard to other farmers, who will render him the harvests in their due time. Jesus said to them: Have you never read in the scriptures: The stone that the builders rejected has come to be at the head of the corner. It was made by the Lord, and is wonderful in our sight. Therefore I tell you that the Kingdom of God shall be taken away from you and given to a nation that produces its harvest. [And he who falls on that stone shall be broken; and he upon whom it falls shall be crushed by it.] And when the high priests and the Pharisees heard his parables they knew that he spoke of them; and they were looking for a way to seize him, but they feared the populace, since these held him to be a prophet.

◀ Then Jesus spoke forth again and talked to them in parables, saying: The Kingdom of Heaven is like a king who held a wedding for his son. And he sent out his slaves to summon the invited guests to the wedding, and they would not come. Again he sent forth more slaves, saying to them: Tell the invited guests: See, I have made the dinner ready, my oxen and calves are sacrificed, and all is ready; come to the wedding. But they paid no heed and went their ways, one to his own lands, one to his house of business, but the others seized the slaves and outraged them and killed them. Then the king was angry and sent out his armies and destroyed those murderers and burned their city. Then he said to his slaves: The wedding feast is ready, but the invited guests were not worthy. Go out then to the street corners and invite any you find there, to the wedding. And those slaves went out into the streets and brought in all they found, bad and good, and the wedding hall was filled with guests at the tables. The king came in to see them at dinner, and saw one man who was not wearing a wedding garment; and he said to him: My friend, how did you come in here without a wedding garment? The man was speechless. Then the king said to his servants: Tie his feet and his hands and cast him into the outer darkness. There will be wailing and gnashing of teeth. For many are invited but few are accepted.

Then the Pharisees went and held a consultation, in order to catch him up in what he said. They sent their disciples along with the Herodians, and they said: Master, we know that you are truthful, and you teach the way of God truthfully, and you care for no man, for you are no respecter of persons. Tell us then what you think. Is it lawful to pay the assessment to Caesar, or not? Jesus guessed at their treachery and said: Hypocrites, why do you tempt me? Show me the coin for the assessment. They showed him a denarius. He said: Whose is the image, and whose name is inscribed? They said: Caesar's. Then he said to them: Then give Caesar what is Caesar's and God what is God's. When they heard this, they were left wondering, and let him be, and went away.

On that day there came to him Sadducees, who say that there is no resurrection. And they questioned him, saying: Master, Moses said: If a man dies without children, his brother shall marry his wife and raise up issue for his brother. But among us there were seven brothers. The first married and died without issue, and left his wife to his brother; and so also did the second and third until all seven had married her. Last of all the woman died. So in the resurrection, whose wife will she be, of the seven? For they all had her as wife. Jesus answered and said to them: You are far astray and do not know the scriptures, nor yet the power of God. For in the resurrection they do not marry, nor are they married, but are as the angels in heaven. But as to the resurrection of the dead, have you not read the word spoken to you by God, saying: I am the

God of Abraham and the God of Isaac and the God of Jacob. God is not God of the dead but of the living. Hearing this the multitude were struck with wonder at his teaching.

But when the Pharisees heard that he had silenced the Sadducees, they assembled together, and one of them who was versed in the law questioned him, making trial of him: Master, in the law, which is the great commandment? He said: That you shall love the Lord your God in all your heart and all your spirit and all your mind. That is the great commandment, and the first. There is a second, which is like it: You shall love your neighbor as yourself. On these two commandments all the law and the prophets depend. And when the Pharisees were gathered together, Jesus questioned them, saying: What do you think concerning the Christ? Whose son is he? They said to him: The son of David. He said: How then did David call him in the spirit, Lord, when he said: The Lord said to my Lord: Sit on my right, so that I may put your enemies beneath your feet. But if David calls him Lord, how can he be his son? And none of them could answer him a word, nor did anyone dare from that day to question him any more.

◖ Then Jesus spoke to the people and to his disciples, saying: The scribes and the Pharisees sit in the chair of Moses. Do and observe all that they tell you, but do not do as they do; for they speak, and do nothing. They tie up heavy bundles and put them on the shoulders of men, but they will not use one finger to carry them. All they do is done for show, before people; they spread their phylacteries and wear large tassels, they love the foremost couch at the dinners and the first seats in the synagogues, and the salutations in the marketplace, and being called rabbi by the people. Do not let yourselves be called rabbi; for you have one teacher, but you are all brothers. And do not call anyone your father on earth; for you have one father, in heaven. And do not let yourselves be called instructors, since you have one instructor, the Christ. He who is greater than you shall be your servant. He who exalts himself shall be brought low, and he who lowers himself shall be exalted.

Woe to you, scribes and Pharisees, hypocrites, because you shut the Kingdom of Heaven in the face of mankind; for neither do you go in yourselves, nor do you let those who are trying to enter go in. Woe to you, scribes and Pharisees, hypocrites, because you sweep the sea and the dry land to make one convert, and when it is done, you make him a son of Gehenna twice over as much as yourselves. Woe to you, blind guides who say: If one swears by the temple, it is nothing, but if one swears by the gold of the temple, he is bound. Fools and blind men, which is greater, the gold or the temple that hallows the gold? Again you say: If one swears by the altar, it is nothing, but if one swears by the offering upon the altar, he is bound. Blind, for which is greater, the offering or the altar that hallows the offering? So one who swears by the altar swears by it and all that is on it; and one who swears by the temple swears by it and by him who dwells in it; and one who swears by heaven swears by the throne of God and by him who sits upon it. Woe to you, scribes and Pharisees, hypocrites, because you pay a tenth on the mint and the anise and the cumin, and have passed over what is weightier in the law, the judgment and the mercy and the faith. These you should have cultivated, nor yet passed over the other things. Blind guides, who filter out the gnat but swallow the camel whole. Woe to you, scribes and Pharisees, hypocrites, because you scour the outside of the cup and the dish, but inside they are filled with rapacity and incontinence. Blind Pharisees, scour first the inside of the cup, so that the outside may be also clean. Woe to you, scribes and Pharisees, hypocrites, because you are like tombs that are whitewashed, which show handsome on the outside, but inside they are full of dead bones and all uncleanness. So you too on the outside seem to men to be just, but on the inside you are full of hypocrisy and lawlessness. Woe to you, scribes and Pharisees, hypocrites, because you build the tombs of the prophets and adorn the monuments of the just, and say: If we had been in the days of our fathers, we should not have been guilty of the blood of the prophets. Thus you bear witness against yourselves that you are the sons of those who murdered the prophets. Fill out, then, the measure of your fathers. Serpents, viper's brood, how can you escape the judgment of Gehenna? Therefore, see, I send you the prophets and the wise men and the scribes; and some of them you will kill and crucify, and some of them you will lash in your synagogues and chase from city to city, so that upon you shall descend all righteous blood that has been poured out upon earth, from the blood of Abel the righteous to the blood of Zachariah the son of Barach, whom you murdered between the temple and the altar. Truly I tell you, all this shall descend upon this generation. Jerusalem Jerusalem, who kill the prophets and stone those who have been sent to you, how many times have I wished to gather in your children, as a bird gathers her fledglings under her wings, and you would not let me. Behold, your house is lost. For I tell you, you shall not see me again,

until you say: Blessed is he who comes in the name of the
Lord.

¶ And Jesus left the temple and was going on his way, and
his disciples came to him, to show him the buildings of
the temple. But he answered them and said: Do you not
see all this? Truly I tell you, nothing here shall escape
destruction and no stone will be left on another. Then he
sat down upon the Mount of Olives, and his disciples
came to him privately and said: Tell us, when shall this
be, and what is the sign of your presence and the end of
the world? Jesus answered and said to them: See to it that
no one leads you astray. For many will come in my name,
saying: I am the Christ. And they will lead many astray.
You will hear wars and rumors of wars. Be watchful, do
not be frightened. For this must be, but the end is not yet.
Nation shall rise up against nation and kingdom against
kingdom, and there shall be famines and earthquakes,
place by place; all these things are the beginnings of the
agony. Then they will hand you over for persecution, and
kill you, and you will be hated by all the nations because
of my name. And at this time many shall be driven astray
and betray and hate each other, and many false prophets
shall rise up, and they shall lead many astray; and
through abundance of lawlessness the love of many shall
grow cold. He who endures to the end shall be saved. And
this gospel of the kingdom shall be preached in all the
inhabited world in testimony to all the nations, and then
the end will come. Thus when you see the abomination of
desolation, that was told by Daniel the prophet, established in the holy place—and let him who reads this take
note of it—then let those who are in Judaea flee to the

mountains, and let him who is on the housetop not come down to take up what is in his house, and let him who is in the field not turn back to pick up his coat. Woe to the women who are with child and the women who are nursing in those days. Pray that your flight may not come in the wintertime, nor on the sabbath. For at that time there will be great affliction, such as there has not been since the beginning of creation and cannot be again. And if those days had not been cut short, there would be no flesh saved; but because of the chosen, those days will be shortened. Then, if anyone says to you: Here is the Christ, or here; do not believe him. For false Christs will rise up and false prophets, and they will present great signs and portents, so as to mislead even the chosen, if that may be done. See, I have warned you. If then they say to you: See, he is in the desert; do not go out; or, see, he is in the countinghouses; do not believe. For as the lightning goes out from the east and shines as far as the west, thus shall be the coming of the son of man. Where the carcass is, there will the eagles be gathered. And at once after the affliction of those days the sun will be darkened and the moon will not give her light, and the stars will fall from the sky, and the powers of the skies will be shaken. And then will appear the sign of the son of man in the sky, and then all the tribes of the earth will beat themselves, and see the son of man coming upon the clouds with power and great glory, and he will send out his angels with a great trumpet, and they will gather the chosen together from the four winds and from end to end of the sky. From the fig tree learn its parable; when its branch is tender and it puts forth leaves, you know that the summer is near; so too when you see all these things, you know that he is near, at your doors. Truly I tell you that this generation will not pass before all these things are done. The sky and the earth will pass away, but my words cannot pass away. But concerning that day and hour none knows, not the angels of heaven nor the son, none but the father alone. For as the days of Noah, thus will be the coming of the son of man. For as in those days before the flood there were people eating and drinking, marrying and making marriages, until the day when Noah went aboard his ark, and they did not know, until the flood came and took them all away; thus also will be the coming of the son of man. Then there will be two in the field, and one taken and one left; two women grinding at the mill, and one taken and one left. Be watchful then, because you do not know on what day your Lord will come. But you know this, that if the master of the house had known the time when the burglar would come, he would have stayed awake and would not have let his house be broken into. Therefore make yourselves also ready, because in the hour when you do not expect him the son of man will come. Who then is the faithful and prudent slave whom the master set over his household, to give them their food when it is due? Blessed is that slave whom his master, when he comes, will find doing so. Truly I tell you that he will put him in charge of all his possessions. But if that other, bad slave says in his heart: My master is long coming; and begins to beat his fellow slaves, and eat and drink with the drunkards; the master of that slave will come on the day when he does not expect him and in the hour when he is unaware, and cut him to ribbons, and make his lot one with the hypocrites; and there will be wailing and gnashing of teeth.

◀ Then the Kingdom of Heaven will be like ten girls who took their lamps and went out to meet the bridegroom. And five of them were thoughtless, and five were thoughtful. For the thoughtless ones, when they took their lamps, did not take oil with them, and the thoughtful ones took oil in their flasks along with their lamps. When the bridegroom was late they all grew sleepy and slept. But in the middle of the night there was a great outcry: Behold, the bridegroom; go out to meet him. Then all those girls woke up and trimmed their lamps, but the thoughtless ones said to those who were thoughtful: Give us some of your oil, since our lamps are going out. But the thoughtful ones answered, saying: There would never be enough for us and for you. Better, go to those who sell it and buy it for yourselves. But while they were gone to buy it, the bridegroom arrived, and those who were ready went in with him to the wedding, and the door was shut. Then later came the other girls, saying: Lord, lord, open to us. But he answered and said: Truly I tell you, I do not know you. Be watchful then, since you do not know the day, or the hour.

For it is like a man who made a journey, and called in his own slaves and handed over to them all his properties. And to one he gave five talents, to one two, to one one, each according to his ability, and went away. At once the one who had received five talents went into business with them, and made five more; so also the one who had received two made another two. But the man who had received one went away and dug a hole in the ground and hid the money of his master in it. Then after a long time the master of those slaves came back and cast up accounts with them. And the one who had received five talents came forward and delivered five talents more, saying: Master, you gave me five talents; see, I have made five talents more. His master said to him: Well done, good and trusty slave; you were trusty in small amounts, I will set you in charge of much. Come in and share your master's festivities. Then he who had received two talents came forward and said: Master, you gave me two talents; see, I have made two talents more. His master said to him: Well done, good and trusty slave; you were trusty in small amounts, I will set you in charge of much. Come in and share your master's festivities. Then he who had received one talent came forward and said: Master, I knew that you were a hard man, that you harvest where you did not sow, that you gather where you did not scatter the seed; and I was afraid and went away and buried your talent in the ground; see, you have what is yours. His master answered and said to him: Wretched timid slave! Did you know that I harvest where I did not sow, that I gather where I did not scatter the seed? You should have put the money out with the bankers, and I could have gone and taken back my own, with interest. Take away his talent and give it to him who has the ten talents; for to everyone who has shall be given, even in excess; but from him who has not, even what he has shall be taken away. And cast this useless slave into the outer darkness; there will be wailing and gnashing of teeth.

When the son of man comes in his glory, and all the angels with him, then he will sit upon the throne of his glory, and all the nations shall be gathered before him, and he will sort them one from another, as the shepherd separates the sheep from the goats, and he will station the sheep on his right hand, and the goats on his left. Then the king will say to those who are on his right: Come, you who are the blessed of my father, inherit the kingdom which has been made ready for you from the beginning of the world. For I was hungry and you fed me, I was thirsty and you gave me to drink, I was a stranger and you took me in, I was naked and you clothed me, I was sick and you visited me, I was in prison and you came to me. Then the just will answer him, saying: Lord, when did we see you hungry and feed you, or thirsty and give you to drink? When did we see you a stranger and take you in, or naked and clothe you? When did we see you sick or in prison and come to you? And the king will answer and say to them: Truly I tell you, inasmuch as you have done it for any one of the least of these my brothers, you have done it for me. Then he will say to those on his left: Go from me, cursed, to the everlasting fire which has been made ready by the devil and his angels. For I was hungry and you did not feed me, I was thirsty and you did not give me to drink, I was a stranger and you did not take me in, I was naked and you did not clothe me, I was sick and in prison and you did not visit me. And they will answer him, saying: Lord, when did we see you hungry or thirsty or a stranger or naked or sick or in prison and not take care of you? Then he will answer them and say: Truly I tell you, inasmuch as you have failed to do this for one of these who are least, you have failed to do it for me. And these shall go to everlasting punishment, but the just to everlasting life.

◀ Then it happened, when Jesus had done with all these sayings, that he said to his disciples: You know tha. after two days the Passover comes, and the son of man will be handed over to be crucified. Then the high priests and the elders of the people gathered in the courtyard of the high priest who was called Caiaphas, and they made plans to capture Jesus by treachery and kill him. But they said: Not during the festival, for fear there may be rioting among the people.

Now when Jesus was in Bethany, in the house of Simon the leper, there came to him a woman with an alabaster vessel full of precious ointment and anointed his head with it as he reclined at dinner. When his disciples saw this they were displeased and said: Why this waste? It could have been sold for a great price and the money given to the poor. Jesus was aware of them and said: Why are you hard on the woman? She has done a good thing to me. For always you have the poor with you, but you do not always have me. When she anointed my body with this ointment, it was for my burial. Truly I tell you, wherever this gospel is preached through all the world, she will be spoken of, and what she did, in memory of her.

And at that time one of the twelve, he who was called Judas Iscariot, went to the high priests and said: What are you willing to give me if I betray him to you? And they paid him thirty pieces of silver. And from that time he looked for an opportunity to betray him.

On the first day of the feast of unleavened bread, his disciples came to Jesus and said: Where do you wish us to make preparations for you to eat the feast of the Passover? He said: Go to the city, to the house of a certain man, and say to him: The teacher says: My time is near. I shall keep the Passover at your house, with my disciples. And his disciples did as Jesus instructed them, and made ready the Passover. When it was evening, he took his place at dinner with the twelve disciples. And as they were eating he said: Truly I tell you that one of you will betray me. They were bitterly hurt and began each one to say: Surely it is not I, Lord? He answered and said: The one who dips his hand in the dish with me, he is the one who will betray me. The son of man goes his way as it has been written for him to do, but woe to that man through whom the son of man is betrayed. It would have been well for that man if he had never been born. Judas, who had betrayed him, answered and said: Master, it is not I? Jesus said to him: It is you who said it. As they ate, Jesus took a loaf of bread, and blessed it, and broke it, and gave it to his disciples, and said: Take it; eat it; this is my body. And he took a cup and gave thanks and gave it to them, saying: Drink from it, all; for this is my blood, of the covenant, which is shed for the sake of many, for the remission of sins. But I tell you, from now on I shall not drink of this produce of the vine, until that day when I drink it with you, new wine, in the kingdom of my father.

And they sang the hymn and went out to the Mount of Olives. Then Jesus said to them: All of you will be made to fail me in the course of this night. For it is written: I will strike the shepherd, and the sheep of his flock will be scattered. But after my resurrection I will lead the way for you into Galilee. Peter spoke forth and said: Though all the others fail you, I will never fail you. Jesus said to him: Truly I tell you that on this night before the cock crows you will disown me three times. Peter said to him: Even if I must die with you, I will never disown you. And so spoke all the disciples.

Then Jesus went with them to a place called Gethsemane; and he said to his disciples: Sit down here, while I go over there and pray. He took with him Peter and the two sons of Zebedee; and then he was in pain and distress. And he said to them: My soul is in anguish to the point of death. Stay here and keep watch with me. Then he went a little farther, and threw himself down on his face, and said in prayer: Father, if it is possible, let this cup pass me by; except only, let it be not as I wish, but as you wish. Then he went back to his disciples and found them asleep, and said to Peter: Are you not then strong enough to keep watch with me for a single hour? Be wakeful, and pray that you may not be brought to the test. The spirit is eager, but the flesh is weak. Again a second time he went off and prayed, saying: Father, if it is not possible for this cup to pass me by, but I must drink it, let your will be done. Then he came back and again found them sleeping, for their eyes were heavy; and leaving them he went back and prayed a third time, saying the same words as before. Then he came back to the disciples and said to them: So you are still asleep, and resting. Behold, the hour is near, and the son of man is betrayed into the hands of sinners. Rise up, let us go; see, my betrayer is near.

And while he was still speaking, behold, Judas came, one of the twelve, and with him a great crowd, with swords and clubs, from the high priests and the elders of the people. And he who betrayed him told them the signal, saying: The one I kiss will be the man. Seize him. And at once he came up to Jesus and said: Hail, master; and kissed him. Jesus said to him: My friend, why are you here? Then they came up and laid hands on Jesus and bound him. And behold, one of those who were with Jesus put out his hand and drew his sword, and struck the slave of the high priest and took off his ear. Then Jesus said: Put away your sword where it belongs; for all who take up the sword shall die by the sword. Or do you not believe that I have the power to call upon my father, and he will at once send more than twelve legions of angels? But then, how to fulfill what has been written, that these things must be. At that time Jesus said to the multitude: You come out to arrest me with swords and clubs as if I were a high-wayman? Day by day I sat in the temple, teaching, and you did not seize me.

But all this took place so that what was written by the prophets should be fulfilled.

At that time all his disciples left him and fled away.

But they who had seized Jesus brought him to the house of Caiaphas the high priest, where the scribes and elders were assembled. But Peter followed him at a distance as far as the courtyard of the high priest, and went inside and sat with the servingmen, to watch the event. And the high priests and the entire council were looking for some false evidence against Jesus, so that they might have him killed, and they could find none, though many false witnesses came forward. But later two came forward and spoke, saying: This man said this: I am able to tear down the temple of God and rebuild it within three days. Then the high priest stood up and said to him: Have you no answer? What is the testimony these bring against you? But Jesus remained silent. And the high priest said to him: I charge you by the living God that you tell us whether you are the Christ, the son of God. Jesus said to him: It is you who said it. But now I say to you, presently you shall see the son of man sitting on the right of the power and walking upon the clouds of the sky. Then the priest rent his clothing, saying: He has blasphemed. Why do we still need witnesses? Behold, you have heard the blasphemy. What is your decision? They answered and said: He has deserved death. Then they spat in his face and struck him with their fists and beat him, saying: Tell us, Christ, by prophecy, who hit you?

But Peter was sitting outside in the courtyard, and a

serving girl came up to him and said: You also were with Jesus the Galilaean. But he denied it before them all, saying: I do not know what you mean. And as he went out to the gate another girl saw him and said to those who were there: This man was with Jesus the Nazarene. And again he denied it, with an oath, saying: I do not know the man. After a little those who were standing by came up to Peter and said: Truly you are one of them, for your way of speaking makes it clear. Then he began to swear with many oaths, saying: I do not know the man. And thereupon the cock crew. And Peter remembered the words of Jesus when he said: Before the cock crows you will disown me three times. And he went out and wept bitterly.

❡ When morning came, all the high priests and elders of the people held a meeting against Jesus, to have him killed. And they bound him and took him away and gave him over to Pilate the governor.

Then when Judas, who had betrayed him, saw that he had been condemned, he repented and proffered the thirty pieces of silver back to the high priests and the elders, saying: I did wrong to betray innocent blood. They said: What is that to us? You look to it. And he threw down the silver pieces in the temple and went away, and when he was alone he hanged himself. The high priests took up the silver pieces and said: We cannot put them in the treasury, since it is blood money. Then they took counsel together and with the money they bought the potter's field to bury strangers in. Therefore that field has been called the Field of Blood, to this day. Then was fulfilled the word spoken by Jeremiah the prophet, saying: I took the thirty pieces of silver, the price of him on whom a price was set, whom they priced from among the sons of Israel, and I gave the money for the field of the potter, as my Lord commanded me.

Now Jesus stood before the governor; and the governor questioned him, saying: Are you the King of the Jews? Jesus answered: It is you who say it. And while he was being accused by the high priests and the elders he made no answer. Then Pilate said to him: Do you not hear all their testimony against you? And he made no answer to a single word, so that the governor was greatly amazed.

For the festival, the governor was accustomed to release one prisoner for the multitude, whichever one they wished. And they had at that time a notorious man, who was called Barabbas. Now as they were assembled Pilate said to them: Which one do you wish me to release for you, Barabbas, or Jesus, who is called Christ? For he knew that it was through malice that they had turned him over. Now as he was sitting on the platform, his wife sent him a message, saying: Let there be nothing between you and this just man; for I have suffered much today because of a dream about him. But the high priests and the elders persuaded the crowd to ask for Barabbas and destroy Jesus. Then the governor spoke forth and said to them: Which of the two shall I give you? They answered: Barabbas. Pilate said to them: What then shall I do with Jesus, who is called Christ? They all said: Let him be crucified. But Pilate said: Why? What harm has he done? But they screamed all the more, saying: Let him be crucified. And Pilate, seeing that he was doing no good and that the disorder was growing, took water and washed his hands before the crowd, saying: I am innocent of the blood of this man. You see to it. And all the people answered and said: His blood is upon us and upon our children. Then Pilate gave them Barabbas, but he had Jesus flogged, and gave him over to be crucified.

Then the soldiers of the governor took Jesus to the residence, and drew up all their battalion around him. And they stripped him and put a red mantle about him, and wove a wreath of thorns and put it on his head, and put a reed in his right hand, and knelt before him and mocked him, saying: Hail, King of the Jews. And they spat upon him and took the reed and beat him on the head. And after they had mocked him, they took off the mantle and put his own clothes on him, and led him away to be crucified. And as they went out they found a man of Cyrene, named Simon. They impressed him for carrying the cross.

Then they came to a place called Golgotha, which means the place of the skull, and gave him wine mixed with gall to drink. When he tasted it he would not drink it. Then they crucified him, and divided up his clothes, casting lots, and sat there and watched him. Over his head they put the label giving the charge against him, where it was written: This is Jesus, the King of the Jews. Then there were crucified with him two robbers, one on his right and one on his left. And those who passed by blasphemed against him, wagging their heads, and saying: You who tear down the temple and rebuild it in three days, save yourself, and come down from the cross, if you are the son of God. So too the high priests, mocking him along with the scribes and the elders, said: He saved others, he cannot save himself. He is King of Israel, let him come down from the cross and we will believe in him. He trusted in

God, let him save him now, if he will; for he said: I am the son of God. And the robbers who were crucified with him spoke abusively to him in the same way.

But from the sixth hour there was darkness over all the earth until the ninth hour. But about the ninth hour Jesus cried out in a great voice, saying: *Elei elei lema sabachthanei?* Which is: My God, my God, why have you forsaken me? But some of those who were standing there heard and said: This man calls to Elijah. And at once one of them ran and took a sponge, soaked it in vinegar and put it on the end of a reed, and gave it to him to drink. But the rest said: Let us see if Elijah comes to save him.

Then Jesus cried out again in a great voice, and gave up his life. And behold, the veil of the temple was split in two from top to bottom, and the earth was shaken, and the rocks were split, and the tombs opened and many bodies of the holy sleepers rose up; and after his resurrection they came out of their tombs and went into the holy city, and were seen by many. But the company commander and those with him who kept guard over Jesus, when they saw the earthquake and the things that happened, were greatly afraid, saying: In truth this was the son of God. And there were many women watching from a distance there, who had followed Jesus from Galilee, waiting on him. Among them were Mary the Magdalene, and Mary the mother of James and Joseph, and the mother of the sons of Zebedee.

When it was evening, there came a rich man of Arimathaea, Joseph by name, who also had been a disciple of Jesus. This man went to Pilate and asked for the body of Jesus. Then Pilate ordered that it be given up to him. And Joseph took the body and wrapped it in clean linen, and laid it in his new tomb, which he had cut in the rock, and rolled a great stone before the door of the tomb, and went away. But Mary the Magdalene and the other Mary were there, sitting before the tomb. On the next day, which is the day after the Day of Preparation, the high priests and the Pharisees gathered in the presence of Pilate, and said: Lord, we have remembered how that impostor said while he was still alive: After three days I shall rise up. Give orders, then, that the tomb be secured until after the third day, for fear his disciples may come and steal him away and say to the people: He rose from the dead. And that will be the ultimate deception, worse than the former one. Pilate said to them: You have a guard. Go and secure it as best you can. And they went and secured the tomb, sealing it with the help of the guard.

◀ Late on the sabbath, as the light grew toward the first day after the sabbath, Mary the Magdalene and the other Mary came to visit the tomb. And behold, there was a great earthquake, for the angel of the Lord came down from heaven and approached the stone and rolled it away and was sitting on it. His look was like lightning, and his clothing white as snow. And those who were on guard were shaken with fear of him and became like dead men. But the angel spoke forth and said to the women: Do not you fear; for I know that you look for Jesus, who was crucified. He is not here. For he rose up, as he said. Come here, and look at the place where he lay. Then go quickly and tell his disciples that he has risen from the dead, and behold, he goes before you into Galilee. There you will see him. See; I have told you. And quickly leaving the tomb, in fear and great joy, they ran to tell the news to his disciples. And behold, Jesus met them, saying: I give you greeting. They came up to him and took his feet and worshipped him. Then Jesus said to them: Do not fear. Go and tell my brothers to go into Galilee, and there they will see me. And as they went on their way, behold, some of the guards went into the city and reported to the high priests all that had happened. And they met with the elders and took counsel together, and gave the soldiers a quantity of money, saying: Say that the disciples came in the night and stole him away while we were sleeping. And if this is heard in the house of the governor, we shall reason with him, and make it so that you have nothing to fear. And they took the money and did as they were instructed. And this is the story that has been spread about among the Jews, to this day.

Then the eleven disciples went on into Galilee, to the mountain where Jesus had given them instructions to go; and when they saw him, they worshipped him; but some doubted. And Jesus came up to them and talked with them, saying: All authority has been given to me, in heaven and on earth. Go out, therefore, and instruct all the nations, baptizing them in the name of the Father and the Son and the Holy Spirit, teaching them to observe all that I have taught you. And behold, I am with you, all the days until the end of the world.

LUKE

Luke is believed by the majority of authorities to be "Luke, the beloved physician" of *Colossians* 4.14. This gospel is generally dated somewhere about A.D. 85, after the fall of Jerusalem in A.D. 70.

¶ SINCE MANY HAVE UNDERTAKEN TO compose an account of those things which have been fulfilled among us, as those who saw for themselves from the beginning and became servants of the word have handed it down to us, it seemed good for me also, since I have followed everything closely from the first, to write it out in order for you, most exalted Theophilus, so that you may learn the truth concerning those stories of which you have been informed.

In the days of Herod, king of Judaea, there was a certain priest, by name Zachariah, of the division of Abiah; and his wife came from the daughters of Aaron, and her name was Elizabeth. They were both righteous people in the sight of God, going blamelessly in all the commandments and judgments of the Lord. And they had no child, because Elizabeth was barren; and they were both well advanced in their days. Now it happened that during his priestly duty, when it was the turn of his division to be in the presence of God, according to the custom of the priesthood, he was the one allotted to go into the temple of the Lord and burn the incense. And all the multitude of people was praying outside at the hour of the incense; and he had a vision of an angel of the Lord standing at the right of the altar for the incense. And Zachariah was shaken when he saw him, and fear fell upon him. But the angel said to him: Do not fear, Zachariah; since your entreaty has been heard, and your wife Elizabeth shall bear you a son, and you shall call his name John; and he will be your joy and your pride, and many will rejoice at his birth. For he will be great in the sight of the Lord, and he will never drink wine or strong drink, and he will be filled with the Holy Spirit while still in the womb of his mother, and he will turn many of the sons of Israel toward the Lord their God; and he will go before him in his presence in the spirit and power of Elijah, to turn the hearts of fathers toward their children, and the disobedient to the wisdom of the righteous; to prepare a people which will be ready for the Lord. And Zachariah said to the angel: How shall I know this? For I am an old man, and my wife is advanced in her days. And the angel answered him and said: I am Gabriel. I stand in the presence of God; and I was sent to talk to you to bring you this good news. And behold, you will be silent and unable to speak until the day when these things come to pass, because you did not believe my words, which will be fulfilled in their time.

Now the people were waiting for Zachariah, and they wondered at the time he took in the temple. But when he came out he could not speak to them, and they realized that he had seen a vision in the temple; and he kept nodding to them, and remained speechless. And it happened that when the days of his service were completed he went back to his own house. And after these days Elizabeth his wife conceived; and she kept herself in concealment for five months, saying: Thus has the Lord done by me in the

days when he consented to take away the reproach that
was mine among men.

In the sixth month the angel Gabriel was sent to a city
of Galilee, whose name is Nazareth, to a virgin engaged to
a man named Joseph, of the house of David; and the name
of this virgin was Mary. And going into her presence, he
said: Hail, favored one; the Lord is with you. She was disturbed at what he said and asked herself what this greeting might mean. And the angel said to her: Do not fear,
Mary, for you have found favor with God; and behold, you
shall conceive in your womb and bring forth a son, and
you shall call his name Jesus. He will be great, and called
son of the Highest, and the Lord God will give him the
throne of David his forefather, and he will be king over
the house of Jacob through the ages, and of his Kingdom
there will be no end. But Mary said to the angel: How
shall this be, since I know no man? And the angel answered and said to her: The Holy Spirit will come to you,
and the power of the highest will overshadow you. Therefore the offspring will be called holy, the son of God. And
behold, Elizabeth your kinswoman, she also has conceived a son, in her old age, and this is the sixth month for
her who had been called barren; because nothing at all
will be impossible for God. Mary said: Here is the slave of
the Lord. May it happen to me as you have said. And the
angel left her.

And Mary rose up in those days and journeyed in haste
into the hill country, to a city of Judah, and entered the
house of Zachariah and greeted Elizabeth. And it happened that when Elizabeth heard the greeting of Mary, the
child leaped in her womb, and Elizabeth was filled with
the Holy Spirit, and she spoke out with a great cry and
said: Blessed are you among women, and blessed the fruit

of your womb. And how did it befall me that the mother of my Lord should come to me? For behold, when the sound of your greeting came to my ears, the child leapt for joy in my womb. And blessed is she who believed that there will be fulfillment of what was told her from the Lord. Then Mary said: My soul exalts the Lord, and my spirit rejoices in God my savior, because he cast down his eyes to the low estate of his slave girl. Behold, after now all the generations will bless me; because the mighty one has done great things for me, and his name is holy; and his mercy is for generations and generations, for those who fear him. He has taken power into his arm, and scattered the proud in the imagination of their hearts. He has pulled down the dynasts from their thrones, and raised up the humble; he has filled the hungry with good things, and sent the rich away empty. He has reached out his hand to Israel his servant, through the memory of mercy; as he said to our fathers, to Abraham and his seed forever.

And Mary remained with her for about three months, and then returned to her own house.

For Elizabeth her time was completed, and she bore a son. And her neighbors and relatives heard that the Lord had made great his mercy in her case, and they rejoiced with her. And it came about that on the eighth day they came to circumcise the baby; and they were calling him by the name of his father, Zachariah. Then his mother spoke forth and said: No, but he shall be called John. And they said to her: There is no one in your kindred who is called by that name. And they made signs to his father, to learn what he wished him to be called. And he asked for a tablet and wrote, saying: John is his name. And all were amazed. But his mouth was set free at once, and his tongue, and he spoke praising God. And fear came upon all those who lived about them, and in all the hill country of Judaea all these sayings were repeated, and those who heard them laid them in their hearts, saying: What will this child be? The hand of the Lord is with him. And Zachariah his father was filled with the Holy Spirit, and he prophesied, saying: Praised be the Lord God of Israel, because he visited his people and wrought their deliverance, and raised up our horn of salvation in the house of David, his servant; as he spoke through the mouth of his holy prophets from of old; safety from our enemies and the hand of all those who hate us, to work mercy with our fathers and to remember his holy convenant; the oath he swore to Abraham our father, to grant that we be rescued without fear from the hand of our enemies, to serve him in piety and righteousness before his presence all our days. And you, child, will be called prophet of the highest, and go before the presence of the Lord to make ready his ways, to grant to his people knowledge of their salvation through the remission of their sins; through the compassionate mercy of our Lord whereby the sunrise shall shine upon us from on high, to illuminate those who sit in darkness and the shadow of death, to guide our feet into the way of peace.

And the child grew and became strong in spirit; and he was in the desert until the day of his appearance before Israel.

◀ It happened in those days that a decree went forth from Augustus Caesar that all the world should be enrolled in a census: This was the first census, when Quirinius was governor of Syria. And all went to be enrolled, each to his own city. And Joseph also went up from Galilee, from the city of Nazareth, to Judaea, to the city of David which is called Bethlehem, because he was of the house and family of David; to be enrolled with Mary his promised wife, who was pregnant. And it happened that while they were there her time was completed, and she bore a son, her first-born, and she wrapped him in swaddling clothes and laid him in a manger, because there was no room for them in the inn. And there were shepherds in that region, camping out at night and keeping guard over their flock. And an angel of the Lord stood before them, and the glory of the Lord shone about them, and they were afraid with a great fear. The angel said to them: Do not be afraid; behold, I tell you good news, great joy which shall be for all the people; because this day there has been born for you in the city of David a savior who is Christ the Lord. And here is a sign for you; you will find a baby wrapped in swaddling clothes and lying in a manger. And suddenly with the angel there was a multitude of the heavenly host, praising God and saying: Glory to God in the highest and peace on earth among men of good will. And it happened that after the angels had gone off from them into the sky, the shepherds began saying to each other: Let us go to Bethlehem and see this thing which has happened, which the Lord made known to us; and they went, hastening, and found Mary and Joseph, and the baby lying in the manger; and when they had seen, they spread the news about what had been told them concerning this baby. And all who heard wondered at what had been told them by the shepherds; and Mary kept in mind all these sayings as she pondered them in her heart. And the shepherds returned, glorifying and praising God over all they had heard and seen, as it had been told them.

And when eight days were past, for his circumcision,

his name was called Jesus, as it was named by the angel
before he was conceived in the womb.

And when the days for their purification according to
the Law of Moses had been completed, they took him up
to Jerusalem to set him before the Lord, as it has been
written in the Law of the Lord: Every male child who
opens the womb shall be called sacred to the Lord; and to
give sacrifice as it is stated in the Law of the Lord, a pair of
turtle doves or two young pigeons. And behold, there was
a man in Jerusalem whose name was Simeon, and this
man was righteous and virtuous and looked forward to
the consolation of Israel, and the Holy Spirit was upon
him; and it had been prophesied to him by the Holy Spirit
that he should not look upon his death until he had
looked on the Lord's Anointed. And in the spirit he went
into the temple; and as his parents brought in the child
Jesus so that they could do for him what was customary
according to the law, Simeon himself took him in his
arms and blessed God and said: Now, Lord, you release
your slave, in peace, according to your word; because my
eyes have looked on your salvation, what you made ready
in the presence of all the peoples; a light for the revelation
to the Gentiles, and the glory of your people, Israel. And
his father and his mother were in wonder at what was
being said about him. And Simeon blessed them and said
to Mary his mother: Behold, he is appointed for the fall
and the rise of many in Israel; and as a sign which is
disputed; and through your soul also will pass the sword;
so that the reasonings of many hearts may be revealed.
And there was Anna, a prophetess, the daughter of
Phanuel, of the tribe of Asher. And she was well advanced
in years, having lived with her husband seven years from
the time of her maidenhood, and now she was eighty-four

years a widow. And she did not leave the temple, serving night and day with fastings and prayers. And at this same time she came near and gave thanks to God and spoke of the child to those who looked forward to the deliverance of Jerusalem.

And when they had done everything according to the Law of the Lord, they went back to Galilee, to their own city, Nazareth.

And the child grew in stature and strength as he was filled with wisdom, and the grace of God was upon him.

Now his parents used to journey every year to Jerusalem for the feast of the Passover. And when he was twelve years old, when they went up according to their custom for the festival and had completed their days there, on their return the boy Jesus stayed behind in Jerusalem, and his parents did not know it. And supposing that he was in their company they went a day's journey and then looked for him among their relatives and friends, and when they did not find him they turned back to Jerusalem in search of him. And it happened that after three days they found him in the temple sitting in the midst of the masters, listening to them and asking them questions. And all who heard him were amazed at his intelligence and his answers. And they were astonished at seeing him, and his mother said to him: Child, why did you do this to us? See, your father and I have been looking for you, in distress. He said to them: But why were you looking for me? Did you not know that I must be in my father's house? And they did not understand what he had said to them. And he returned with them and came to Nazareth, and was in their charge. And his mother kept all his sayings in her heart. And Jesus advanced in wisdom and stature, and in the favor of God and men.

❡ In the fifteenth year of the reign of Tiberius Caesar, when Pontius Pilate was governor of Judaea, and Herod was tetrarch of Galilee, and Philip his brother was tetrarch of the region of Ituraea and Trachonitis, and Lysanias was tetrarch of Abilene, when Annas, with Caiaphas, was high priest, the word of God came to John the son of Zachariah in the desert. And he went into all the region about Jordan preaching the baptism of repentance for the remission of sins, as it is written in the book of the words of Isaiah the prophet: The voice of one crying in the desert, prepare the way of the Lord, make straight the roads before him. Every watercourse will be filled, and every mountain and hill will be brought low; and the crooked will turn straight and the rough roads will turn smooth; and all flesh will look on the salvation of God. And he said to the multitudes that came out to be baptized by him: You viper's brood, who warned you to flee from the anger to come? Then produce fruits that are worthy of your repentance; and do not begin to say among yourselves: We have Abraham for our father. For I say to you that out of these stones God can raise up children to Abraham. And by now the ax is set against the root of the trees; so that every tree that does not bear fruit is cut out and thrown into the fire. And the people questioned him saying: What then shall we do? He answered and said to them: Let him who has two tunics share with him who has none, and let him who has food do likewise. And tax collectors also came to him to be baptized and said to him: Master, what shall we do? He said to them: Collect nothing except what is assigned to you. And soldiers in service also questioned him, saying: And we too, what

shall we do? And he said to them: No extortion, no false
accusation, and live on your wages. And as the people had
great hopes and all were wondering in their hearts about
John, whether he might even be the Messiah, John spoke
forth saying to all: I baptize you with water; but one is
coming who is stronger than I, and I am not fit to untie
the fastening of his shoes. He will baptize you in the Holy
Spirit and in fire. His winnowing fan is in his hand, to
clear his threshing floor and gather his grain into his
storehouse, and he will burn the chaff in quenchless fire.

There was much else also that he advised the people to
do as he announced the good news. But Herod the tetrarch, who had been reproved by him in the matter of
Herodias his brother's wife, and for all his other misdeeds,
added this one to the rest: he had John confined in prison.

And it happened that in the baptizing of all the people
Jesus also was baptized; and as he prayed the sky opened
and the Holy Spirit in bodily form like a dove descended
upon him, and there came a voice from the sky saying:
You are my son, whom I love, in whom I am well pleased.

And Jesus when he began was about thirty years old,
and was the son, as it was believed, of Joseph, the son
of Heli, the son of Mathat, the son of Levi, the son of
Melchi, the son of Jannai, the son of Joseph, the son of
Matathias, the son of Amos, the son of Nahum, the son
of Esli, the son of Naggai, the son of Maath, the son of
Matathias, the son of Semein, the son of Josech, the son of
Joda, the son of Joanan, the son of Rhesa, the son of
Zerubbabel, the son of Salathiel, the son of Neri, the son
of Melchi, the son of Addi, the son of Cosam, the son of
Elmadam, the son of Er, the son of Jesus, the son of
Eliezer, the son of Jorim, the son of Mathat, the son
of Levi, the son of Symeon, the son of Judah, the son of

Joseph, the son of Jonam, the son of Eliacim, the son of
Melea, the son of Menna, the son of Matatha, the son
of Nathan, the son of David, the son of Jesse, the son of
Jobed, the son of Boaz, the son of Sala, the son of Nahshon, the son of Aminadab, the son of Admin, the son of
Arni, the son of Hezron, the son of Perez, the son of Judah,
the son of Jacob, the son of Isaac, the son of Abraham, the
son of Terah, the son of Nachor, the son of Serug, the son
of Reu, the son of Peleg, the son of Eber, the son of Sala,
the son of Cainan, the son of Arphaxad, the son of Shem,
the son of Noah, the son of Lamech, the son of
Methuselah, the son of Enoch, the son of Jared, the son of
Mahahaleel, the son of Cainan, the son of Enos, the son of
Seth, the son of Adam, the son of God.

¶ And Jesus, filled with the Holy Spirit, turned away from
Jordan and was guided by the spirit in the desert for forty
days, being tested by the devil. And he ate nothing in
those days, and when they were finished he was hungry.
And the devil said to him: If you are the son of God, tell
this stone to become bread. Jesus said to him in answer: It
is written: Not by bread alone shall man live. Then he led
him on high and showed him all the kingdoms of the
world in a flash of time; and the devil said to him: I will
give you this power entire and the glory of these things,
because this has been turned over to me, and I give it to
whom I will. If then you will worship me, it shall all be
yours. Jesus answered and said to him: It is written: You
shall worship the Lord your God, and shall serve him
only. Then he took him to Jerusalem and set him on the
gable of the temple, and said to him: If you are the son of
God, throw yourself down from here; for it is written: He

will charge his angels concerning you, to guard you; and that: Upon their hands they will support you, so that never may you strike your foot against the stone. And Jesus answered and said to him: It is said: You shall not tempt the Lord your God. So when he had done with every temptation, the devil left him until a better time.

And Jesus, in the power of the Spirit, returned to Galilee; and rumor about him went through the entire region; and he himself taught in their synagogues, honored by all. And he came to Nazareth, where he had been raised, and entered the synagogue as was his custom on the day of the sabbath, and stood up to read. And he was handed the book of the prophet Isaiah, and opening the book he found the place where it was written: The spirit of the Lord is upon me, because of which he has anointed me, to bring good news to the poor; he sent me forth to announce release to captives, and eyesight to the blind; to set those who are broken at liberty; to proclaim the accepted year of the Lord. And folding the book he gave it back to the servant and sat down; and the eyes of all who were in the synagogue were fixed upon him. And he began to say to them: Today this scripture is fulfilled in your hearing. And all spoke well of him and marveled at the grace in the words that came from his mouth, and said: Is not this the son of Joseph? And he said to them: Surely you will tell me the parable: Physician, cure yourself; do here also in your own country all we have heard of that was done in Capernaum. And he said: Truly I tell you, no prophet is accepted in his own country. But this is true that I tell you: There were many widows in Israel in the days of Elijah, when the sky was closed for three years and six months, so that there was famine in all the land; but to none of them was Elijah sent, but only to a widowed

woman of Sarepta in Sidon. And there were many lepers
in Israel in the time of Elisha the prophet, but none of
them was made clean except Naaman the Syrian. And all
those in the synagogue were filled with anger when they
heard this, and they rose up and cast him out of the city,
and they took him to the brink of the cliff on which was
built their city, to fling him over. But he passed through
their midst and went on his way.

And he went down to Capernaum, a city of Galilee.
And he was teaching them on the sabbath, and they were
astonished at his teaching, because he spoke with authority. And in the synagogue there was a man who had the
spirit of an unclean demon and he cried out in a great
voice: Ha. What is there between us and you, Jesus of
Nazareth? Did you come to destroy us? I know you, who
you are, God's holy one. Jesus reproved him, saying: Be
silent and go out from him. And the demon flung him
down in their midst and came out of him, without doing
him any harm. And wonder came upon all and they
talked among themselves, saying: What is this speech,
that in authority and power he gives orders to unclean
spirits, and they come out? And the rumor of him went
forth to every place in the region.

But he rose up and left the synagogue and went into the
house of Simon. The mother-in-law of Simon was suffering from a great fever, and they besought him for her
sake. He stood over her and reproved the fever, and it left
her; and at once she stood up and served them. And when
the sun set, all those who had people sick with various
sicknesses brought them to him, and he laid his hands on
each one of them, and healed them. And also demons
came out of many, crying out and saying: You are the son
of God. But he forbade them and told them not to speak,

because they knew that he was the Christ. When day came he went out to a deserted place, and the multitudes went looking for him, and came up with him, and held him back so that he could not go from them. But he said to them: I must bring the good news of the Kingdom of God to the other cities also, since for this I was sent forth. And he went preaching through the synagogues of Judaea.

◖ It happened that, while the crowd was pressing upon him and listening to the word of God, he himself was standing by the Lake of Gennesaret, and he saw two boats standing beside the lake, but the fishermen had disembarked and were washing their nets. He went aboard one of the boats, which was Simon's, and asked him to take him out a little way from the land, and he sat in the boat and taught the multitudes. And when he was through speaking, he said to Simon: Go on out into the deep water and let down your nets and fish. Simon answered and said: Master, all through the night we wore ourselves out and got nothing; but on your word I will let down our nets. And when they did so, they netted a great haul of fish, and their nets were breaking. And they beckoned to their partners in the other boat to come and help them. And they came, and both boats were filled so they began to sink. Seeing this, Simon Peter flung himself at the knees of Jesus and said: Go from me, for I am a sinful man, Lord. For amazement had seized him and all who were with him over the haul of fish they had taken, and also James and John, the sons of Zebedee, who were partners with Simon. And Jesus said to Simon: Do not be afraid. From now on your catch will be men. And they beached their boats and left everything and followed him.

It happened that he was in one of the cities, and behold, there was a man covered with leprosy; and when he saw Jesus, he flung himself down on his face and implored him, saying: Lord, if you wish you can make me clean. And he stretched out his hand and touched him, saying: I wish it; be clean. And immediately the leprosy left him. And he told him not to tell anyone; but go and show yourself to the priest, and bring him the gift for your purification that Moses ordained, in witness to these things. But the word went around all the more about him, and multitudes came together to hear him and to be healed of their sicknesses. But he for a while was withdrawn into the desert, praying.

And it happened on one of those days, he himself was teaching, and also there were Pharisees seated there and teachers of the law, who had come out from every village of Galilee and Judaea, and from Jerusalem; and the power of the Lord was with him, to heal. And behold, men carrying on a bed a man who was paralyzed, and they tried to carry him inside and set him before Jesus. And failing to find any way to get him in through the crowd, they went up on top of the house and let him down, bed and all, between the tiles and into the middle, before Jesus. And he, seeing their faith, said: Fellow, your sins are forgiven you. Then the scribes and the Pharisees began to discuss this, saying: Who is this man who speaks blasphemies? Who can forgive sins, except God alone? Jesus realized what they were saying to each other, and spoke forth and said to them: Why do you question in your hearts? Which is easier, to say: Your sins are forgiven you, or to say: Arise and walk about? But so that you may know that the son of man has authority on earth to forgive sins—he said to the paralyzed man: I say to you, rise, take up your bed and go to your house. And at once he stood up before them all, and lifted up what he had been laid on, and went away to his house, glorifying God. And they were all transported, and they glorified God and were filled with fear and said: We have seen incredible things today.

And after that he went forth and saw a tax collector named Levi sitting in the tollhouse, and said to him: Follow me. And he left everything and got up and followed him. And Levi held a great reception for him in his house; and there was a throng of tax collectors and others who dined with them. Then the Pharisees and their scribes muttered to his disciples: Why do you eat and drink with tax collectors and sinners? Jesus answered and said to them: The healthy do not need a physician but those who are in poor health. I did not come to summon the just to repentance, but the sinners. But they said to him: The disciples of John fast often and say prayers, and so likewise do the disciples of the Pharisees, but yours eat and drink. But Jesus said to them: Surely you cannot make the members of the wedding party fast while the bridegroom is with them? But the days will come, and when the bridegroom is taken away from them, then in those days they will fast. And he told them a parable: No one tears a piece from a new coat to put on an old coat; if he does, he will be tearing the new one, and the patch from the new will not fit the old. And no one puts new wine into old skins; if he does, the new wine will break the skins and the wine will all be spilled and the skins will be destroyed; but new wine is to be put into new skins. And no one drinking old wine wants new; for he says: The old is good.

◀ It happened on the sabbath he went walking through the sown fields, and his disciples picked and ate the ears of grain, rubbing them in their hands. And some of the Pharisees said: Why do you do what is forbidden on the sabbath? Jesus answered and said to them: Have you not read what David did when he was hungry and those with him? How he went into the house of God and took the show bread and ate it and gave it to those who were with him; which it is not lawful for any to eat except only the priests? And he said to them: The son of man is lord of the sabbath.

And it happened that on another sabbath he went into the synagogue and taught; and there was a man there, and his right arm was withered. And the scribes and the Pharisees were watching him to see whether he healed on the sabbath, so that they might find a charge to bring against him. But he read their thoughts and said to the man with the withered arm: Rise up and stand in our midst. And he rose and stood there. And Jesus said to them: I ask you, is it lawful to do good or evil on the sabbath, to save a life or destroy it? And he looked around at them all and said to the man: Stretch out your arm. And he did, and his arm became sound. They were filled with fury, and talked with each other about what they could do to Jesus.

And it happened in those days that he went out to the mountain to pray, and he spent all the night in prayer to God. And when it was day, he summoned his disciples, and chose twelve of them, whom he also named apostles: Simon, whom he also named Peter, and Andrew his brother, and James and John and Philip and Bartholomew, and Matthew and Thomas, and James the son of Alphaeus and Simon, who was called the zealot, and Judas the son of

James, and Judas Iscariot, who turned traitor: and went down with them and stood in a place in the plain: and there was a great crowd of his disciples, and a great multitude of the people from all of Judaea and Jerusalem and the seaboard of Tyre and Sidon, who had come to hear him and be healed of their sicknesses: and those troubled with unclean spirits were cured of them: and all the multitude sought to touch him, because power went forth from him and he healed all. And he himself, raising his eyes to his disciples, said:

Blessed are you who are poor, because yours is the Kingdom of God.

Blessed are you who are hungry now, because you shall be fed.

Blessed are you who weep now, because you shall laugh.

Blessed are you when men hate you, and when they segregate you and blame you and cast out your name as wicked, because of the son of man. Rejoice on that day and frolic, for behold your reward is great in heaven. For in the same way their fathers treated the prophets.

But woe to you who are rich, because you have had all your consolation.

Woe to you who are filled now, because you shall be hungry.

Woe to you who laugh now, because you shall mourn and weep.

Woe when all men speak well of you, for in the same way their fathers treated the false prophets.

But I say to you who hear me, love your enemies, do well by those who hate you, praise those who curse you, pray for those who revile you. When one strikes you on the cheek, offer him the other; if one seizes your coat, do

not keep him from taking your shirt also. Give to any
who asks you and from him who takes what is yours ask
for nothing back. And as you wish men to do by you, so do
by them. And if you love those who love you, what
thanks do you have? For even the sinners love those who
love them. And if you do good to those who do good to
you, what thanks do you have? For even the sinners do
the same. And if you lend to those from whom you hope
for a return, what thanks do you have? Even sinners lend
to sinners so they may get an equal return. But love your
enemies and do good and lend without hope of return; and
your reward will be great, and you will be sons of the
Highest, because he is good to the ungrateful and the
wicked. Be compassionate as your father is compassionate; and do not judge, and you shall not be judged; and do
not condemn, and you shall not be condemned. Forgive,
and you will be forgiven. Give, and it will be given you.
They will pour into your lap good measure, pressed down,
shaken down, running over. For by the measure by which
you measured it will be measured back to you.

And he told them a parable: Surely a blind man cannot
guide a blind man? Will they not both fall into the pit?
Nor is the disciple above the teacher, but every disciple
will end by being like his teacher. Why do you look at the
straw that is in the eye of your brother, and not perceive
the log that is in your own eye? How can you say to your
brother: Brother, let me take out the straw that is in your
eye? When you cannot see the log that is in your eye? You
hypocrite, first take the log out of your eye, and then you
can see to take the straw out of the eye of your brother.
There is no good tree that bears rotten fruit, nor again a
rotten tree that bears good fruit. For every tree is known
from its own fruit; men do not gather figs from thorns, or

harvest grapes from brambles. The good man brings forth good from the good treasure house of his heart, and the bad brings forth bad from the bad. For out of the fullness of his heart his mouth speaks. Why do you call me Lord Lord and not do what I say? Whenever any man comes to me and listens to my words and does as I say, I will show you what that man is like. He is like a man building a house who dug deep down and placed his foundation upon the rock; and the flood came and the river burst out against that house, and could not shake it because it was well built. But the man who listens to me but does not do as I say is like a man who built his house on the ground, without any foundation, and the river burst forth against it, and at once it collapsed, and the ruin of that house was great.

¶ After he had completed all his discourse for the people to hear, he went to Capernaum. And the slave of a certain centurion, who was prized by him, was sick and about to die. When he heard about Jesus, he sent the elders of the Jews to him, asking him to come and rescue his slave. When they came to Jesus they entreated him earnestly, saying: This man for whom you will do this is worthy of it, for he loves our people and he himself built our synagogue. And Jesus went along with them. And when he was no long way from the house, the centurion sent friends from the house saying to him: Lord, do not trouble yourself, for I am not fit to have you come under my roof. Therefore I did not take it upon myself to come to you. But say it in a word, and let my servant be healed. For I myself am a man set under orders, and I have soldiers under me, and I say to this man: Go, and he goes, and to another: Come, and he comes, and to my slave: Do this, and he does it. Jesus hearing this wondered at him, and turned about and said to the crowd that was following him: I tell you, I have not found such faith in Israel. And those who had been sent to him returned to the house and found the slave in good health.

And it happened after this that he went to a city called Nain, and his disciples and a great multitude went along with him. As he approached the gate of the city, behold, there was a dead man being carried out, the only son of his mother, and she was a widow; and a good crowd from the city was with her. And when he saw her the Lord took pity on her and said to her: Weep no more. And he went up and laid hands on the coffin, and those who were carrying it stopped; and he said: Young man, I tell you, rise up. And the corpse sat up and began to talk, and he gave him to his mother. And fear seized all of them, and they glorified God, saying: A great prophet is risen among us, and: God has looked on his people. And the word about him went forth over all Judaea and all the land about.

John's disciples brought him news about all these things. And John summoned two of his disciples and sent them to the Lord, saying: Are you the one who is to come or shall we look for another? And when the men reached him, they said: John the Baptist sent us to you, saying: Are you the one who is to come or shall we look for another? In that time he healed many from diseases and afflictions and evil spirits, and he gave to many who were blind the joy of sight. He answered them and said: Go and tell John what you have seen and heard. The blind see again, the lame walk, lepers are made clean and deaf-mutes hear, the dead rise up, beggars are told good news; and blessed is he who does not go wrong where I am concerned. When the messengers of John went away, he began to speak to the multitudes about John: What did you come out into the desert to see? A reed shaken by the wind? But what did you come out to see? A man dressed in soft clothing? Behold, those who are in splendid clothing and luxury are in the houses of the kings. But what did you come out to see? A prophet? Yes, I tell you, and more than a prophet. This is he about whom it was written: Behold, I send forth my messenger before your face, who will make ready your way before you. I tell you, among men born of women there is none greater than John; but one who is a lesser one in the Kingdom of God is greater than he. (And all the people who listened, and the tax collectors, called God righteous, since they had been baptized with the baptism of John; but the Pharisees and the legalists rejected the will of God for themselves, since they had not been baptized by him.) To what shall I liken the people of this generation, and what are they like? They are like children sitting in the public places who call to each other, who say: We played the flute for you and you did not dance; we lamented and you did not weep. For John came neither eating bread nor drinking wine, and you say: He has a demon. The son of man came eating and drinking, and you say: See, this man is an eater and a wine drinker, a friend of tax collectors and sinners. And wisdom is justified from all its children.

One of the Pharisees asked him to dine with him; and he went into the house of the Pharisee and reclined for dinner. And behold, there was a woman of the town who was a sinner; and when she learned that he was dining in the house of the Pharisee, she brought a jar of ointment and stood behind by his feet, weeping, and with her tears she began to wash his feet, and dried them with her hair and kissed his feet and anointed him with the ointment.

The Pharisee who had invited him saw this and said to himself: If this were a prophet, he would have known who she was and what sort of woman is handling him, that she is a sinner. Jesus spoke forth and said to him: Simon, I have something to say to you. He said: Speak, master. There were two who were in debt to a certain lender. One owed him five hundred denarii, the other fifty. When they could not repay him, he forgave both. Then which of them will love him more? Simon answered and said: I suppose the one whom he forgave the greater amount. He said: You judge rightly. Then turning to the woman he said to Simon: Do you see this woman? I came into your house, you did not give me water for my feet. But she washed my feet with her tears and dried them with her hair. You gave me no kiss. But she from the time when I came in did not leave off kissing my feet. You did not anoint my head with oil; but she anointed my feet with ointment. In thanks for which, I tell you, her sins are forgiven, which are many, because she loved much. But one who is forgiven little loves little. And he said to her: Your sins are forgiven. And those who were dining with him began to say among themselves: Who is this who even forgives sins? But he said to the woman: Your faith has saved you. Go in peace.

◀ And it happened after this that he was traveling, city by city and village by village, preaching and bringing the good news of the Kingdom of God; both himself and the twelve with him, and there were certain women who had been healed of evil spirits and sicknesses, Mary who was called the Magdalene, from whom seven demons had been driven, and Joanna the wife of Chuza, Herod's steward, and Susannah and many others. These ministered to them from their own possessions. And when a great multitude gathered and the people of the city came out also, he spoke to them through a parable: The sower went out to sow his seed. And as he sowed it, some fell beside the way, and it was trodden down and the birds of the sky ate it. And some fell on the rock, and after growing it withered because it had no moisture. And some fell in the midst of thorns, and the thorns grew together and stifled it. And some fell upon good soil and grew and bore fruit, a hundredfold. When he had told them this, he said: He who has ears to hear, let him hear. His disciples asked him what that parable was. And he said: To you it is given to understand the secrets of the Kingdom of God, but to the rest in parables, so that though they have sight they may not see and though they have hearing they may not understand. But this is the parable. The seed is the word of God. Those who fall beside the way are those who hear, and then the devil comes and plucks the word from their heart, so that they may not believe and be saved. Those on the rock are those who when they hear the word accept it with joy, and these have no root, who believe for the time and in the time of trial give way. What falls among the thorns, that means those who listened, and then as they go along they are stifled by concerns and money and the pleasures of life, and bring nothing to fulfillment. And what falls on the good soil, that means those who when they hear the word keep it fast in their good and worthy hearts, and bear fruit for their steadfastness.

No one lights a lamp and covers it with stuff or puts it under a bed, but one puts it on a stand, so that those who come in may see the light. For there is nothing hidden which will not be manifest, and nothing obscure which will not be known and come to light. Look to it how you listen. For when a man has, it will be given him, and if one has not, even what he thinks he has will be taken away from him.

His mother and his brothers came to see him, and they could not reach him because of the crowd. Word was brought to him: Your mother and your brothers are standing outside, and wish to see you. He answered and said to them: My mother and my brothers are these people, who listen to the word of God and perform it.

It happened on one of these days that he went aboard a ship, he and his disciples, and said to them: Let us cross to the other side of the lake. And they put out, and as they sailed he fell asleep. And a great wind storm descended upon the lake, and they were filling, and in peril. They went to him and woke him, saying: Master, master, we are lost. But he woke, and reproved the wind and the waves on the water, and they stopped, and it fell calm. And he said to them: Where is your faith? And they were afraid, and wondered, saying to each other: Who is this who gives orders even to the winds and the water, and they obey him?

And they put in at the country of the Gerasenes, which is across from Galilee. And as he stepped ashore a man from the city met him, a man beset by demons; for some time he had worn no clothing, and would not stay in a house, but only among the tombs. When he saw Jesus he cried out aloud and threw himself down before him and said, in a great voice: What have I to do with you, Jesus son of the most high? I pray you, do not torture me. For he had been commanding the unclean spirit to go out of the man. For at many times it had seized upon him, and he had been bound in chains and shackles and kept under guard, and he would break his bonds and go driven by the demon into the desert. But Jesus asked him: What is your name? And he said: Legion; because many demons had entered him. And they begged him not to order them to vanish into the bottomless pit. But there was a considerable herd of swine feeding there on the hillside. And they begged him to give them leave to enter into these; and he gave them leave. And when the demons came forth from the man they entered into the swine, and the whole herd rushed over the cliff into the lake and were drowned. And when those who were herding them saw what had happened, they fled and brought the news to the city and the countryside. And they came out to see what had happened, and came to Jesus, and they saw the man, from whom the demons had gone forth, sitting at the feet of Jesus, clothed and in his right mind: and they were afraid. Those who had seen it told them how the possessed man had been saved. And the whole population of the region of the Gerasenes asked him to go away from them, because they were constrained by a great fear; and he went to the ship and returned. The man from whom the demons had gone forth begged to be with him; but he dismissed him, saying: Go back to your house and describe what God has done for you. And he went through the whole city announcing what Jesus had done for him.

As Jesus returned the multitude welcomed him, for they were all expecting him. And behold, a man came to him whose name was Jairus; and this man was a leader in the synagogue, and he threw himself at the feet of Jesus and begged him to enter his house, because he had an only daughter about twelve years old, and she was dying. As he went the people were crowding close about him. And there was a woman who had been bleeding for twelve years, who could not be healed by anyone. She came behind him and touched the hem of his mantle, and immediately her flow of blood stopped. And Jesus said: Who is the one who touched me? When they all denied that they had, Peter said: Master, the crowds are squeezing you and pressing in upon you. But Jesus said: Someone touched me, for I felt the power going forth from me. And when the woman saw that she had not gone unnoticed, she came, trembling, and threw herself down before him, and in the presence of all the people she told why she had touched him and how she had been healed at once. And he said: My daughter, your faith has saved you. Go in peace. While he was still talking, a man came from the house of the leader of the synagogue, saying: Your daughter is dead: do not trouble the master any longer. But when Jesus heard, he answered him: Have no fear, only believe, and she will be saved. And he entered the house, and would not let anyone come in with him except Peter and John and James and the father of the child, and her mother. And all were weeping and mourning for her. But he said: Do not weep, for she has not died, but she is asleep. And they laughed at him, knowing that she had died. But he took her hand and spoke and said: Child, awake. And her breath came back, and at once she stood up, and he directed that something be given her to eat. And her parents were astonished; but he told them to tell no one what had happened.

¶ And calling together the twelve, he gave them power and authority against all demons, and to treat sicknesses, and he sent them out to preach the Kingdom of God and to heal, and he said to them: Take nothing with you for the journey, no staff, no bag, no bread, no money, nor have two tunics. And if you go into a house, stay there and make your excursions from there. And when any will not receive you, as you go out of that city shake the dust from your feet, in testimony against them. And they went forth and went through the villages preaching the gospel and healing people everywhere.

And Herod the tetrarch heard of all that was happening, and he was perplexed because it was said by some that John was risen from the dead, and by some that Elijah had appeared, and by others that one of the ancient prophets had risen up. And Herod said: John I beheaded. But who is this about whom I hear such things? And he sought to see him.

And the apostles returned and told him what they had done. And taking them with him he withdrew privately to a city called Bethsaida. And the multitudes learned of it and followed him. And he welcomed them and talked to them about the Kingdom of God, and those who needed treatment he healed. And the day began to decline; and the twelve came to him and said: Dismiss the people, so that they can go to the villages and farms which are round about and put up there and find something to eat, since here we are in a deserted place. But he said to them: Give them something to eat yourselves. But they said: We have nothing but five loaves and two fish; unless we go and buy food for all these people. For there were some five thousand men. But he said to his disciples: Place them by companies, by about fifties. And they did so and placed them all. And taking the five loaves and the two fish he looked up into the sky, and blessed them and broke them and gave them to his disciples to set before the multitude. And they ate and all were fed, and what was left of the broken pieces was picked up, twelve baskets.

It happened that while he was praying, alone, his disciples joined him, and he questioned them, saying: Who do the masses say I am? And they said in answer: John the Baptist; but others say Elijah, and others that one of the ancient prophets has risen up. He said to them: And you, who do you think I am? Peter answered and said: The Christ of God. But he warned them and directed them to tell this to no one, saying: The son of man must suffer much, and be rejected by the elders and the high priests and the scribes, and be killed, and rise up on the third day. And he said to all: If anyone wishes to go after me, let him deny himself and take up his cross day by day and follow me. For he who wishes to save his life will lose it; and he who loses his life for my sake, will save it. For what will it advantage a man if he gains the whole world, but loses himself or is punished? For he who is ashamed of me and my words, of him will the son of man be ashamed when he comes in the glory of himself and his father and the holy angels. But I tell you truly, there are some of those who stand here who will not taste of death until they see the Kingdom of God.

And it happened about eight days after these sayings that taking with him Peter and John and James he went up the mountain to pray. And it happened while he was praying that the look of his face became different, and his clothing was flashing white. And behold, two men were talking with him. They were Moses and Elijah, and they were seen in their glory as they spoke of his outward journey which he was to complete in Jerusalem. Now Peter and those with him had been heavy with sleep; but wakening they saw his glory, and the two men who were standing with him. And it happened as they were going from him that Peter said to Jesus: Master, it is good for us to be here, and let us make three shelters, one for you and one for Moses and one for Elijah. He did not know what he was saying. But as he was saying this there came a cloud, and it covered them; and they were frightened as they went into the cloud. And a voice came from the cloud, saying: This is my son, the chosen; listen to him. And in the coming of the voice Jesus was found to be alone. And they kept silence and reported to no one, in those days, anything of what they had seen.

And it happened on the next day, as they came down from the mountain, a great multitude met them. And behold, out of the crowd a man cried out, saying: Master, I beg you to look upon my son; because he is my only child, and see, a spirit takes hold of him, and suddenly he screams, and it racks him with foaming and bruises him and barely leaves him. And I begged your disciples to cast him out, and they were not able to. Jesus answered and said: O generation without faith and perverse, how long shall I be with you and endure you? Bring your son here. While he was still coming forward the demon tore him and convulsed him. But Jesus reproved the unclean spirit and healed the boy and gave him back to his father. And all were astounded at the greatness of God.

And as all were wondering over all the things he was doing, he said to his disciples: Store these words in your ears; for the son of man is about to be betrayed into the hands of men. But they did not understand this saying, and it was hidden from them so that they might not be aware of it, and they were afraid to ask him about this saying. But there arose a dispute among them as to which was the greater; and Jesus, knowing the disputation of their hearts, took a child and set him beside himself and said to them: He who accepts this child in my name accepts me, and he who accepts me accepts him who sent me. For he who is smaller among you all, that one is great.

And John spoke forth and said: Master, we saw a man driving out demons in your name, and we tried to stop him, because he was not one of our following. Jesus said to him: Do not stop him; for he who is not against you is for you.

And it happened in the filling out of the days before his assumption, that he himself set his face toward the journey to Jerusalem and also that he sent messengers out before his presence. And they on their journey entered a village of the Samaritans, to make things ready for him. And they would not receive him, because his face was set on the journey to Jerusalem. And learning of this the disciples James and John said: Lord, do you wish us to summon fire to come down from heaven and consume them? But Jesus turned on them and reproved them. And they went to another village.

And as they journeyed along the way, a man said to him: I will follow you wherever you go. And Jesus said to him: Foxes have holes, and the birds of the sky have nests, but the son of man has no place to lay his head. And he said to another: Follow me. But the man said: Give me leave first to go and bury my father. But he said to him: Leave the dead to bury their own dead, but you go and announce the Kingdom of God. And another man said: I will follow you, Lord; but first allow me to take leave of the people in my house. But Jesus said to him: No one who has put his hand to the plow and then looked back is fit for the Kingdom of God.

❡ After this the Lord appointed seventy other men and sent them out two by two before his presence to every city and place where he was going to go. And he said to them: The harvest is abundant, but the laborers few. Beg the master of the harvest to send out laborers to his harvest. Go forth. See, I send you out like sheep into the midst of wolves. Take no purse, no bag, no shoes, and greet no one on the road. Whenever you enter any house, say: Peace to this house. And if a son of peace is there, your peace will stay with him; and if not, it will return to you. Remain in the same house, eating and drinking what they give you, for the laborer is worthy of his wages. Do not move about from house to house. And when you go into any city, and they receive you, eat what is put before you, and treat the sick who are there, and say to them: The Kingdom of God has come near you. But when you go into any city and they do not receive you, as you go into the open places of that city say: Even the dust of your city which has stuck to our feet we wipe off, against you. Only know this, that the Kingdom of God is near. I tell you that on the Day it will be more tolerable for Sodom than for that city. Woe, to you, Chorazin. Woe to you, Bethsaida. For if there had been shown in Tyre and Sidon the powers that have been shown among you, long since they would have repented in sackcloth and ashes. But for Tyre and Sidon it will be more tolerable at the judgment than it will be for you. And you, Capernaum, will you be exalted to the sky? You will go down to Hades.

He who listens to you listens to me, and he who rejects you rejects me. And he who rejects me rejects him who sent me.

And the seventy returned in joy, saying: Lord, even the demons submit to us in your name. He said to them: I saw Satan falling from the sky like a flash of lightning. See, I have given you authority to tread on snakes and scorpions, and against every power of the enemy, and nothing can injure you. Except do not rejoice in this, that the spirits submit to you, but rejoice because your names are written in heaven.

In that same hour, he rejoiced in the Holy Spirit and said: I thank you, father lord of heaven and earth, because you have hidden these things away from the clever and the understanding, and revealed them to the simple. Yes, father, that thus it has been your pleasure in your sight. All was given to me by my father, and no one knows who is the son except the father, and who is the father except the son and anyone to whom the son wishes to reveal it. And he turned to the disciples and said to them alone: Blessed are the eyes that have seen what you have seen. For I tell you that many prophets and kings have wished to see what you have seen, and have not seen it, and to hear what you have heard and have not heard it.

And behold, a man versed in the law stood up, making trial of him and saying: Master, what shall I do to inherit everlasting life? He said to him: What is written in the law? How do you read it? The man answered and said: You shall love the Lord your God from all your heart and in all your spirit and in all your strength and in all your mind; and you shall love your neighbor as yourself. He said to him: You have answered right. Do this and you will live. But the man, wishing to justify himself, said to Jesus: And who is my neighbor? Jesus answered and said: There was a man who went down from Jerusalem to Jericho and fell in with robbers who stripped him and beat him and went away leaving him half dead. And by chance a priest went down that road, and when he saw him passed by on the other side; and so likewise a Levite coming to the place and seeing him passed by on the other side. But a certain Samaritan came there on his journey, and when he saw him he pitied him, and went to him and bound up his wounds, pouring oil and wine on them, and set him on his own beast and took him to an inn, and took care of him. And on the next day he put out two denarii and gave them to the innkeeper and said: Take care of him, and any extra expense you have I will repay you on my return journey. Which of these three do you think was the neighbor of the man who fell among robbers? He said: The man who treated him with mercy. Jesus said to him: Go on, you also, and do likewise.

And it happened on their journey that he came to a certain village; and there was a woman, Martha by name, who took him into her house. And she had a sister named Mary who sat at the feet of the Lord and listened to what he was saying. But Martha was distracted with much serving, and she stood near him and said: Lord, does it not matter to you that my sister has left me to serve all by myself? Tell her to help me. But the Lord answered and said to her: Martha, Martha, you worry and are troubled over much, but there is need of few things, or only one. For Mary has chosen the good portion, which shall not be taken away from her.

❡ And it happened that while he was praying in a certain place, when he stopped, one of his disciples said to him: Lord, teach us to pray, as John also taught his disciples. He said to them: When you pray, say: Father, may your name be hallowed. May your kingdom come. Give us our sufficient bread day by day; and forgive us our sins, for we also forgive everyone who is our debtor. And do not bring us into temptation.

And he said to them: Which of you will have a friend and go to him in the middle of the night and say to him: My friend, lend me three loaves, because a friend has come in from the road to visit me and I have nothing to set before him? And he answers from inside and says: Stop making difficulties for me. Now the door is locked, and my children are in bed with me. I cannot get up and give it to you. I tell you, if he will not get up and give it to the man because he is his friend, he will wake up and give him what he needs because of his insistence. And I tell you, ask, and it shall be given you; seek, and you shall find; knock, and the door will be opened for you. For everyone who asks receives, and he who seeks finds, and for him who knocks the door is opened. Or who is there among you whose son will ask his father for a fish, and he will give him a snake? Or ask for an egg, and will give him a scorpion? If then you, who are corrupt, know how to give good gifts to your children, by how much more your father in heaven will give the Holy Spirit to those who ask him.

He was casting out a deaf-mute demon, and it happened as the demon went out the deaf-mute talked. And the people marveled, but some of them said: It is through Beelzebub the prince of the demons that he drives out the demons. But others, making trial of him, demanded of him a sign from heaven. But he knew their thoughts and said to them: Every kingdom that is divided against itself is made desolate, and house that is against house collapses. And if even Satan is divided against himself, how shall his kingdom stand? Since you say that through Beelzebub I drive out the demons. But if I drive out the demons through Beelzebub, through whom do your sons drive them out? Therefore they will be judges of you. But if through the finger of God I drive out demons, then the Kingdom of God has come suddenly upon you. When the strong man, well armed, guards his own estate, his possessions are in peace; but when one stronger than he attacks and overcomes him, he takes away the armor in which he had trusted, and he gives away his spoils. He who is not with me is against me; and he who does not gather with me, scatters. When the unclean spirit goes forth from a man, it wanders through waterless regions looking for a place to rest, and when it does not find one it says: I will return to my house that I came out from; and it comes and finds it swept and furnished. Then it goes and picks up other spirits worse than itself, seven of them, and they go in and settle there; and the end for that man is worse than the beginning.

While he was saying this, it happened that a woman in the crowd raised her voice and cried to him: Blessed is the womb that carried you, and the breasts that you sucked. But he said to her: Blessed rather are those who listen to the word of God and obey it.

As the crowds gathered he began to say: This generation is a corrupt generation. It asks for a sign, but no sign shall be given it unless it be the sign of Jonah. For as Jonah was a sign to the people of Nineveh so is the son of man to this generation. The Queen of the South will rise up on the day of judgment with the men of this generation, and condemn them; because she came from the ends of the earth to listen to the wisdom of Solomon, and behold, there is more than Solomon here. The men of Nineveh will arise on the day of judgment with this generation and condemn it; because they repented upon the proclamation of Jonah, and behold, there is more than Jonah here. No one lights a lamp and then puts it in a hiding place or under a basket, but on a lampstand, so that those who come in may see the light. The lamp of the body is your eye. When your eye is clear, the whole of your body is also full of light; but when it is soiled, your body also is in darkness. Consider then whether the light in you may not be darkness. If then your whole body is full of light, having no part that is dark, it will all be light as when the lamp illuminates you with its beam.

While he was talking, a Pharisee asked him to dine with him; and when he entered, he took his place at table. And the Pharisee seeing this was surprised that he had not washed before the meal. But the Lord said to him: Now you Pharisees scour the outside of the cup and the plate, but what is inside you teems with rapacity and corruption. You fools. Did not he who made the outside make the inside also? But give away what is inside as charity, and see, all is clean with you. But woe to you Pharisees, because you pay a tenth on the mint and the rue and every kind of potherb, but you pass over the judgment and the love of God; but you should have done that, without neglecting the other. Woe to you Pharisees, because you love the first seats in the synagogues and the salutations in the public places. Woe to you, because you are like concealed unmarked graves, and people walk upon you without knowing it. One of those expert in the law spoke up and said to him: Master, in saying this you attack us also. But he said: And woe to you, experts in the law, because you load people with burdens that are hard to carry, and you yourselves do not put a finger to the burdens. Woe to you, because you build the tombs of the prophets, but your fathers killed them. But you are witnesses, and you join in approval of their actions, because they killed them and you build their tombs. Therefore even the wisdom of God has said: I will send them prophets and apostles, and some of these they will kill and persecute, so that the blood of all the prophets that has been spilled since the establishment of the world may be exacted from this generation, from the blood of Abel to the blood of Zachariah who was killed between the altar and the temple. Yes, I tell you, it will be exacted from this generation. Woe to you, experts in the law, because you have taken away the key to knowledge. You did not go in yourselves, and you prevented those who tried to go in. And when he went away from them, the scribes and Pharisees began to hate him terribly, and to try to make him speak carelessly about more matters, lying in wait to catch him up on something he might let fall.

❡ As the multitude gathered by tens of thousands, so that they trampled each other, he began to speak first to his disciples: Guard yourselves against the leaven, that is, the hypocrisy, of the Pharisees. There is nothing concealed that shall not be revealed, nothing secret that shall not be known. Because of which, what you say in the dark will be heard in the light, and what you have said in someone's ear in inner rooms will be proclaimed on the housetops. But I say to you, my friends, do not fear those who kill the body but are able to do nothing more after that. I will show you which one to fear. Fear the one who has authority after killing you to throw you into Gehenna. Yes, I tell you, fear that one. Are not five sparrows sold for

two coppers? And not one of them is forgotten in the sight
of God. But even the hairs of your heads are all numbered.
Have no fear; you are worth many sparrows. I tell you,
everyone who will acknowledge me before men the son of
man will acknowledge before the angels of God; but he
who denies me in the sight of men shall be denied in the
sight of the angels of God. And everyone who speaks a
word against the son of man shall have it forgiven him;
but for the one who blasphemes against the Holy Spirit it
shall not be forgiven. And when they bring you before the
synagogues and the powers and the authorities, do not be
concerned about how you will defend yourselves and
what you will say; for the Holy Spirit will teach you in
that very hour what you must say.

Someone in the crowd said to him: Master, tell my
brother to divide the inheritance with me. But he said to
him: My good man, who appointed me your judge or your
arbitrator? And he said to them: Look to it and keep yourselves from all greed, because a man's life does not consist
in the abundance of his possessions. And he told them a
parable, saying: There was a certain rich man whose land
was fruitful. And he deliberated within himself, saying:
What shall I do, since I have no place where I can store all
my crops? And he said: Here is what I will do. I will tear
down my granaries and build bigger ones, and I will bring
all my grain and my goods together there, and I will say to
my soul: Soul, you have many good things stored away,
for many years. Rest, eat, drink, enjoy yourself. But God
said to him: You fool, they demand that soul of you
tonight. Who will have what you provided? So much for
him who stores up treasures for himself rather than being
rich for God.

And he said to his disciples: Therefore I tell you, do not

take thought for your life, what you will eat, or for your body, what you will wear. For life is more than food, and the body is more than clothing. Think of the ravens, that they do not sow or harvest, they have neither storehouse nor granary, and God feeds them. How much more are you worth than the birds! Which of you by taking thought can add one cubit to his growth? If then you cannot achieve the least, why are you concerned about the rest? Think of the lilies, how they grow. They do not toil or spin; yet I tell you, not even Solomon in all his glory was clothed like one of these. But if God so arrays the grass in the field which grows today and tomorrow is thrown in the oven, how much more will he array you, you men of little faith! Do not you then keep searching for what you can eat and what you can drink, and do not be troubled, for all the nations of the world search for these things, and your father knows that you need them; only search for his kingdom, and all these things will be added also. Do not fear, little flock; because your father has been well pleased to give you the kingdom. Sell what you own and give it away as charity; make yourselves purses that do not wear out, an infallible treasure house in heaven, where no thief attacks, no moth corrupts; for where your treasure is, there also will be your heart.

Let your loins be girt up and your lamps burning, and yourselves like men who are expecting their master when he comes back from the wedding, so that when he comes and knocks they can open promptly to him. Blessed are those slaves whom this master returning finds wide awake; truly I tell you, he will gird himself up and set them down to dine and go about and wait on them. And if he comes in the second watch or the third and finds them thus, blessed are they. But know this, that if the master of the house had known at what time the thief was coming, he would have been watchful and not let his house be broken into. And you, be ready, because the son of man comes in the hour when you do not expect him. Peter said: Lord, are you telling this parable to us or to all? And the Lord said: Who is the faithful steward, the prudent one, whom his master will set over the servants of his household to give them their measure of food when it is due? Blessed is that slave whom his master arriving finds doing thus; truly I tell you that he will put him in charge of all his possessions. But if that slave says in his heart: My master is late returning; and begins to beat the men-servants and the maidservants, and to eat and drink and get drunk; the master of that slave will come on a day when he does not expect him in the hour when he is unaware, and cut him to ribbons, and make his lot one with the unfaithful. That slave who knows the will of his master, and does not make ready or act according to his will, will be beaten with many strokes; but the one who knows nothing and does what deserves whipping will be beaten with few strokes. Everyone to whom much is given will have much required of him; from him to whom much was entrusted they will demand more.

I came to cast fire upon the earth, and what is my will if it has already been lit? I have a baptism to undergo, and how I am oppressed until it is done with. Do you think that I came to give peace on earth? No, I tell you, dissension rather. For from now there will be five in one house at odds with each other, three against two and two against three, and father will be at odds with son and son with father, mother with daughter and daughter with mother, mother-in-law with her daughter-in-law and daughter-in-law with mother-in-law.

And he said to the multitudes: When you see a cloud rising in the west, you say at once: Rain is coming. And so it happens. And when you see the south wind blowing, you say: There will be hot weather. And so it happens. You hypocrites, you know how to read the face of the earth and the sky, but how is it you do not know how to read this time? And why do you not judge what is right of your own will. As you go with your adversary at law to the magistrate, make an effort to be reconciled with him on the way there, for fear he may drag you before the judge, and the judge turn you over to the bailiff, and the bailiff throw you in prison. I tell you, you cannot come out of there until you pay the last penny.

◀ At that time some people came to him and brought him news about the Galilaeans whose blood Pilate had mixed with their sacrifices. And he answered and said to them: Do you suppose that these Galilaeans, because they suffered this, were sinners as compared with the rest of the Galilaeans? No, I tell you, but unless you repent, you will all be destroyed like them. Or those eighteen when the tower at Siloam fell on them and killed them. Do you suppose they were guilty as compared with all the rest of the people who live in Jerusalem? No, I tell you, but unless you repent you will all be destroyed in the same way. And he told them this parable: A man had a fig tree planted in his vineyard, and he went looking for fruit on it and did not find any. And he said to the gardener: It is three years now since I began coming and looking for fruit on this fig tree without finding it. Cut it down. Why should it be wasting the soil? But he answered and said to

him: Master, let it go for this year too, until I have cultivated it and put manure on it. And if it bears fruit after
that, well: . . . but if it does not, you will cut it down.

He was teaching in one of the synagogues on the sabbath. And behold, there was a woman who had had a
spirit of infirmity for eighteen years, and she was bent
over and unable to straighten up at all. And Jesus saw her
and spoke to her and said: Woman, you are loosed from
your infirmity, and laid his hands on her. And immediately she straightened up and glorified God. But the head
of the synagogue, angered because Jesus had given treatment on the sabbath, said to the congregation: There are
six days in which one must work. Come then and be
healed on those days and not on the day of the sabbath.
The Lord answered him and said: You hypocrites, does
not each of you on the sabbath loose his ox or his donkey
from the crib and lead him to water? And she, who is a
daughter of Abraham, whom Satan had kept bound for
eighteen years, must she not be loosed from this bondage
on the day of the sabbath? And when he said this, all who
were set against him were put to shame, and all the
masses were happy over all the glorious things that came
to be through him.

Then he said: What is the Kingdom of God like, and to
what shall I liken it? It is like a grain of mustard, which a
man took and sowed in his garden, and it grew and became a tree, so that the birds of the air came and nested in
its branches. And again he said: To what shall I liken the
Kingdom of God? It is like leaven, which a woman took
and buried in three measures of dough, so that it all rose.

And he journeyed through the cities and villages, teaching and making his way toward Jerusalem. And a man

said to him: Lord, will those who are saved be few? And
he said to them: Struggle to go in through the narrow
door, because many, I tell you, try to get in and are not
able to, from the time when the master of the house wakens and bars the door, and you begin to stand outside and
knock on the door, saying: Lord, open to us. And he will
answer and say to you: I do not know you or where you
come from. Then you will begin to say: We ate and drank
in your presence, and you taught in our public places.
Then he will speak and say to you: I do not know where
you come from. Go away from me, all you workers of
iniquity. There will be weeping and gnashing of teeth,
when you see Abraham and Isaac and Jacob and all the
prophets in the Kingdom of God, and yourselves cast outside. And they will come from the east and the west, and
the north and the south, and be feasted in the Kingdom of
God. And behold, they are last who will be first, and they
are first who will be last.

In the same hour some Pharisees came to him and said:
Go and make your way from here, because Herod wants
to kill you. And he said to them: Go and say to that fox:
Look, I cast out demons and effect my cures today and
tomorrow, and the third day I am done. But I must go
forward today and tomorrow and the next day, because
there is no way for a prophet to be killed outside
Jerusalem. Jerusalem, Jerusalem, who kills the prophets
and stones those who have been sent to her! How often I
have wished to gather your children together as a bird
gathers her brood under her wings, and you were unwilling. Behold, your house is deserted. I tell you, you cannot
see me until you say: Blessed is he who comes in the
name of the Lord.

❡ And it happened that when he went to the house of one of the leading Pharisees, and dined, that they were watching him closely. And behold, there was a man before him who suffered from dropsy. And Jesus spoke forth and said to the legal experts and the Pharisees: Is it lawful or not to give treatment on the sabbath? They held their peace. He took hold of him, and healed him, and dismissed him. And he said to them: Which of you will have a son, or an ox, fall down a well, and will not immediately pull him out on the day of the sabbath? And they were not able to answer that.

And he told the guests a parable, applying it to the way they apportioned their places of honor, and said to them: When you are invited by someone to a wedding, do not recline in the first place, for fear someone he honors more than you may have been invited by him, and he who invited you both may come and say to you: Give this man the place. And then you will begin, with shame, to occupy the last place. But when you are invited, go and set yourself in the last place, so that when your host comes he will say to you: My friend, come on up higher. Then you will have dignity in the sight of all your fellow guests; because everyone who exalts himself will be humbled, and he who humbles himself will be exalted.

And he said to the man who had invited him: When you give a lunch or a dinner, do not invite your friends, or your brothers, or your relatives, or your rich neighbors, lest they too invite you in return and some recompense befall you. But when you are receiving, invite the poor and the maimed and the lame and the blind; and you will be blessed, because they are not able to repay you; for it will be repaid you at the resurrection of the righteous.

Hearing this, one of his fellow guests said: Blessed is he

who dines in the Kingdom of God. Jesus said to him: A certain man was holding a great feast, and he invited many, and at the time for the feast he sent out his slave to say to those who were invited: Come, since everything is now ready. Then they all at once began to make excuses. The first one said to him: I have bought a piece of land and I must go out and look at it; I pray you, hold me excused. Another said: I have bought five yoke of oxen, and I am on my way to try them out. I pray you, hold me excused. And another said: I took a wife in marriage, and therefore I cannot come. And the slave came back and reported all this to his master. Then the master of the house was angry and said to his slave: Go out quickly into the squares and streets of the city and bring here the poor and the maimed and the blind and the lame. And the slave said: Master, what you ordered has been done, and there is still room. And the master said to his slave: Go out to the highways and the hedgerows and force them to come in, so that my house may be full; for I tell you that not one of those other men who were invited shall taste of my feast.

Many multitudes followed him along the way, and he turned and said to them: If someone comes to me and does not hate his father and mother and wife and children and brothers and sisters, and even his own life also, he cannot be my disciple. He who does not take up his cross and come after me cannot be my disciple. For which of you who desires to build a tower does not first sit down and reckon the cost, to see if he has enough for its completion? For fear that, after he has set down the foundation and cannot finish it, all the people watching him may begin to tease him and say: This man began to build, and he could not finish. Or what king, on his way to encounter another king in battle, will not first sit down and think out whether with his ten thousand he is strong enough to meet the man who comes against him with twenty thousand? If he is not, while the other is still far off, he sends an embassy to ask for peace. So, therefore, any of you who does not renounce all his possessions cannot be my disciple. Salt is good: but if the salt loses its power, with what will it be seasoned? It is fit for neither the land nor the dunghill. They throw it out. He who has ears to hear, let him hear.

¶ All the tax collectors and the sinners kept coming around him, to listen to him. And the Pharisees and the scribes muttered, saying: This man receives sinners and eats with them. But he told them this parable, saying: Which man among you who has a hundred sheep and has lost one of them will not leave the ninety-nine in the wilds and go after the lost one until he finds it? And when he does find it, he sets it on his shoulders, rejoicing, and goes to his house and invites in his friends and his neighbors, saying to them: Rejoice with me, because I found my sheep which was lost. I tell you that thus there will be joy in heaven over one sinner who repents, rather than over ninety-nine righteous ones who have no need of repentance. Or what woman who has ten drachmas, if she loses one drachma, does not light the lamp and sweep the house and search diligently until she finds it? And finding it she invites in her friends and neighbors, saying: Rejoice with me, because I found the drachma I lost. Such, I tell you, is the joy among the angels of God over one sinner who repents.

And he said: There was a man who had two sons. And

the younger of them said to his father: Father, give me my appropriate share of the property. And the father divided his substance between them. And not many days afterward the younger son gathered everything together and left the country for a distant land, and there he squandered his substance in riotous living. And after he had spent everything, there was a severe famine in that country, and he began to be in need. And he went and attached himself to one of the citizens of that country, who sent him out into the fields to feed the pigs. And he longed to be nourished on the nuts that the pigs ate, and no one would give to him. And he went and said to himself: How many hired servants of my father have plenty of bread while I am dying of hunger here. I will rise up and go to my father and say to him: Father, I have sinned against heaven and in your sight, I am no longer worthy to be called your son. Make me like one of your hired servants. And he rose up and went to his father. And when he was still a long way off, his father saw him and was moved and ran and fell on his neck and kissed him. The son said to him: Father, I have sinned against heaven and in your sight, I am no longer worthy to be called your son. But his father said to his slaves: Quick, bring the best clothing and put it on him, and have a ring for his hand and shoes for his feet, and bring the fatted calf, slaughter him, and let us eat and make merry because this man, my son, was a dead man and came to life, he was lost and he has been found. And they began to make merry. His older son was out on the estate, and as he came nearer to the house he heard music and dancing, and he called over one of the servants and asked what was going on. He told him: Your brother is here, and your father slaughtered the fatted calf, because he got him back in good health. He was angry and did not want to go in. But his father came out and entreated him. But he answered and said to his father: Look, all these years I have been your slave and never neglected an order of yours, but you never gave me a kid so that I could make merry with my friends. But when this son of yours comes back, the one who ate up your livelihood in the company of whores, you slaughtered the fatted calf for him. But he said to him: My child, you are always with me, and all that is mine is yours; but we had to make merry and rejoice, because your brother was a dead man and came to life, he was lost and has been found.

❡ And he said to his disciples: There was a rich man who had a steward, and this steward was accused to his master of wasting the property. And he called him and said to him: What is this I hear about you? Give the statement of your stewardship, since you can no longer be the steward. And the steward said to himself: What shall I do now that my master has taken away my stewardship from me? I am not strong enough to dig, I am ashamed to beg. Now I have seen what to do, so that I can be removed from my stewardship but people will still take me into their houses. And he called in each one of his master's debtors, and he said to the first one: How much do you owe my master? And he said: A hundred measures of oil. He said to him: Take your note and sit down quickly and write fifty. Then he said to another: And how much do you owe? He said: A hundred measures of grain. He said to him: Take your note and write eighty. And the master praised the steward for his dishonesty because he had acted prudently; because the sons of this age are wiser than the sons of light for this generation that is theirs. And

I tell you, make friends for yourselves by means of the mammon of dishonesty, so that when it gives out they may receive you into everlasting tabernacles. He who is trustworthy in the least matter is also trustworthy in the great one, and he who is dishonest in the least matter is also dishonest in the great one. If then you were not trustworthy in the dishonest mammon, who will entrust the true to you? And if you were not trustworthy in what belonged to others, who will give you what is yours? No servant can serve two masters. For he will either hate the one and love the other, or he will cling to the one and despise the other. You cannot serve God and mammon.

The Pharisees, who are fond of money, heard all this and they sneered at him. He said to them: You are the ones who justify yourselves in the eyes of men, but God knows your hearts; because what is exalted among men is an abomination in the eyes of God. Until John, it was the law and the prophets; but from then on, the good news of the Kingdom of God is announced, and everyone tries to force his way into it. But it is easier for heaven and earth to pass away than for one letter end of the law to fail. Everyone who divorces his wife and marries another is committing adultery, and he who marries a woman divorced from her husband is committing adultery.

There was a certain rich man, and he would put on purple and fine linen and feast in his splendor day after day. And a beggar, Lazarus by name, would throw himself down at his door, covered with sores, and longing to eat of the crumbs that fell from the rich man's table. And the very dogs would come out and lick his sores. And it happened that the beggar died, and he was transported by angels to recline close by Abraham; and the rich man died and was buried. And in Hades he lifted up his eyes, being in torment, and from far away he could see Abraham, and Lazarus reclining close by him. And he called out and said: Father Abraham, have pity and send Lazarus to dip his fingertip in water and refresh my tongue, because I am in agony in this flame. But Abraham said: My child, remember that you got your share of good things in your life, and Lazarus likewise his misfortunes. But now he is thus comforted and you are in pain. And in any case, there is a great chasm fixed between us and you, so that those who wish to cross over to you are not able to, nor can they cross from there to us. Then he said: I beg you then, father, to send him to my father's house, for I have five brothers, to warn them so that they may not come into this place of torment. But Abraham said: They have Moses and the prophets. Let them listen to them. But he said: No, father Abraham, but if someone goes to them from the dead, they will repent. But he said to him: If they do not listen to Moses and the prophets, they will not be persuaded though one rise from the dead.

◀ And he said to his disciples: It is impossible that there should come no causes to make man go astray; but woe to him through whom they come. It is better for him to have a millstone hung around his neck and be thrown into the sea than to cause one of these little ones to go astray. Watch yourselves. If your brother does wrong, charge him with it, and if he repents, forgive him. And if he does you wrong seven times in a day and seven times turns to you and says: I repent, you shall forgive him. The apostles said to the Lord: Give us more faith. But the Lord said: If you have faith the size of a grain of mustard, you could have said to this sycamine tree: Be uprooted and grow in the sea; and it would have obeyed you. Or which of you has a slave who plows or herds the flocks and will say to him when he comes in from the fields: Come now and eat with me? Will he not rather say: Prepare me something to dine on, and tuck yourself up and wait on me while I eat and drink, and after that you eat and drink? Surely he does not feel thankful to the slave because he has done as he was told? So you, when you have done all that you were told to, should say: We are worthless slaves. What we have done was what we were obliged to do.

And it happened on his journey to Jerusalem that he passed between Samaria and Galilee. And as he went into a certain village ten men who were lepers met him, and they stood at a distance, and raised their voices, saying: Jesus, master, pity us. And when he saw them he said: Go and show yourselves to the priests. And it happened that as they went they became clean. And one of them, seeing that he was healed, turned, glorifying God in a great voice, and fell on his face at his feet, thanking him. And this man was a Samaritan. Jesus answered him and said: Were not all ten made clean? Where are the nine? Were none found turning back and glorifying God except only this alien? And he said to him: Rise and go. Your faith has saved you.

When he was asked by the Pharisees when the Kingdom of God was to come, he answered them and said: The Kingdom of God is not coming in an observable way, nor will they say: Look, it is here; or: There. For see, the Kingdom of God is inside you. And he said to his disciples: Days will come when you will long to see one of the days of the son of man, and you will not see it. And they will say to you: Look, it is there; or: See, this way. Do not follow them. For as the lightning flashes and lights up, from one side to the other, what is under the sky, such will be the son of man. But first he must suffer much and be rejected by this generation. And as it was in the days of Noah, so will it be in the days of the son of man. They ate, they drank, they married, they were given in marriage, until the day when Noah went into the ark and the flood came and destroyed them all. Or as it was in the days of Lot. They ate, they drank, they bought, they sold, they planted, they built houses. But on the day when Lot went out from Sodom, it rained fire and sulphur from the sky and destroyed them all. It will be the same way on the day when the son of man is revealed. On that day, if one is on his roof and his goods are in the house, let him not come down to take them up: and so likewise let him who is in the field not turn back. Think of Lot's wife. He who tries to preserve his life will lose it, and he who loses it will bring it to life. I tell you, on that night there will be two in one bed, and one will be taken and the other left; there will be two women grinding at the same place, and one will be taken and the other left. And they answered and said to him: Where, Lord? He said to them: Where the body is, there will the eagles be gathered.

◀ And he told them a parable about the need to be always praying and not weakening, saying: In a certain city there was a judge who neither feared God nor heeded man. But there was a widow in that city and she kept going to him and saying: Vindicate me against my adversary. And for a time he would not, but later he said to himself: Even though I neither fear God nor heed man, because this widow gives me trouble I will vindicate her, so that she may not end by wearing me out with her visits. And the

Lord said: Hear what this judge of injustice says. Will God
not accomplish the vindication of his chosen ones who
cry out to him day and night? Will he be patient in their
case? I tell you that he will accomplish their vindication
with speed. But when the son of man comes, will he find
faith on earth?

And he told this parable against those who were confident that they were righteous and despised all others:
Two men went out to the temple to pray; one was a
Pharisee, the other a tax collector. And the Pharisee stood
and prayed thus within himself: O God, I thank you that I
am not like the rest of mankind—rapacious, dishonest,
adulterous—or even like this tax collector. I fast twice
a week, I pay a tithe on all I have. But the tax collector,
standing at a distance, would not even raise his eyes to the
sky, but beat his breast and said: O God, have mercy upon
sinful me. I tell you, this man went back to his house
justified as compared with the other; because everyone
who exalts himself will be humbled, and he who humbles
himself will be exalted.

They brought him even their babies for him to touch.
And seeing this the disciples scolded them. But Jesus
called them to him and said: Let the children come to me
and do not prevent them: for of such is the Kingdom of
God. Truly I tell you, he who does not receive the Kingdom of God like a child may not enter into it.

And an official questioned him, saying: Good master,
what must I do to inherit life everlasting: Jesus said to
him: Why do you call me good? No one is good but God
alone. You know the commandments: Do not commit
adultery, do not murder, do not steal, do not bear false
witness, honor your father and your mother. But he said: I
have kept all these from my youth. Hearing this Jesus said

to him: You have one thing missing. Sell all you have and give it to the poor, and you shall have a treasury in heaven; and come and follow me. He was greatly pained when he heard this, for he was very rich. Watching him, Jesus said: How hard it is for those with money to enter the Kingdom of God. For it is easier for a camel to enter the eye of a needle than for a rich man to enter the Kingdom of God. But his listeners said: And who can be saved? He said: What is impossible for men is possible for God. But Peter said: See, we have given up all that was our own and followed you. But he said to them: Truly I tell you, there is no one who has given up house or wife or brothers or parents or children for the sake of the Kingdom of God who will not receive many times as much in this time, and in the age to come life everlasting.

Then taking the twelve aside he said to them: Behold, we are going up to Jerusalem, and all that has been written by the prophets about the son of man will be fulfilled. He will be given over to the Gentiles, and he will be mocked and outraged and spit upon, and they will flog him and kill him, and on the third day he will rise. And they understood nothing of all this, and this saying was hidden from them, and they did not know what was being said.

And it happened as he drew near Jericho there was a blind man sitting by the road, begging. And when he heard the crowd going through he asked what was going on; and they told him that Jesus of Nazareth was passing by. And he cried out, saying: Jesus, son of David, have pity on me. Those who were escorting him scolded the man, to silence him, but he screamed all the harder: Son of David, have pity on me. Jesus stopped and ordered that he be brought before him. And as he approached he asked him: What do you want me to do for you? He said: Lord, let me see again. And Jesus said to him: See again; your faith has saved you. And immediately he could see again, and he followed him, glorifying God. And all the people, seeing this, gave praise to God.

◀ And he entered Jericho and was passing through it. And behold, there was a man called Zacchaeus, and he was a chief tax collector, and he was rich. And he was trying to see which one was Jesus and could not see him from the crowd, because he was short of stature. So he ran on ahead and climbed a sycamore tree so that he could see him, because he was going to pass by it. And as he came to the place Jesus looked up and said to him: Zacchaeus, hurry and come down, for I must stay in your house today. And he hastened and came down, and welcomed him with joy. And when they saw this everybody muttered, saying: He has gone in to stay with a sinful man. But Zacchaeus stood before the Lord and said: See, Lord, I am giving half of my possessions to the poor, and if I have made anything dishonestly at someone's expense, I give it back fourfold. Jesus said to him: Salvation has come to this house today, because this man also is a son of Abraham; for the son of man came to seek out and save the lost.

As they were listening to him, he told an additional parable because he was close to Jerusalem and they thought that the Kingdom of God would appear very soon. So he said: A certain highborn man went on a journey to a far country to get a kingdom for himself and then return. And he summoned ten slaves who belonged to him and gave them ten minas and told them: Engage in business until I come. But his citizens hated him, and they sent an embassy after him, saying: We do not want this man to be king over us. And it happened on his return, after he had got the kingdom, he ordered those slaves to whom he had given the money to be summoned, so that he might learn what business they had got done. And the first appeared, and said: Master, your mina has earned ten more minas. And he said: Well done. Good slave, because in the least matter you were trustworthy, know that you now have power over ten cities. And the second one came and said: Master, your mina has made five minas. And to this one also he said: Know that you are set over five cities. And the other one came and said: Master, here is your mina which I kept hidden away in a napkin. For I was afraid of you because you are a severe man, who pick up what you did not put down and harvest what you did not sow. He said to him: Out of your own mouth I judge you, bad slave. You knew that I am a severe man, who pick up what I did not put down and harvest what I did not sow? Then why did you not put out my money to the bankers? Then when I returned I could have taken it out with interest. And to those who were standing by he said: Take his mina away and give it to the one who has ten minas—and they said to him: Master, he has ten minas— I tell you that to everyone who has it shall be given, and from him who does not have even what he has shall be taken away. But those enemies of mine, who did not want me to be king over them, bring them here and slaughter them in my presence.

And when Jesus had said this he went on with his journey up to Jerusalem.

And it happened that when he came near Bethphage and Bethany, near the hill which is called the Mount of Olives, he sent two of his disciples ahead, saying to them:

Go into the village that lies before you, and as you go in you will find a colt tethered, on which no man has ever ridden. And when you have untied him bring him. And if anybody asks you: Why are you untying him? answer thus: His master needs him. And those whom he had sent on this errand went and found it as he had said they would. And as they were untying the colt his masters said to them: Why are you untying the colt? And they said: His master needs him. And they brought the colt to Jesus and threw their clothing upon him and mounted Jesus on him; and as he went on they strewed their clothing in the road. And as he approached the descent from the Mount of Olives, all the multitude of his disciples, rejoicing, began to praise God in a great voice for all the powers they had seen displayed, saying: Blessed is he who comes, the King, in the name of the Lord; peace in heaven, and glory in the highest. And some of the Pharisees in the crowd said to him: Master, reprove your disciples. And he answered and said: I tell you, if these are silent, the stones will cry out.

And as he approached and looked at the city he wept over it, saying: If you only knew on this day, even you, what leads to peace! But now it is hidden from your eyes. For the days will come when your enemies will run an entrenchment around you and encircle you and crush you from every side, and they will level you to the ground, and your children in you, and they will not leave stone upon stone in you, because you did not recognize the time of your visitation.

And he went into the temple and began to drive out those who sold there, saying to them: It is written: And my house shall be a house of prayer. But you have made it into a den of robbers.

And he was teaching day by day in the temple. But the high priests and the scribes looked for a way to destroy him, and so also did the leading men among the people, but they could not think of what to do, for all the populace hung on his words.

⟨ And it happened on one of those days when he was teaching the people in the temple and preaching the gospel, the high priests and the scribes came up to him, along with the elders, and they said to him: Tell us by what authority you do this, or who it is who gave you this authority. He answered and said to them: I too will ask you a question, and you tell me. Was the baptism of John from heaven or from men? They discussed this among themselves, saying: If we say: From heaven, he will say: Why did you not believe him? But if we say: From men, the whole populace will stone us to death, for they are convinced that John was a prophet. And they answered that they did not know whence it came. And Jesus said to them: Neither will I tell you by what authority I do this.

And he began to tell the people this parable: A man planted a vineyard, and let it out to farmers, and left the country for some time. And when the time came he sent his slave to the farmers so that they could give him some of the fruits of the vineyard. But the farmers lashed him and sent him away empty-handed. He sent another slave in addition and they lashed him too and outraged him and sent him away empty-handed. He added still a third and sent him, and they wounded him and threw him out. Then the lord of the vineyard said to himself: What shall I do? I will send them my beloved son; perhaps they will respect him. But when they saw him the farmers dis-

cussed it with each other, and they said: This is the heir.
Let us kill him, so that the inheritance will be ours. And
they threw him out of the vineyard and killed him. What
will the lord of the vineyard do to them? He will come
and destroy those farmers and give the vineyard to others.
When they heard it, they said: May it never happen! But
he looked at them and said: What then is this that is
written? The stone that the builders rejected has come to
be at the head of the corner. And anyone who falls on that
stone shall be broken; and he on whom it falls shall be
crushed by it. And the scribes and the high priests were
looking for a way to lay their hands on him at that very
time, and they were afraid of the people, for they knew
that he had spoken that parable against them. And they
watched their opportunity and sent spies who pretended
to be righteous men, so that they could seize on something he said and be able to turn him over to the government and the authority of the governor. And they questioned him, saying: Master, we know that you speak and
teach straight, and do not take account of persons, but
truthfully teach the way of God. Is it lawful to pay the tax
to Caesar or not? But he knew their knavery and said to
them: Show me a denarius. Whose is the image and
whose name is inscribed? They said: Caesar's. And he
said to them: Then give Caesar what is Caesar's and God
what is God's. And they could not get a hold on this
saying before the people, and they wondered at this answer and were silent.

Then there came to him certain of the Sadducees, who
say that there is no resurrection, and they questioned
him, saying: Master, Moses wrote for us that if a man's
brother dies, married but without children, his brother
should take his wife and raise up issue for his brother.

Now there were seven brothers; and the first one took a wife and died without children; and the second took her, and the third, and in the same way all seven left no children, and died; and finally the woman died. So in the resurrection, whose wife will the woman be? For all seven had her as wife. Jesus said to them: The sons of this life marry and are given in marriage, but those who have been called worthy to attain that other life, and the resurrection from the dead, neither marry nor are given in marriage. For they can no longer die, for they are like angels, and being sons of the resurrection they are sons of God. But that the dead waken Moses bore witness, at the bush, when he says: The Lord God of Abraham and the God of Isaac and the God of Jacob; for he is not God of the dead but of the living, for all live in him. Then some of the scribes answered and said: Master, you have spoken well; for they no longer dared question him on anything. But he said to them: How do they say that the Christ is the son of David? For David himself says in the Book of Psalms: The Lord said to my Lord: Sit on my right, so that I may put your enemies beneath your feet. So David calls him Lord, and how can he be his son?

And in the hearing of all the people he said to his disciples: Beware of the scribes, who like to walk about in their robes, who love the salutations in the marketplaces and the first seats in the synagogues and the foremost couches at the dinners, who eat up the houses of the widows and pray long as an excuse. The greater the condemnation these will receive.

¶ Then he looked out and saw the people throwing their gifts into the treasury, rich people; and he saw a poor widow tossing in two little coins. And he said: Truly I tell you, this widow who is poor has put in more than all. For they all put in their gifts out of their surplus, but she put in out of her deficit, her whole livelihood.

And when some said concerning the temple that it was made beautiful with fine stones and dedications, he said: There will come days when of all this that you see there will be no stone set on stone that will escape falling to ruin. But they questioned him, saying: Master, when will this be, and what will be the sign when this is about to happen? He said: See to it that you are not led astray. For many will come in my name saying: I am he, and: The time is near. Do not follow them. But when you hear of wars and dissensions, do not be frightened. For all this must come first, but the end will not be soon. Then he said to them: Nation shall rise up against nation and kingdom against kingdom, there will be great earthquakes, and in places there will be pestilences and famines, and horrors and great signs from the sky. But before all these things they will lay their hands on you and persecute you, turning you over to the synagogues and prisons, as you are brought before kings and chiefs because of my name. This will be your time to testify. Then store it in your hearts that you must not study beforehand how you will defend yourselves, for I will give you such lips and such skill that all your antagonists will be unable to stand against you or speak against you. But you will be betrayed even by parents and brothers and kinsmen and friends, and they will put some of you to death, and you will be hated by all because of my name. But not one hair of your head shall be destroyed. Through your endurance you will possess your own souls. But when you see Jerusalem encircled by encampments, then know that her desolation is near. Then let those who are in Judaea flee to the mountains, and those who are in the middle of the city go out, and those who are in the provinces not go into her, because these are the days of her retribution, for all the scriptures to be fulfilled. Woe to the women who are with child in those days and the women who are nursing in those days. For there will be great stress upon the land and anger against this people, and they will fall to the edge of the sword and be led captive into all the nations, and Jerusalem will be trampled by the nations until the times of the nations are fulfilled. And there will be portents in the sun and the moon and stars, and on earth distress of nations in bewilderment of the sound of the sea and its surf, as people faint from fear and expectation of what is advancing upon the world, for the powers of the skies will be shaken. And then they will see the son of man coming upon the cloud with power and great glory. As these things begin to happen, look up and raise your hands, because the time of your deliverance is near.

And he told them a parable: Look at the fig tree and all the trees. When they put forth leaves, you look at them for yourselves and know that the summer is now near; so also when you see these things happening you know that the Kingdom of God is near. Truly I tell you that this generation will not pass by before all these things are done. The sky and the earth will pass away but my words may not pass away. But look to yourselves so that your hearts may not become heavy with surfeit and drunkenness and thoughts of this life, lest that day come upon you suddenly like a trap; for it will come upon all those who are settled upon the face of the whole earth. Be wakeful at every moment, praying for strength to escape all those things that are going to happen, and to stand before the son of man.

And during the days he would teach in the temple, but for the nights he would go out and stay at the Mount of Olives; and all the people would go out at dawn to the temple to hear him.

❡ The festival of the unleavened bread drew near, which is called the Passover. And the high priests and the scribes were looking for a way to destroy him, for they were afraid of the people. And Satan entered into Judas, the one called Iscariot, who was one of the number of the twelve. And he went and talked with the high priests and generals about how to betray him to them. And they were delighted and contracted to give him money. And he agreed, and looked for an opportunity to betray him, when the crowd was not there.

And the day of unleavened bread came, when it was time to sacrifice the paschal lamb. And Jesus sent out Peter and John, saying: Go and make preparations for us to eat the feast of the Passover. And they said to him: Where shall we prepare it? And he said to them: See, as you go into the city, a man carrying a pot of water will meet you. Follow him into whatever house he enters. And say to the master of the house: The master says to you: Where is my guest chamber where I can eat the Passover dinner with my disciples? And he will show you a large upper room, furnished. There prepare it. And they went and found it as he had told them, and made ready the Passover. And when the time came, he took his place, and the apostles with him. And he said to them: I greatly desired to eat this Passover dinner with you, before my suffering; for I tell you that I shall not eat it again until there is fulfillment in the Kingdom of God. And he accepted a cup and gave thanks and said: Take this and divide it among yourselves; for I tell you, I will not drink of the produce of the vine from now until the Kingdom of God arrives. And he took a loaf and gave thanks and broke it and gave it to them, saying: This my body [which is given for your sake; do this in remembrance of me. And so too with the cup, after dinner, saying: This cup is the new covenant in my blood, which is poured out for your sake]. But see, the hand of the betrayer is with me, on the table. Because the son of man goes the way appointed, but woe to that man through whom he is betrayed. And they began to ask among themselves which of them it could be who was going to do this thing.

And a dispute arose among them over which of them was thought to be the greatest. But he said to them: The kings of the Gentiles are as lords over them, and those who exercise authority are called their benefactors. Not so you; but let the greater among you be as the younger, and let him who leads be as him who serves. For who is greater, he who dines, or he who serves him? Is it not he who dines? Yet I am among you as the one who serves. But you are the ones who have stayed with me in my times of trial; and I appointed for you, as my father appointed a kingdom for me, that you shall eat and drink at my table in my kingdom, and sit upon thrones and judge the twelve tribes of Israel. Simon, Simon, behold, Satan asked for you, to sift you like grain, but I asked for you that your faith should not fail you. So you, one day, turn to your brothers and strengthen them. But he said to him:

Lord, with you I am ready to go to prison and to death. But he said: I tell you, Peter, the cock will not crow today until you have denied three times that you knew me.

And he said to them: When I sent you forth without purse or bag or shoes, surely you did not lack for anything? They said: Nothing. But he said to them: But now, let him who has a purse, take it; let him who has a bag, likewise; let him who has no sword sell his coat and buy one. For I tell you, this that has been written must be fulfilled in me: He was even counted among the outlaws. For what is said about me comes to fulfillment. They said: Lord, here are two swords. But he said to them: It is enough.

And he went out and proceeded according to his custom to the Mount of Olives. And when he had reached the place he said to them: Pray that you do not come to the time of trial. And he himself withdrew from them about a stone's throw, and went on his knees and prayed, saying: Father, if you will, take this cup from me; but let, not my will, but yours, be done. And an angel from the sky was seen by him, giving him strength. And as he came into his agony he prayed the more intensely, and his sweat became like drops of blood falling on the ground. And he stood up from his prayer and went to his disciples and found them asleep after their sorrow, and said to them: Why do you sleep? Get up and pray that you do not come to the time of trial.

And while he was still speaking, behold, a crowd came, and the man called Judas, one of the twelve, was leading them, and he came up to Jesus to kiss him. But Jesus said to him: Judas, are you betraying the son of man with a kiss? When his companions saw what was going to happen, they said: Lord, shall we strike with the sword? And one of them struck the slave of the high priest and took off his right ear. But Jesus spoke forth and said: Let that be enough. And he took hold of the man's ear and healed him. But Jesus said to the high priests and generals of the temple and elders who were present: Did you come out with swords and clubs as if I were a highwayman? Day by day I was with you in the temple and you did not put forth your hands against me. But this is your time, and the power of darkness.

They seized him and led him away and took him to the house of the high priest; and Peter followed him at a distance. And when they lit a fire in the middle of the courtyard and sat by it together, Peter sat among them. A serving girl saw him sitting by the fire, and she stared at him and said: This man was with him too. But he denied it, saying: Woman, I do not know him. And after a little while someone else saw him and said: You are one of them too. But Peter said: Man, I am not. But after an interval of about an hour another man insisted on it, saying: Truly this man was with him; he is a Galilaean. But Peter said: Man, I do not know what you are talking about. And at that moment while he was still talking the cock crew. And the Lord turned and looked at Peter, and Peter remembered the Lord's saying, how he had told him: Before the cock crows this morning you will deny me three times. And he went outside and wept bitterly.

And the men who had hold of Jesus mocked him, lashing him and covering his head and asking him: Which one hit you? Prophesy! And they said many other things against him, reviling him.

And when it was day, the elders of the people were

assembled, the high priests and the scribes, and they brought him before their council, saying: If you are the Christ, tell us. But he said to them: If I tell you, you will not believe me; and if I ask you you will not answer. From now on the son of man will be sitting on the right of the power of God. And they all said: Are you then the son of God? But he said to them: You are saying that I am. And they said: Why do we still need testimony? For we ourselves have heard it from his mouth.

⁋ And their whole assemblage rose up and brought him before Pilate. And they began to accuse him, saying: We found that this man was corrupting our people and interfering with the payment of taxes to Caesar and calling himself the King anointed. Pilate questioned him, saying: Are you the King of the Jews? He answered him and said: It is you who say it. And Pilate said to the high priests and the mob: I find no guilt in this man. But they insisted, saying: He is disturbing the people with his teaching throughout Judaea, all the way from Galilee to here. When Pilate heard this he asked if the man were a Galilaean, and understanding that he was from Herod's sphere of authority, he sent him off to Herod, who was himself in Jerusalem during these days. Herod was greatly pleased at seeing Jesus, for he had wished to see him for some time, because he had heard about him, and he hoped to see some miracle performed by him. And he questioned him at considerable length, but Jesus gave him no answer. And the high priests and the scribes stood there strenuously accusing him. And Herod despised him and put shining clothing on him in mockery and sent him back with his guards to Pilate. And Herod and Pilate became friends with each other on that same day, after having been at enmity before.

Now Pilate called together the high priests and the chief men and the people and said to them: You brought me this man as one who was corrupting the people, and look, I have judged him in your presence and found him not guilty of any of the things you charge him with. Nor did Herod either, for he sent him back to us. And see, nothing has been done by him to deserve death. So I will teach him a lesson and let him go. But they screamed in full cry, saying: Take him away and let our Barabbas go. He was a man who had been thrown into prison on account of an uprising with bloodshed that had taken place in the city. And again Pilate spoke to them, wishing to let Jesus go. But they cried out saying: Crucify, crucify him. A third time he said to them: But what harm has this man done? I have found nothing about him to deserve death. I will teach him a lesson and let him go. But they kept at him, demanding in loud voices that he be crucified, and their voices prevailed. And Pilate decided that they should have what they demanded; and he set free the man they asked for, who had been thrown into prison for insurrection and murder, and he gave Jesus up to their will.

And as they led him away, they seized on a certain Simon of Cyrene who was on his way in from the country, and loaded him with the cross to carry behind Jesus. And a great multitude of the people followed him and women who mourned and lamented for him. And Jesus turned to them and said: Daughters of Jerusalem, do not cry for me, but for yourselves and your children, because, behold, the days are coming when they will say: Blessed are the barren, and the wombs that did not breed and the breasts that did not nurse. Then they will begin to say to the mountains: Fall upon us; and to the hills: Cover us. For if they do these things when the wood is green, what will happen when it is dry?

Two others also, who were malefactors, were led along with him to be put to death. And when they came to the place which is called The Skull, there they crucified him and the malefactors, one on the right and one on the left. And Jesus said: Father, forgive them, for they do not know what they are doing. They divided up his clothing and cast lots for it. And the people stood there watching. But the chief men sneered at him, saying: He saved others, let him save himself, if this is the anointed of God, the chosen one. And also the soldiers came up to him and mocked him, offering him vinegar and saying: If you are the King of the Jews, save yourself. There was also an inscription above him, saying: This is the King of the Jews. And one of the malefactors hanging there reviled him and said: Are you not the Christ? Save yourself and us. But the other answered, reproving him, and said: Do you not fear God because you share his sentence? And we are justly punished, for we are getting what we deserve for what we have done; but he has done nothing out of the way. And he said: Jesus, remember me when you enter upon your kingdom. He said to him: Truly I tell you, this day you will be with me in paradise. And now it was about the sixth hour, and darkness came over the whole earth until the ninth hour, with the sun eclipsed, and the veil of the temple was split down the middle. And Jesus cried out in a great voice and said: Father, into your hands I give my spirit; and when he had said this he breathed his last. And when the company commander saw what happened, he glorified God, saying: Truly this was a righteous man. And all those crowds who had gathered together for this spectacle, when they had watched what happened, beat their breasts and went away. But those who were known to him stood at a distance, and also the women who had followed him from Galilee, watching all this.

And behold, there was a man named Joseph who was one of the council, a good and righteous man, who had not agreed with the council and their action. He was from Arimathaea, a city of the Jews; and he was expecting the Kingdom of God. He came to Pilate and asked for the body of Jesus, and he took it down and wrapped it in fine linen, and laid him in a tomb cut in the rock, where no one had ever been buried. It had been the Day of Preparation and the sabbath was beginning to dawn. And the women who had come with him from Galilee followed and saw the tomb and how the body was placed there. Then they returned and prepared spices and ointments.

❡ And for the sabbath they rested, according to the commandment; but on the first day after the sabbath just before daylight they came bringing the spices which they had prepared. And they found the stone rolled away from the tomb, and they went in but did not find the body of the Lord Jesus. And it happened that as they were at a loss about this, behold, two men stood before them in radiant clothing. And as the women were full of fear and bowed their faces toward the ground, the men said: Why do you look for the living among the dead? He is not here, he has wakened. Remember how he talked to you when he was still in Galilee, saying that the son of man must be betrayed into the hands of sinful men, and be crucified, and rise again on the third day. And they remembered his

words, and returned from the tomb and reported all these
matters to the eleven and all the others. The women were
Mary the Magdalene and Joanna and Mary the mother of
James; and the other women who were with them told
the apostles the same story. And to them these words
seemed to be madness, and they did not believe the
women. But Peter started up and ran to the tomb, and
stooped and saw only the linen bindings, and came back
to them marveling over what had happened.

And behold, on the same day, two of them were making
their way toward a village named Emmaus sixty furlongs
away, and they were talking with each other about all
these things that had occurred. And it happened that during their talk and discussion Jesus himself came up and
went along with them, but their eyes were prevented
from recognizing him. And he said to them: What is this
you are talking about, tossing it back and forth as you go?
And they stopped, frowning. And one, whose name was
Cleopas, answered and said to him: Are you the only vis-
itor to Jerusalem who does not know what happened in it
during these days? He said: What things? They said: The
story of Jesus of Nazareth, who was a powerful prophet in
act and word before God and all the people, and how our
high priests and those who rule over us gave him over to
the judgment of death and crucified him. We had been
hoping that he was the one who was going to liberate
Israel. But with all that, this is now the third day since
these things happened to him. But also some women of
our group astonished us. They went at dawn to the tomb
and did not find his body, and came back saying that they
had even seen a vision of angels, who say that he is alive.
And some of those who were with us went back to the

tomb, and found it as the women had said, but did not see him. And he said to them: O mindless and slow in the heart to believe all that the prophets have told you. Did not the Christ have to suffer this and enter into his glory? And beginning from Moses, and through the prophets, he expounded to them all that was in the scriptures concerning himself. And they approached the village they were making for, and he pretended to be going on farther. And they pressed him, saying: Stay with us, because it is nearly night and the sun is already set. And he went in to stay with them. And it happened that as he took his place to eat with them he took a loaf and blessed it and broke it and gave some to them. And their eyes were opened and they recognized him. But he himself vanished from their sight. And they said to each other: Were our hearts not burning when he talked with us on the road, when he unfolded the scriptures to us? And they rose up in that same hour and returned to Jerusalem, and found the eleven and their companions assembled and saying that truly the Lord had awakened and been seen by Simon. And they described what had happened on the road and how he had been recognized by them in the breaking of the bread. While they were saying these things he himself stood in their midst and said to them: Peace be with you. They were startled and full of fear and thought they were looking at a ghost. And he said to them: Why are you shaken, and why do doubts arise in your hearts? Look at my hands and my feet and see that I am myself. Touch me and see, because a ghost does not have flesh and bones as you see that I have. And as he said this he showed them his hands and his feet. And when they still could not believe for joy, and were full of wonder, he said to them:

Do you have anything to eat here? And they gave him a portion of cooked fish; and he took it and ate it in their presence.

And he said to them: These are my words which I spoke to you while I was still with you, that there must be fulfillment of all that was written in the law of Moses and the prophets and the psalms about me. Then he opened their minds to the understanding of the scriptures. And he said to them that thus it was written for the Christ to suffer, and rise from the dead on the third day, and for the preaching in his name of repentance for the forgiveness of sins, to all the nations; beginning from Jerusalem; of these things you are witnesses. And behold, I send forth the promise of my father to you. And do you rest in the city until you are clothed with power from on high.

And he led them out as far as Bethany, and raised his hands and blessed them. And it happened that in the act of blessing he departed from them and was carried up to heaven. And they did obeisance to him and turned back to Jerusalem with great joy, and they were constantly in the temple praising God.

JOHN

John is probably not the apostle, but a follower or disciple of his. The gospel is now generally thought to have been written between A.D. 80 and 120.

◖IN THE BEGINNING WAS THE WORD, and the word was with God, and the word was God. He was in the beginning, with God. Everything came about through him, and without him not one thing came about. What came about in him was life, and the life was the light of mankind; and the light shines in the darkness, and the darkness did not understand it.

There was a man sent from God; his name was John. This man came for testimony, to testify concerning the light, so that all should believe through him. He was not the light, but was to testify concerning the light. The light was the true light, which illuminates every person who comes into the world. He was in the world, and the world came about through him, and the world did not know him. He went to his own and his own people did not accept him. Those who accepted him, he gave them power to become children of God, to those who believed in his name, who were born not from blood or from the will of the flesh or from the will of man, but from God.

And the word became flesh and lived among us, and we have seen his glory, glory as of a single son from his father, full of grace and truth. John bears witness concerning him, and he cried out, saying (for it was he who was speaking): He who is coming after me was before me, because he was there before I was; because we have all received from his fullness, and grace for grace. Because the law was given through Moses; the grace and the truth came through Jesus Christ. No one has ever seen God; the only-born God who is in the bosom of his father, it is he who told of him.

And this is the testimony of John, when the Jews sent priests and Levites from Jerusalem to ask him: Who are you? And he confessed, and made no denial, but confessed: I am not the Christ. And they asked him: What then? Are you Elijah? And he said: I am not. Are you the prophet? And he answered: No. Then they said to him: Who are you? So that we can give an answer to those who sent us. What do you say about yourself? He said: I am the voice of one crying in the desert: Make straight the way of the Lord; as Isaiah the prophet said. Now they had been sent by the Pharisees. And they questioned him and said to him: Why then do you baptize, if you are not the Christ, or Elijah or the prophet? John answered them saying: I baptize with water; but in your midst stands one whom you do not know, who is coming after me, and I am not fit to untie the fastening of his shoe. All this happened in Bethany beyond the Jordan, where John was baptizing.

The next day he saw Jesus coming toward him and said: See, the lamb of God who takes away the sinfulness of the world. This is the one of whom I said: A man is coming after me who was before me, because he was there before I was. And I did not know him. But so that he might be made known to Israel, this was why I came baptizing with water. And John bore witness, saying: I have seen the Spirit descending like a dove from the sky, and it remained upon him; and I did not know him, but the one who sent me to baptize with water was the one who said to me: That one, on whom you see the Spirit descending and remaining upon him, is the one who baptizes with the Holy Spirit. And I have seen, and I have borne witness that this is the son of God.

The next day John was standing with two of his disciples, and he saw Jesus walking about and said: See, the lamb of God. His two disciples heard what he said and followed Jesus. Jesus turned about and saw them following him and said: What are you seeking? They said to him: Rabbi (which translated means master), where are you staying? He said to them: Come and see. So they came, and saw where he was staying, and stayed with him for that day. It was about the tenth hour. Andrew, one of the two who heard Jesus and followed him, was the brother of Simon Peter. He went first and found his brother Simon and said to him: We have found the Messiah (which is, translated, the Christ). He took him to Jesus. Jesus looked at him and said: You are Simon, the son of John. You shall be called Cephas (which means Peter).

The next day Jesus wished to go out to Galilee. And he found Philip and said to him: Follow me. Philip was from Bethsaida, the city of Andrew and Peter. Philip found Nathanael and said to him: We have found the one of whom Moses wrote in the law, and the prophets: Jesus the son of Joseph, from Nazareth. And Nathanael said to him: Can anything good come from Nazareth? Philip said to him: Come and see. Jesus saw Nathanael coming toward him and said of him: See, a true son of Israel, in whom there is no guile. Nathanael said to him: How is it that you know me? Jesus answered and said to him: I saw you when you were under the fig tree, before Philip called you. Nathanael answered: Master, you are the son of God, you are the King of Israel. Jesus answered and said to him: Because I told you I saw you under the fig tree, you believe? You will see greater things than that. And he said to him: Truly truly I tell you, you will see the heaven open and the angels of God ascending and descending to the son of man.

❡ And on the third day a wedding took place at Cana, in Galilee, and the mother of Jesus was there; and Jesus also, and his disciples, had been invited to the wedding. And when the wine gave out, Jesus' mother said to him: They have no wine. Jesus said to her: What is that to you and me, madam? My time has not yet come. His mother said to the servants: Do whatever he tells you. Now there were six stone water jars set by for the lustration, which is the custom of the Jews, each holding two or three measures. Jesus said to them: Fill the jars with water. And they filled them to the brim. And he said to them: Now pour it out and take it to the master of the feast. And they took it to him. When the master of the feast tasted the water that had turned into wine—and did not know where it came from, but the servants who had poured it knew—the master of the feast called the bridegroom and said to him: Everybody first puts out the good wine and the poorer wine after they have drunk well; but you kept the good wine until now. This was the first of his miracles Jesus performed, at Cana in Galilee, and displayed his glory, and his disciples believed in him.

After this he went down to Capernaum, himself and his

mother and his brothers and disciples, and they stayed there for a few days.

And the Passover of the Jews drew near, and Jesus went up to Jerusalem. And in the temple he found people selling oxen and sheep and doves, and the money changers sitting there; and he made a scourge out of ropes and drove them all out of the temple, and the sheep and the oxen, and he scattered the coins of the money changers and overturned their tables, and to the sellers of doves he said: Take these things out of here; stop making the house of my father a house of business. His disciples remembered that it is written: Jealous concern for your house consumes me. The Jews spoke forth and said to him: What sign do you give us that you can do this? Jesus answered and said to them: Destroy this temple and in three days I will raise it up again. But the Jews said: This temple was built in forty-six years; and you will raise it up in three days? But he had been speaking of the temple of his body. Thus when he rose from the dead, his disciples remembered that he had said this, and believed in the scripture and the word that Jesus had spoken. But when he was in Jerusalem at the Passover, at the festival, many believed in his name, seeing the miracles he performed. But Jesus himself did not entrust himself to them, because he knew them all, and knew that he had no need for anyone to tell him about man, for he himself knew what was in man.

❡ There was a man among the Pharisees, Nicodemus by name, a councillor of the Jews. He came to Jesus at night and said to him: Master, we know that you came as a teacher from God; for no one could perform the miracles you perform if God were not with him. Jesus answered and said to him: Truly truly I tell you, if one is not born from above, he cannot see the Kingdom of God. Nicodemus said to him: How can a man be born when he is old? Surely he cannot enter his mother's womb a second time and be born? Jesus answered: Truly truly I tell you, if one is not born from water and spirit, he cannot enter the Kingdom of God. What is born from the flesh is flesh, and what is born from the spirit is spirit. Do not wonder because I told you: You must be born from above. The wind blows where it will, and you hear its sound, but you do not know where it comes from or where it is going. So it is with everyone who is born from the spirit. Nicodemus answered and said to him: How can this happen? Jesus answered and said to him: You are the teacher of Israel and do not understand this? Truly truly I tell you that we tell you what we know, and testify to what we have seen, and you do not accept our testimony. If I tell you of earthly matters and you do not believe, how will you believe if I tell you of heavenly matters? And no one has gone up to heaven except the one who came down from heaven, the son of man. And as Moses raised up the snake in the desert, so must the son of man be raised up, so that everyone who believes in him may have everlasting life. For God so loved the world that he gave his only son, so that everyone who believes in him may not be destroyed but may have everlasting life. For God did not send his son into the world to judge the world, but so that the world could be saved through him. He who believes in him is not judged. He who does not believe in him has already been judged, because he did not believe in the name of the only son of God. This is the judgment, be-

cause the light came into the world and people loved the
darkness more than the light because their actions were
wicked. For everyone who does bad things hates the light
and does not come toward the light, lest his actions be
discovered; but he who accomplishes the truth comes
toward the light, so that it may be made clear that his
actions were with God.

After this Jesus and his disciples went into the land of
Judaea, and there he spent some time with them and baptized. And John also was baptizing at Aenon near Salim,
because there were many waters there, and the people
came to him and were baptized. For John had not yet been
thrown into prison. Now there was a dispute between the
disciples of John and a Jew about lustration. And they
came to John and said to him: Master, the one who was
with you beyond Jordan, to whom you testified, see, he is
baptizing and all come to him. John answered and said: A
man cannot receive anything unless it is given to him
from heaven. You yourselves bear witness that I said: I am
not the Christ. But I said: I am sent before him. He who
has the bride is the bridegroom; but the friend of the
bridegroom, who stands by and listens to him, rejoices
with a joy that comes from the voice of the bridegroom.
This is my joy which is fulfilled. He must increase, and I
must be diminished. He who comes from above is above
all. He who comes from the earth is of the earth and
speaks from the earth. He who comes from heaven is
above all. What he testifies to is what he has seen and
heard, and no one accepts his testimony. He who accepts
his testimony proves that God is true. For he whom God
sent speaks the words of God, for there is no measure to
what the spirit gives. The father loves the son and has

given all things into his hand. He who believes in the son has everlasting life; but he who disbelieves in the son will not see life, but the anger of God remains upon him.

◀ When the Lord realized that the Pharisees had heard that Jesus was making more converts than John and baptizing them (in fact, Jesus himself was not baptizing but his disciples were), he left Judaea and went back to Galilee. He had to pass through Samaria. So he came to the city in Samaria which is called Sychar, near the piece of land which Jacob gave to Joseph his son. There was a well of Jacob there. Now Jesus was tired from his journey and thus sat down by the well. It was about the sixth hour. A woman of Samaria came to draw water. Jesus said to her: Give me a drink. For his disciples had gone off to the city to buy provisions. So the Samaritan woman said to him: How is it that you, a Jew, are asking for a drink from me, a Samaritan woman? [For Jews have no dealings with Samaritans.] Jesus answered and said to her: If you knew the gift of God, and who it is that says to you: Give me a drink; *you* would have asked *him,* and he would have given you living water. She said to him: Lord, you have no bucket to let down, and the well is deep. From where then do you have the living water? Surely you are not greater than Jacob our forefather, who gave us this well, who drank from it himself, as did his sons and his cattle. Jesus answered and said to her: Whoever drinks from this water will be thirsty again; but he who drinks from the water I shall give will not be thirsty forevermore, but the water I shall give him will turn within him into a spring of water jetting up into everlasting life. The woman said to him: Lord, give me this water so I shall not

be thirsty or have to come here to draw it up. He said to
her: Go and tell your husband and come back. The
woman answered and said to him: I have no husband.
Jesus said to her: You did well to say: I have no husband.
You have had five husbands and the one you have now is
not your husband. What you said was true. The woman
said to him: Lord, I see that you are a prophet. Our fathers
worshipped on this mountain; but you people say that
Jerusalem is the place where one should worship. Jesus
said to her: Believe me, madam, the time is coming when
you will worship the father neither on this mountain nor
in Jerusalem. You worship what you do not know; we
worship what we do know, because salvation comes from
the Jews. But the time is coming and it is now when the
true worshippers will worship the Father in the spirit and
in truth, for the Father looks for such worshippers. God is
spirit and those who worship him must worship in the
spirit and in truth. The woman said to him: I know that
the Messiah, who is called the Christ, is coming. When he
comes, he will tell us all. Jesus said to her: I am he, talking to you.

Thereupon his disciples came and were surprised that
he had been talking to a woman, but no one said: What
are you looking for? Or: Why are you talking with her?
Then the woman left her water jar and went off to the
city, and said to the people: Come and see a man who told
me everything I have done. Might he not be the Christ?
They went forth from the city and came to him. In the
meanwhile his disciples questioned him and said to him:
Master, eat. But he said to them: I have food to eat which
you do not know of. So the disciples said to each other:
Could someone have brought him something to eat? Jesus
said to them: My food is to do the will of him who sent

me and finish his work. Do you not say: There are four more months, and then comes the harvest? But see, I tell you, raise up your eyes and look at the fields, see that they are white for harvesting. And now he who reaps takes his wages and gathers the crop for everlasting life, so that sower and reaper alike can be happy. For in this matter it is true to say that the sower is one person and the reaper another. I sent you to harvest what you never labored on. Others labored, and you came in upon their labor.

And many Samaritans from that city believed in him because of what the woman said when she testified: He told me everything I have done. So when the Samaritans came to him they invited him to stay with them, and he stayed there for two days. And many more believed in him because of what he himself said, and they said to the woman: It is no longer because of your talk that we believe; we ourselves have heard, and we know that this is truly the savior of the world.

At the end of the two days he went from there to Galilee; for Jesus himself had testified that a prophet has no honor in his own country. But when he came to Galilee the Galilaeans welcomed him, for they had seen what he did in Jerusalem at the festival, since they had themselves gone to the festival. So then he returned to Cana in Galilee where he had made the water into wine. And there was a certain prince, whose son was sick, in Capernaum. This man, hearing that Jesus had come from Judaea to Galilee, went to him and asked him to come to his house and heal his son, for he was going to die. Then Jesus said to him: Unless you see miracles and wonders, you will not believe. But the prince said to him: Lord, come to my house before my little boy dies. Jesus said to him: Go on your way; your son lives. The man believed in the word Jesus had spoken to him and went on his way. And just as he was coming home his slaves met him saying that his son was alive. So he asked them at what hour he had got better; and they said: Yesterday at the seventh hour the fever left him. So the father realized that it was at the time when Jesus had said: Your son lives; and he, with all his household, believed. This was the second miracle Jesus performed, when he came from Judaea to Galilee.

◀ After that, there was a festival of the Jews, and Jesus went up to Jerusalem. In Jerusalem by the Sheep Gate there is a pool for which the name in Hebrew is Bethzatha. It has five porches. There would lie a crowd of afflicted people, blind, lame, paralyzed, [waiting for the water to be disturbed. For an angel of the Lord would come down to the pool from time to time, and the water would be disturbed. And whoever was first to enter the pool after the disturbing of the water would be healed of the infirmity that afflicted him]. There was one man there who had had his sickness for thirty-eight years. And seeing him lying there, and knowing that he had had it for a long time, Jesus said to him: Do you wish to be healthy? The sick man answered: Lord, I have no man to put me into the pool when the water is disturbed; and while I am on my way someone else gets there ahead of me. Jesus said to him: Arise, take up your bed, and walk. And immediately the man was healthy, and he took up his bed and walked. It was the sabbath on that day; so the Jews said to the man who had been healed: It is the sabbath, and it is not lawful for you to carry your bed. But he answered them: The man who made me healthy was the

one who told me: Take up your bed and walk. They asked
him: Which is the man who said to you: Take it up and
walk? But the man who had been healed did not know
who it was, since Jesus had disappeared into the crowd
that was there. Afterward Jesus found him in the temple
and said to him: See, you have become healthy. Sin no
more, lest it be the worse for you. The man went away
and told the Jews that it was Jesus who had made him
healthy. And that was why the Jews persecuted Jesus,
because he did this on the sabbath. But he answered
them: Until now my father has been doing his work, and I
too am doing my work. For this the Jews sought all the
more to kill him, because he not only was breaking the
sabbath but even called God his own father, making himself the equal of God. But Jesus answered and told them:
Truly truly I tell you, the son cannot do anything by himself unless he sees the father doing it; for what he does the
son does likewise. For the father loves the son and shows
him everything he himself does, and he will show him
greater deeds than these for you to wonder at. For as the
father wakes the dead and gives them life, so the son also
gives life to whom he will. Nor does the father judge
anyone, but he has given all judgment to his son, so that
all may honor the son as they honor the father. He who
does not honor the son does not honor the father who sent
him. Truly truly I tell you that he who listens to my
words and believes in him who sent me has life everlasting, and does not come to judgment, but has gone over
from death to life. Truly truly I tell you, the time is coming, and it is now, when the dead shall hear the voice of
the son of God, and those who have heard shall live. For as
the father has life in himself, so he has given the son life
to have in himself. And he gave him authority to pass

judgment, because he is the son of man. Do not wonder at this, because the hour is coming when those who are in the graves will hear his voice and come out, those who have done good, to the resurrection of life, and those who have done evil to the resurrection of judgment. I cannot do anything by myself. I judge as I hear, and my judgment is just, because I do not seek my own will but the will of him who sent me. If I testify about myself, my testimony is not true; he who testifies about me is someone else, and I know that the testimony he gives about me is true. You have sent to John and he has testified to the truth; but I do not take my testimony from man, but I say this so that you may be saved. He was the lamp that burns and shines, and you wished to exult for a time in his light; but I have testimony greater than John's, for the works that my father gave me, for me to fulfill them, these same works that I do, testify concerning me that the father sent me, and the father who sent me has testified concerning me. You have never heard his voice or seen his shape, and you do not have his word remaining among you, because you do not believe the one he sent to you. You search the scriptures, because you think they have life everlasting in them; and it is they who testify to me; and you are not willing to come to me to have life. I do not receive glory from men; but I know you and that you do not have the love of God in you. I came in the name of my father and you do not accept me; if someone else comes in his own name, you will accept him. How can you believe, when you receive your glory from each other, and do not look for the glory that comes from God alone? Do not suppose that I shall accuse you to my father. Your accuser is Moses, in whom you put your hopes. If you believed Moses, you would believe me, for he wrote about me. But if you do not believe his writings, how shall you believe my sayings?

◀ After this Jesus went across the Sea of Galilee, that is, Tiberias. And a great crowd was following him, for they saw the miracles he worked for the sick. Jesus went up onto the mountain, and sat there with his disciples. And the Passover, the festival of the Jews, was near. So Jesus lifted up his eyes and saw that a great crowd had come to him, and he said to Philip: Where shall we buy bread so that these can eat? He said this, making trial of him, for he knew what he was going to do. Philip answered: Two hundred denarii worth of bread is not enough for everyone to have a little bit. Andrew, the brother of Simon Peter and one of the disciples, said to him: There is a boy here who has five barley loaves and two little fishes; but what is that for all these people? Jesus said: Have the people take their places on the ground. There was plenty of grass in the place. So the men took their places, to the number of five thousand. Then Jesus took the loaves and gave thanks and passed them out to the people who were lying there, and so too with the fishes, as much as they wanted. And when they were filled, he said to his disciples: Gather up the broken pieces that are left over so that nothing will be lost. So they gathered them up and filled twelve baskets from what was left of the five barley loaves after the people had eaten. When the people saw what miracles he had done, they said: Truly this is the prophet who is coming into the world. Jesus, realizing that they were going to come and carry him off to make him king, withdrew back up the mountain, all by himself. When night came his disciples went down to the sea, and embarking on a ship, they began to cross over the sea to Capernaum. And now it was dark and Jesus had not yet come to them; and the sea was rough from a great wind blowing. When they had rowed about twenty-five or thirty furlongs they saw Jesus walking on the sea and coming close to the ship, and they were frightened. But he said to them: It is I, do not be afraid. They wanted to take him aboard the ship, and immediately it was at the shore for which they were making.

The next day the crowd that was standing on the other side of the sea had seen that there had been no other ship there except the one, and that Jesus had not gone aboard the ship with his disciples, but the disciples had gone away without him. But ships from Tiberias arrived near the place where they had eaten the bread after the Lord had given thanks. So when the crowd saw that neither Jesus nor his disciples were there, they themselves boarded the ships and went to Capernaum in search of Jesus. And when they found him on the other side of the sea, they said to him: Master, when did you reach here? Jesus answered them and said: Truly truly I tell you, you look for me not because you saw signs but because you ate the loaves and were fed. Try to earn, not the food that perishes, but the food that remains into life everlasting, which the son of man will give you, for God the Father set his seal upon him. Then they said to him: What shall we do, to do the work of God? Jesus answered and said to them: This is the work of God, to believe in the one he sent. Then they said to him: What sign are you accomplishing, for us to see and believe you? What work are you doing? Our fathers ate the manna in the desert, as it is written: He gave them bread from heaven to eat. Then Jesus said to them: Truly truly I tell you, it was not Moses who gave you bread from heaven, but my father gives you the true bread from heaven; for the bread of God is what comes down from heaven and gives life to the world. Then they said to him: Lord, give us always this bread. Jesus said to them: I am the bread of life. He who comes to me will not be hungry, and he who believes in me will not be thirsty, ever. But I have said to you that you have seen but do not believe. All that my father gives me will come to me, and the one who comes to me I will not drive out, because I have come down from heaven not to do my own will but the will of him who sent me; and this is the will of him who sent me, that I should lose nothing of all he gave me but raise it up again on the last day. For this is the will of my father, that everyone who sees the son and believes in him shall have life everlasting, and I shall raise him up on the last day.

Now the Jews murmured about him because he had said: I am the bread which came down from heaven; and they said: Is not this Jesus the son of Joseph, whose father and mother we know? How is it that he now says: I have come down from heaven? Jesus answered and said to them: Do not murmur among yourselves. No one can come to me unless the father who sent me pulls him; and I will raise him up on the last day. It is written in the prophets: And they shall all be taught from God. Everyone who has listened and learned from the father comes to me. Not because anyone has seen the father, except for the one who is beside God; he has seen the father. Truly truly I tell you, he who believes has life everlasting. I am the bread of life. Your fathers ate the manna in the desert and died. This is the bread which comes down from heaven so that one may eat of it and not die. I am the bread which lives, which came down from heaven. If one eats of this bread he will live forever, and the bread I will give, for the sake of the life of the world, is my flesh.

The Jews quarreled with each other, saying: How can this man give us his flesh to eat? Jesus said to them: Truly truly I tell you, unless you eat the flesh of the son of man and drink his blood, you have no life in you. He who eats my flesh and drinks my blood has life everlasting, and I will raise him up on the last day. For my flesh is the true food, and my blood is the true drink. He who eats my flesh and drinks my blood stays in me, and I in him. As the living father sent me and I live through the father, so he who eats me will also live through me. This is the bread which came down from heaven; not as our fathers ate and died, he who eats this bread will live forever.

All this he said as he taught in the synagogue in Capernaum. Then many of his disciples hearing him said: This is a hard saying. Who can listen to it? And Jesus knew in his heart that his disciples were murmuring about this, and said to them: Is this too difficult for you? What if you were to see the son of man going up to where he was before? It is the spirit that makes life, the flesh is no help. The words I have spoken to you are spirit and life. But there are some of you who do not believe. For Jesus knew from the beginning who were the ones who did not believe and who was the one who would betray him. And he said: This is why I told you that no one can come to me unless it is given him from the father. Because of this, many of his disciples left him thenceforth and no longer went about with him. So Jesus said to the twelve: You do not wish to go away? Simon Peter answered him: Lord, to whom shall we go? You have the words of everlasting life, and we have believed, and we know that you are the holy one of God. Jesus answered them: Did I not choose you twelve? And one of you is an enemy. He meant Judas, the son of Simon Iscariot; for he, one of the twelve, was going to betray him.

❡ And after that Jesus went about in Galilee; for he did not wish to go about in Judaea, because the Jews were seeking to kill him. Now the festival of the Jews which is the Feast of the Tabernacles was at hand. And his brothers said to him: Remove from here and go to Judaea, so that your disciples also can see the works that you perform; for no one acts in secret and then hopes to be well known. If you are doing these things, show yourself to the world. For even his brothers did not believe in him. And Jesus said to them: My time is not yet come, but your time is always ready at hand. The world cannot hate you, but it hates me, because I testify concerning it that what it does is wicked. You go up to the festival. I will not yet go up to this festival, because my time is not yet completed. He told them this and remained in Galilee. But when his brothers went up to the festival, then he went too, not openly but in secret. So then the Jews looked for him at the festival and said: Where is he? And there was much murmuring about him in the crowds. Some said: He is good; and others said: No. He leads the people astray. But none spoke openly about him, through fear of the Jews.

And now the festival had gone halfway, and Jesus went up to the temple and taught. And the Jews were astonished and said: How does this man have learning when he was never a student? Jesus answered them and said: My teaching is not my own but his who sent me; if anyone wishes to do his will, he will know about the teaching, whether it comes from God or whether I speak on my own account. He who speaks on his own account is looking for his own glory; but he who looks for the glory of him who sent him is the true man, and there is no wrong in him. Did not Moses give you the law? And not one of you obeys the law. Why are you trying to kill me? The crowd answered: You are possessed. Who is trying to kill you? Jesus answered and said to them: I did one thing and you all are astonished. This was why Moses gave you circumcision—not that it comes from Moses but from the fathers—and you circumcise a man on the sabbath. If a man receives circumcision on the sabbath so that the law of Moses may not be broken, are you angry with me because I made a whole man healthy on the sabbath? Do not judge by appearance, but make the judgment that is just. Then some of the people of Jerusalem said: Is not this the man they are trying to kill? And see, he speaks in public and they say nothing to him. Might it be that the authorities have seen that this is the Christ? But we know where this man comes from. But when the Christ comes, no one will know where he comes from. Jesus cried aloud as he taught in the temple: You know me and you know where I come from. But I came not on my own account, but he is the true one who sent me, and you do not know him. I know him, because I am from him and it was he who sent me. Then they sought to seize him, but no one laid a hand on him because his time had not yet come. Many in the crowd believed in him, and they said: When the Christ comes, can he perform more miracles than this one has done?

The Pharisees heard the crowd murmuring thus about him, and the high priests and the Pharisees sent officers to seize him. Then Jesus said: For a little more time I am with you and then I go to him who sent me. You will look for me and you will not find me, and where I am you cannot go. Then the Jews said among themselves: Where does this man mean to go where we shall not find him? He cannot be going to go where we are settled among the Greeks, and teach the Greeks? What is this that he said: You will look for me and you will not find me, and where I am you cannot go?

On the last great day of the festival Jesus stood forth and made a declaration, saying: If anyone is thirsty, let him come to me and drink. For one who believes in me, as the scripture says, streams of living water shall flow from deep within him. This he said concerning the spirit, of which those who had put their faith in him would partake; but the spirit was not yet because Jesus was not yet glorified. And some in the crowd who listened to these words said: This is in truth the prophet. And others said: This is the Christ. But others said: Surely the Christ cannot come out of Galilee? Did not the scripture say that the Christ would be of the seed of David, and from Bethlehem, David's village? So there was division in the multitude over him. And some of them wished to seize him, but no one laid hands on him.

Then the officers came back to the high priests and the Pharisees, who said to them: Why did you not bring him? The officers answered: Never has a man spoken like that. The Pharisees answered: Surely you have not been led astray? Do you think that one of the council or of the Pharisees believes in him? Only this rabble which does not know the law and is accursed. Nicodemus, who had gone to Jesus before, who was one of them, said to them: Surely our law does not judge a man without first giving him a hearing and being told what he does. They an-

swered and said to him: Could it be that you are from
Galilee too? Study the matter, and know that no prophet
originates in Galilee. [And they went away each to his
own house.

❡ But Jesus went to the Mount of Olives; but at dawn he
came back to the temple, and all the people came to him,
and he sat and taught them. And the scribes and the
Pharisees brought a woman who had been caught in adultery, and they set her in their midst. And they said to
him: Master, this woman was caught in the act of adultery. In the law Moses charged us to stone such women to
death. But what do you say? This they said to entrap him,
so that they could bring a charge against him. Jesus
stooped down and wrote with his finger in the dust. But
when they continued to question him he stood up and
said: Let the one of you who is without sin be the first to
throw a stone at her. And again he stooped and wrote in
the dust. And when they heard they went out, one by one,
the eldest first, and he was left alone, and the woman who
had been in their midst. And Jesus stood up and said to
her: Woman, where are they? Has no one condemned
you? She said: No one, Lord. And Jesus said: Nor do I
condemn you. Go, and from now on sin no more.]

Then Jesus talked with them again and said: I am the
light of the world; he who follows me will not walk about
in darkness but will have the light of life. Then the
Pharisees said to him: You are testifying about yourself;
your testimony is not true. Jesus answered and said to
them: Even if I am testifying about myself, my testimony
is true, because I know where I came from and where I am
going. But you do not know where I come from or where I

am going. You judge according to the flesh but I judge no one. And if I do judge, my judgment is true, because I am not alone but am I and the one who sent me. And in your law it is written that the testimony of two persons is true. I am he who testifies about myself, and my father who sent me testifies about me. Then they said to him: Where is your father? Jesus answered: You know neither me nor my father. If you knew me, you would also know my father. These words he spoke in the treasury as he taught in the temple. And no one seized him, because his time had not yet come.

Then again he said to them: I am going, and you will look for me, and in your sin you will die. Where I am going you cannot go. Then the Jews said: Will he kill himself when he says: Where I am going you cannot go? And he said to them: You come from things below, I come from things above. You are of this world, I am not of this world. I told you that you will die in your sins; for if you do not believe that I am, you will die in your sins. Then they said to him: Who are you? Jesus said to them: What I have been telling you from the beginning. I have much to say about you and much to judge. But he who sent me is true, and what I heard from him is what I speak to the world. They did not realize it was his father he told them about. Then Jesus said: When you raise the son of man aloft, then you will know that I am, and that of myself I do nothing, but what I say is according to what my father taught me. And he who sent me is with me. He did not leave me alone, because what I do is his pleasure, always. When he said this, many believed in him.

Then Jesus said to the Jews who had believed him: If you remain with my teaching, then you are truly my disciples and you will know the truth, and the truth will set

you free. They answered him: We are the seed of Abraham
and have never been enslaved to anyone; how is it that
you say: You will be made free? Jesus answered them:
Truly truly I tell you that everyone who commits sin is
the slave of his sin. But the slave does not remain in the
house forever. The son remains forever. If then the son
sets you free, you will be free in truth. I know that you are
the seed of Abraham. But you are trying to kill me, because my teaching does not work in you. What I have
seen with my father, I tell you; do then what you have
heard from the father. They answered and said to him:
Our father is Abraham. Jesus said to them: If you are the
children of Abraham, then do what Abraham did. But
now you are trying to kill me, a man who has told you the
truth I heard from God. Abraham did not do that. You are
doing what your father did. They said to him: We were
not bred from promiscuity. We have one father, God.
Jesus said to them: If God were your father, you would
love me, since I issued from God and come from God; for I
did not come on my own account, but he sent me. Why do
you not understand what I say? Because you are not able
to listen to my reasoning. The father you come from is the
devil and you wish to do your father's will. He has been a
man killer from the beginning, and he does not stand
upon the truth because there is no truth in him. When he
speaks his lie he speaks from what is his own, because he
is a liar and so is his father. And because I speak the truth
you do not believe me. Which one of you proves me in
error? If I speak the truth, why do you not believe me? He
who is from God listens to the words of God. That is why
you do not listen, because you are not from God. The Jews
answered and said to him: Are we not right in saying you
are a Samaritan, and possessed? Jesus answered: I am not

possessed, but I honor my father, and you dishonor me. I do not seek my own glory. He who seeks it is he who judges. Truly truly I tell you, he who follows my teaching shall not look on death, forever. The Jews said to him: Now we know that you are possessed. Abraham died, and the prophets died, and you say: He who follows my teaching shall not taste of death, forever. Can you be greater than our father Abraham, who died? And the prophets died. Who do you think you are? Jesus answered: If I glorify myself, my glory is nothing. It is my father who glorifies me, whom you call your God; and you do not know about him, but I know him. And if I say that I do not know him, I shall be a liar like you. But I know him and I follow his teaching. Abraham your father was joyful over seeing my day, and he did see it, and was glad. Then the Jews said to him: You are not yet fifty years old; and you have seen Abraham? Jesus said to them: Truly truly I tell you, I am from before Abraham was born. Then they picked up stones to throw at him, but he effaced himself and left the temple.

◀ On his way he saw a man who had been blind from birth. And his disciples questioned him, saying: Master, who sinned, this man or his parents, for him to be born blind? Jesus answered: Neither he nor his parents sinned; it was so that the workings of God might be made manifest in him. We must do the work of him who sent me while it is day. The night is coming, when no one can work. While I am in the world, I am the light of the world. So saying, he spat on the ground and made mud out of the spittle, and put mud on the man's eyes, and said to him: Go and wash in the pool of Siloam (which translated means the one who has been sent). So he went and washed, and came away seeing. So his neighbors, and those who had seen him before when he was a beggar, said: Is not this the man who sat and begged? Some said: It is he. Others said: No, but it is someone like him. But he said: It is I. Then they said to him: How were your eyes opened? He answered: The man called Jesus made mud and smeared it on my eyes and said to me: Go to Siloam and wash. So I went and washed, and I saw. And they said to him: Where is he? He said: I do not know. Then they took the man who had once been blind to the Pharisees. The sabbath was the day on which Jesus had made the mud and opened the man's eyes. Then the Pharisees in turn asked him how he had got his sight. And he told them: He put mud on my eyes, and I washed, and I see. And some of the Pharisees said: This is no man from God, since he does not keep the sabbath. But others said: How can a sinful man work such miracles? And there was division among them. So they said, once more, to the blind man: What do you have to say about him, because he opened your eyes? He said: He is a prophet. But the Jews did not believe it about him, that he had been blind and got his sight, until they called in the parents of the man who had got his sight and questioned them, saying: Is this your son, who, you say, was born blind? How is it that he can now see? His parents answered and said: We know that this is our son and that he was born blind. We do not know how it is that he now can see, and we do not know who opened his eyes. Ask him; he is of age and he will tell you about himself. His parents said this because they were afraid of the Jews, because the Jews had agreed that anyone who confessed that he was Christ should be barred from the synagogue. That is why his parents said:

He is of age, ask him. Thus for the second time they summoned the man who had been blind, and said to him:
Give glory to God. We know that this man is sinful. The
man answered and said: Whether he is sinful I do not
know. One thing I do know, that I was blind and now I
see. Then they said to him: What did he do to you? How
did he open your eyes? He answered them: I told you
before, and you did not listen. Why do you want to hear it
again? Could it be that you want to be his disciples? And
they reviled him and said: You are his disciple. We are
disciples of Moses. We know that God talked with Moses;
but we do not know where this man is from. The man
answered and said to them: Here is what is astonishing,
that you do not know where he is from and he opened my
eyes. We know that God does not listen to sinners, but if
someone is pious and does his will, to that man he listens.
From the beginning of time it has never been heard of that
anyone opened the eyes of one born blind; if this man
were not from God, he could not have done anything.
They answered and said to him: You were born all in sin;
and you are teaching us? And they cast him out. Jesus
heard that they had cast him out, and he found him and
said: Do you believe in the son of man? The man answered: Who is that, Lord? So that I may believe in him.
Jesus said to him: You have seen him; and it is he who is
talking with you. And he said: I believe, Lord. And worshipped him. And Jesus said: I have come into this world
for judgment, so that those who do not see may see, and
those who see may go blind. The Pharisees who were
with him heard this, and they said to him: Surely, even
we are not blind? Jesus said to them: If you were blind,
you would have no sin. But now you say: We see. Your sin
remains.

¶ Truly truly I tell you, he who does not enter the sheep-fold through the gate but climbs into it from another place is a thief and a robber; but he who enters through the gate is the shepherd of the sheep. To him the gatekeeper opens, and the sheep listen to his voice, and he summons his own sheep by name and leads them out. When he has put all of his own outside, he goes ahead of them, and the sheep follow him, because they know his voice. But they will not follow a stranger but run away from him, because they do not know the voice of strangers. This is a parable Jesus told them; but they did not know what he was talking about. Again Jesus said: Truly truly I tell you, I am the gate for the sheep. All those who came before me are thieves and robbers; but the sheep did not listen to them. I am the gate. Whoever enters through me shall be saved and go in and out and find pasturage. The thief does not come except to steal and slaughter and destroy; I came so that they may have life, and have abundance. I am the good shepherd. The good shepherd lays down his life for the sheep. The man who is hired, who is no shepherd, whose sheep are not his own, sees the wolf coming and lets the sheep go and runs away; and the wolf ravages and scatters them; because he is hired and the sheep are of no concern to him. I am the good shepherd, and I know mine and they know me, as the father knows me and I know the father, and I lay down my life for the sheep. And I have other sheep which are not from this fold; and I must bring them, and they will listen to my voice, and they will become one flock, one shepherd. That is why the father loves me, because I lay down my life, so that I may take it back again. No one took it from me, but I lay it down of my own will. I have authority to lay it down and authority to take it back. This is the command I had from my father.

Once more there was division among the Jews because of those words. And many of them said: He is possessed, and raves. Why do you listen to him? Others said: These are not the words of a man possessed. Could a fiend open the eyes of the blind?

Then it was the Feast of Dedication in Jerusalem. It was winter, and Jesus walked about in the temple, in the Porch of Solomon. The Jews surrounded him and said to him: How long will you go on agitating our spirits? If you are the Christ, tell us plainly. Jesus answered them: I told you, and you do not believe. The acts I perform in the name of my father, these bear me witness; but you do not believe, for you are not of my flock. My sheep listen to my voice, and I know them, and they follow me, and I give them life everlasting, and they shall not perish forever, and no one will snatch them out of my hand. What my father gave me is greater than all, and no one can snatch it from the hand of the father. I and the father are one. Then the Jews picked up stones once more, to stone him. Jesus answered them: I have shown you many good acts from my father. For which of these acts do you stone me? The Jews answered him: We stone you not for any good act, but for blasphemy, and because you, who are a man, make yourself God. Jesus answered them: Is it not written in your law: I have said: You are gods? If he called those gods to whom the word of God came, and scripture cannot be voided, then do you say of one whom the father hallowed and sent into the world: You blaspheme; because I said I am the son of God? If I do not do the acts of my father, do not believe me. But if I do them, even if you do not believe me, believe the acts, so that you may see and know that the father is in me and I am in the father. Then once again they tried to seize him; and he passed through their hands.

And he went back beyond Jordan to the place where John had been baptizing before, and remained there. And many came to him and said: John wrought no miracle for us, but all that John said about him was true. And many there believed in him.

❧ There was a man who was sick, Lazarus, from Bethany, the village of Mary and Martha her sister. It was Mary who anointed the Lord with ointment and wiped his feet with her hair, and it was her brother Lazarus who was sick. So the sisters sent to him saying: Lord, see, a man you love is sick. When Jesus heard it he said: This sickness is not to the death but is for the glory of God so that the son of God may be glorified through it. And Jesus loved Martha and her sister and Lazarus. Now when he heard that he was sick, he remained in the place where he was for two days, after which he said to his disciples: Let us go back to Judaea. His disciples said to him: Master, just now the Jews were trying to stone you; and will you go back there? Jesus answered: Are there not twelve hours in the day? If a man walks in the daytime, he does not stumble, because he sees the light of this world; but if he walks in the night, he stumbles, because the light is not there. This he said, and after this he said to them: Lazarus our friend has gone to his rest, but I am on my way to waken him. So the disciples said to him: Lord, if he has gone to his rest he will be safe. Jesus had been speaking of his death, but they thought he was talking about the rest which comes from sleep. So then Jesus said to them plainly: Lazarus is dead; and I am glad on your account, so that you may believe, that I was not there. But let us go to him. Then Thomas, called the Twin, said to his fellow disciples: Let us also go, so that we may die with him.

When Jesus arrived he found that he had been four days in the tomb. Now Bethany was near Jerusalem, about twenty-five furlongs off. And many of the Jews had come to Martha and Mary to console them for their brother. When Martha heard that Jesus was coming she went out to meet him; but Mary was sitting in the house. Then Martha said to Jesus: Lord, if you had been here, my brother would not have died; even now I know that all that you ask of God God will give you. Jesus said to her: Your brother will resurrect. Martha said to him: I know that he will resurrect in the resurrection on the last day. Jesus said to her: I am the resurrection and the life. He who believes in me shall live, even if he dies, and everyone who lives and believes in me shall not die, ever. Do you believe this? She said to him: Yes, Lord; I believe that you are the Christ, the son of God, who is coming into this world. So saying, she went back and called Mary her sister, saying to her privately: The master is here and calls for you. When Mary heard this, she rose up quickly and went to him; and Jesus had not yet come into the village but was still in the place where Martha had gone to meet him. So the Jews who had been with her in the house, comforting her, seeing that Mary rose up quickly and went out, followed her, supposing that she was on her way to the tomb to lament there. When Mary came to where Jesus was, and saw him, she fell at his feet, saying to him: Lord, if you had been here, my brother would not have died. When Jesus saw her weeping, and saw the Jews who had come with her weeping, he raged at his own spirit, and harrowed himself, and said: Where have you laid him? They said to him: Lord, come and see. Jesus wept. Then the Jews said: See how he loved him. But some of them said: Could not he, who opened the eyes of the blind man, make it so that this man also might not die? Jesus once more was inwardly raging, and went to the tomb. It was a cave, and a stone was set in front of it. Jesus said: Take away the stone. Martha, the sister of the dead man, said to him: Lord, by now he smells, since he has been there four days. Jesus said to her: Did I not tell you that if you believe you will see the glory of God? So they took away the stone. And Jesus lifted up his eyes and said: Father, I thank you for hearing me, and I know that you always hear me; but because of the crowd which surrounds me, I said it so that they should believe that you sent me. After saying this he cried out in a great voice: Lazarus, come out here. And the man who had died came out, with his hands and feet wrapped in bandages, and his face tied up in cloth. Jesus said to them: Untie him and let him go.

Then many of the Jews, who had gone to Mary and seen what he did, believed in him; but some of them went to the Pharisees and told them what Jesus had done. So the high priests and the Pharisees called a council and said: What are we doing about this man who performs so many miracles? If we let him go on like this, all will believe in him, and the Romans will come and take away our country and our nationality. But one of them, Caiaphas, who was high priest for that year, said to them: You know nothing: nor do you understand that it is for your advantage for one man to die, for the sake of the people, and not have the whole nation destroyed. This he said not of himself, but as high priest for that year he prophesied that Jesus would die for the sake of the nation, and not only for the sake of the nation, but so that he might bring together the scattered children of God.

From that day on they plotted to kill him.

But Jesus no longer went about publicly among the Jews, but he went away from there to a place near the desert, to a city called Ephraim, and there he stayed, with his disciples. The Passover of the Jews was approaching, and many went up from the country to Jerusalem before the Passover, to purify themselves. They were looking for Jesus, and they said to each other as they stood in the temple: What do you think? That he will not come to the festival? But the high priests and the Pharisees had given orders that if anyone knew where he was, he should inform on him, so that they could seize him.

◖ But six days before the Passover Jesus came to Bethany, where Lazarus was, the one Jesus had raised from the dead. So they prepared a supper for him there, and Martha served them, and Lazarus was one of those who dined with him. And Mary brought a measure of ointment of nard, pure and precious, and anointed the feet of Jesus and wiped his feet with her hair; and the house was full of the fragrance of ointment. One of his disciples, Judas the Iscariot, who was about to betray him, said: Why was not this ointment sold for three hundred denarii and given to the poor? But he said this not because he cared anything about the poor but because he was a thief and, being keeper of the purse, used to make off with what had been put into it. But Jesus said: Let her be, so that this can serve for the day of my burial; for the poor you have always with you, but you do not always have me.

The great populace of the Jews knew that Jesus was there, and they came, not only because of Jesus, but to see Lazarus, whom he had raised from the dead. But the high priests plotted to kill Lazarus also, since many of the Jews were going away because of him, and believed in Jesus.

The next day the great crowd which had come to the festival, hearing that Jesus was coming into Jerusalem, took palm branches and went out to meet him, and they cried: Hosanna. Blessed is he who comes in the name of the Lord, and the King of Israel. And Jesus found a young donkey and rode on it, as it is written: Do not fear, daughter of Zion. Behold, your King is coming, riding on the colt of a donkey. His disciples did not understand this at first, but after Jesus was glorified they remembered that these scriptures were for him, and they had done this for him. And the crowd which had been with him when he called Lazarus from the tomb and raised him from the dead bore witness to it. That was why the crowd went to meet him, because they heard that he had performed the miracle. So the Pharisees said to each other: See how little good you are doing. Look, the world has gone after him.

There were some Greeks among those who had gone up to worship at the festival. These approached Philip, from Bethsaida in Galilee, and made a request, saying: Sir, we wish to see Jesus. Philip went and spoke to Andrew; Andrew and Philip went and spoke to Jesus. Jesus answered them, saying: The hour has come for the son of man to be glorified. Truly truly I tell you, when the grain of wheat falls to the ground, unless it dies, it remains only itself, but if it dies it bears a great crop. He who loves his life loses it, and he who hates his life in this world shall keep it for the life everlasting. If one serves me, let him follow me, and wherever I am, there will my servant also be. If one serves me, my father will honor him. Now my soul is shaken, and what shall I say? Father, save me from this hour? But this is why I came to this hour. Father, glorify your name. Then a voice came from the sky: I have glorified it, and I shall glorify it again. The people who were standing by and heard said it had thundered. Others said: An angel has talked with him. Jesus answered and said: This voice came not for my sake but for yours. Now is the judgment of this world, now the leader of this world will be cast out; and if I am lifted aloft from the earth, I will draw all to myself. This he said, signifying the kind of death he was to die. But the multitude answered him: We heard from the law that the Christ remains forever; and how is it that you tell us that the son of man must be lifted aloft? Who is this son of man? So Jesus said to them: For a little time yet the light is among you. Walk about while you have the light, so that the darkness may not overtake you; and he who walks in darkness does not know where he is going. While you have the light, believe in the light, so that you may be sons of light.

Jesus said this and went away and was hidden from them. But though he had done all these miracles before them, they did not believe in him, so that the word spoken by Isaiah the prophet might be fulfilled: Lord, who believed in the rumor of us? And to whom was the arm of the Lord revealed? This is why they could not believe, because Isaiah said, once more: He has blinded their eyes and hardened their hearts, so that they may not see with their eyes or understand with their hearts and be con-

verted; for me to heal them. Isaiah said this because he
knew his glory, and he was talking about him. Even so,
many of the chief men believed in him, but they did not
admit it because of the Pharisees and for fear of being
denied the synagogue, for they cared more for the opinion
of men than for the glory of God. But Jesus cried out and
said: He who believes in me believes not in me but in him
who sent me, and he who looks on me looks on him who
sent me. As light I came into the world, so that everyone
who believes in me may not stay in the dark. And if one
hears my words and does not keep them, I will not judge
him, for I did not come to judge the world but to save the
world. He who rejects me and does not accept my words
has his judge. The word I have spoken, that will judge him
on the last day. Because I did not speak from myself, but
the father who sent me himself gave me his commandment, what to say and how to talk. And I know that his
commandment is life everlasting. So what I say is said as
my father told me to say it.

¶ Before the feast of the Passover Jesus knew that the
hour had come for him to pass from this world to his
father. He had loved his own people in the world and he
loved them to the end. And when supper was served, and
the devil had already resolved in his heart that Judas Iscariot, the son of Simon, should betray him, Jesus, knowing that his father had put everything into his hands, and
that he had come from God and was going to God, rose up
from the supper and laid aside his clothing and took a
towel and girt himself with it. Then he poured water into
the basin and began to wash the feet of the disciples and
dry them on the towel he was girt with. So he came to

Simon Peter. He said to him: Lord, are you washing my feet? Jesus answered and said to him: What I do you do not now know, but you will know it afterwards. Peter said to him: You shall never wash my feet. Jesus answered him: Unless I wash you you have no part in me. Simon Peter said to him: Lord, not only my feet, but also my hands and my head. Jesus said to him: He who is bathed has no need to wash, except for his feet, but is clean all over. And you are clean; but not all of you. For he knew his betrayer; that is why he said: Not all of you are clean. So when he had washed their feet and resumed his clothing and taken his place at supper, he said to them again: Do you know what I have done for you? You call me the master and the lord, and what you say is right, for I am. If then I, the master and lord, have washed your feet, you also have the duty of washing each other's feet; for I have given you an example, for you to do as I have done to you. Truly truly I tell you, there is no slave greater than his master or any apostle greater than him who sent him. If you know these things, you are blessed if you do them. I am not speaking of all of you. I know which ones I chose. But so as to fulfill what is written: He who ate my bread has raised his heel against me. I tell you now before it happens, so that when it happens you will believe that I am *I*. Truly truly I tell you, he who accepts anyone I send accepts me, and he who accepts me accepts him who sent me.

After he had said this, Jesus was shaken in spirit, and bore witness, and said: Truly truly I tell you that one of you will betray me. The disciples looked at each other, wondering which was the one he spoke of. One of the disciples, whom Jesus loved, was lying close beside the breast of Jesus; so Simon Peter nodded to this man and said to him: Tell us which is the one of whom he is speaking. So this man leaned back so that he was close to the breast of Jesus and said to him: Lord, who is it? Jesus answered: It is the one for whom I will dip a crust and give it to him. So he took a crust and dipped it and gave it to Judas the son of Simon Iscariot. Then after the crust Satan entered into him. So then Jesus said to him: Do what you are doing quickly. But no one of those at dinner understood what he meant when he said this to him; for some thought, since Judas kept the purse, that Jesus was saying to him: Buy what we need for the festival; or, something to give the poor. But he took the crust and went out at once. Now it was night.

When he went out, Jesus said: Now the son of man has been glorified, and God has been glorified in him. And God will glorify him in himself, and he will glorify him at once. My children, I am with you still for a little while. You will look for me, and as I said to the Jews, where I go you will not be able to go, so I say it to you now, I give you a new commandment, to love each other, as I have loved you and as you do love each other. By this all will know that you are my disciples; if you have love for each other. Simon Peter said to him: Lord, where are you going? Jesus answered: Where I am going you cannot follow me now, but you will follow me later. Peter said to him: Lord, why can I not follow you now? I will lay down my life for you. Jesus answered: You will lay down your life for me? Truly truly I tell you, the cock will not crow before you have disowned me three times.

❡ Let your hearts not be disturbed. Believe in God and believe in me. In my father's house there are many rooms.

Were there not, I would have said to you that I was going
to make ready a place for you. And if I go, and make ready
a place for you, I will come back and take you to myself,
so that where I am you may also be. And you know the
way to where I am going. Thomas said to him: Lord, we
do not know where you are going. How can we know the
way? Jesus said to him: I am the way and the truth and
the life. No one goes to the father except through me. If
you had known me you would also have known my
father. Now you know him and you have seen him. Philip
said to him: Lord, show us the father, and that is enough
for us. Jesus said to him: All this time I have been with
you and you do not know me, Philip? He who has seen me
has seen the father. How can you say: Show us the father?
Do you not believe that I am in the father and the father is
in me? The words I speak to you I do not say for myself.
But my father remaining in me does his works. Believe
me that I am in my father and my father is in me. And if
not, believe because of the works themselves. Truly truly
I tell you, he who believes in me will do, he also, the
works that I do, and he will do greater ones than I do,
because I am going to my father. And whatever you ask in
my name, this I will do, so that the father may be glorified
in the son. If you ask for something in my name, I will do
it. If you love me, you will keep my commandments. And
I will ask my father, and he will give you another comforter to be with you forever: The spirit of truth, which the
world cannot accept, because it does not see it or know it;
but you know it, because it stays with you and is in you. I
will not leave you orphans, I will come to you. A little
time and the world will no longer see me, but you will see
me, because I live and you will live. On that day you will
know that I am in my father and you are in me and I in

you. He who has my commandments and keeps them, this is the one who loves me; and the one who loves me shall be loved by my father, and I will love him and show myself to him. Judas (not the Iscariot) said to him: Lord, what has happened that you mean to show yourself to us and not to the world? Jesus answered and said to him: If anyone loves me, he will do as I say, and my father will love him, and we will come to him and make our dwelling place with him. He who does not love me will not do as I say; and what I say, which you hear, is not mine, but is from the father who sent me.

This I have said to you while I stay with you. But the comforter, the Holy Spirit whom the father will send in my name, he is the one who will teach you all and make you remember all I have said to you. I leave you peace, I give you my peace. I give it to you, not as the world gives it. Let your hearts not be disturbed or afraid. You have heard me say to you: I am going away and I will come back to you. If you loved me you would rejoice, because I am going to my father, because my father is greater than I. And now I have told you before it happens so that when it happens you will believe. I will no longer talk much with you, for the ruler of the world is coming; and he owns no part of me; but so that the world may know that I love my father, and as my father gave me his orders, thus I do. Rise up, let us go from here.

❡ I am the true vine, and my father is the grower. Every branch which bears no fruit he takes off, and every one that does bear fruit he keeps clean so that it may bear more fruit. You are already clean, because of the word I have spoken to you. Stay with me, as I with you. As the branch cannot bear fruit by itself, unless it stays on the vine, so cannot you unless you stay with me. I am the vine, you are the branches. The one who stays with me as I with him is the one who bears much fruit, because without me you can do nothing. If one does not stay with me, he is cast out like the branch, and dries up, and they gather these and throw them in the fire, and they burn. If you stay with me, and my sayings stay in you, ask whatever you wish and it will be given you. Herein is my father glorified, so that you may bear much fruit and be my disciples. As my father loves me, and I love you, stay in my love. If you keep my commandments, you will stay in my love, as I have kept the commandments of the father and stay in his love. This I have said to you so that my joy may be in you and your joy may be full. This is my commandment, that you love each other as I loved you. No one has greater love than this, to lay down his life for his friends. You are my friends if you do what I tell you to. No longer do I call you slaves, because the slave does not know what his master is doing; but I call you friends, because I made known to you all that I heard from my father. You did not choose me, but I chose you, and I placed you where you may go and bear fruit, and your fruit may last, so that whatever you ask of the father in my name he may give you. This is my commandment to you, to love each other.

If the world hates you, you know that it has hated me before you. If you were of the world, the world would love its own, but because you are not of the world, but I chose you out of the world, therefore the world hates you. Remember the saying I gave you: The slave is not greater than his master. If they persecuted me, they will persecute you also. If they hold to my word, they will hold to yours also. But all this they will do to you because of my name, because they do not know him who sent me. If I had not come and spoken to them, they would have no guilt; but now they have no excuse for their guiltiness. He who hates me hates my father also. If I had not done among them things that no one else has done, they would have no guilt; but now they have seen, and they have conceived hate both for me and for my father. But, to fulfill the word that is written in their law: They hated me, gratuitously. When the comforter comes, whom I will send you from my father, the spirit of truth who comes from my father, he will bear witness concerning me. Do you also bear witness, since you have been with me from the beginning.

¶ I have told you this so that you may not be driven astray. They will put you out of the synagogue. But the time is coming when anyone who kills you will be thought to be doing a service to God. And they will do this because they know neither my father nor me. But I have told you these things so that when their time comes you may remember that I told you about them. I did not tell you these things from the beginning because I was with you. But now I am going to him who sent me, and not one of you asks me: Where are you going? But because I have told you these things grief has filled your hearts. But I am telling you the truth; it is to your advantage for me to go away. If I do not go, the comforter cannot come to you, but if I go, I will send him to you. And when he comes he will confute the world concerning error and righteousness and judgment: error, because they do not believe in me; righteousness, because I am going away to my father and you will see me no more; and judgment, because the ruler of this world has been judged. I have much else to tell you, but you cannot handle it now; but when he, the spirit of truth, comes, he will be your guide to the whole truth, for he will speak, not on his own authority, but will tell you what he hears, and will report to you of what is to come. He will glorify me, because he will take from what is mine and report it to you. All that the father has is mine; that is why I said that he takes from me and will report to you.

A little while and you will look on me no longer; and again a little while, and you will see me. So some of his disciples said to each other: What is this that he is telling us? A little while and you will not look on me, and again a little while and you will see me? And: Because I am going to my father? So they said: What is this little while he is talking about? We do not know what he means. Jesus perceived that they wished to question him, and said to them: Is this what you are seeking together to understand, what I meant by: A little while and you will not look upon me; and again a little while and you will see me? Truly truly I tell you that you will weep and mourn, but the world will rejoice. You will have pain, but your pain will turn to joy. A woman has pain when she is giving birth, when her time has come, but when she has borne her child she no longer remembers her affliction, through joy that a human being has been born into the world. So now you also feel pain; but I will see you again, and your hearts will rejoice, and no one will take that joy away from you. And on that day you will not ask me anything. Truly truly I tell you, if you ask the father for anything he will give it to you in my name. Until now you asked for nothing in my name. Ask and you will receive, so that your joy may be complete.

I have told you this in riddles; but the time is coming when I shall speak in riddles no longer but will tell you in plain language about the father. On that day you will ask in my name, and I say that I will not ask my father on your behalf, for the father himself loves you because you have loved me and believed that I came from the father. I came from my father and went into the world. I leave the world again and go back to my father. His disciples said: See, now you are talking in plain language and tell us no more riddles. Now we know that you know all and have no need for anyone to ask you. By this we believe that you came from God. Jesus answered them: Now you believe? The time is coming, and it has come, for you to be scattered each to his own place and leave me alone. And I am not alone, because my father is with me. These things I have told you so that you may have peace in me. In the world you will have affliction; but do not fear, I have defeated the world.

❡ Jesus spoke thus, then lifted his eyes to heaven and said: Father, the hour has come. Glorify your son, so that your son may glorify you; as you gave him authority over all flesh, so that he will give life everlasting to all you have given him. And this is the life everlasting, that they know you, the only true God, and Jesus Christ, whom you sent. I have glorified you on earth by completing the work you gave me to do; and now, father, glorify me, in your own presence, with the glory I had with you before the world began. I made your name known to the people you gave me from the world. They were yours and you gave them to me, and they have kept your word. Now they have recognized that all that you gave me was from you; because I gave them the sayings that you gave me, and they accepted them and recognized rightly that I came from you, and believed that you sent me. I ask for their sake; I ask not for the sake of the world but for the sake of those you gave me, because they are yours, and all that is mine is yours and all that is yours is mine, and I am glorified in them. And I am no longer in the world, but they are in the world, and I am going to you. Holy father, keep them by your name, which you gave me, so that they may be one as we are. When I was with them I kept them, by the name which you gave me, and I protected them, and not one of them was lost except the son of perdition, so that the scripture might be fulfilled. But now I am going to you, and I say this in the world so that they may have my joy fulfilled in themselves. I gave them your word, and the world hated them, because they are not of the world, as I am not of the world. I do not ask you to take them from the world, but to keep them from evil. They are not of the world, as I am not of the world. Consecrate them in the truth. Your word is truth. As you sent me into the world, so I sent them into the world; and for their sake I consecrate myself, so that they also may be consecrated in the truth.

I ask not for the sake of these only, but also for the sake of those who believe in me because of the word of these, so that all may be one, as you, father, are in me and I in you, so that they also may be in us, so that the world may believe that you sent me. And I have given them the glory that you gave me, so that they may be one as we are one, I

in them and you in me, so that they may be made perfect
as one, so that the world may learn that you sent me and
loved them as you loved me. Father, I wish that wherever
I am, those whom you gave me may be with me also, so
that they may look upon my glory which you gave me,
because you loved me before the establishment of the
world. Righteous father, even the world did not recognize
you, but I recognized you, and these realized that you sent
me, and I made your name known to them and will make
it known, so that the love you had for me may be in them,
and I may be in them.

◀ After this prayer Jesus went with his disciples out beyond the brook Cedron to where there was a garden, and
he and his disciples went into it. And Judas, who had
betrayed him, knew this place, since Jesus had often gone
there with his disciples. So Judas got the guard, and the
servingmen from the high priests and the Pharisees, and
went there with lights and torches and weapons. Then
Jesus, who knew everything that was in store for him,
went out and said to them: Whom do you seek? They
answered him: Jesus of Nazareth. He said to them: I am
he. And Judas, who betrayed him, was standing with
them. When he said to them: I am he, they drew back and
fell to the ground. Again he asked them: Whom do you
seek? And they said: Jesus of Nazareth. Jesus answered: I
told you that I am he. So if you are looking for me, let
these go. To fulfill what he had said: I have not lost one of
those whom you gave me. Now Simon Peter had a sword,
and he drew it and struck the slave of the high priest and
cut off his right ear. The slave's name was Malchus. But

Jesus said to Peter: Put away your sword in its sheath. Shall I not drink the cup which my father gave me?

The guard and its commander and the serving-men of the Jews seized Jesus and bound him and took him first to Annas; for he was the father-in-law of Caiaphas, who was the high priest that year. And it was Caiaphas who had advised the Jews that it was better for one man to die for the sake of the people. And Simon Peter and another disciple followed Jesus. And that disciple was an acquaintance of the high priest, and he went with Jesus into the high priest's court, but Peter stood outside by the door. Then the other disciple, the acquaintance of the high priest, went out and spoke to the doorkeeper and brought Peter inside. Then the girl who was at the door said to Peter: Are you not one also of that man's disciples? He said: I am not. The slaves and the servingmen had made a charcoal fire, because it was cold, and stood by it and warmed themselves; and Peter was standing with them and warming himself.

So then the high priest questioned Jesus about his disciples and about his teaching. Jesus answered him: I have spoken openly to the world. I have taught always in the synagogue and the temple, where all the Jews come together, and I have said nothing in secret. Why do you ask me? Ask my listeners what I said to them. See, they know what I said. When he said this, one of the servingmen standing there gave Jesus a slap, saying: Is this how you answer the high priest? Jesus answered him: If I spoke evil, specify what the evil was. But if I spoke well, why strike me? So then Annas sent him in in bonds to Caiaphas the high priest.

Simon Peter was standing and warming himself. So

they said to him: Are you not also one of his disciples? He denied it and said: I am not. One of the high priest's slaves, who was related to the one whose ear Peter had cut off, said: Did I not see you with him in the garden? Once again Peter denied it; and immediately the cock crew.

Now they took Jesus from the house of Caiaphas to the residence. It was early morning. And they themselves did not enter the residence, so as to keep from defilement and be able to eat the Passover. So Pilate came out to them and said: What charge do you bring against this man? They answered and said to him: If he had not been doing evil, we should not have turned him over to you. Pilate said to them: You take him, and judge him according to your law. The Jews said to him: It is not lawful for us to put anyone to death. This was to fulfill the word of Jesus when he foretold the kind of death he was going to die.

Then Pilate went back into the residence and called Jesus in and said to him: Are you the King of the Jews? Jesus answered: Are you speaking for yourself, or did others tell you about me? Pilate answered: I am not a Jew, am I? Your own people and the high priests turned you over to me. What had you done? Jesus answered: My kingdom is not of this world. If my kingdom were of this world, my servingmen would fight to keep me from being turned over to the Jews. But as it is, my kingdom is not here. So Pilate said to him: Then you are a king? Jesus answered: It is you who are saying that I am a king. For this I was born and for this I came into the world, to testify to the truth. For everyone who is on the side of truth listens to my voice. Pilate said to him: What is truth?

And so saying he went back out to the Jews and said to

them: I find no fault in him. But you have this custom, that I should release one man for you at the Passover. Do you want me to release the King of the Jews? They shouted back saying: Not this man, but Barabbas. Barabbas was a robber.

¶ Then Pilate took Jesus and had him scourged. And the soldiers wove a crown of thorns and put it on his head, and they put a purple cloak about him, and came before him and said: Hail, King of the Jews. And they slapped him. And Pilate came out again and said to them: See, I am bringing him out to you, so that you may know that I find no fault in him. So Jesus came out, wearing the crown of thorns and the purple cloak. And Pilate said to them: Behold the man. When the high priests and their servingmen saw him they shouted: Crucify crucify. Pilate said to them: Take him yourselves and crucify him, since I find no fault in him. The Jews answered: We have a law, and by that law he must die, because he made himself out to be the son of God. When Pilate heard them say this, he was more frightened, and he went back into the residence and said to him: Where do you come from? But Jesus did not give him an answer. So Pilate said to him: Do you say nothing to me? Do you not know that I have authority to let you go, and authority to crucify you? Jesus answered him: You would not have had any authority whatever over me, if it had not been given you from above. Therefore, he who betrayed me to you has the greater guilt. Thereupon Pilate sought to release him; but the Jews cried aloud and said: If you let him go, you are no friend of Caesar's; anyone who makes himself out to be a king is challenging Caesar. When Pilate heard these words, he brought Jesus outside and sat down on the judgment seat at a place called the Stone Pavement, in Hebrew Gabbatha. It was the Day of Preparation for the Passover, at about the sixth hour. And he said to the Jews: Behold your king. They shouted: Off with him, off with him, crucify him. Pilate said to them: Shall I crucify your king? The high priests answered: We have no king except Caesar. So then he gave him to them to be crucified.

So they took Jesus. And carrying his own cross he went out to what was called the Place of the Skull, which is called in Hebrew Golgotha, where they crucified him, and with him two others, on this side and on that, with Jesus in the middle. And Pilate wrote a label and put it on the cross: and what was written was: Jesus of Nazareth, the King of the Jews. Many of the Jews read this inscription, because the place where Jesus was crucified was near the city; and it was written in Hebrew and Latin and Greek. So the high priests of the Jews said to Pilate: Do not write: the King of the Jews; but write that he said: I am the King of the Jews. Pilate answered: What I have written, I have written.

Then, when they had crucified Jesus, the soldiers took his clothes and divided them into four parts, one for each soldier; and took also his tunic. But the tunic was without a seam, woven in one piece from the top down; so they said to each other: Let us not split it, but draw lots for it, to see whose it shall be. So as to fulfill the scripture: They divided my clothes among themselves, and they threw lots for my apparel.

This is what the soldiers did. But by the cross of Jesus stood his mother; and his mother's sister, Mary the wife of Clopas; and Mary the Magdalene. So Jesus, seeing his mother with the disciple whom he loved standing beside her, said to his mother: Mother, here is your son. Then he said to the disciple: Here is your mother. And from that moment the disciple took her into his own household.

After this Jesus, knowing that all was completed for the fulfillment of the scripture, said: I am thirsty. A bowl full of vinegar was lying by; so they put a sponge soaked with the vinegar on hyssop and held it up to his mouth. So when he received the vinegar, Jesus said: It is ended; and bowing his head he gave up his life.

Now since it was the Day of Preparation the Jews asked Pilate to have the legs of the crucified men broken and the men taken off, so that the bodies would not still be on the cross on the sabbath, since that sabbath day was an important day. So the soldiers came and broke the legs of the first man, and then of the other man who had been crucified with him; but when they came to Jesus, and saw that he was already dead, they did not break his legs, but one of the soldiers stabbed him in the side with his spear, and at once blood and water came out. And he who saw it has testified to it, and his testimony is true, and he knows that he is speaking the truth, so that you also may believe. For all this took place to fulfill the scripture: They shall not break any bone in him. And again another scripture says: They shall look upon him whom they stabbed.

After that, Joseph of Arimathaea, who was a disciple of Jesus, but secretly, for fear of the Jews, asked Pilate if he could take off the body of Jesus. And Pilate gave permission. So he came and took off his body. And Nicodemus, who had gone to him first by night, also arrived, bringing a mixture of aloes and myrrh, about a hundred pounds weight. Then they took the body of Jesus and wrapped it in strips of linen along with the perfumes, as it is customary for the Jews to prepare bodies for burial. And in the region where he was crucified there was a garden, and in the garden a new tomb where no one had ever been buried. There they placed Jesus, because of the Day of Preparation of the Jews, since the tomb was nearby.

¶ Early on the first day of the week, when it was still dark, Mary the Magdalene came to the tomb and saw that the stone had been removed from it. So she ran back until she came to Simon Peter and the other disciple, whom Jesus loved, and said to them: They have taken our Lord from the tomb, and we do not know where they have put him. So Peter and the other disciple came out, and went to the tomb. The two ran together, but the other disciple ran faster than Peter and reached the tomb first, and stooped and looked in and saw the wrappings lying there, but he did not go inside. Then Simon Peter came, following him, and he went into the tomb; and he saw the wrappings lying there, and the napkin, which had been on his head, lying not with the wrappings but away from them and rolled up in a ball. And then the other disciple, who had reached the tomb first, also entered it, and he saw, and believed; for they had never yet known of the scripture, that he was to rise from the dead. Then the disciples went back to where they were staying.

But Mary stood by the tomb, lamenting. And as she lamented, she stooped and looked inside the tomb, and she saw two angels, in white, sitting where the body of Jesus had been lying, one at the head and one at the feet. And they said to her: Lady, why are you lamenting? She said to them: Because they have taken my Lord away, and I do not know where they have put him. So speaking, she turned about, and she saw Jesus standing there and did not know that it was Jesus. Jesus said to her: Lady, why are you lamenting? Whom do you seek? She thought he was the gardener and said to him: Sir, if you took him away, tell me where you put him, and I will take him. Jesus said to her: Mary. Then she turned and said to him, in Hebrew: Rabbuni (which means master). Jesus said to her: Do not hold me, since I have not yet gone up to my father. Go to my brothers and tell them I am going up to my father, and your father, and my God and your God. Mary the Magdalene went and announced to the disciples: I have seen the Lord. And that he had said these things to her.

When it was evening on that day, the first of the week, and the doors of the place where the disciples were staying were locked, through fear of the Jews, Jesus came and stood in their midst and said: Peace be with you. And when he had said this, he showed them his hands and his side. And the disciples were joyful at seeing the Lord. So he said to them once more: Peace be with you. As the father sent me forth, so I also send you. And so saying he breathed his spirit into them, and said to them: Receive the Holy Spirit. For any whose sins you forgive, their sins are forgiven. For any whose sins you keep fast, they are kept fast.

One of the twelve, Thomas, called the Twin, was not with them when Jesus came. So the other disciples said to him: We have seen the Lord. But he said to them: Unless I see the holes from the nails, and put my finger into the holes from the nails, and put my hand into his side, I will not believe. And eight days later the disciples were in the house once again, and Thomas was with them. Jesus came, though the doors were locked, and stood in their midst and said: Peace be with you. Then he said to Thomas: Put your finger here, and examine my hands, and take your hand and put it into my side, and be not an unbeliever but a believer. Thomas answered and said to him: My Lord and my God. Jesus said to him: You have believed me because you have seen me? Blessed are they who have not seen, and believe.

Jesus performed many other such miracles, in the presence of the disciples, which have not been written down in this book; but these have been written down, so that you may believe that Jesus is the Christ, the son of God, and so that, believing, you may have life in his name.

❡ After this, Jesus again showed himself to his disciples, by the Sea of Tiberias. And this is how he showed himself. There together were Simon Peter and Thomas called the Twin and Nathanael from Cana in Galilee and the sons of Zebedee and two others of the disciples. Simon Peter said to them: I am going fishing. They said to him: And we are going with you. So they went and manned the ship, and that night they caught nothing. Early in the morning Jesus was standing on the beach, but the disciples did not know that it was Jesus. Jesus then said to them: Children, have you caught anything to eat? They answered him: No. And he said to them: Cast your net in the waters to the right of the ship, and you will find some. So they cast, and they could no longer pull it in because of the quantity of fish. Then that disciple whom Jesus loved said to Peter: It is the Lord. So Simon Peter, when he heard that it was the Lord, put on his outer clothes, for he had been stripped down, and threw himself into the sea. And the other disciples came with the boat, for they were not far from the land but about three hundred feet off, dragging the net full of fish. When they came out on the shore they saw a charcoal fire laid, and a small fish placed on it, and bread. Jesus said to them: Bring some of the fish that you caught just now. So Simon Peter went aboard and hauled ashore the net full of big fish, a hundred and fifty-three of them; and though there were so many, the net did not break. Jesus said to them: Come to breakfast. Not one of the disciples dared ask him: Who are you? For they knew that it was the Lord. Jesus came and took the bread and gave it to them, and the fish likewise.

This was now the third time since he had risen from the dead that Jesus showed himself to the disciples.

When they had breakfasted Jesus said to Simon Peter: Simon son of John, do you love me more than these? He said to him: Yes, Lord, you know that I love you. He said to him: Feed my lambs. He said to him a second time: Simon son of John, do you love me? He said to him: Yes, Lord, you know that I love you. He said to him: Take care of my little sheep. He said to him for the third time: Simon son of John, do you love me? Peter was hurt because he had asked him for the third time: Do you love me? And he said to him: Lord, you know all things, you know that I love you. Jesus said to him: Feed my little sheep. Truly truly I tell you, when you were younger, you girded yourself up and walked about wherever you wished; but when you are old, you will stretch out your hands, and another will gird you and carry you where you do not wish to go. This he said, indicating the kind of death by which he was to glorify God. And when he had said this, he told him: Follow me.

Peter turned about and saw following them the disciple whom Jesus loved, the very one who at the dinner had leaned back close to the breast of Jesus and said: Lord, which one is your betrayer? So seeing this man, Peter said to Jesus: Lord, what of him? Jesus said to him: If I wish him to remain until I come, what is that to you? You, follow me. Therefore the story went out among the brothers that that one was not to die. But Jesus did not tell him that he was not to die, but: If I wish him to remain until I come, what is that to you?

This is the disciple who testifies to these things, and who wrote this, and we know that his testimony is true.

And there are many other things which Jesus did. If they were written down one by one, I do not think the very world could hold all the books that would be written.

ACTS

The Acts
of the Apostles

¶THE FIRST BOOK I WROTE, O THEOPH-
ilus, was about all the acts and teachings of Jesus until
that day when, after giving instructions through the Holy
Spirit to the apostles whom he had chosen, he was taken
aloft. It was to these that he showed himself after his
ordeal with many proofs that he was alive, and for forty
days he would appear to them and tell them about the
Kingdom of God. And while he was staying with them
he told them not to remove from Jerusalem, but said:
Await my father's promise which you have heard of from
me; because John baptized with water, but after not many
days you will be baptized with the Holy Spirit. So those
who were with him questioned him, saying: Lord, are
you restoring the Kingdom of Israel in this time? He said
to them: It is not yours to know the times and occasions
which the Father has appointed by his own authority;
but when the Holy Spirit comes upon you, you will be
given power, and you will be my witnesses in Jerusalem
and all Judaea and Samaria and as far as the end of the
earth. When he had said this and as they watched he was
raised aloft and a cloud hid him from their eyes. And as
they stared into heaven where he went, behold, two men

clothed in white stood near them and said: You men of
Galilee, why do you stand there looking toward heaven?
This same Jesus who was taken up from you to heaven
will come back in the same way that you saw him going
to heaven. Then they returned to Jerusalem from the hill
which is called the Mount of Olives; it is near Jerusalem,
a sabbath's walk away. And when they were indoors, they
went to the upper story where they were staying. They
were Peter and John and James and Andrew, Philip and
Thomas, Bartholomew and Matthew, James the son of
Alphaeus and Simon the zealot and Judas the son of
James. All these together were devoting themselves to
prayer, along with some women, and Mary the mother
of Jesus, and his brothers.

On one of those days Peter stood up in the midst of
the brothers. There was a crowd of about a hundred and
twenty persons assembled. And Peter said: Men and
brothers, the scripture was bound to be fulfilled which
the Holy Spirit gave us as prophecy through the mouth
of David, concerning Judas, who acted as guide for the
men who seized Jesus. For he was numbered among us
and had his share of this ministry. Judas bought a piece
of property with the money he got for his crime, and
there he fell on his face and burst open in the middle
and all his bowels spilled out of him. This became known
to all who live in Jerusalem, so that that property is called
in their language *Akeldamach*, which means the Field of
Blood. For it is written in the Book of Psalms: May his
dwelling place be desolate, and may there be no one living in it; and again: Let someone else take over his office. Therefore, out of those men who were with us in
all the time when the Lord Jesus came and went among
us, beginning from his baptism by John until the day

when he was taken aloft from us, out of all these men one should join us as witness to his resurrection. Then they put forward two men, Joseph called Barsabbas, who was surnamed Justus, and Matthias. Then they spoke, praying: Lord, you who know the hearts of all, show us which one of these two you have chosen to take the place in this ministry and mission which Judas forsook for his own place. And they gave them the lots, and the lot fell on Matthias, and he was added by vote to the eleven apostles.

¶ Now as the day of Pentecost had come, they were all together in one place; and suddenly there came from the sky a noise like the blowing of a great wind, and it filled all the house where they were sitting. And they saw what was like separate tongues of fire, and one settled on each of them, and they were all filled with the Holy Spirit, and they began to speak in different languages according as the Spirit gave each one the gift of speaking them.

Now there were Jews living in Jerusalem who were devout men from every nation under heaven; and at the sound of these voices the crowd came together, and they were confused, because each one heard them speaking in his own language; and they were full of astonishment and wonder, and said: See, are not all these speakers Galileans? And how is it that each of us hears them speaking in the language he was born to? Parthians and Medes and Elamites, and inhabitants of Mesopotamia, Judaea and Cappadocia, Pontus and Asia, Phrygia and Pamphylia, Egypt and the parts of Libya by Cyrene; and the Romans who are here in town, Jews and proselytes, Cretans and Arabs: we all hear them speaking in our own languages of the greatness of God. They were astonished and puzzled and said, one to another: What can this mean? But others scoffed and said: They are drunk on new wine.

But Peter stood forth with the eleven and raised his voice and said to them: Men, Jews and all who live in Jerusalem, let this be understood by you and listen to my words. These men are not drunk as you suppose, for it is only the third hour of the day, but this is what was spoken of by the prophet Joel: And it will come about in the final days, says God, that I will inspire all flesh with my spirit, and your sons and your daughters will prophesy, and your young men will see visions, and your old men will dream dreams; and in those days I will inspire my slaves and my slave women with something of my spirit, and they will prophesy. And I will present portents in the sky above, and signs upon the earth below, blood and fire and clouds of smoke. The sun will turn to darkness and the moon to blood before the coming of the day of the Lord, the great and glorious day. And it will come about that everyone who calls upon the name of the Lord will be saved.

Men of Israel, listen to these words. There was Jesus of Nazareth, a man attested to you by God through powers and portents and the miracles God wrought through him in your presence, as you yourselves know. This man was delivered up by the definite plan and purpose of God, and you nailed him to the cross by the hands of heathen men, and killed him. But God destroyed the pangs of death and resurrected him, because it was not possible for him to be overcome by death. For David says, meaning him: Throughout all I see the Lord close by me, since he is on my right to keep me unshaken. Therefore my heart is gladdened and my tongue rejoices, and my flesh

will still live with hope; because you will not abandon
my soul to Hades, nor make him who is sacred to you
look upon destruction. You have made me know the ways
of life, and with your countenance will fill me with glad-
ness.

Men and brothers, it is possible to speak confidently
about the patriarch David because he did die and was
buried and his tomb is with us, down to the present day.
He was a prophet, and knew that God had sworn to him
an oath that he would seat upon his throne one sprung
from the issue of his loins; and he said with foreknowl-
edge of the resurrection of the Christ that he was not
abandoned to Hades, and that his flesh knew no corruption. God resurrected this Jesus; to that we are all witnesses. And raised to the right hand of God, and having
received the promise of the Holy Spirit from his father,
he inspired this which you see and hear. For David did
not go up to heaven; he himself says: The Lord said to
my Lord: Sit on my right, so that I may make your enemies a footstool for your feet. Then let every house in
Israel know for sure that God made him Lord and Christ,
this Jesus whom you crucified.

When they heard it they were stricken to the heart,
and they said to Peter and the rest of the apostles: Men
and brothers, what shall we do? Peter said to them: Repent, and let each one of you be baptized in the name of
Jesus Christ for the remission of your sins, and you will
receive the gift of the Holy Spirit; since for you is the
promise, and for your children and for all those far away
whom the Lord our God summons to him.

And in many more words he charged them and ex-
horted them, saying: Be saved from this crooked generation. And those who accepted his word were baptized,

and something like three thousand souls were brought over on that day. And they held fast to the teaching of the apostles, their life in common, their breaking of bread, and their prayers. And there was fear in every soul, and many portentous things and miracles were wrought by the apostles. And all those who believed had everything in one place and in common, and they sold their property and belongings and shared all as each one might have need; and every day they would attend at the temple together, and break their bread at home, and share their food in cheerfulness and innocence of heart, praising God and in favor with the whole population. And every day the Lord added more who were saved to their number.

¶ Peter and John went up to the temple at the hour for prayer, the ninth hour; and there was a man being carried there who had been lame from his mother's womb. Every day they would lay him down by the gate of the temple which is called the Beautiful Gate, to beg for charity from the people going into the temple. When this man saw Peter and John about to enter the temple, he asked for charity. Peter, together with John, stared at him and said: Look at us. The man turned toward them, expecting to get something from them. But Peter said: I have no silver or gold. But what I do have, I give you. In the name of Jesus Christ of Nazareth, walk. And he gripped him by the right hand and pulled him up; and suddenly his feet and his ankles became strong, and he sprang up and stood and walked, and went into the temple with them, walking and bounding and praising God. And all the people saw him walking and praising God, and they knew that this was the man who had sat begging by the Beautiful Gate of the temple, and they were filled with wonder and amazement at what had happened to him.

As he clung to Peter and John, all the people, in wonderment, ran up to them at the porch which is called the Porch of Solomon. When Peter saw them he spoke forth to the people, saying: Men of Israel, why do you wonder at this? Or why do you stare at us as if by our own power or piety we had made this man walk? The God of Abraham and Isaac and Jacob, the God of our fathers, glorified his son Jesus, whom you betrayed and denied before Pilate, when Pilate judged that he should be released; but you denied the holy and righteous man, and demanded that a murderer be given you as your gift; and you killed the author of life, whom God raised from the dead. To this we are witnesses. And by faith in his name, his name gave strength to this man whom you see before your eyes, and the faith, through him, gave this man full health in the sight of you all.

Now I know, brothers, that you acted in ignorance, and so did your leaders; but God thus fulfilled the sufferings of his Christ which he had foretold through the mouths of all the prophets. Repent, therefore, and turn yourselves to wiping out your sins, so that times may come for relief from the face of the Lord and for him to send Jesus, appointed to be your Christ, whom heaven must receive until the time of the restoration of all things, time of which God has spoken from eternity through the mouths of his holy prophets. Moses said: The Lord God will raise up a prophet from among your brothers; as he did me. Listen to everything he says to you.

And every soul which does not listen to that prophet

shall be eradicated from the people. And all the prophets
who have spoken, from Samuel and his successors, have
predicted these days. You are the sons of the prophets
and of the covenant which God made with your fathers,
saying to Abraham: And in your seed all the nations of
the earth shall be blessed. It was for you first that God
raised up his son and sent him to you to bless you by
turning each one of you away from his wickedness.

¶ As they were speaking to the people, the high priests
and the captain of the temple and the Sadducees were
upon them, angry because they were teaching the people
and announcing in the name of Jesus the resurrection
from the dead; and they laid hands on them and put them
in prison until the next day, since it was now evening.
But many of those who had heard the word believed, and
the number of these men came to about five thousand.

And it happened that on the next morning the chief
men and the elders and the scribes assembled in Jerusalem; and also Annas the high priest, and Caiaphas and
John and Alexander and all who were of the high priest's
family; and they stood them in their midst and questioned them, saying: By what power and in what name
have you done this? Then Peter, filled with the Holy
Spirit, said to them: Chief men of the people and elders,
if, in the matter of helping a sick man, we are being asked
today by whom he has been saved, let it be known to
you all and to all the people of Israel that it was in the
name of Jesus Christ of Nazareth, whom you crucified,
whom God raised from the dead; it is through him that
this man stands before you, a healthy man. He is the
stone that was despised by you, the builders, which has
come to be at the head of the corner. And salvation is

not in anyone else, for there is no other name given to men under heaven by which we must be saved.

And seeing the boldness of Peter and John, and realizing that they were plain, unlettered men, they marveled, and they knew that they had been with Jesus, and when they saw the man standing with them, healed, they had nothing to say in reply. So they told them to leave the council, and they consulted together, saying: What shall we do with these men? Since a proved miracle has been done by them which is plain to all who live in Jerusalem, and we cannot deny it; but to keep this from being spread about further among the people, let us order them under threat to say no more to anyone in this name. Then they called them back in and ordered them absolutely not to speak and not to teach in the name of Jesus. But Peter and John answered and said to them: Judge whether it is right before God to listen to you rather than to God; since we are not able to keep from speaking of what we have seen and heard. They threatened them and let them go without finding any way to punish them, because of the people, since all were glorifying God over what had happened; for the man whom this miracle of healing had befallen was over forty years old.

When they were let go they went back to their own people and reported to them what the high priests and the elders had said. When they heard, of one accord they raised their voices to God and said: Lord, you who made the sky and the earth and the sea and all things that are in them, you said through the Holy Spirit by the mouth of David, our father and your servant: Why were the nations enraged and the peoples full of vain designs? The kings of the earth came on, and their leaders were gathered together against the Lord and against his Christ. For

ACTS: 4.27 | 5.3

in truth in this city there were gathered against your holy son Jesus, whom you anointed, Herod and Pontius Pilate with the nations and peoples of Israel, to do what your hand and your will had foreordained to be done. And now, Lord, take note of their threats and grant to your slaves that they may speak your word with freedom, through your stretching out your hand to make healing and miracles and portents take place through the name of your holy son Jesus. And when they prayed, the place in which they were assembled was shaken, and they were all filled with the Holy Spirit and spoke the word of God with freedom.

There was one heart and one spirit in the whole body of the believers, nor did any one of them call any of his possessions his own, but they had everything in common. And with great force the apostles bore witness to the resurrection of the Lord Jesus, and there was great good will among them all. Nor was anyone among them in need, for all those who happened to own lands or houses would sell them and bring in the proceeds of what had been sold and lay them at the feet of the apostles; and they were distributed, to each one as he had need. And there was Joseph, surnamed by the apostles Barnabas, which means, translated, Son of Consolation, a Levite and a Cyprian by birth, who owned an estate. He sold it, and brought the money and laid it at the feet of the apostles.

¶ But a certain man, Ananias by name, whose wife was Sapphira, sold some property but, with the connivance of his wife, withheld some of the proceeds and brought only a part and laid it at the feet of the apostles. But Peter said to Ananias: Why was it that Satan put it into

your heart to lie to the Holy Spirit and withhold some
of the proceeds from the property? If you had let it remain, would it not have remained yours and, even when
sold, still been at your disposal? Why did you let this
deed be put in your heart? You lied, not to men but to
God. When Ananias heard these words he fell down and
died; and great fear came upon all those who heard. Then
the younger men rose up and covered him and carried
him out and buried him. There was an interval of about
three hours and his wife came in, not knowing what had
happened. Peter said to her: Tell me, was this the amount
for which you sold the property? She said: Yes, this
amount. Peter said to her: Why did you both agree to
make trial of the Spirit of the Lord? See! The feet of
those who buried your husband are at the door; and they
will carry you out. And immediately she fell at his feet
and died; and the young men came in and found her
dead, and they carried her out and buried her by her husband. And great fear came upon the whole congregation
and on all who heard about these things.

And many miracles and portentous things were
wrought among the people by the hands of the apostles.
And they all kept gathering in the Porch of Solomon; but
none of the other people dared try to join their number,
but the people thought them very great, and more and
more a multitude of men and women came over to the
Lord, believing in him; so that they even carried their
sick out into the streets and set them there on cots and
beds so that Peter's shadow at least might fall on them
as he went by. And also a multitude from the cities round
about Jerusalem gathered there, bringing their sick and
those troubled by unclean spirits; and they were all
healed.

Then the high priest and all who were with him, that is, the sect of Sadducees, rose up and were filled with jealousy and laid hands on the apostles and put them in the public prison. But an angel of the Lord opened the doors of the prison by night, and as he led them out he said: Go and stand in the temple and tell the people all the words of this life. When they heard this they went into the temple at dawn and began teaching. But the high priest and those with him came and called together the council and the whole board of elders of the sons of Israel, and sent to the prison to fetch them. But when the servingmen arrived, they did not find them in the prison, and came back and reported, saying: We found the prison locked quite securely and the guards standing at the doors, and we opened them and found no one inside. When the captain of the temple and the high priest heard these words they were puzzled about them, as to how this could be. But a man arrived and told them: See, the men you put in prison are standing in the temple and teaching the people. Then the captain went with his servingmen and took them, not forcibly, for they were afraid of the people and that they might be stoned, and they brought them and stood them before the council. And the high priest questioned them, saying: We gave you a formal order not to teach in this name, and see, you have filled Jerusalem with your teaching; and you want to put the blood of that man upon us. Peter and the apostles answered and said: We must obey God rather than men. The God of our fathers raised Jesus, whom you killed by hanging him on the cross. God elevated him to his right hand as ruler and savior, to give Israel repentance and remission of sins. And we are witnesses to these things, we and the Holy Spirit which God gave to those who obey him.

When they heard this, they were convulsed with rage and wanted to kill them. But a certain Pharisee who was in the council, Gamaliel by name, a teacher of the law honored by all the people, stood up and urged them to have the men removed for a little while, and said to the others: Men of Israel, be careful how you go about dealing with these people. For before these days Theudas set himself up, claiming to be important, and men inclined to him to the number of about four hundred; he was killed, and all who believed in him were dispersed and came to nothing. And after him Judas of Galilee set himself up in the days of the census and won people over to his following; and he, too, was killed, and all those who believed in him were scattered. And as for now, I tell you, let these men be and release them. For if this purpose and this work come from men, they will come to nothing; but if they come from God, you will not be able to bring them to nothing. Do not be caught fighting against God.

They were persuaded by him, and they called back the apostles and had them lashed and ordered them not to speak in the name of Jesus, and released them. And they went away from the presence of the council rejoicing because they had been found worthy to suffer outrage for the sake of the name; and every day, in the temple and at home, they never stopped teaching and preaching the Christ, Jesus.

¶ During those days, as the number of disciples grew, loud complaints developed from the Hellenists against the Hebrews, that in the daily distribution the widows among their number were being overlooked. Then the twelve summoned the general body of disciples and said: It is not to our liking that we should neglect the word of God in order to see to the distribution of food. But, brothers, select from among yourselves seven men who are well recommended and who are full of the Spirit and wisdom, whom we shall put in charge of this service; and we shall devote ourselves to prayer and the ministry of the word. And this word was pleasing to all the people, and they chose Stephen, a man filled with faith and the Holy Spirit, and Philip and Prochorus and Nicanor and Timon and Parmenas and Nicolaus, a proselyte from Antioch, and these they set before the apostles, who said a prayer and laid their hands on them.

And the word of God increased, and the number of disciples in Jerusalem grew greatly, and a great number of the priests submitted to the faith.

And Stephen, filled with grace and power, accomplished portentous things and miracles among the people. But some people from the synagogue which is called that of the freedmen, and some of the Cyreneans and Alexandrians, and some from Cilicia and Asia, set themselves up against Stephen and disputed with him, but they were not able to stand up against the wisdom and spirit with which he spoke. Then they suborned certain men, who said: We have heard him speaking blasphemous words against Moses and God. And they stirred up the people and the elders and the scribes, and they set upon him and seized him and brought him before the council, and they set up false witnesses who said: This fellow never stops speaking against this holy place and the law, for we have heard him say that Jesus of Nazareth will destroy this place and change the customs which Moses handed down to us. And all who were sitting in the council stared at him and saw his face, which was like the face of an angel.

¶ Then the high priest said: Is this so? He replied: Men, my brothers and fathers, listen. The God of glory appeared to our forefather Abraham when he was in Mesopotamia, before he settled in Harran; and God said to him: Go out from your own country and your own people and come here to a country which I will show you. Then he left the country of the Chaldeans and settled in Harran. And from there, after his father died, God moved him to this land where you now live; and he did not give him any property in it, not one foot of land; but he promised to give it into his possession and to his seed after him. He had then no child. And God spoke to him thus, saying that his descendants would be alien in the land of others, and these would enslave them and afflict them for four hundred years. And I, he said, will judge that nation whom they will serve as slaves, and after that they will go from it and serve me in this place. And he gave him the covenant of the circumcision; and thus Abraham begot Isaac and circumcised him on the eighth day, as did Isaac to Jacob and Jacob to the twelve patriarchs.

The patriarchs were jealous of Joseph and sold him into Egypt; but God was with him and rescued him from all his afflictions, and gave him favor and wisdom in the eyes of Pharaoh the King of Egypt; and Pharaoh established him as governor over Egypt and all his household.

But there came a famine in all of Egypt and Canaan, and great affliction, and our fathers could find no food.

But Jacob, hearing that there was food in Egypt, sent our fathers on their first visit; and on the second visit Joseph was recognized by his brothers, and the origin of Joseph was made known to Pharaoh. And Joseph sent and summoned Jacob his father and all his family, some seventy-five souls, and Jacob went to Egypt. And he died, and so did our fathers, and they were transported to Shechem and buried in the tomb which Abraham had bought for a sum of silver from the sons of Hamor in Shechem.

When the time drew near for the promise which God had agreed to with Abraham, his people in Egypt increased and multiplied, until another king was set over Egypt, one who had not known Joseph. This one contrived against our people and did evil to our fathers by causing their babies to be exposed so that they should not survive. In this time Moses was born, and he was pleasing to God. He was reared for three months in the house of his father; and when he was exposed, the daughter of Pharaoh took him up and raised him as her own son. And Moses was educated in all the wisdom of the Egyptians, and he was powerful, in words and actions.

And when he was fully forty years old, it came into his heart to visit his brothers, the sons of Israel. And when he saw one of them being injuriously treated he came to the defense of the man abused, by striking the Egyptian down. He thought that his brothers understood that God through his hand was rescuing them; but they did not understand. And the next day he appeared to them as they were fighting each other, and he tried to reconcile them and make peace, saying: Sirs, you are brothers. Why are you injuring each other? But the man who had been injuring his neighbor thrust him away, saying: Who set you up as leader and judge over us? Could it be that you want to kill me the way you killed the Egyptian yesterday?

At that word Moses went into exile and lived as an alien in Midian, where he had two sons. And when forty years had passed, an angel appeared to him in the desert of Mount Sinai, in the flame of the burning bush. When Moses saw him he wondered at the vision, but as he approached to look, there came the voice of the Lord: I am the God of your fathers, the God of Abraham and Isaac and Jacob. Moses trembled and did not dare look; but the Lord said to him: Take off your shoes from your feet, for the place where you stand is holy. I looked and saw the evil done to my people in Egypt, and I heard their groaning, and I came down to bring them out; and now, come, I send you back to Egypt.

This was that Moses whom they had denied, saying: Who set you up as leader and judge? This was he whom God sent as leader and deliverer, helped by the hand of the angel who appeared to him at the bush. He led them out, after accomplishing portentous things and miracles in Egypt and in the Red Sea and in the desert for forty years. This is the Moses who said to the sons of Israel: God will raise up a prophet for you from among your brothers; as he did me. This is he who was in the congregation in the desert, with the angel who talked with him on Mount Sinai and with our fathers.

He received living oracles to give you. But our fathers would not obey him, but they thrust him away and turned in their hearts toward Egypt, saying to Aaron: Make us gods who will go before us; for as for this Moses who led us out of Egypt, we do not know what became of him. And they made the calf in those days, and they sacrificed to the idol, and they were pleased with the work of their hands. But God turned them about and committed them to the worship of the host of the sky, as it is written in the book of the prophets: House of Israel, did you bring me victims and sacrifices for forty years in the desert? No, but you took up the tabernacle of Moloch, and the star of the god Rhompha, the figures you made, to worship them. And I will move you beyond Babylon.

Our fathers had the tabernacle of testimony in the desert, as he who talked with Moses told him to make it in the image of what he had seen; and our fathers inherited it and also brought it here when with Joshua they dispossessed the Gentiles, whom God drove from the sight of our fathers. Until the days of David; and David found favor in the eyes of God and asked leave to devise a tabernacle for the God of Jacob. But Solomon built him a house. But the Highest does not live in what has been made by hands; as the prophet says: Heaven is my throne, and the earth is a footstool for my feet; what kind of house will you build for me, says the Lord, or what place will be my resting place? Did not my hand make all these things?

Stiff-necked, like the uncircumcised in your hearts and ears, you struggle always against the Holy Spirit. As your fathers did, so do you. Which one of the prophets did your fathers not drive out? And they killed those who foretold the coming of the righteous one whose betrayers and murderers you are now shown to be. You received the law on the orders of angels, and you did not keep it.

When they heard this they were convulsed with rage in their hearts and gnashed their teeth at him. But, filled with the Holy Spirit, he gazed into the sky and saw the glory of God, and Jesus standing on the right hand of

God, and he said: See, I behold the heavens opened and
the son of man standing on the right hand of God. They
cried aloud in a great voice and covered their ears, and
they made a concerted rush at him and threw him out
of the city and began to stone him. And the witnesses
laid their coats at the feet of a young man named Saul.
And they stoned Stephen as he made his invocation and
said: Lord Jesus, receive my spirit. Then he fell on his
knees and cried out in a great voice: Lord, do not hold
this sin against them. And as he said this, he fell asleep.

¶ And Saul approved of their killing him.

And on that day a great persecution began against the
church in Jerusalem; and all, except the apostles, were
scattered about the countryside of Judaea and Samaria.
Certain devout men buried Stephen and made a great lament over him. But Saul continued to outrage the church,
breaking into houses, dragging out men and women, and
sending them to prison.

Those who had been scattered went about proclaiming
the word of the gospel. Philip went to the city of Samaria
and preached the Christ to the people. And the masses
followed the sayings of Philip with enthusiasm as they
listened to n. m and saw what miracles he was working.
For many who had unclean spirits were relieved of them,
crying aloud as they went, and many who were paralysed
and many who were lame were made whole. And there
was great joy in that city.

But a certain man named Simon had been in the city
before Philip, practicing sorcery and astonishing the people of Samaria, claiming to be a great man, and all followed him, from the small to the great, saying: This is
the power of God which is called great. They followed

him because for some time he had been astonishing them with his sorceries. But when they believed Philip as he preached the gospel of the Kingdom of God and the name of Jesus Christ, they were baptized, both men and women. And Simon himself believed, and when he was baptized he attached himself to Philip, and when he saw the miracles and great powers that were shown, he was astonished.

The apostles in Jerusalem, hearing that Samaria had accepted the word of God, sent Peter and John to them. When these arrived, they prayed for their sake that they might receive the Holy Spirit. For this had not yet come to any of them, but they had been baptized only in the name of the Lord Jesus. Then they laid their hands upon them and they received the Holy Spirit. When Simon saw that the Holy Spirit was given by the laying on of the hands of the apostles, he brought them money, saying: Give me also this power, so that anyone on whom I lay my hands may receive the Holy Spirit. But Peter said to him: May your silver go to perdition and you along with it, since you thought you could buy the gift of God for money. You have no part or rightful share in this word, since your heart is not straightforward in the sight of God. Then repent of this baseness and beg of the Lord that the intention of your heart will be forgiven; for I see that you are in the gall of bitterness and the bondage of unrighteousness. Simon answered and said: Yourselves pray to the Lord for my sake, that nothing of what you have spoken of will happen to me.

They then, bearing witness and speaking the word of the Lord, turned back toward Jerusalem, and they brought the gospel to many villages of the Samaritans.

An angel of the Lord spoke to Philip, saying: Rise up and go south to the road that comes down from Jerusalem to Gaza. This is desert. And he rose up and went on his way, and behold, there was an Ethiopian man, a eunuch, influential with Candace the Queen of the Ethiopians, who was in charge of all her treasure. He had come to worship in Jerusalem, and now he was on his way back, sitting in his carriage and reading the prophet Isaiah. And the Spirit said to Philip: Go and attach yourself to that carriage. Then Philip ran up to him, and he heard him reading the prophet Isaiah aloud, and said: Do you understand what you are reading? He answered: Why, how could I be able to, unless someone were to guide me? And he invited Philip to mount up and sit by him. And this is the passage of scripture which he had been reading: He was led like a sheep to slaughter, and as a lamb is speechless before his shearer, even so he does not open his mouth. He was condemned to humiliation. Who can tell of his posterity? His life is taken off the earth.

And the eunuch spoke forth and said: Please tell me, about whom does the prophet say this? About himself or someone else? Then Philip opened his mouth and, beginning from this scripture, told him the whole gospel of Jesus. And as they went on along the road they came to some water, and the eunuch said: See, water. What prevents me from being baptized? So he ordered the carriage to stop, and both of them, Philip and the eunuch, went into the water, and Philip baptized him. But when they came out of the water, the Spirit of the Lord caught Philip up and away, and the eunuch did not see him any more, for he was continuing on his way, rejoicing. But Philip found himself in Ashdod, and he brought the gospel to all the cities as he passed through until he came to Caesarea.

¶But Saul, still breathing threats and slaughter against the disciples of the Lord, went to the high priest and asked him for letters to the synagogues in Damascus, so that if he could find any disciples of the Way, man or woman, he could bring them in bonds to Jerusalem. And on his journey it befell him that he was approaching Damascus, and suddenly there was a flash of light from the sky around him, and he fell to the ground and heard a voice saying to him: Saul, Saul, why do you persecute me? And he said: Who are you, Lord? And he said: I am Jesus; whom you persecute. But rise up and go into the city, and you will be told what you must do. And the men who were traveling with him had been standing there speechless; they heard the voice but they saw no one. Saul got up from the ground but when his eyes were opened he could see nothing, and they led him by the hand and brought him into Damascus. And he was three days without seeing, and he ate nothing and drank nothing.

There was a disciple in Damascus named Ananias, and the Lord said to him in a vision: Ananias. And he said: Here I am, Lord. The Lord said to him: Rise up and go to the street which is called Straight and look in the house of Judas for one, Saul by name, from Tarsus; for behold, he is praying, and he saw in a vision a man named Ananias coming in and laying his hands upon him, to make him see again. But Ananias answered: Lord, I have heard from many people about this man, and all the evil things he has done to your saints in Jerusalem; and he has such authority from the high priests that he can imprison all who call upon your name. The Lord said to him: Go on, because this man is my chosen instrument to carry my name before the nations and the Kings and sons of Israel, for I will show him all that he must suffer for the sake of my name. So Ananias went off and entered the house, and laid his hands upon him and said: Brother Saul, the Lord has sent me; Jesus, who appeared to you on the road where you were going; so that you may see again and be filled with the Holy Spirit. And immediately there fell from his eyes what was like scales, and he saw again, and rose up and was baptized; and when he had taken some nourishment, he got his strength.

He was with the disciples in Damascus for some days; and immediately he began proclaiming Jesus in the synagogues, and saying that he was the son of God. And all who heard were startled and said: Is not this the man who in Jerusalem preyed on those who called upon that name, and did he not come here to bring them in bonds before the high priests? But Saul grew all the stronger and confounded the Jews who lived in Damascus, demonstrating that this was the Christ. And after a number of days had passed, the Jews plotted to kill him; but their plot was made known to Saul. They were watching the gates, night and day, to kill him; but his disciples got him across the wall at night and eased him down in a basket.

Arriving in Jerusalem, he tried to attach himself to the disciples, but all were afraid of him, not believing that he was a disciple. But Barnabas took him by the hand and led him before the apostles and told them how he had seen the Lord on the road and talked with him, and how he had spoken out in Damascus in the name of Jesus. And he was with them, going in and out of Jerusalem, and speaking out in the name of the Lord; and he spoke and argued against the Hellenists. These were trying to kill him; but when the brothers learned of this, they got him down to Caesarea and sent him off to Tarsus.

So now in all Judaea and Galilee and Samaria the church had peace and was building up, and proceeding in the fear of the Lord, and the comforting of the Holy Spirit, it increased.

It happened that Peter traveled about among them all and came to the saints who lived in Lydda. And there he found a man named Aeneas who had been lying in bed for eight years. He was paralysed. And Peter said to him: Aeneas, Jesus Christ heals you. Get up and make your bed. And at once he stood up. And all those saw him who lived in Lydda and Sharon, those who had turned to the Lord.

In Joppa there was a disciple named Tabitha, which translated means Dorcas. She was full of good works and the acts of charity which she did. And it happened that in those days she fell sick and died; and they washed her and laid her out in an upper room. Lydda is close to Joppa, and the disciples, hearing that Peter was there, sent two men to him who said to him in entreaty: Do not hesitate, come to us. Peter rose up and went with them; and when he arrived they took him to the upper room, and all the widows came to him, weeping and displaying the tunics and mantles which Dorcas had made when she was with them. Peter put everyone out and went on his knees and prayed and turned to the body and said: Tabitha, rise up. She opened her eyes and when she saw Peter she sat up. He gave her his hand and raised her up, and called to the saints and the widows and set her before them, alive. This became known throughout Joppa, and many believed in the Lord. And it happened that he stayed for some days in Joppa with a certain Simon, a tanner.

¶ There was a man in Caesarea named Cornelius, a centurion of the cohort called the Italian cohort; a pious man who feared God, together with all his household, who did many acts of charity for the people and prayed to God in everything he did. In a vision about the ninth hour he saw plainly an angel of God who came into his house and said to him: Cornelius. He gazed at him and was full of fear and said to him: What is it, Lord? He said to him: Your prayers and your acts of charity have gone up and come to the attention of God. Now send men to Joppa, and invite a man named Simon, surnamed Peter; he is the guest of Simon the tanner, whose house is by the sea. And when the angel who spoke to him left him, he called in two of his servants, and a pious soldier out of those who were under his command, and told them everything and sent them to Joppa.

On the next day, as these men were on their way and approaching the city, Peter went up to the roof to pray at about the sixth hour. And he was hungry and wished to eat; and as people were preparing something for him, a trance came over him, and he saw the sky opened, and coming down from it an arrangement that was like a great sheet let down by its four corners upon the earth; and on it were all the four-footed beasts and creeping things of the earth, and the birds of the sky. And a voice came to him: Rise up, Peter; kill, and eat. But Peter said: Surely not, Lord; since I have never eaten anything profane and unclean. And the voice spoke to him again: What God has made clean do not you make profane. This happened three times; and immediately the arrangement was taken back up into the sky.

As Peter was wondering to himself over the meaning of the vision he had seen, behold, the men sent by Cornelius had found their way to the house of Simon and stood before the gate, and called out to ask whether Simon, surnamed Peter, were a guest there. And as Peter was still pondering his vision the Spirit said: Behold, here are three men looking for you; rise, and go down, and go along with them without hesitation; because I sent them. Peter came down to the men and said: Here I am, the one you were looking for. What is the reason for your being here? They said: Cornelius the centurion, a man who is righteous and fears God, as is attested by all the Jewish people, was told by a holy angel to invite you to his house and listen to what you have to say. So Peter asked them in and made them his guests.

On the next day he rose up and went with them, and some of the brothers from Joppa went with him. And on the day after that he entered Caesarea; and Cornelius was expecting them and had called in all his relatives and his close friends. And at the time when Peter entered, Cornelius went to meet him and threw himself at his feet and did obeisance to him. But Peter raised him and said: Stand up. I myself am also a man. And he went inside, talking with him, and found many gathered together, and said to them: You understand that it is not lawful for a Jewish man to approach or mingle with an alien. But God has shown me that I must not call any person profane or unclean. Therefore I came without objection when I was invited. So I ask, for what reason did you invite me? And Cornelius said: Four days before this time I was praying at the ninth hour in my house, and behold, a man stood before me in shining clothes, and said: Cornelius, your prayer has been heard and your acts of charity have come to the attention of God. Send therefore to Joppa and invite Simon, who is surnamed Peter; he is the guest of Simon the tanner, by the sea. So I sent men to you at once, and you have been kind enough to come. Here then we are all gathered in the sight of God to hear all that the Lord has commanded you to say.

Then Peter opened his mouth and said: I understand the truth, that God has no favorites, but in any nation he who fears him and practices righteousness is acceptable to him. He sent out the word to the sons of Israel, bringing the gospel of peace through Jesus Christ. He is the Lord of all. You know the word that went through all Judaea, beginning from Galilee after the baptism which John preached: Jesus, from Nazareth, when God anointed him with the Holy Spirit and with power, who went about doing good and healing those who were in the power of the devil, because God was with him. And we are witnesses to all that he did in the land of the Jews and in Jerusalem. And they killed him by hanging him on the cross. God raised him on the third day and granted that he should become visible, not to all the people but to witnesses who were foreordained by God; to us, who ate and drank with him after his resurrection from the dead; and he told us to preach to the people and testify that this is the one appointed by God as judge of the living and the dead. And all the prophets testify to him, that through his name everyone who believes in him shall have forgiveness of his sins.

While Peter was still speaking these words, the Holy Spirit descended upon all who were listening to his discourse. And the faithful from among the circumcised who had come with Peter were astonished that the gift of the Holy Spirit had been diffused upon the Gentiles also; for they heard them speaking with tongues and glorifying God. Then Peter spoke forth: Surely no one can forbid the water for the baptism of those who have received the Holy Spirit, as we also have done. And he ordered that they should be baptized in the name of Jesus Christ. Then they asked him to stay with them for a few days.

¶ The apostles and the brothers who were in Judaea heard that the Gentiles also had received the word of God. And when Peter went up to Jerusalem, the circumcised took issue with him, saying that he had visited uncircumcised men and eaten with them. But Peter explained everything in order from the beginning, saying: I was in the city of Joppa, praying, and in a trance I saw a vision: an arrangement like a great sheet let down by its four corners from the sky, and it came close to me. And I gazed at it and studied it, and I saw the four-footed beasts of the earth and the wild animals and the creeping things and the birds of the sky. And I heard a voice saying to me: Rise up, Peter; kill, and eat. But I said: Surely not, Lord; since nothing profane or unclean has ever entered my mouth. But the voice answered me again from the sky: What God has made clean do not you make profane. This happened three times and then everything was drawn up again into the sky. And behold, presently three men stood before the house where we were, sent to me from Caesarea; and the Spirit told me to go along with them without hesitation. These six brothers went with me and we entered the man's house. And he described to us how he had seen the angel standing in his house and saying: Send to Joppa and invite Simon, surnamed Peter, who will tell you words which will be the salvation of yourself and all your household. And as I began to speak, the Holy Spirit descended upon them as it did upon us at the outset. And I remembered the words of the Lord, how he said: John baptized in water, but you shall be baptized in the Holy Spirit. If, then, God has given them a gift equal to that which he gave us when we believed in the Lord Jesus Christ, who was I to be able to stand in the way of God?

When they heard this, they held their peace and glorified God, saying: In truth then, God has granted repentance to the Gentiles, to give them life.

Those who had been scattered abroad after the persecution that came over the matter of Stephen traveled to Phoenicia and Cyprus and Antioch, announcing the word to no one except Jews. But some of them were men from Cyprus and Cyrene, and these when they came to Antioch spoke also to the Greeks, preaching the gospel of the Lord Jesus. And the hand of the Lord was with them, and a great number believed and turned to the Lord. Word of them came to the ears of the church which was in Jerusalem, and they sent Barnabas to Antioch. When he arrived and saw the grace of God there, he was filled with joy, and he urged them all to remain true to the Lord in the devotion of their hearts; since he was a good man and full of the Holy Spirit and faith. And a considerable number was brought over to the Lord. Then he went to Tarsus to look for Saul, and when he found him he brought him to Antioch. And it befell them that they met for a whole year in the church and taught a considerable number of people; and it was in Antioch that, for the first time, the disciples came to be called Christians.

In those days prophets came down from Jerusalem to Antioch; and one of them, by name Agabus, stood up and, through the Spirit, foretold that there would be a great famine over all the world. This took place in the time of Claudius. And they ordained that each of the disciples, according to his means, should send something to take care of the brothers who lived in Judaea. This they did, sending it to the elders through the agency of Barnabas and Saul.

¶ At that time Herod the King laid hands upon some members of the church to destroy them. He had James, the brother of John, killed with the sword. And seeing that this was pleasing to the Jews, he added the arrest of Peter. It was during the days of Unleavened Bread. He seized Peter and put him in prison, and gave four squads of soldiers the duty of guarding him, meaning to bring him before the people after the Passover. So Peter was kept under guard in the prison, and there was continual prayer to God from the church for his sake.

When Herod was about to produce him, Peter was sleeping that night between two soldiers, bound with two chains, and guards were keeping watch before the door. And behold, an angel of the Lord stood there, and light flashed in the cell; and he struck Peter in the side and wakened him, saying: Rise up in speed. And his chains fell off his hands. Then the angel said to him: Dress and put on your shoes. And he did so. Then he said to him: Put on your mantle and follow me. And he followed him out, and he did not know that this was really being done by the angel, but thought he was seeing a vision. They passed through the first guard and the second and came to the iron gate which leads to the city, and this opened to them of its own accord; and they went out and walked to the next street, and suddenly the angel left him. And Peter came to himself and said: Now I know that the Lord really did send his angel and rescue me from the hand of Herod and all that the Jewish people had been hoping to do against me. And when he realized this, he went to the house of Mary, the mother of John, who was surnamed Mark, where a number of people were gathered together and praying. When he knocked on the courtyard door a maid named Rhoda came to answer, and when she recognized the voice of Peter, in her joy instead of opening the door she ran inside and announced that Peter was standing before the courtyard. They said to her: You are mad; but she insisted that it was so. But they said: It is his angel. But Peter continued to knock, and when they opened they saw him and were astonished. But motioning with his hand for them to be quiet, he described to them how the Lord had led him out of the prison, and said: Report this to James and the brothers. Then he went out and removed to another place.

When day came, there was no little consternation among the soldiers over what had become of Peter. And Herod, having searched for him and not found him, interrogated the guards and ordered them to be taken away and executed, and then went down from Judaea to Caesarea and stayed there. He was furious with the Tyrians and Sidonians; but they came to him in a body, after persuading Blastus, the king's chamberlain, and sued for peace, because their country was supported from the royal territory. And on an appointed day Herod put on his royal robes and sat on the platform and made a speech to them; and the people cried aloud: The voice of God, not of man. And suddenly an angel of the Lord struck him down because he had not given the glory to God, and he was eaten by worms and died.

And the word of the Lord grew and increased.

And Barnabas and Saul returned from Jerusalem after fulfilling their mission, taking along with them John, who was surnamed Mark.

¶ At the church which was in Antioch, there were prophets and teachers, Barnabas and Simeon surnamed Niger, and Lucius of Cyrene, and Manaen, a close friend of Herod the Tetrarch, and Saul. And while they were serving the Lord and fasting, the Holy Spirit said to them: Appoint Barnabas and Saul to do for me the work I have called them to. Then after fasting and prayer and laying their hands upon them they sent them on their way.

So these men, sent forth by the Holy Spirit, arrived at Seleucia, and from there sailed to Cyprus, and in Salamis preached the word of God in the synagogues of the Jews. And they had John with them as a helper. And after traveling through the entire island as far as Paphos they found there a certain man, a magician and false prophet, a Jew, whose name was Barjesus, who was in the company of the proconsul Sergius Paulus, an intelligent man. This man invited Barnabas and Saul in and desired to hear the word of God. But the magician Elymas, for this is how his name is translated, opposed them, trying to turn the proconsul away from the faith. But Saul, who is also Paul, was filled with the Holy Spirit and stared at him and said: O full of every trick and every deception, son of the devil, enemy of everything righteous, will you not stop trying to twist the straight ways of the Lord? And now, behold, the hand of the Lord is against you, and you will be blind and not see the sunlight for a while. And immediately a mist and darkness fell upon him, and he went about looking for people to lead him by the hand. Then the proconsul, seeing what had happened and struck by the teaching of the Lord, believed.

Sailing from Paphos, Paul and his party came to Perge in Pamphylia, but John left them and returned to Jerusalem. And traveling from Perge, they arrived at the Pisidian Antioch, and entered the synagogue on the day of the sabbath and sat down. After the reading of the law and the prophets, the heads of the synagogue sent them a message saying: Men and brothers, if you have any word of exhortation before the people, speak. Then Paul stood up and gestured with his hand and said: Men of Israel, and all who fear God, listen. The God of this people, Israel, chose our fathers, and exalted their people in their stay in Egypt, and with his mighty arm he brought them out of there; and when for a period of forty years he had nursed them in the desert, then by overcoming seven nations in the land of Canaan he made that land their heritage for some four hundred and fifty years. And after that he gave them judges, until Samuel the prophet; and after that they asked for a King, and God gave them Saul the son of Kish, a man from the tribe of Benjamin, for forty years. Then putting him aside he raised up David to be their King, to whom he bore witness and said: I have found David the son of Jesse, a man after my own heart, who will carry out all my wishes.

It was from his seed, according to his promise, that he brought Israel its savior, Jesus, before the coming of whose presence John had preached the baptism of repentance to all the people of Israel. And as John ran his course, he would say: What do you suppose I am? I am not he. But behold, there is one coming after me, and I am not fit to take his shoes off his feet.

Men and brothers, sons of the stock of Abraham, and all among you who fear God, the word of this salvation was sent to us. For the dwellers in Jerusalem and their chiefs did not recognize him, and by judging him they fulfilled the utterances of the prophets which are read aloud on every sabbath; and without finding any true cause for his death they demanded that Pilate should have him killed. And when they had fulfilled everything that was written about him, they took him down from the cross and laid him in a tomb. But God raised him from the dead; and he appeared for some days to those who had come up with him from Galilee to Jerusalem, who are his witnesses before the people. And we bring you the gospel of the promise that was made to our fathers, that God has fulfilled this for us their children by resurrecting Jesus, as it is written in the Second Psalm: You are my son, this day I begot you.

And that he raised him from the dead to be one who would never more return to corruption, this he has said, thus: I will give you the sacraments of David, which are to be believed. Since in another place he says: You shall grant your holy one that he shall not know corruption. For David, after serving the will of God, in his own lifetime died and was laid beside his fathers and knew corruption, but he whom God raised did not know corruption.

Therefore let it be understood by you, men and brothers, that remission of sins through him is promised to you, and for all those matters where you could not be justified by the law of Moses, everyone who believes is justified by him. Look to it then that what was spoken of by the prophets may not come upon you: Look, you scoffers, and marvel and be brought to nothing, because in your days I will do a deed, a deed which you would not believe if someone described it to you.

When Paul and Barnabas went out, they requested that these matters should be spoken of on the next sabbath. And when the meeting broke up, many Jews and faithful proselytes followed Paul and Barnabas; and they talked to them and urged them to remain true to the grace of God. And on the next sabbath almost the entire city was gathered together to listen to the word of God. But the Jews, when they saw the crowds, were filled with envy and attacked the speeches of Paul, reviling him. But Paul and Barnabas spoke out boldly and said: It was necessary that the word of God should be told first to you; but since you reject it and judge yourselves to be unworthy of everlasting life, we are turning to the Gentiles. For thus the Lord has commanded us: I have appointed you to be the light of the Gentiles, and for you to bring salvation as far as the end of the earth. When the Gentiles heard this they were joyful and glorified the word of God, and all those who were destined to life everlasting believed; and the word of the Lord was spread through the entire country. But the Jews stirred up the prominent women who were worshippers and the foremost men of the city, and they started a persecution of Paul and Barnabas and drove them out of their territory. And they shook the dust from their feet against them and went to Iconium, and their disciples were filled with joy and the Holy Spirit.

¶ In the same way it happened in Iconium that they went into the synagogue of the Jews and spoke in such a way that a great number of Jews and Greeks believed. But the Jews who would not believe stirred up the minds of the Gentiles and poisoned them against the brothers. They spent some time there, speaking boldly, trusting in the Lord, who testified to the word of his grace by granting that miracles and portentous things should be brought about at their hands. But the population of the city was split, and some were with the Jews and some were with the apostles. But when there was a movement among the Gentiles and Jews, together with their leaders, to use violence and stone them, they got wind of it and fled to the cities of Lycaonia, Lystra and Derbe and their vicinity; and there they went on bringing the gospel.

Now there was a certain man, crippled in his feet, who sat in Lystra. He was lame from his mother's womb and had never walked. This man was listening to Paul as he spoke; and Paul gazed at him, and seeing that he had faith that he could be saved, he said in a great voice; Get on your feet and stand upright. And he sprang up and walked. And when the crowds saw what Paul had done, they cried aloud in their own Lycaonian language, saying: The gods have made themselves like men and come down to us. And they called Barnabas Zeus and Paul Hermes, because he was the chief speaker. And the priest of the Zeus whose temple was before the city brought bulls and garlands into the courtyard and, together with the crowds, wanted to sacrifice to them. When the apostles Barnabas and Paul heard of this, they tore their robes and leaped into the crowd, crying out and saying: Men, why are you doing this? We also are men who feel and suffer as you do, who are bringing you the gospel to turn you away from these idiocies, to the living God, who made the sky and the earth and the sea and all that is in them. In past ages he let all nations go their own ways; and yet he has not let himself be without proof for his good works, giving you rains from the sky and fruitful seasons, filling your hearts with sustenance and good cheer. And by saying these things they finally managed to stop the crowds from sacrificing to them.

But Jews arrived from Antioch and Iconium, and won over the masses, and stoned Paul and dragged him out of the city, believing that he was dead. But his disciples made a circle around him and he got up and went into the city. And on the next day he set out with Barnabas for Derbe. And after bringing the gospel to that city and making a number of converts they returned to Lystra and Iconium and Antioch, strengthening the spirits of the disciples, urging them to endure in their faith, and telling them that it is only through much suffering that we can enter the Kingdom of God. And they selected elders for them, church by church, and with prayer and fasting committed them to the Lord in whom they had put their faith.

Then, passing through Pisidia, they came to Pamphylia, and after preaching the word in Perga they came to the sea at Attalia and sailed from there to Antioch; from which place they had by the grace of God been appointed to the work which they had now completed. And arriving there and convening the church they reported all that God had done through them, and that he had opened the door of faith to the Gentiles. And they spent a considerable amount of time with the disciples there.

¶ Then certain men came down from Judaea and began to teach the brothers, saying: Unless you are circumcised by the rite of Moses, you cannot be saved. And when considerable dissension and debate arose between Paul and Barnabas and these men, they decreed that Paul and Barnabas and some others of their number should go up to see the apostles and elders in Jerusalem to discuss this question. So those who were sent by the church passed through Phoenicia and Samaria describing the conversion of the Gentiles, and brought great joy to all the brothers. And arriving in Jerusalem, they were received by the church and the apostles and the elders, and they reported all that God had done through them. But some believers from the sect of the Pharisees rose up, saying that they must circumcise them in order to keep the law of Moses.

The apostles and the elders assembled to look into this question. And after much discussion Peter stood up and said to them: Men and brothers, you know well that in our early days God made his choice among us that from my lips the Gentiles should hear the word of the gospel and believe; and God, who knows the heart, proved it to them by giving the Holy Spirit to them, as he did to us, and did not discriminate between us and them, purifying their hearts through faith. Why then do you make trial of God by putting on the necks of the disciples a yoke that neither our fathers nor ourselves were strong enough to bear? Rather through the grace of the Lord Jesus we believe that we are saved in the same way as they. Then all the congregation fell silent, and they listened to Barnabas and Paul describing all the portentous acts and miracles that God had worked through them among the Gentiles.

And when they had fallen silent, James answered, saying: Men and brothers, listen to me. Simon has told how the Lord was first concerned to accept a people in his name from among the Gentiles. And the words of the prophets accord with this, as it is written: After this I will return, and I will rebuild the fallen tabernacle of David and restore its ruins and raise it up again, so that the rest of mankind may seek out the Lord, and all the nations to whom my name has been spoken. Thus says the Lord, making all this known, since eternity.

Therefore I believe we should not make difficulties for those of the Gentiles who turn to God, but instruct them to abstain from the pollution of idols, and from lechery, and from what has been strangled, and from blood. For Moses has had since ancient generations those who preach him in every city, and he is read in the synagogues every sabbath.

Then the apostles and elders, together with the whole church, resolved to send men picked from among them to Antioch along with Paul and Barnabas. They were Judas, surnamed Barsabbas, and Silas, prominent men among the brothers. And they wrote a letter, for them to deliver by hand, saying: The apostles and elders, brothers, to the Gentile brothers in Antioch and Syria and Cilicia, greetings. Since we have heard that some of us have disturbed and distracted your minds by their words, without instructions from us, we have unanimously resolved to select two men and send them to you together with our beloved Barnabas and Paul, men who have risked their lives for the name of the Lord Jesus Christ. We have sent, then, Judas and Silas, who will give you the same message by word of mouth. It seemed best to the Holy Spirit, and to us, not to burden you with any commandments except these, which are fundamental: to abstain from idol offerings, and blood, and what has been strangled, and lechery. If you keep yourselves from these, you will be acceptable. Farewell.

So they were sent on their way and went down to Antioch, and they assembled the congregation and delivered the letter; and when they read it they rejoiced over the advice. And Judas and Silas, who were themselves also prophets, talked much with them and advised and strengthened the brothers; and after staying some time they went in peace from these brothers to those who had sent them. But Paul and Barnabas stayed on in Antioch, teaching and, with many others, carrying the gospel of the word of the Lord.

Then after some days Paul said to Barnabas: Let us return and visit our brothers in every city in which we preached the word of the Lord, to see how they are faring. Barnabas wished to take John Mark along; but Paul thought it would be wrong to take that man who had deserted them in Pamphylia and not gone on with them to their work. And some bitterness arose, so that they separated from each other, and Barnabas sailed for Cyprus, taking Mark with him. But Paul chose Silas and left, commended to the grace of the Lord by the brothers, and journeyed through Syria and Cilicia strengthening the churches.

¶ He also visited Derbe and Lystra. And behold, there was a disciple there named Timothy, the son of a Jewish woman believer and a Greek father, and he was recommended by the brothers in Lystra and Iconium. And Paul wished to have him travel with him, and he took him and circumcised him, on account of the Jews who were in those parts, since all knew that his father was a Greek. And as they journeyed through the cities, they delivered to the people the commandments decreed by the apostles and elders in Jerusalem, for them to obey. And the churches were strengthened in their faith and grew in number day by day.

They passed through Phrygia and the Galatian territory, being prevented by the Holy Spirit from preaching the word in Asia; and going by Mysia they tried to go on to Bithynia, but the Spirit of Jesus would not let them; and passing by Mysia they landed at Troas. And a vision appeared in the night to Paul; a Macedonian man was standing there inviting him and saying: Cross over into Macedonia and come to our aid. And when he had seen the vision, we sought to go to Macedonia, concluding that God had invited us to bring the gospel to those people.

So sailing from Troas we ran a straight course to Samothrace, and on the next day to Neapolis, and from there to Philippi, which is the first city in the district of Macedonia, a colony. We spent some days in this city. And on the day of the sabbath we went outside the gate beside the river where we thought there was a place of prayer, and we sat down and talked to the women who gathered there. And one woman named Lydia, a seller of purple cloth, from the city of Thyatira, one who worshipped God, listened, and the Lord opened her heart to receive what was said by Paul. And when she and her household had been baptized, she invited us, saying: If you have judged me to be faithful to the Lord, come into my house and stay with me. And she made us do so.

And it happened that as we were on our way to the place of prayer, we encountered a maidservant who pos-

sessed a spirit of prophecy; she made a great deal of
money for her masters by her divining; and she followed
Paul and the rest of us and cried aloud, saying: These
people are slaves of the highest God, and they announce
to you the way of salvation. She did this for many days.
But Paul was annoyed and turned on the spirit and said:
I command you in the name of Jesus Christ to go forth
from her. And it went forth in that same hour. But when
her masters saw that their hope for profit was gone, they
seized on Paul and Silas and dragged them into the market place before the authorities, and led them up to the
chief magistrates and said: These people, who are Jews,
are upsetting our city and preaching usages which we,
who are Romans, cannot accept. And the mob joined in
the attack against them, and the chief magistrates tore
the men's clothing to pieces and ordered them to be
beaten, and after inflicting many blows they threw them
in prison, ordering the warden to keep them under close
guard; and he on receiving such an order threw them into
the innermost part of the prison and fastened their feet
in the stocks. But in the middle of the night Paul and
Silas were praying and singing hymns to God, and the
prisoners were listening to them; and suddenly there was
a great earthquake, so that the foundations of the prison
were shaken, and all the doors came open, and the chains
fell off all of them. The warden woke up, and when he
saw that the doors of the prison were open, he drew his
sword and was about to kill himself, believing that the
prisoners had escaped. But Paul called out in a great voice,
saying: Do not do yourself an injury, for we are all here.
And the man called for a light and leaped inside, and
threw himself down trembling before Paul and Silas, then
led them outside and said: Lords, what must I do to be

saved? And they said: Believe in the Lord Jesus and you and your household will be saved.

And they preached the word of God to him, with all who were in his house; and he took them at that hour of the night and washed their wounds, and he himself and all who were in his house were baptized on the spot; and he took them into his house and set a table before them, and rejoiced with all his household that he had come to believe in God.

When day came the chief magistrates sent their lictors, saying: Release those men. The warden brought the message to Paul, to this effect: The chief magistrates have sent to have you released; so now come out and go on your way in peace. But Paul said to them: After lashing us publicly without trial, us who are Roman citizens, they threw us in prison. And now they are putting us out secretly? Not so; let them come themselves and conduct us out. The lictors reported these words to the chief magistrates; and they were frightened when they heard that they were Romans, and came and apologized and conducted them out and asked them to leave the city. And they left the prison and went to Lydia's house; and they saw the brothers and encouraged them and left.

¶ Making their way through Amphipolis and Apollonia, they came to Thessalonica, where there was a synagogue of the Jews. And following his custom, Paul visited them and for three sabbaths lectured to them on the scriptures, demonstrating and proving that the Christ had to suffer and rise from the dead, and saying, This is the Christ, Jesus, whom I proclaim to you. And some of them believed and attached themselves to Paul and Silas, a great number of Greek believers, and not a few prominent women. But the Jews became jealous, and they enlisted the help of some tough men from the market place rabble and started a riot and threw the city into confusion; and they besieged the house of Jason and demanded that he bring them out before the people. But not finding them, they dragged Jason and some of the brothers before the authorities, shouting: These men who are upsetting the Empire are here now, and Jason has taken them in; and all of them are acting against the decrees of Caesar, saying that there is another who is King, Jesus. And they stirred up the mob and the authorities, but after getting bail from Jason and the others they let them go.

The brothers immediately took Paul and Silas to Beroea by night, and arriving there they went to the synagogue of the Jews. These people were more honorable than the ones in Thessalonica, and they received the word in all eagerness, studying the scriptures day by day to see if this were really so. And many of them believed, and not a few of the prominent Greek women and men. But when the Jews of Thessalonica learned that the word of God had been proclaimed in Beroea by Paul, they went there also, upheaving and disturbing the masses. But then the brothers promptly sent Paul on his way to the sea; and Silas and Timothy stayed there. Then those who had Paul in their charge brought him to Athens and, after receiving his instructions to Silas and Timothy that they should come to him with all speed, they returned.

In Athens, while Paul was awaiting them, his spirit was exasperated within him as he saw that the city was full of idols. And he would have discussions with the Jews and the worshippers in the synagogue and in the market place every day with anyone he happened to meet. And some of the Stoic and Epicurean philosophers encountered him, and some of them said: What might this vagabond be trying to tell us? And others said: He seems to be an announcer of foreign divinities. Because he brought the gospel of Jesus and the resurrection. So they took him in hand and led him up to the Areopagus, saying: Can we discover what is this new teaching of which you are telling us? You are bringing something new to our ears. So we wish to learn what this means. All the Athenians and their visitors from abroad spent their time on nothing except saying or hearing something novel.

Then Paul, standing on the middle of the Areopagus, said: Gentlemen of Athens, I perceive that you are in every way more god-fearing than others; for as I went about and observed your sanctuaries I even found an altar inscribed: To the Unknown God. What you worship, without knowing what it is, this is what I proclaim to you. God, who made the world and everything in it, being Lord of heaven and earth, does not live in hand-built temples, nor, as one who needs anything, is he ministered to by human hands, since he himself gave life and breath and everything else to all. And out of one he made every nation of men to live on every face of the earth, decreeing the seasons in their order and the boundaries of their habitations; and he made them search for God, to try to feel their way to him, since indeed he is not far from any one of us. For in him we live and move and are, since, as some of your own poets have said: We are his offspring.

Being then as we are the offspring of God, we ought not to believe that divinity is like gold or silver or stone, the carving of art and the thought of man. God, then, overlooking our times of ignorance, now announces to men that all men everywhere must repent; because he has set a day on which he will judge the inhabited world in justice through a man whom he has appointed to do this, after giving sure proof to all by resurrecting him from the dead.

When they heard about the resurrection from the dead, some scoffed but some said: We will listen to you again concerning this matter.

So Paul went from their midst; but some men attached themselves to him and believed, among them Dionysius the Areopagite and his wife, who was named Damaris, and some others with them.

¶ After that he left Athens and went to Corinth. There he found a Jew named Aquila, from Pontus by origin, who had recently come from Italy with his wife, Priscilla, because Claudius had decreed that all Jews must leave Rome. He went to them and, because they shared the same craft, he stayed with them and they all worked together. Their craft was tent-making. And every sabbath he would speak in the synagogue, and he converted both Jews and Greeks.

But when Silas and Timothy arrived from Macedonia, Paul gave himself over to preaching the word, testifying to the Jews that the Christ was Jesus. And when they opposed him and abused him, he shook out his clothing and said: Your blood be upon your own heads. My hands are clean. From now on I shall go to the Gentiles. And leaving the place, he went to the house of a man named Titius Justus, who worshipped God, and whose house was next to the synagogue. And Crispus, the head of the synagogue, believed in the Lord, together with all his household; and many Corinthians when they heard him believed and were baptized. And in a vision by night the

Lord said to Paul: Do not fear, but speak on and do not be silent; because I am with you, and no one will attack you to do you harm; because I have many people in this city.

And he stayed for a year and six months teaching them the word of God. But when Gallio was proconsul of Achaea, the Jews made a concerted attack on Paul and brought him to the tribunal, saying: This man persuades people to worship God contrary to the law. But as Paul was about to open his mouth to speak, Gallio said to the Jews: If there were some crime or flagrant villainy, you Jews, I would reasonably have put up with you; but if your complaints concern a word or names or the law that you have, you must see to it yourselves. I do not wish to be judge of these matters. And he drove them from the tribunal. Then they all seized on Sosthenes, the head of the synagogue, and beat him in front of the tribunal; but none of all this was of any concern to Gallio.

Paul stayed on for a number of days and then, after saying farewell to the brothers, sailed for Syria, and Priscilla and Aquila went with him, and he cut his hair short in Cenchreae, for he had taken a vow. They put in at Ephesus, and he left the others there and went himself into the synagogue and talked with the Jews. And when they asked him to stay for a longer time, he refused, but after saying farewell and telling them: I will return to you again, God willing, he sailed from Ephesus; and went ashore at Caesarea and went up and greeted the church, and went down to Antioch, and after spending some time there left; and passed from place to place through the territory of Galatia and Phrygia, strengthening the disciples.

There was a certain Jew, Apollos by name, an Alexandrian by origin, who came to Ephesus: an eloquent man, strong in the scriptures. This man was a student in the way of the Lord and, seething with enthusiasm, he spoke and taught accurately the facts about Jesus, but he knew only the baptism of John. And he began to speak freely in the synagogue; but when Priscilla and Aquila heard him, they took him aside and explained to him more exactly about the Way of God. When he wished to go to Achaea, the brothers encouraged him and wrote to the disciples that they should accept him. And when he arrived, he was very helpful to those who, through grace, had become believers; for he strenuously confuted the Jews, proving in public, through the scriptures, that the Christ was Jesus.

¶ While Apollos was in Corinth, it happened that Paul, after traveling through the interior, came to Ephesus, and there found some disciples and said to them: When you believed, did you receive the Holy Spirit? They said: We have not even heard whether there is a Holy Spirit. Paul said: Then in what were you baptized? They answered: In the baptism of John. Paul said: John baptized in the baptism of repentance, telling the people to believe in the one who was coming after him, that is, in Jesus. When they heard this, they were baptized in the name of the Lord Jesus; and after Paul had laid his hands upon them, the Holy Spirit came over them, and they began to speak with tongues and prophesy. There were about twelve men in all.

Then he went into the synagogue and spoke freely for three months, lecturing and arguing about the Kingdom of God. But when some men began to scoff and disbelieve, speaking ill of the Way of God before the congregation, Paul left them and took away his disciples, lecturing every day in the school of Tyrannus. And this went on for two years, so that all the inhabitants of Asia heard the word of the Lord, Jews and Greeks alike. And God displayed no ordinary powers through the hands of Paul, so that even if only handkerchiefs or towels he had touched were brought to the sick, their diseases would leave them and the evil spirits would go out of them. And some of the traveling Jewish exorcists tried naming the name of the Lord Jesus to those who possessed evil spirits, saying: I adjure you by Jesus, the one Paul preaches. There were seven sons of a certain Sceva, a Jewish high priest, who did this. But the evil spirit answered and said to them: Jesus I know, and I know about Paul, but who are you? And the man who had been controlled by the evil spirit leaped upon these men and overpowered and defeated them so that they fled from the house naked and bleeding. This became known to all the Jews and Greeks living in Ephesus, and fear fell upon them all, and the name of the Lord Jesus was exalted. And many of those who had come to believe began confessing and reporting their magical practices, and a number of those who had been practicing magic brought their books together into one place and burned them in the sight of all; and they counted the value of these and found that they came to fifty thousand pieces of silver. Thus powerfully did the word of the Lord grow and gain strength.

After these matters were concluded, Paul took it into his mind to make a tour through Macedonia and Achaea and go on to Jerusalem, saying: After I have been there,

I must also see Rome. Then he sent off two of his assistants, Timothy and Erastus, to Macedonia, and himself stayed for some time in Asia.

And at that time there arose a considerable disturbance over the Way of the Lord. For there was a certain man, Demetrius by name, a silversmith, who built shrines of Artemis and so gave considerable employment to the craftsmen. He assembled those and others who did this kind of work, and said: My men, you understand that our prosperity comes from this work; and you can see, and hear, that this man Paul has converted by his persuasion a large crowd not only in Ephesus but in almost all of Asia, saying that gods who are made by hands are not gods. This threatens not only to make our trade fall into disrepute, but also to make the temple of the great goddess Artemis be set at naught, and to put her, whom all Asia and the world worships, in danger of being brought down from her greatness. When they heard this, they were filled with anger and shouted: Great is Artemis of the Ephesians. And the whole city was filled with confusion, and they made a concerted rush to the theater, seizing and carrying along with them Gaius and Aristarchus, Macedonians and traveling companions of Paul. Paul wanted to go before the people, but the disciples would not let him; and also some of the Asiarchs who were friendly to Paul sent to him and urged him not to present himself in the theater.

Now some were shouting one thing and some another, for the meeting was in confusion, and most people did not know why they had been assembled. And some from the crowd told Alexander what to say; the Jews had pushed him forward. And Alexander, gesturing with his hand, tried to speak in defense before the people; but when they recognized that he was a Jew, a single voice came from them all as they shouted for something like two hours: Great is Artemis of the Ephesians. But the secretary of the city quieted the crowd and said: Men of Ephesus, what living person does not know that the city of the Ephesians is the temple keeper of the great Artemis and the image that fell from heaven? Since all that is indisputable, you should remain quiet and not do anything reckless. For you brought these men here when they had neither blasphemed against our goddess nor injured her temple. So now if Demetrius and his fellow craftsmen have anything to say against anyone, the courts are in session and the proconsuls are there, let them bring their charges. If you demand anything more, it will be settled in the regular assembly. For we are in danger of being charged with lawlessness over today; since there is no excuse we can give for this disturbance. And so saying, he closed the meeting.

¶ After the excitement was over, Paul sent for his disciples and encouraged them and said his farewells and set off on his journey to Macedonia. And after passing through those parts and encouraging the people with much speaking, he arrived in Greece. When he had spent three months there and was about to sail to Syria, he decided to return by way of Macedonia because of a plot against him by the Jews. Along with him went Sopater the son of Pyrrhus, from Beroea, Aristarchus and Secundus of the Thessalonians, Gaius and Timothy of Derbe, and the Asians Tychicus and Trophimus. These went on ahead and awaited us at Troas; and we sailed from Philippi after the days of Unleavened Bread, and we came to them at Troas after five days, and for seven days we remained there.

On the first day of the week when we were gathered together to break bread, Paul was discoursing, and since he intended to leave the next day, he drew out his discourse until midnight. There were plenty of lamps in the upper room where we were gathered together. But a young man named Eutychus was sitting in the window, and he fell into a deep sleep as Paul talked on at length, and overcome as he was by sleep, he fell all the way from the third story and was picked up dead. Paul went down and lay over him and embraced him, then said: Do not be alarmed, his life is there within him. Then he went up and broke bread and ate it and talked until sunrise, and then left. And they took away the boy, and he was alive; and they were greatly comforted.

We went on board the ship and sailed for Assos, intending to take Paul on board there, for so he had directed; he himself was going to go there by land. And when he met us at Assos, we took him aboard and went to Mitylene, and sailed from there, and on the next day we were off Chios; on the day after that we crossed over to Samos, and on the following day came to Miletus. For Paul had decided to bypass Ephesus so as not to lose time in Asia, since he was hastening to be in Jerusalem on the day of the Pentecost if that might be possible.

From Miletus he sent to Ephesus and summoned the elders of the church. And when they were in his presence he said to them: You know well, from the first day I set foot in Asia, what I was like all the time I was with you, serving the Lord in all humility and through the tears and trials that befell me from the plots of the Jews against me; how I never gave up doing what was to your advantage, bringing the news to you and teaching you, both in public and in your houses, attesting, to Jews and Hellenes alike, repentance and faith in our Lord Jesus. And now, behold, I am on my way to Jerusalem, in bondage to the Holy Spirit; not knowing what will happen to me there, except that the Holy Spirit testifies to me in every city that imprisonment and afflictions await me. But I do not count my life as of any great value to me, so long as I finish my course and the ministry which I accepted from the Lord Jesus, to testify to the gospel of the grace of God. And now, behold, I know that you will never see my face again: not any of you among whom I went about preaching the Kingdom.

Therefore I testify to you, upon this very day, that I am clean of the blood of all of you; for I never gave up announcing all God's will to you. Take heed, then, for yourselves and for all the flock in which the Holy Spirit has set you as guardians, to be shepherds of the church of God which he brought about with his own blood. I know that after I leave you, fierce wolves will come among you who will not spare the flock; and men from your own number will rise up and speak perversely, to pull the disciples into their own following. Therefore be watchful, remembering how for three years I never ceased, night and day, from counseling each one of you, with tears. And now I give you into the charge of the Lord and the word of his grace, which has power to restore you and give you your inheritance among all who have been consecrated. I never wanted anyone's silver or gold or clothing; you yourselves know that these hands of mine provided for my needs and for my companions. I have always shown you that thus you should toil to help those who are weak and remember the words of the Lord Jesus Christ which he himself spoke: It is more blessed to give than to receive.

So saying, he knelt with all of them and prayed. And there was much lamentation by all, and they fell on Paul's neck and kissed him. What had grieved them the most was when he said that they would never see his face again. And they escorted him to his ship.

¶ When we had to tear ourselves away from them and put out to sea, we made a straight run to Cos, and on the next day to Rhodes, and from there to Patara; and finding there a ship that was crossing to Phoenicia we went aboard and sailed. After sighting Cyprus and leaving it behind on the left, we sailed to Syria and came ashore at Tyre, for it was there that the ship unloaded her cargo. We found the disciples and stayed there seven days; and they warned Paul, because of what the Spirit had told them, not to go on to Jerusalem. But when we had come to the end of our days there, we left and started on our way, and they all escorted us, with their wives and children, outside the city; and we all knelt down on the beach and prayed and said our farewells; and then we boarded the ship, and they turned back to their homes.

We ended our sea voyage from Tyre by reaching Ptolemais, and there we greeted the brothers and stayed with them for a day. And on the next day we set forth and reached Caesarea and went to the house of Philip the evangelist, one of the seven, and stayed with him. He had four maiden daughters, who were prophetic. After we had stayed there for a number of days, there came down from Judaea a prophet named Agabas, who came up to us and took off Paul's belt and bound his own feet and his hands, saying: Thus says the Holy Spirit. The Jews will thus bind the man, whose belt this is, in Jerusalem, and they will give him over into the hands of the heathens. When we heard this, we, together with the people who lived there, implored him not to go up to Jerusalem. Then Paul answered: Why are you doing this, crying and breaking my heart? I am ready not only to be bound but to die in Jerusalem for the name of the Lord Jesus. So when he would not be persuaded we held our peace, saying: The Lord's will be done.

After these days we made our preparations and went up to Jerusalem; and some of the disciples from Caesarea went with us and took us where we could be the guests of a certain Mnason of Cyprus, a disciple of long standing, and when we arrived in Jerusalem the brothers welcomed us gladly. On the next day Paul went with us to the house of James, and all the elders were there. And Paul greeted them and recounted to them one by one all the things that God had made happen among the Gentiles through his ministry. When they heard, they glorified God; but they said to Paul: You can see, brother, how many tens of thousands there are among the Jews who have come to believe; and all of them are zealots for the law. And they have been told concerning you that you are teaching all the Jews who live among the Gentiles to turn away from Moses, telling them not to circumcise their children and not to follow his customs.

What to do, then? They will surely learn that you are here. So do as we tell you, thus. There are four men among us who have taken a vow, of their own free will. Take them along with you and be purified along with them, and pay their expenses so that they can shave their heads; and all will realize that what they were told about you is not true, but you also hold to serving the law. Concerning the Gentiles who have come to believe, we have sent word decreeing that they must keep themselves from idol offerings, and blood, and what has been strangled, and lechery.

Then on the next day Paul took the men with him, and was purified along with them and entered the temple, giving notice of the time when the days of purification would be completed, at which time the offering should be made for each one of them. But when the seven days were about to be completed, the Jews from Asia, who had seen him in the temple, stirred up the whole populace, and they laid hands on him, shouting: Men of Jerusalem, help us. This is the man who teaches all men everywhere, going against the people and the law and this place; and now he has even brought Greeks into the temple and profaned this holy place. For they had previously seen Trophimus of Ephesus with him in the city, and they thought Paul had brought him into the temple. The whole city was aroused, and the people made a rush and seized Paul and dragged him out of the temple; and immediately the doors were shut. And as they were demanding his death, word got to the tribune of the Roman cohort that all Jerusalem was rioting; and he, taking with him his soldiers and their centurions, ran at once to where they were, and when they saw the tribune and the soldiers they stopped beating Paul. Then the tribune went to Paul and seized him and ordered him to be bound with double chains, and asked who he was and what he had done. Some in the crowd said one thing and some said another. And when the tribune could not find out for sure because of the uproar, he ordered him to be taken into the barracks. But when he got to the steps, he had to be carried by the soldiers, because of the violence of the mob, for most of the population followed him crying: Kill him.

When he was about to be taken into the barracks, Paul said to the tribune: May I say something to you? He said: You know Greek? Then you are not that Egyptian who started a riot some days ago and went off into the desert with four thousand of the assassins? Paul said: I am a Jew, from Tarsus in Cilicia, a citizen of no insignificant city; and I request of you, give me leave to speak to the people. When he gave him leave, Paul stood on the steps and motioned with his hand to the people; and when there was mostly silence, he spoke to them in Hebrew, saying:

¶ Brothers, fathers, listen to the defense I make before you now. And when they heard him speaking to them in Hebrew they were the more quiet. And he said: I am a Jew, born in Tarsus in Cilicia, and brought up in this city at the feet of Gamaliel, instructed in the strict style of the law of our fathers, and I was a zealot for God as all of you are today. I persecuted this Way to the death, binding men and women and delivering them to the prisons, as the high priest and the entire council of elders will testify. From them I received letters to the brothers in Damascus and I was on my way to bring those who were there in bonds to Jerusalem to be punished. And it befell me that as I was on my way and approaching Damascus, about noon, a great light from the sky suddenly flashed about me, and I fell to the ground and I heard a voice saying: Saul, Saul, why do you persecute me? And I answered: Who are you, Lord? And he said to me: I am Jesus of Nazareth; whom you persecute. And the men

who were with me saw the light but they did not hear
the voice which spoke to me. And I said: What shall I
do, Lord? And the Lord said to me: Rise up and go on to
Damascus, and there you will be told about all the things
that you have been appointed to do.

But since from the glory of that light I could not see, I
came to Damascus with my companions leading me by
the hand. Then a certain Ananias, a man devout in the
law and well spoken of by all the Jews who live in Damascus, came and stood over me and said: Brother Saul,
regain your sight; and in that moment I saw him. And
he said: The God of our fathers has chosen you to learn
his will, and to see the Just One and to hear the voice
from his mouth; because you will be his witness, to all
men, of what you have seen and heard. And now, why
delay? Rise up and be baptized and wash away your sins,
calling upon his name.

Then it befell me that when I returned to Jerusalem
and was praying in the temple I fell into a trance, and I
saw him and he was saying to me: Make haste and go
from Jerusalem quickly, because they will not accept your
testimony concerning me. And I said: Lord, they themselves know that I kept imprisoning and flogging those
in one synagogue after another who believed in you; and
when the blood of Stephen your martyr was shed, I myself was standing by and approving and keeping the coats
of the men who were killing him. But he said to me: Go,
because I shall send you far from here, among the Gentiles.

They had been listening to him up until this word, but
then they cried aloud, saying: Rid the earth of him; such
a man has no right to live. And as they clamored and
threw off their coats and raised a cloud of dust in the air

the tribune ordered him to be taken into the barracks, telling them to whip him so as to get it out of him and find out why they cried out so against him. But when they stretched him out for the lashes, Paul said to the centurion who stood by: Are you permitted to whip a Roman citizen, and that without a trial? When the centurion heard this, he went and told it to the tribune, saying: What do you mean to do? This man is a Roman citizen. The tribune went to him and said: Tell me, are you a Roman citizen? He said: Yes. The tribune said: I paid a great deal to get this citizenship. Paul said: I was born to it. Then those who had been going to interrogate him immediately withdrew from him; and the tribune was frightened, realizing that he was a Roman, and that he had put him in chains.

The next day, wishing to find out precisely what he was accused of by the Jews, he released him, and ordered the high priests and the entire council to assemble, and then brought Paul in and set him before them.

¶ Paul looked hard at the council and said: Men and brothers, I have been God's citizen in full good conscience down to this very day. Then the high priest Ananias ordered the men who stood beside him to strike him on the mouth. Then Paul said to him: God will strike you, you whitewashed wall. And do you sit there and judge me according to the law while you unlawfully order me to be struck? The men who stood beside him said: Do you revile the high priest of God? Paul said: I did not know, brothers, that he was the high priest; for it is written: You shall not insult the leader of the people.

Then Paul, knowing that one part of them was Sadducees and the other Pharisees, cried aloud in the council: Men and brothers, I am a Pharisee, the son of Pharisees; I am being tried for my hope for the resurrection of the dead. When he said this, there was strife between the Pharisees and the Sadducees, and the assembly was split in two. For the Sadducees say that there is no resurrection, and neither angel nor spirit, but the Pharisees believe in both of these. And there was a great uproar, and some of the scribes of the Pharisaean sect rose up and dissented, saying: We find no evil in this man. It may be that a spirit has spoken to him, or an angel. And as the quarrel grew violent, the tribune, fearing that Paul might be torn to pieces by them, ordered his soldiers to go down and snatch him out of their midst and take him into the barracks.

On the following night the Lord stood over him and said: Take heart; for as you testified concerning me in Jerusalem, so you must also testify in Rome.

When day came, the Jews formed a gang and bound themselves by oath neither to eat nor drink until they had killed Paul. There were more than forty men in this conspiracy; and these went to the high priests and elders and said: We have bound ourselves by oath to taste nothing until we kill Paul. Do you now explain to the tribune, along with the council, that he should bring the man before you, since you wish to learn more accurately about him; and we are ready to kill him before he gets to you.

But the son of Paul's sister heard of the ambush, and he went to the barracks and got in and reported it to Paul. Paul called over one of the centurions and said: Take this young man to the tribune, since he has something to report to him. So the centurion took him to the tribune and said: The prisoner Paul called me over and asked me to bring this young man to you; he has something to tell you. The tribune took him by the hand and led him to a place apart and asked him: What is this you have to tell me? He said: The Jews have decided to ask you to bring Paul before the council tomorrow, as if for the purpose of learning more accurately about him. But do not do as they say; for more than forty of them are lying in wait for him, and they have bound themselves by oath neither to eat nor drink until they kill him; and now they are ready and waiting for the word from you.

The tribune let the young man go, saying to him: Do not tell anyone that you gave me this information. Then he called in two of his centurions and said: Have two hundred infantrymen, and seventy horsemen, and two hundred light troops ready to start for Caesarea at the third hour of the night; and have horses for Paul to ride, and get him safely to Felix, the governor. And he wrote a letter which read as follows: Claudius Lysias to Felix the most mighty governor, greetings. When this man had been seized by the Jews and was on the point of being killed by them, I went with an armed force and rescued him, having learned that he is a Roman citizen, and I brought him before their council, wishing to learn what was their case against him. And I found that he was accused because of questions concerning their law, but not on any charge that would deserve death or imprisonment. And being informed of a plot against the man I immediately sent him to you, having also ordered his accusers to charge him in your presence.

So the soldiers, as ordered, took Paul by night and brought him to Antipatris; and the next day, leaving the horsemen to go on with him, they returned to the barracks. And the cavalry went on to Caesarea and delivered the letter to the governor and also brought Paul to him. When he had read it, and asked from what province he came and learned that he was from Cilicia, he said: I will hear you when your accusers are also here. And he ordered him held in the residence of Herod.

¶ After five days the high priest Ananias came down from Jerusalem with some of the elders and a certain orator, Tertullus, and they brought a charge against Paul before the governor. And when Paul had been summoned, Tertullus began to accuse him, saying: We have had much peace because of you, and reforms of every kind have come from everywhere in this country through your forethought, which, most mighty Felix, we acknowledge in all gratitude. But, not to weary you, I beg you in your graciousness to give us a brief hearing. For we have found this man to be a plague, one who stirs up dissensions among all the Jews in the empire, and the ringleader of the heretical sect of Nazarenes. He even tried to profane the temple. We seized him, and wanted to try him by our own law, but the tribune Lysias came and forcibly took him out of our hands and said that his accusers must go to you. You yourself will be able to learn by questioning him about all that we accuse him of. And the Jews joined in the attack, saying that this was true.

Then Paul answered, when the governor nodded his permission to speak: Knowing that for many years you have been judge over this nation, I will speak in my own defense with a good will; since you can verify that it is not more than twelve days since I went up to Jerusalem to worship, and they have not found me talking to anyone or attracting a mob either in the temple or the synagogues or about the city; nor are they able to prove any of the things of which they now accuse me. But I do admit this to you, that the Way which they call heresy is the Way in which I serve the God of our fathers (for I believe all that is written in the law and the prophets) with hope in God, a hope these men also share, that there will soon be a resurrection of the just and the unjust. In this matter I myself make it my study to have a clear conscience before God and man throughout.

Now, after a number of years, I went to Jerusalem to effect some charities for my people and to bring offerings; during which they found me in the temple after my purification, but not with any crowd or causing disturbance. But there are some Jews from Asia, who ought to be here before you and accusing me, if they have anything against me; or else let these men say what wrongdoing they found in me when I stood before the council other than that one cry that I uttered when I stood among them: I am being judged by you today over the resurrection of the dead.

Then Felix, who knew a great deal about the Way, put them off, saying: When the tribune Lysias comes here I will decide your case. And he ordered the centurion to have him kept under guard, but to give him some freedom, and not to prevent any of his own people from ministering to him.

And after a few days, Felix came with Drusilla, his own wife, who was Jewish, and sent for Paul, and heard him tell about belief in Christ Jesus. But when Paul discoursed about righteousness and continence and the judgment to come, Felix was frightened and said: For the present, go, but I will send for you again when I find another occasion. Also, he was hoping to be given money by Paul, for which reason he sent for him and talked with him the more frequently.

After a full two years, Felix was succeeded by Porcius Festus; and wishing to store up some favor with the Jews, Felix left Paul still a prisoner.

¶ Three days after setting foot in his province Festus went up from Caesarea to Jerusalem; and the high priests and the foremost men of the Jews brought charges against Paul; and they urged Festus, asking to be favored against Paul, to have him transferred to Jerusalem. They were planning to lie in wait for him and kill him on the way. But Festus answered that Paul was being held in Caesarea, and that he himself was about to leave for there very soon. So, he said, let your chief men come down with me, and if there is anything wrong about the man, charge him with it.

Then, after spending no more than eight or ten days among them, he went down to Caesarea; and the next day he sat in the tribunal and ordered Paul brought in. When he arrived the Jews who had come down from Jerusalem surrounded him and brought many serious charges against him, which they could not prove; since Paul said in his defense: I have not sinned in any way against the law of the Jews, nor against the temple, nor against Caesar.

But Festus, wishing to store up some favor with the Jews, answered and said to Paul: Are you willing to go up to Jerusalem and there be tried on these charges, before me? But Paul said: I have taken my stand at the tribunal of Caesar, and there I must be tried. I have done the Jews no wrong, as you yourself know quite well. If I

am guilty and have done something that deserves death,
I do not protest against dying; but if there is nothing in
what they charge against me, no one can give me to them
as a favor. I appeal to Caesar. Then Festus, after talking
with the council, answered: You have appealed to Caesar; to Caesar you shall go.

After a few days had gone by, King Agrippa and Bernice visited Caesarea to welcome Festus. And as they spent
some days there, Festus referred Paul's case to the King,
saying: There is a man whom Felix left behind as a prisoner; and concerning him the high priests and the elders
of the Jews brought charges when I was in Jerusalem,
demanding his condemnation. To these I answered that
it is not the Roman way to hand any man over as a favor; not until the accused has his accusers before his face
and is given some chance to defend himself against the
accusation. So when they assembled here I made no delay but the next day I sat in the tribunal and ordered the
man brought in. When his accusers stood up they did not
accuse him of any of the evildoings I had expected, but
they had against him only some questions concerning
their own religiosity, and concerning one Jesus; who is
dead but who, as Paul says, is alive. Not knowing what
to do about investigating these matters, I asked him if
he would be willing to go to Jerusalem and there be tried
on these charges. But Paul appealed to be held for the
attention of Augustus; so I ordered him held until I
can send him to Caesar. Agrippa said to Festus: I would
like to hear the man myself. Tomorrow, said Festus, you
shall hear him.

So on the next day Agrippa arrived, and Bernice, with
much circumstance, and they entered the audience room
along with the tribunes and the men of prominence in

the city; and at the command of Festus, Paul was brought in. And Festus said: King Agrippa, and all you gentlemen who are here with us, you are looking at the man for whose sake the whole population of the Jews has been after me, both in Jerusalem and here, crying that he should not go on living. I myself judged that he had done nothing to deserve death; but since he himself appealed to Augustus, I decided to send him. But I have nothing definite to write to our master about him; which is why I have brought him before all of you, and above all before you, King Agrippa, so that when he has been questioned I can have something to write; for it seems absurd to me to send a prisoner without indicating the charges against him.

¶ Then Agrippa said to Paul: You have leave to speak for yourself. Then Paul extended his hand and began his defense, saying: I count myself most fortunate, King Agrippa, that I am to defend myself against the charges of the Jews in your presence today; for I know that you are supremely well informed in all the customs and questions which are the concern of the Jews. Therefore I beg you to listen to me with patience.

All Jews know about my life, from youth onward, both in my own country and in Jerusalem, and they know from the past, if they will admit it, that I lived according to the strictest sect in our religion, as a Pharisee. And now I stand on trial for hope in that promise which was given by God to our fathers, that expectation which our twelve tribes hope to realize by serving strenuously night and day. It is for this hope, O King, that I am being accused by the Jews. If God wakens the dead, why is that accounted incredible by you Jews?

Now, I thought to myself that I had to do much to oppose the name of Jesus of Nazareth. And this I did in Jerusalem, and with authority granted me by the high priests I confined many of the saints in prison, and when they were killed I cast my vote for it, and in all the synagogues by frequent punishment I tried to force them to blaspheme; and in my immoderate rage against them I even pursued them into cities abroad.

One of these was Damascus, where I was on my way with authority and a commission from the high priests when in the middle of the day on the road I saw, O King, a light surpassing the brightness of the sun which flashed about me and my fellow travelers. And as all of us fell to the ground I heard a voice saying to me in Hebrew: Saul, Saul, why do you persecute me? It is hard for you to kick against the goads. And I said: Who are you, Lord? And the Lord said: I am Jesus, whom you persecute. But rise up and stand on your feet; since it was for this that I appeared to you, to choose you as my minister and my witness to the things which you have seen and to the times I shall be seen by you; choosing you out of my people and the Gentiles, to whom I shall send you, so as to open their eyes, to turn them from darkness to light and from the power of Satan to God; for them to receive remission of sins and a share among those who have been sanctified by their belief in me.

Therefore, King Agrippa, I have not disobeyed the heavenly vision, but to those in Damascus first and Jerusalem, to the whole land of Judaea, and to the Gentiles I have preached repentance and turning to God and the doing of acts to match their repentance. For these reasons the Jews seized me in the temple and tried to kill me. But having been given the help of God until this day, I stand here and testify to great and small, saying nothing but what the prophets and Moses said must be going to happen, that the Christ must suffer, that after the resurrection of the dead he will be the first to proclaim the light to his people and to the nations.

When he made this defense, Festus said in a great voice: Paul, you are mad. Too many books are driving you mad. But Paul said: No, I am not mad, most mighty Festus; my words are those of truth and good sense. The King, to whom I speak openly, knows about these matters; I think there is not one thing that has escaped him, for it was not done in a corner. Do you, King Agrippa, believe in the prophets? I know that you believe. Agrippa said to Paul: Soon you will persuade me to become a Christian. Paul said: Late or soon, I would pray to God that not only you but all who listen to me today would become like me—except for these chains.

Then the King and the governor and Bernice and those who had sat with them got up, and talked with each other as they went out, saying: This man is doing nothing to deserve death or imprisonment. And Agrippa said to Festus: This man could have gone free, if he had not appealed to Caesar.

¶ When it was decided that we should sail for Italy, they turned Paul and some other prisoners over to a centurion named Julius, from the Augustan cohort. We went aboard a ship of Adramyttium which was to sail to places in Asia, and put out to sea. Aristarchus, a Macedonian from Thessalonica, was with us. On the next day we put in at Sidon, and Julius, who treated Paul humanely, allowed him to visit his friends and receive some kindnesses from them. Then putting out from there, we sailed under the lee of Cyprus because the winds were against us, and crossing the open sea by Cilicia and Pamphylia we came to Myra in Lycia. There the centurion found an Alexandrian ship bound for Italy and put us aboard it. Then, sailing slowly for a number of days and barely getting to Cnidus, when the wind would let us go no farther, we sailed under the lee of Crete, by Salmone, and barely managed to coast along until we came to a place called Fair Haven, with the city of Laseia near by.

Since a good deal of time had been spent and sailing was now dangerous, with the Day of Atonement already past, Paul advised them, saying: I can see, gentlemen, that our sailing will be stormy, with much damage not only to the cargo and the ship but to our own lives. But the centurion trusted the steersman and the captain more than Paul's advice. Since the harbor was unsuitable for wintering, most were in favor of leaving there and, if they could somehow make Phoenix, a harbor of Crete which looks both northwest and southwest, they would spend the winter there. And with the south wind blowing gently they thought they had achieved their purpose and put out and coasted along Crete. But not much later the hurricane wind which is called the northeaster struck from the land, and the ship was caught up in it and could not face the wind, so we gave in to it and were swept along. Then, running under shelter of a little island named Cauda, we were barely able to recover the lifeboat, which they hoisted aboard, and then undergirded the ship with cables; and then, fearing that they might be driven on to the shoals of Syrtis, they let down the sea anchor and so were carried along. But we were battered by the storm, and on the second day they began to jettison, and on the third they threw the ship's gear overboard with their own hands. But when neither sun nor stars could be seen for a number of days, and we were being beset by a great storm, all hope that we would survive was finally lost.

And there had been no eating for a long time. Then Paul stood in their midst and said: You should, gentlemen, have paid attention to me and not put out from Crete and so got yourselves this battering and damage. But now I advise you to be of good courage, for there will be no loss of life from among you, only of the ship. For last night the angel of God, to whom I belong, whom I serve, stood by me and said: Have no fear, Paul. You must stand before Caesar. And behold, God has granted you the lives of all who sail with you. Therefore be of good courage, gentlemen; for I believe in God and that it will be as he has told me. But we must be driven upon some island.

And when it was our fourteenth day of being adrift on the Adriatic, in the middle of the night the sailors thought that some land was near. And they took soundings and found twenty fathom, and after a little interval they took soundings again and found fifteen; and fearing that we might be driven on rugged shores they dropped four anchors from the stern and prayed for day to break. But when the sailors tried to abandon the ship and were lowering the lifeboat into the sea, pretending that they were going to set out anchors from the prow, Paul said to the centurion and the solders: Unless these men stay on the ship, you cannot be saved. Then the soldiers cut the ropes on the lifeboat and let it drop.

Now Paul urged everyone to take some food before the coming dawn, saying: This is the fourteenth day that you have gone without food in your anxiety, tasting nothing; therefore I urge you to take some food, since this has to do with your safety. For not one hair from any of your heads shall be lost. And so saying, he took a loaf and gave thanks to God before them all and broke it and began to eat. Then all became cheerful and they also took some food. We were seventy-six souls in all on the ship. When they had eaten their fill they lightened the ship by throwing the grain into the sea.

When day came, they did not recognize the land, but they could see a bay, with a beach where they planned to get the ship safely ashore, if they could. So they cast off the anchors and let them go, and at the same time loosening the bands on the rudders and hoisting the foresail they went before the wind toward the shore. But they struck upon a shoal surrounded by water and ran the ship aground, and the prow stuck and remained fixed, but the stern began to break up in the surf. There was a plan among the soldiers to kill the prisoners, to keep any from swimming away and escaping; but the centurion wished to keep Paul alive and prevented them from that purpose; and he ordered those who could swim to plunge in first and get to shore, and the rest to use boards or anything else from the ship. And so it came about that all got safe to shore.

¶ After our escape we learned that the island is called Malta. And the natives showed us no ordinary kindness, for they lit a fire and brought us all to it, because of the rain which had set in and the cold. And Paul had gathered a load of brushwood and laid it on the fire when a viper came out to escape the heat and fastened on his hand. And when the natives saw the creature dangling from his hand they said to each other: This man is surely a murderer; he was saved from the sea but justice would

not let him live. But he shook off the creature into the
fire and suffered no hurt; while they waited for him to
begin to swell up or suddenly drop dead. But when they
waited a long time and saw nothing extraordinary happening to him, they changed their minds and said that
he was a god.

In the neighborhood of this place were the estates of
the chief man of the island, Publius by name, who invited us in and entertained us hospitably for three days.
It happened that the father of Publius was lying sick with
a fever and dysentery, and Paul went in to him and prayed
and laid his hands upon him and healed him. When that
happened the other people on the island who had sicknesses came to him and were treated; and they honored
us with many honors, and when we sailed away they
gave us all that we needed.

After three months we sailed aboard an Alexandrian
ship which had wintered at the island. It carried the in-
signia of Castor and Pollux. And we went to Syracuse
and stayed there three days, and removing from there
proceeded to Rhegium. And after one day, with the arrival of a south wind, we reached Puteoli on the second
day. There we found brothers, and were invited to stay
with them for seven days. And so we went to Rome. And
from Rome the brothers, who had heard about us, came
out to meet us as far as the Appian Forum, and the Three
Taverns; and when he saw them Paul gave thanks to God,
and took courage.

When we entered Rome, Paul was permitted to stay
by himself, with the soldier who was guarding him.

It happened that after three days he called together
those who were the chief men among the Jews; and when
they were gathered together he said to them: Men and

brothers, though I had done nothing against our people
or contrary to the laws of our fathers, I was turned over
as a prisoner from Jerusalem into the hands of the Romans; who after interrogating me wanted to set me free
because there was nothing in my case that deserved
death. But when the Jews objected I was forced to appeal
to Caesar, though not as one who had any charge to bring
against my own people. For this reason I have invited
you, to see you and to talk with you; because it is on
account of the hope of Israel that I wear these chains.
They said to him: We have received no letters about you
from Judaea, nor has any of the brothers arrived and reported or spoken any evil of you. But we desire to hear
from you what you think; for concerning this sect, it is
known to us that people everywhere speak against it.

Then they agreed on a day with him and came to him
at his lodgings in greater numbers, and he lectured to
them from dawn until evening, testifying to the Kingdom of God and trying to persuade them about Jesus from
the law of Moses and the prophets. And some were persuaded by what was said, and others would not believe;
and they broke up, at variance with each other, as Paul
said one thing to them: Well did the Holy Spirit speak
through the prophet Isaiah to your fathers, saying: Go to
this people and say: With your hearing you shall hear
and not understand, and you shall use your sight and look
but not see. For the heart of this people is stiffened, and
they hear with difficulty, and they have closed their eyes;
so that they may never see with their eyes, or hear with
their ears, and with their hearts understand and turn
back, so that I can heal them.

Let it be known to you that this salvation of God was
sent forth to the Gentiles; and they will listen.

He remained a full two years, in his own rented place, and he received all who came to him, preaching the Kingdom of God and teaching about the Lord Jesus Christ, quite openly, without any interference.

LETTERS

The Letter
to the Romans

¶PAUL, THE SLAVE OF JESUS CHRIST, called to be an apostle, set apart for the gospel of God which God proclaimed through his prophets in the holy scriptures concerning his son, who was born, in the way of the flesh, from the seed of David; but who is declared to be the son of God in power, which is according to the spirit of sanctity, by his resurrection from the dead; Jesus Christ our Lord, from whom we have received grace, and the rank of apostle to make the faith obeyed among all the nations for the sake of his name; among which nations you also are called by Jesus Christ; to all who in Rome are the beloved of God, chosen saints: grace to you and peace from God our Father and our Lord Jesus Christ.

First I thank my God through Jesus Christ concerning all of you, that your faith is proclaimed through all the world. For God, whom I serve in my spirit in the gospel of his son, is my witness how constantly I make mention of you always in my prayers, asking if somehow at last I may be guided by the will of God to come to you. For I long to see you, so that I may impart to you some spiritual gift for your strengthening, that is, for you to be comforted among yourselves through our faith in each

[329]

other, yours and mine. I do not wish you not to realize, brothers, that I have often proposed to come to you (but I have been prevented until now), so that I may make some harvesting among you as among the rest of the nations. To Greeks and Barbarians, wise and unwise, I am indebted; thus for my part I am eager to bring the gospel to you in Rome also. For I am not ashamed of the gospel, for it is the power of God for the salvation of everyone who believes, Jew and Greek; since the justice of God is revealed in it from faith to faith, as it is written: The righteous man shall live by faith.

For from heaven is revealed the anger of God against all the impiety and unrighteousness of people who in their unrighteousness suppress the truth; since what can be known about God is plain to them because God made it plain to them. Since the creation of the world, what is his and invisible, his eternal power and divinity, has been perceived by the mind through what he has made, so that they have no excuse; because, while knowing God, they did not glorify or thank him as God, but they were beguiled in their reasonings and their uncomprehending hearts were made dark. They thought that they were wise but they were fools, and they gave up the glory of imperishable God in exchange for the likeness of an image, of perishable man, or of creatures that fly and walk on all fours and crawl.

Therefore God gave them up in the lusts of their hearts to immorality, to the disgracing of their own bodies among themselves. They exchanged the truth of God for falsehood, and they worshipped and served the creature rather than the Creator, who is to be praised forevermore. Amen. Because of this God delivered them over to disgraceful passions. For their females changed their natural relations into what is against nature; and so likewise the males, forsaking the natural intercourse with the female, were inflamed with desire for each other, males for males, acting shamefully and receiving the retribution due them for their misguided ways. And as they did not see fit to keep God in mind, so God delivered them over to a state of mind that was unworthy, and to unbecoming conduct; being filled with every wrong, wickedness, greed, badness; stuffed with envy bloodthirstiness contentiousness treachery malignity; whisperers gossips god haters violent proud pretentious; devisers of evil, disobedient to parents; mindless faithless loveless pitiless; who though they knew well about the verdict of God, that those who do such things deserve death, nevertheless not only do them but encourage others who do.

¶ Thus you, whoever you are, who are human, and judge, have no defense. In judging another you convict yourself, for you who judge do the same thing; but we know that the judgment of God is truly against those who do such things. Then you, who are human, and judge those who do such things while you do them yourself, do you count on escaping the judgment of God? Or do you misunderstand the wealth of his goodness and forbearance and patience, not realizing that the goodness of God means to lead you to repentance? Through your hardness and your unrepentant heart you are storing up for yourself anger on the day of anger and the revelation of the righteous judgment of God, who will give to each according to his actions: to those who, through steadfastness in doing good, strive for glory and honor and incorruptibility, he will give everlasting life; but for those who out of contentiousness are disobedient to the truth but obey unrighteousness there shall be rage and anger, affliction and anguish for every soul of a man who does evil, Jew first, but also Greek; but glory and honor and peace for everyone who does good, Jew first, but also Greek, for there is no discrimination with God.

For those who sinned outside the law will also perish outside the law: and those who sinned while within the law will be judged according to the law. For it is not those who listen to the law who are righteous in the sight of God, but it is those who do what is in the law who will be justified. For when Gentiles who do not have the law do by nature what is in the law, they, without having the law, are their own law; and they display the work of the law engraved on their hearts; with their conscience bearing them witness, as their arguments attack or defend each other, on that day when God will judge the secrets of men, as it is said in my gospel, through Jesus Christ.

But if you call yourself a Jew, and rely on the law, and glory in God and know his will, and pass judgment on what is important, being educated in the law; and are confident that you are the guide of the blind, light for those in the dark, instructor of the ignorant, teacher of the simple, possessing, in the law, the shape of knowledge and truth; do you then, who teach someone else, not teach yourself? You who preach no stealing, do you steal? You, who forbid adultery, do you commit it? And you, who loathe idols, do you steal from temples? Do you, who glory in the law, dishonor God by breaking the law? Because, as it is written, the name of God is ill spoken of among the Gentiles, because of you.

Circumcision is helpful if you do obey the law, but if you transgress the law, your circumcision becomes uncircumcision. If, then, the uncircumcised man keeps the requirements of the law, shall not that uncircumcision be counted as circumcision? And the uncircumcised, who by nature fulfill the law, shall judge you who have the circumcision and the letter of the law, but break it. For one is not a Jew by what can be seen, nor is circumcision in what can be seen in the flesh; but one is a Jew in what cannot be seen, and circumcision is a thing of the heart, in the spirit, not in the letter, for one whose approval comes not from men but from God.

¶ What then is the Jew's advantage, and what is the use of circumcision? Great, in every way. In the first place, to them were entrusted the oracles of God. But what then? If some were unfaithful, will not their unfaithfulness make void the good faith of God? Never! God must be truthful and every man a liar, as it is written: So that you may be justified in your words and triumph when you are brought to judgment. But if our unrighteousness demonstrates the righteousness of God, what are we to say? Can God be unfair in visiting his anger? (I speak in human terms.) Never: since then how shall God judge the world? But if, through my falseness, God's truthfulness redounds to his glory, why am I condemned as a sinner? Am I not what my detractors call me, when certain people say that I say: Let us do evil so that good may come of it? Their condemnation is just.

What then? Are we Jews better? Not altogether, for we have already charged all Jews and Greeks with being subject to sin, as it is written: There is not one righteous man, not one, there is not one who understands, not one who seeks out God. They have all gone off the course, and with that they have become useless; there is none who practices honesty, there is not so much as one. Their throat is an open grave, with their tongues they are deceitful; the poison of asps is on their lips, their mouth is full of cursing and bitterness. Their feet are swift toward bloodshed. Ruin and wretchedness are in their ways, and they have not learned the way of peace. Their eyes know no fear of God.

We know that the law says what it says to those who are within the law, so that every mouth may be stopped and all the world be subject to the judgment of God; because it is not from the works of the law that all flesh will be justified in his presence, since through the law comes consciousness of sin. But now the righteousness of God has been made evident apart from the law. It was testified to by the law and the prophets, but the righteousness of God is through belief in Jesus Christ; for all who believe, for there is no distinction. For all sinned and come short of the glory of God, but are justified by the gift of his grace through their redemption by Christ Jesus, whom God put forward for propitiation through faith in his blood, for the demonstration of his righteousness by the forgiveness of sins committed before, through the indulgence of God; for the demonstration of his righteousness in the present time, that he is righteous himself and justifies one who believes in Jesus.

Where then is the exultation? It is excluded. By what law? The law of actions? No, but by the law of faith. For we hold that a man is justified through faith without the actions of the law. Is God the God of the Jews alone? Not of the Gentiles also? Yes, of the Gentiles also, since God is one, and he will justify the circumcised from faith and the uncircumcised through faith. Are we then making the law void through faith? Never. We are confirming the law.

¶ What then shall we say of Abraham, our forefather in the way of the flesh? If Abraham was justified because of his actions, he has reason for glorying; but not before God, since what does the scripture say? Abraham believed God, and it was counted as righteousness in him. For one who does something, repayment is counted not as grace but as his due; but for one who does nothing, but believes in him who justifies the impious man, his faith is counted as righteousness. So David also says of the blessedness of the man whom God counts as righteous, apart from his actions: Blessed are they whose lawless acts have been forgiven and whose sins have been hidden away. Blessed is the man whose sin the Lord does not count.

Now, is this blessedness for the circumcised or also for the uncircumcised? Since we say the faith of Abraham was counted as righteousness. How then was it counted? In his circumcised or uncircumcised state? It was when he was not yet circumcised, but still uncircumcised. And he received the mark of circumcision, the seal upon the righteousness of that faith he had when he was still uncircumcised; to be the father of all those who are believers through their uncircumcised state so that righteousness could be counted for them, and also to be the father of the circumcised for those who not only have been circumcised but also walk in his footsteps through the faith, which our father Abraham had when he was still uncircumcised. For the promise to Abraham, or his seed, that he should be the inheritor of the world, was not on account of the law, but of the righteousness of his faith. For if the inheritors are those who belong to the law, then the faith is made void and the promise is gone; for the law causes anger, but where there is no law there is no lawbreaking.

Thus (it is) because of faith, and thus by grace, that the promise should hold good for all his seed; not only for him who has the law but for him who has the faith of Abraham. He is the father of us all, as it is written: I have made you the father of many nations. It held good in the sight of God, in whom he believed, the God who puts life into the dead and summons into existence the things that do not exist. He against hope believed in the hope that he would become the father of many nations according to what had been said, that is: Thus shall your seed be. And Abraham, without weakening in his faith, knew that his own body was that of a dead man, since he was about a hundred years old, and he knew the dead state of Sarah's womb, but he was not distracted with unbelief in God's promise but was strengthened in his belief, giving glory to God and assured that God was able to do as he had promised.

Thus it was that faith counted as righteousness in him. But it was not written for him alone that it was so counted for him, but also for us for whom it is to be counted, for us who believe in him who raised from the dead Jesus our Lord, who was betrayed for our sins and raised up again for our justification.

¶ Justified therefore through faith, let us keep peace with God through our Lord Jesus Christ, through whom we have got by faith access to that grace in which we stand, and let us exult in the hope of the glory of God. Not only that, let us even exult in afflictions, knowing that affliction causes endurance, and endurance quality, and quality, hope, and hope does not disappoint us. Because God's love is diffused in our hearts through the Holy Spirit who was given to us; if indeed when we were sick Christ died in time for the sake of us, who were sinful. Indeed, one will scarcely die for a righteous man. Perhaps one does even dare to die for a good man. But God shows his love for us; because it was when we were still sinners that Christ died for us. All the more then, being justified now by his blood, shall we be saved from the anger to come. For if when we were enemies we were reconciled through the death of his son, all the more, now reconciled, shall we be saved by his life; not only that, but exulting in God through our Lord Jesus Christ, through whom we have now got this reconciliation.

Therefore, just as sin came into the world through one man, and through sin, death, so also death went about among all men, because all sinned. Before there was the law there was sin in the world, but when there was no law it was not reckoned as sin. But death was king from Adam until Moses, even over those who did not sin after the example of the transgression of Adam, who is the type of what was to come.

But the gift of grace is not like the transgression; for if by the transgression of one many died, far more has been the abundance, for the many, of the grace of God and his gift in the grace of one man, Jesus Christ. And the gift is not as when one man sinned; for the judgment from one leads to condemnation, but the gift of grace, after many transgressions, leads to justification. For if by the transgression of one man death was king because of the one, so all the more shall they be kings in life, who have received the abundance of grace and righteousness, through one, Jesus Christ.

So then, just as one blunder meant condemnation for all men, so also one righteous act shall mean the vindication of life for all men; for just as through the disobedience of the one man the many were made sinful, so also through the obedience of the one man the many shall be made righteous. The law came in to increase the transgression; but where the sin has increased, grace has increased even more, so that just as sin was king in death, so also grace shall be king through righteousness for life everlasting, because of Jesus Christ our Lord.

¶ What then shall we say? Shall we persist in our sin, so that the grace may be multiplied? Never. How shall we, who died to sin, still live in it? Or do you not know that we, who were baptized for Christ, were baptized for his death? So we were buried with him through the baptism for death; so that, as Christ was raised from the dead through the glory of his father, so we too may walk in a renewal of life. For if we were united with him in the same kind of death, so shall we share his resurrection; knowing that the old person who was in us was crucified with him, so the body of our sin might be destroyed, and we shall no longer be the slaves of sin, since one who has died is absolved of sin. But if we died with Christ, we believe that we shall also live with him, knowing that Christ, raised from the dead, dies no more, for death no longer has lordship over him. When he died, he died to sin, once for all; but when he lives, he lives for God. Thus do you also count yourselves as dead for sin, but living for God, in Jesus Christ.

Do not then let sin be king in your mortal body so that

you obey its desires, and do not give your limbs to sin as the weapons of wrongdoing, but give yourselves to God, as living people who have been dead, and give your limbs to God as the weapons of righteousness. For sin will have no lordship over you, for you are subject not to law but to grace.

What then? Shall we sin because we are subject not to the law but to grace? Never. Do you not know that when you give yourselves as slaves to someone, to obey him, you are the slaves of him whom you obey, either of sin, for death, or of obedience, for righteousness? Thanks be to God, though you were the slaves of sin, you obeyed from the heart that form of teaching which had been made traditional for you; and when set free from sin you were enslaved to righteousness. I speak in human terms because of the weakness of your flesh. For as you gave your bodies over as slaves to debauchery and lawlessness, so now give over your bodies as slaves to righteousness, to be sanctified. For when you were the slaves of sin, you were free for righteousness. What was then the harvest you reaped from those acts of which you are now ashamed? Their end is death. But now, set free from sin and enslaved to God, you have your harvest, to be sanctified, and the end is life everlasting. For the stipend of sin is death, but God's gift of grace is life everlasting through Christ Jesus our Lord.

¶ Are you not aware, brothers—I am speaking to those who know the law—that the law has power over a person only as long as he is alive? Thus a married woman is bound by the law to her husband while he is alive; but if her husband dies, she is set free from the law of her husband. So while her husband lives she will be called an adulteress if she goes to another man; but if her husband dies, she is free from the law, so that she is not an adulteress if she goes to another man. Thus, my brothers, you also have died for the law through the body of the Christ, to belong to another, to him who was raised from the dead so that we may bear harvest to God. For when we were in the flesh, the passions of our sins, because of the law, worked in our bodies to make us bear harvest to death. But now, by dying, we have been set free from the law, to which we had been subjected, so as to be slaves, in a new way, of the Spirit, and not, in the old way, of the letter.

What then shall we say? That the law is sin? Never. But I never would have known sin except through the law, for I never would have known desire if the law had not said: You shall not desire what is not yours. But it was by getting a starting point through the commandment that sin caused every kind of desire in me, since without the law sin is a dead thing. I once did live without the law; but when the commandment came the sin came to life, and I died, and my commandment for life was found to be for my death. So it was by getting a starting point through the commandment that sin distracted me and, through the commandment, killed me.

Thus the law is holy, and the commandment is holy and just and good. Then was this good thing death for me? Never. But it was sin, so that sin might be shown, through the good, to be accomplishing my death; so that sin might be surpassingly sinful, because of the commandment. For we know that the law is spiritual; but I am carnal, sold into subjection to sin. I do not know what I am doing. I do not do what I want, but what I hate;

that is what I do. But if what I do is what I do not want,
I agree that the law is good. But now it is no longer I
who do this but the sin that lives in me. For I know that
good does not live in me, not, that is, in my flesh; for it
is in my power to wish for the good, but not to do good.
I do not do the good that I want, but the bad that I do
not want. That is what I do. But if I do what I do not
want, it is no longer I who do it but the sin that lives in
me.

I find that the law, for me, who wish to do good, comes
as an evil. I rejoice, in my inner person, in the law of
God, but I see another law in my body arrayed for battle
against the law of my mind, and it takes me captive by
means of the law of sin which is in my body. I am a
wretched human being. Who will rescue me from this
body which belongs to death? Thanks be to God, it will
be through Jesus Christ our Lord. I myself am slave by
the mind to the law of God, but slave by the flesh to the
law of sin.

¶ Thus there is no condemnation for those who are in
Christ Jesus; for the law of the Spirit of life in Christ
Jesus set you free from the law of sin and death. God did
what the law could not do, because it was weakened by
the flesh; he sent his own son in the likeness of the sinful flesh, and found sin in the flesh guilty of sin; so that
the requirements of the law might be fulfilled in us who
walk not in the way of the flesh but in the way of the
Spirit. For those who are in the flesh think the thoughts
of the flesh, but those who are in the spirit think the
thoughts of the Spirit. The thinking of the flesh is death,
but the thinking of the Spirit is life and peace; because

the thinking of the flesh is hostility against God, since it is not obedient to the law of God, for it cannot be. Those who are in the flesh cannot please God.

But you are not in the flesh but in the Spirit if the Spirit of God lives in you. One who does not have the Spirit of Christ is not his. But if Christ is in you, your body is a dead thing, because of sin, but your spirit is life, because of righteousness. But if the Spirit of him who raised Jesus from the dead lives in you, then he who raised Christ Jesus from the dead will make your mortal bodies live through his Spirit that dwells in you.

So then, brothers, we are under obligation, but not to the flesh to live according to the flesh, since if you live according to the flesh you will die; but if by spirit you make the activities of the body die, you will live. For all who are led by the Spirit of God are the sons of God. You did not receive the spirit of slavery, to be afraid again, but you received the spirit of adoption as sons, in which we cry aloud: Abba, Father! This spirit bears witness to our spirit, that we are the children of God. If we are children, we are also heirs: heirs of God, co-heirs with Christ, if we are suffering with him so that we may be glorified with him.

I reason that the sufferings of the present time are not comparable to the glory that is going to be revealed to us. For the expectation of the world awaits the revelation of the sons of God. For the world is subjected to vanity not because it wishes to be but because of him who subjected it; but there is hope, because this world will be set free from slavery to decay into the freedom of the glory of the children of God. For we know that the whole world groans and is in labor together, until now; not only that, but even we who have some foretaste of the Spirit also groan within ourselves as we await adoption and the redemption of the body. It was by hope that we were saved; but hope that sees is not hope, since who hopes for what he sees? But if we hope for what we do not see, we await it steadfastly.

So also the Spirit takes a hand to help our weakness. We do not know what we should rightly pray for, but the Spirit itself intercedes for us with inarticulate groans, and he who scrutinizes our hearts knows the will of the Spirit, that by the will of God it intercedes for the saints. We know that God helps make everything good for those who love God, those who are summoned by preference. Those whom he foreknew, he foreordained to share the likeness of his son so that that son should be the first-born among many brothers; and those whom he foreordained, he also summoned; and those whom he summoned, he also justified; and those whom he justified, he also glorified.

What then shall we say to that? If God is for us, who is against us? For he did not spare his own son, but sacrificed him for the sake of us all. How, with his help, will not every grace be given us? Who will speak against the chosen of God? It is God who justifies us. Who will condemn us? It is Christ who died, or rather was raised from the dead, who is on the right hand of God, it is he who intercedes for us. Who will take us away from the love of the Christ? Will it be affliction or distress or persecution or starvation or nakedness or peril or the sword? It is written: For your sake we are killed all day long, we are counted like sheep for the slaughter. But in all this we are more than winners because of him who loves us. For I believe that neither death nor life; neither angels nor authorities; neither things that are nor things to come; not powers, nor height nor depth nor any other state of the world will be able to take us away from the love of God which is in Christ Jesus our Lord.

¶ I am speaking the truth, in Christ, I am not lying, and my conscience in the Holy Spirit bears me witness: there is great sorrow and incessant pain in my heart. I could have wished to be outcast from the Christ myself for the sake of my brothers, who are my blood kindred. They are Israelites. Theirs is the adoption and the glory, theirs the covenants and the giving of the law and the service and the promises. From them are the fathers, from them, in the way of the flesh, the Christ, who is over all, God to be praised forever. Amen. But it is not possible that the word of God has failed. For not all who are from Israel are Israel; nor, because they are the seed of Abraham, are they all his children, but: Your seed shall be named through Isaac. That is, it is not the children of the flesh who are children of God, but the children of his promise are counted as his seed. For this is what the promise says: I will come at that time, and Sarah shall have a son. Not only that, but there was Rebeccah whose children were conceived from a single person, Isaac our forefather. Then, when her children had not yet been born, when they had done nothing either good or bad, so that the purpose in the choice of God might hold good, not because of what they had done but because of him who called them, she was told: The elder shall be the slave of the younger. As it is written: I loved Jacob and I hated Esau.

What then shall we say? Could there be any unfairness in God? Never! To Moses he says: I will pity whom I pity, and I will have mercy on him on whom I have mercy. But that is not a matter of wish or effort but of God's mercy. For scripture says to Pharaoh: For this I have raised you up, to show my power through you, and for you to make my name known in all the earth. He pities the one he wishes to pity, and he makes insensitive the one he wishes to be so.

Will you then ask me: What fault can he still find? Who ever stood up against his will? My good man, who are you to argue with God? Shall the work of art say to the artist: Why did you make me the way you did? Does not the potter have power over his clay to make, from the same material, one piece that is to be prized and another to be despised? But if God, while wishing to show his anger and make known his power, endured with great patience the vessels of anger which were made for destruction, it was to make known the abundance of his glory given to the vessels of mercy which he had foreordained for glory: ourselves, whom he summoned not only from among the Jews but also from among the Gentiles. So he says in Hosea: I will call what is not my people my people, and her who was not beloved, beloved; and in the place where it was said to them: You are not my people, they shall be called sons of the living God. Isaiah cries aloud concerning Israel: Though the number of the sons of Israel is as the sands of the sea, only a remnant will be saved; for the Lord will complete and conclude his sentence upon the earth. And as Isaiah said before: If the Lord of Hosts had not left us children, we would have been like Sodom, and we would have been in the likeness of Gomorrah.

What then shall we say? That the Gentiles, who did not pursue righteousness, found righteousness, but it was the righteousness which comes from faith; while Israel, pursuing the law of righteousness, did not achieve that law. Why so? Because it was not by faith but by actions, and they stumbled against the stone of stumbling, as is written: Behold, I place on Zion the stone of stumbling and the rock of misdirection; but he who has faith in him shall not be brought to shame.

¶ Brothers, the desire in my heart and my prayer to God are for them, that they may be saved. For I bear these brothers witness that they have the longing for God; but not in the way of understanding; for they are ignorant of the righteousness of God, and when they tried to set up their own righteousness, they did not submit to the righteousness of God. Christ is the fulfillment of the law and means righteousness for everyone who has faith. Moses writes that everyone who acts righteously according to the law shall live through that. But the righteousness which comes from faith speaks thus: Do not say in your heart: Who will go up to heaven? This is to bring Christ down. Or say: Who will go down into the bottomless pit? This is to bring Christ up from the dead. Then what does it say? That the word is close to you, it is in your mouth and in your heart. This is the word of the faith which we preach: that if you confess to the word that is in your mouth, that Jesus is Lord, and believe in your heart that God raised him from the dead, you will be saved. For faith in the heart means righteousness, and confession by the mouth means salvation; Since scripture says: No one who has faith in him shall be put to shame. There is no distinction between Jew and Greek, since the same Lord is Lord of all, and he is bountiful toward all who call upon him. For everyone who calls upon the name of the Lord shall be saved. How then shall they call upon one in whom they do not believe? How shall they believe in one of whom they have not heard? How shall they hear without one to preach him? How shall they preach unless they are sent forth? As it is written: How beautiful are the feet of those who bring the good news, the gospel.

But not all heeded the gospel. For Isaiah says: Lord, who believed in our report? Faith comes from what they hear, and what they hear is of the word of Christ. But do I say, they did not hear? Rather: Their voice went out over all the earth, and their words to the ends of the world. But I say, did Israel not understand? First Moses says: I will make you jealous of what is no nation, against a nation without understanding I will rouse your anger. And Isaiah is bold to say: I was found by those who did not seek me, I was made manifest to those who did not want to know me. And to Israel he says: All day I have stretched out my hands to a people who would not obey and contradicted me.

¶ Then I ask, could God have rejected his people? Never! I myself am an Israelite, of the seed of Abraham, of the tribe of Benjamin. God did not reject his people, not those whom he had chosen before. Or do you not know that the scripture says, in Elijah, how he pleads with God against Israel: Lord, they killed your prophets, they wrecked your altars, and I alone am left, and they are after my life. But then, what is the divine response to him? I have put aside for myself seven thousand men who did not bend the knee to Baal. So even in the present time there is a remnant by way of election for grace; but if by grace, not because of their actions, since such grace is grace no longer. How then? Israel did not find what Israel sought; but the elect found it. But the rest were made insensitive, as it is written: God gave them a spirit of stupidity, and eyes that would not see and ears that would not hear, even down to the present day. And David says: Let their table turn into a snare to entrap them, and a stumbling block, so that they will be punished. Let their eyes be darkened so that they may not see, and their backs forever bent double.

I ask then, did they stumble in order to fall? Never! But by their transgression came the salvation of the Gentiles, to make the Jews emulate them. But if their transgression meant good fortune for the world, and their defeat meant good fortune for the Gentiles, how much more will their success mean!

But this I say to you, the Gentiles: Insofar as I am the apostle of the Gentiles, I enlarge my ministry, to stir up if I can my own flesh and blood and so save some of them. For if their rejection means the reconciliation of the world, what will their acceptance mean? Surely, life after death. But if the first fruits are blessed, so is the main mass; and if the root is blessed, so are the branches.

But if some of the branches have been broken off, and you, a wild olive, have been grafted in their place and share with the root the richness of the olive tree, do not glory over those branches. Though you may glory, it is not you who support the root, the root supports you. You will say: The branches were broken off so that I could be grafted on. Very well. They were broken off for lack of faith and you took their places because of your faith. Do not be too confident; but be full of fear. For if God did not spare the branches that were naturally his, he will not spare you. Behold the goodness, and the severity, of God: his severity toward those who have fallen away, but for you the goodness of God, so long as you endure in that goodness; since you too could be cut off. And those others, unless they persist in their unbelief, will be grafted, for God has the power to graft them in again. For if you were cut away from your natural wild olive tree and grafted against your nature onto the good olive tree, how much the sooner will they be grafted onto the olive tree which is naturally their own.

For I would not have you think yourselves wise, brothers, through failure to understand this mystery: that a part of Israel has been made uncomprehending until such time as the number of the Gentiles is full; and thus all Israel shall be saved, as it is written: The deliverer will come from Zion, and he will turn impiety away from Jacob; this will be my covenant with them, when I take away their sins. In the matter of the gospel they are enemies because of you, but in the matter of being chosen they are beloved because of their fathers; for the favors and the summons of God are not to be reversed. Just as you once disbelieved in God, but now have been granted mercy through their disbelief; so now they have disbelieved, so that, by the mercy given to you, they may also receive mercy; since God has included all in one disbelief so that he may have mercy on all.

Oh, the depth of the riches and wisdom and understanding of God! How inscrutable are his judgments, how untraceable his ways! For who knows the mind of the Lord? Who was ever his counselor? Who ever advanced him anything, and will be repaid? Since from him and through him and to him come all things; his is the glory forever. Amen.

¶I urge you, brothers, by God's mercy, to offer your bodies as a living holy sacrifice pleasing to God. This is your reasonable service. And do not pattern yourselves after this age, but transform yourselves through a renewal of the mind, to study the nature of the will of God, what is good, and pleasing, and perfect.

For through the grace that has been granted me I say to every one among you: Do not think thoughts beyond the thoughts you should have, but think to be moderate, according to the measure of faith God has given to each. As in our bodies we have many parts, but the parts do not all have the same function, so we many are one body in Christ, and individually parts of each other. We have different gifts which vary according to the grace that has been given us. If the gift is for prophecy, it should be based on faith. If one is gifted for service, he should serve; the teacher should teach, the comforter should bring comfort; the contributor should show his generosity, the leader his energy, the charitable man his graciousness. Let love be sincere. Hate the bad, hold fast to the good; love each other as brothers, prize each other more than yourselves; be unflagging in energy, seething with enthusiasm, serving the Lord, rejoicing in hope, steadfast against oppression, devoted in prayer; contribute to the needs of the saints, cultivate hospitality. Bless your persecutors, bless them, do not curse them. Rejoice with those who rejoice and weep with those who weep. Agree with each other in your thoughts, and do not be haughty but accommodate yourselves to modest thoughts. Do not be wise in your own estimation. Return no one evil for evil. Have good intentions in regard to all men. If it is possible, be for your part at peace with all men. Do not avenge yourselves, dear friends, but give way to God's anger, since it is written: Mine is the vengeance, mine the retribution, says the Lord. Then if your enemy is hungry, feed him; if he is thirsty, give him something to drink; so doing, you will heap coals of fire on his head. Do not let yourselves be overcome by evil, but overcome evil through good.

¶ Let every soul subject itself to the authorities that are set over it, for there is no authority except by God's will, and those which exist are appointed by God. Thus anyone who sets himself against authority is rebelling against the ordinance of God, and the rebels will bring judgment upon themselves. The men in power are nothing for good conduct to fear, only for bad conduct. Do you wish not to be afraid of authority? Then continue to do good, and you will have praise from it, for authority is God's minister for your good. But if you do evil, then be afraid, since it is not for nothing that that minister wears a sword, since he is God's minister, vindictive in anger against the evildoer. So it is necessary for you to subject yourself, not only because of the anger but because of your conscience. This is also why you pay your taxes. These are the servants of God devoted to this very purpose. Pay all men what you owe them; pay the tax to whom you owe the tax, the toll to whom you owe the toll; fear him you ought to fear, honor whom you ought to honor.

Do not be obliged to anyone for anything, except to love each other; he who loves has fulfilled all the rest of the law. For: You shall not commit adultery, you shall not murder, you shall not steal, you shall not covet, and any other commandment there may be, all are summed up in this statement: You shall love your neighbor as yourself. Love does your neighbor no harm, so love is the fulfillment of the law. And do this knowing what time it is, that now is the hour for you to waken from sleep, since our salvation is now much closer to us than when we got our faith. The night is advanced, the day is near. Let us put away the works of darkness and put on the armor of light. As in daylight let us go about decently, without reveling and drunkenness, without lovemaking and debauchery, without contentiousness and jealousy. But arm yourselves in the Lord Jesus Christ, and do not take thought for your body and its desires.

¶ Welcome the company of the man who is weak in faith, but not to dispute over fine points. For some have faith that they can eat anything, but the weak man eats only vegetables. Let the man who does eat not ridicule the one who abstains, and let the one who abstains not judge the one who eats, for God has accepted him. Who are you to judge the servant of another? He stands or falls by his own master. But he will stand, for the Lord has the power to make him stand.

One man prefers one day to another; another man approves of every day. Let each one be convinced in his own mind; for he who favors a day favors it for the Lord. The eater eats for the Lord, since he gives thanks to God; the abstainer abstains for the Lord, and he too gives thanks to God. For not one of us lives for himself, and not one of us dies for himself; if we live, we live for the Lord, and if we die, we die for the Lord. Whether we live or die, we belong to the Lord. For that was why Christ died and came to life, to be Lord over the dead and the living. You, why do you judge your brother? Or you, why do you, in turn, ridicule your brother? For we shall all stand before the judgment seat of God; since it is written: I live, says the Lord, that every knee shall bend to me, and every tongue shall confess to God. So each of us shall account for himself to God.

Then let us stop judging each other; rather, use your judgment to keep from offending your brother or putting a stumbling block in his way. I know and believe through the Lord Jesus that nothing is unclean in itself; only if one thinks that something is unclean, it is unclean for him. If your brother is hurt by what you eat, you are not walking in the way of love. Do not undo him, for whom Christ died, through what you eat. Do not let what is good for you be cause for ill repute. For the Kingdom of God is not food and drink, but righteousness and peace and joy in the Holy Spirit; and he who in this Spirit serves the Christ is pleasing to God and respected by men. Let us then pursue the ways of peace and the edification of each other. Do not undo the work of God for the sake of food. All things are pure, but it is bad for a man to eat in a way that will mislead. It is good not to eat meat or drink wine or do anything else if by this your brother is misled; as for you, keep your own faith before God. Happy is he who does not have to judge himself in the matter of what he approves. If one doubts but eats, he is guilty, because he does not do it from faith; and anything done without faith is a sin.

¶ We who are strong have a duty to put up with the weaknesses of those who are not strong, rather than pleasing ourselves. Let every man try to please his neighbor, to build up the community; for Christ also did not please himself, but, as it is written: The revilements of those who reviled you fell upon me. All that was written in days before was written for our instruction so that, through steadfastness and through the exhortation of the scriptures, we may have hope. May the God of steadfastness and exhortation grant you concord among yourselves after the example of Christ Jesus, so that together with one voice you may glorify God the Father of our Lord Jesus Christ.

So welcome each other, as Christ has welcomed us, for the glory of God. For I say that Christ was born to be the minister of the circumcised for the sake of God's truth, to confirm the promises made to our fathers; but also, for the Gentiles to glorify God for his mercy, as it is written: Therefore I shall acknowledge you among the Gentiles, and I will sing the praises of your name. And again it says: Rejoice, Gentiles, along with his people; and again: All nations, praise the Lord, and let all peoples praise him. And, once more, Isaiah says: There shall be a scion of Jesse who shall rise up to rule the nations, and in him the nations will have hope. May the God of hope fill you with all joy and peace, by your faith, so that your hope will be abundant through the power of the Holy Spirit.

Concerning you, my brothers, I am convinced that you yourselves are full of goodness, and complete in all understanding, and able to advise each other. But I have written to you rather boldly in part, to remind you, because God gave me the privilege of being the minister of Christ Jesus to the Gentiles, serving as priest the gospel of God; so that the offering up of the Gentiles to him may be acceptable and sanctified by the Holy Spirit. I am full of exultation before God because of Christ Jesus, for I will not dare speak of anything except Christ working through me to make the Gentiles obedient to his will;

by word and act, by the power of miracles and portents, by the power of the Holy Spirit. Thus I have toured about from Jerusalem as far as Illyria to complete the preaching of the gospel of Christ, so ambitious was I to bring the gospel where the name of Christ was not known, so as not to build on someone else's foundation but, as it is written: They who had not been told of him shall see him, and they who never heard of him shall know him.

Because of all this, I have been constantly prevented from coming to you. But now I no longer find any place for me in these regions, and for some years I have been longing to visit you, and then go on to Spain; for I hope to become acquainted with you as I pass through, and that you will see me on my way after I have first enjoyed something of your company. But now I am on my way to Jerusalem in the service of the saints. For Macedonia and Achaea have decided to make a contribution for the poor who are among the saints in Jerusalem. They have so decided and they are indebted to them; for since the Gentiles shared with them in matters of the spirit, they owe it to them to help them in a material way. When I have finished this business and set my seal upon this bounty for them, then I shall leave for Spain, stopping with you on the way; and I know that when I come to you I shall come with the full blessing of Christ.

Now I entreat you, by our Lord Jesus Christ and by the love of the Spirit, to aid me in my struggle, through your prayers to God, for me, so that I may be kept safe from the faithless in Judaea and my ministry in Jerusalem may prove acceptable to the saints, and so by God's will I may come to you in joy and take some rest with you. And may the God of peace be with you all. Amen.

¶I recommend to you Phoebe, our sister, who is deaconess of the church in Cenchreae; to receive her, in the Lord's name, in a manner befitting the saints, and help her in anything she needs from you, for she has been the benefactor of many, myself among them.

Give greetings to Prisca and Aquila, my fellow workers in Christ Jesus. They have risked their necks for my life, and not only am I grateful to them but so are all the churches among the Gentiles. Give greetings also to the church that is in their own house. Give greetings to my beloved Epaenetus, who is Asia's first offering to Christ. Give greetings to Mary, who has worked very hard for you. Give greetings to Andronicus and Junias, my fellow countrymen and fellow prisoners, who are distinguished among the apostles and were with Christ even before me. Give greetings to Ampliatus, my beloved in the Lord. Give greetings to Urbanus, our fellow worker in Christ, and to my beloved Stachys. Give greetings to Apelles, honored in Christ. Give greetings to the household of Aristobulus. Give greetings to Herodian, my fellow countryman. Give greetings to those of the household of Narcissus who are in the Lord. Give greetings to Tryphaena and Tryphosa, who have worked hard for the Lord. Give greetings to the beloved Persis, who has worked very hard for the Lord. Give greetings to Rufus, excellent in the Lord, and to his mother, who is a mother to me. Give greetings to Asyncritus, Phlegon, Hermes, Patrobas, Hermas, and the brothers who are with them. Give greetings to Philologus and Julia, Nereus and his sister, and Olympas, and all the saints who are with them. Give greetings to each other with the sacred kiss. All the churches of Christ give you greetings.

And I entreat you, brothers, to mark well those who

cause dissension and misguidance, which are counter to the doctrine you have learned; and avoid them. Such people are the slaves not of our Lord Christ but of their own bellies; but by fair speech and flattery they deceive the hearts of the simple. Your obedience has become known to everyone. Therefore I rejoice in you, and I wish you to be wise for good, but innocent for evil. The God of peace will crush Satan under your feet soon.

The grace of our Lord Jesus be with you.

Timothy, my fellow worker, sends you greetings, as do Lucius and Jason and Sosipater, my fellow countrymen. And I, Tertius, who wrote down this letter send you greetings in the Lord. Gaius, who is host to me and to the entire church, sends you greetings. And Erastus, the treasurer of the city, sends you greetings, as does Quartus, his brother.

To the one who has power to strengthen you, as in my gospel and the preaching of Jesus Christ; by the revelation of a mystery which was silenced through the ages but now has been brought to light, and has been made known through prophetic scriptures to all the nations by order of the everlasting God, to make them obedient to the faith; to the one God, who is wise, may the glory be given, through Jesus Christ, forever. Amen.

The First Letter
to the Corinthians

¶PAUL, CALLED TO BE AN APOSTLE OF Jesus Christ by the will of God, and Sosthenes, his brother, to the church of God which is in Corinth, to those who are consecrated in Christ Jesus, called to be saints; together with all those who invoke the name of our Lord Jesus Christ in every locality, theirs and ours: grace to you and peace from God our Father and the Lord Jesus Christ.

I thank God at all times on your account for the grace of God given you in Christ Jesus, that in every way you have been made rich in him, in every word and all understanding, as the testimony to the Christ has been confirmed among you, so that you do not come short in any gift of grace, as you look for the revelation of our Lord Jesus Christ. He will keep you firm until the end, without reproach on the Day of our Lord Jesus. One must believe in God, by whom you were summoned to the fellowship of his son Jesus Christ our Lord.

Still, I entreat you, brothers, in the name of our Lord Jesus Christ, all to agree with each other, so that there will be no schisms among you, but you will be united in the same mind and the same understanding. For, my brothers, I have been told about you by Chloe and her people; that there are rivalries among you. I mean this: each of you says: I am for Paul; or else: I am for Apollos; or: I am for Peter; or: I am for Christ. Christ is partitioned! Was Paul ever crucified for you? Or were you baptized in the name of Paul? I am thankful that I baptized no one of you (except Crispus and Gaius), so that no one can say that you were baptized in my name. I did also baptize the household of Stephanas. For the rest, I do not know whether I baptized anyone else. For Christ did not send me forth to baptize, but to preach the gospel; not in accomplished oratory, but so that the cross of the Christ might not be made meaningless.

For the word of the cross is folly to those who go the way of perdition, but to us who go the way of salvation it is the power of God. Since it is written: I will destroy the wisdom of the wise, and I will make void the intelligence of the intelligent.

Where is the sage? Where is the scholar? Where is the student of this age? Did not God turn the wisdom of the world to folly? For since by the wisdom of God the world did not, because of its wisdom, know God, God saw fit to save the believers through the folly of what was preached to them. For the Jews demand miracles and the Greeks look for wisdom; but we preach Christ crucified, a stumbling block to the Jews and folly to the heathens, but to us who are chosen, Jews and Greeks alike, Christ the power of God and the wisdom of God. Since the folly of God is wiser than men, and the weakness of God is stronger than men.

For consider your calling, brothers: that not many of you are wise in the way of the flesh, not many are strong, not many are well born. But God chose out the fools of the world, to shame the wise, and God chose out the weak of the world, to shame the strong, and God chose out the humble and despised of the world; and what is not, to abolish what is; so that no flesh may take pride before God. For you are from him, in Christ Jesus, who was born our wisdom from God, and our righteousness and sanctification and redemption, so that, as it is written: Let him who takes pride take pride in the Lord.

¶ And I myself when I came to you, brothers, did not come to you with any superiority of speech or wisdom when I proclaimed to you the mystery of God; for I did not judge that, among you, I knew anything except only Jesus Christ, that is, Jesus Christ crucified. And I came to you in weakness and much fear and trembling, and my message and my preaching did not consist in persuasive words of wisdom but in the revelation of spirit and power, so that your faith might not rest on the wisdom of men but on the power of God. Still, what we say is wisdom, to the initiates, but not the wisdom of this age or of the leaders of this age, who are doomed; but what we say is the wisdom of God in a mystery, the hidden wisdom, which God foreordained before the ages for our glory; which not one of the leaders of this age understood, since if they had understood it they would not have crucified the Lord of glory. But, as it is written: All that God made ready for those who love him; which the eye did not see and the ear did not hear, nor did it enter into the heart of man.

For God made his revelation to us through the Spirit; for the Spirit explores everything, even the depths of God. Who among men knows what is in a man except the spirit of man which is in him? So also no one knows what is in God except the Spirit of God. And we did not receive the spirit of the world but the Spirit which is from God, so that we may know what grace we were given by God; which we also now speak of, not in words which are the teaching of human wisdom, but in words which are the teaching of the Spirit, combining the spiritual with the spiritual. The sensual man does not accept what belongs to the Spirit of God, since it is folly to him, and he cannot understand, because these things are judged spiritually; but the spiritual man judges all things, while he himself is judged by no man. For who knows the mind of the Lord, which will instruct him? But we do have the mind of Christ.

¶ And I, brothers, could not speak to you as to spiritual persons, but as fleshly ones, little children in Christ. I gave you milk to drink, not solid food, for you were not yet strong enough. Nor are you even now, since you are still of the flesh. For when there is jealousy and rivalry among you, are you not of the flesh, and going the way of mankind? When one of you says: I am for Paul, and another: I am for Apollos, are you not being human? What then is Apollos? And what is Paul? Servants, through whom you got belief, and each as the Lord gave it. I planted, Apollos watered, but God made it grow. So he who plants is nothing, nor he who waters; only God who makes it grow. He who plants and he who waters are one, but each will receive his own wages for his own labor. We are the fellow workers of God; you are God's field, God's architecture.

By the grace of God given to me I laid the foundation like a skilled architect, but another builds upon it. Let every man look to it how he builds; for no one can lay down any foundation beside the one that has been laid down, which is Jesus Christ. And if anyone builds upon the foundation in gold, silver, precious stones, wood, hay, straw, the work of each will become manifest, for the Day will make it plain; because revelation comes by fire, and the fire itself will prove the nature of each man's work. If the work a man has built endures, he will have his reward; if anyone's work burns up, he will be penalized, but he himself will be saved; but as if through fire.

Do you not know that you are God's temple and God's Spirit lives in you? If anyone destroys God's temple, God will destroy him. For the temple of God is holy. This you are.

Let no one deceive himself. If anyone thinks he is wise among you in this age, let him become a fool, so that he may become wise, for the wisdom of this world is folly with God. Since it is written: He who catches the wise in their shiftiness; and again: The Lord knows the reasonings of the wise; that they are vain. So let no one take pride among men; for all things are yours, whether it be Paul or Apollos or Peter or the world or life or death or present or future; all are yours, but you are Christ's and Christ is God's.

¶ So let a man think of us as servants of Christ and stewards of the mysteries of God. But it is required of any steward that he be found reliable. It means very little to me to be judged by you or by any human day of judgment; nor again do I judge myself, for I am not conscious of any guilt; but I am not justified by that, but he who judges me is the Lord. Do not, therefore, make any judgment before it is time, not until the Lord comes; and he will illuminate what is hidden in darkness and bring to light the counsels of men's hearts; and that will be the time for each man's praise from God.

I have put this in terms of Apollos and myself for your sake, brothers, so that in us you may understand the saying: Nothing beyond what is written; so that you may not become too emotional each in favor of one against another. For who marks you out for distinction? What do you have which you were not given? And if you did receive something, why do you take pride as if you had been given nothing? Have you had your fill yet? Have you grown rich yet? Have you been made kings, without us? I wish you had been made kings, so that we could be kings along with you.

For I believe God displayed us, the apostles, at the end of the show like men condemned to death; because we have turned into a spectacle for the world, for angels and men alike. We are fools for Christ but you are wise in Christ. We are weak, you are strong. You are respected, we are despised. For until this very day we have been hungry and thirsty and naked, and beaten and driven from place to place, and worn ourselves out working with our own hands. We are reviled and give blessings; we are persecuted and put up with it; we are abused and are conciliatory. We have become the outcasts of the world, the offscouring of everything; to this very day.

I write you this, not to make you ashamed, but as if I were admonishing my own beloved children; for even if you have ten thousand tutors in Christ, you do not have many fathers; but I am your father in Christ Jesus through the gospel. So I implore you: copy me. For this reason I have sent you Timothy, who is my child, beloved and faithful in the Lord, and he will recall to you my ways in Christ, as I teach everywhere in every church.

Some of you became inflated with pride as if I were not coming to you; but if the Lord is willing, I shall come to you soon, and learn of the proud ones not what they say but what they can do, since the Kingdom of God is not in speech but in power to act. Which do you want? Shall I come to you with a stick, or in love and the spirit of gentleness?

¶ In very truth, a case of immorality is reported in your community, and such immorality as is not found even among the heathens: a man has taken his father's wife. And are you pleased with yourselves, rather than so grieved that the man who did this thing must be removed from your presence? For I, absent in body but present in spirit, have already judged the man who did this as if I were really there; in the name of our Lord Jesus; with yourselves and my spirit gathered together, with the power of our Lord Jesus; to hand over a man like this to Satan for the destruction of the flesh, so that his soul may be saved on the Day of the Lord. Your pride is not good. Do you not know that a little leavening raises the whole mass of dough? Clean out the old leavening so that you may be a new baking, unleavened as you are. For even Christ, our paschal lamb, was sacrificed; so let us keep the festival, not in the old leavening, nor in the leavening of baseness and corruption, but in the unleavened bread of purity and truth.

I wrote in my letter to you that you should have nothing to do with lechers; not, that is, meaning the lechers of this world in general, nor the covetous or the rapacious or the idolatrous, since then you would have had to take leave of the world; but in fact I wrote to you that you should have nothing to do with one who is named a *brother* if he is a lecher, or covetous or idolatrous or abusive or drunken or rapacious; not even to eat with such a one. For what have I to do with judging those who are outside our number? Do you not judge those who are inside our number, while God judges those who are outside? Drive the evil one out from among you.

¶ Does any one of you, who has a case against any other one of you, presume to have it judged before the unjust rather than before the saints? Do you not know, then, that the saints will judge the world? And if the world is judged by you, are you then unfit for the most trivial lawsuits? Do you not know that we shall be judging angels, let alone ordinary cases? And if you have ordinary cases, do you seat in judgment those who are of no account in the church? I say this to your shame. Is there among you no man wise enough to be able to decide between brother and brother? Does brother go to law with brother, and before unbelievers too? It is a real fault in you that you have lawsuits against each other at all. Why not rather let yourselves be wronged? Why not rather let yourselves be robbed? But you do wrong and rob, and to brothers too. Or do you not know that wrongdoers shall not inherit the Kingdom of God? Do not be deceived. Neither lechers nor idolators nor adulterers nor effeminates nor pederasts nor thieves nor the covetous, none who are drunken or abusive or rapacious, shall inherit the Kingdom of God. And some of you have been these very things; but you have been washed clean and sanctified and justified in the name of our Lord Jesus Christ and in the Spirit of our God.

All things are lawful for me; but not all things are advantageous. All things are lawful for me, but I shall not be in the power of anything. Foods are for the belly, and the belly is for food; but God will put an end to both the one and the other. But the body is not for lechery but for the Lord and the Lord is for the body; and God both raised the Lord from the dead and also will raise us by his power. Do you not know that your bodies are the limbs of Christ? Then shall I take the limbs of Christ and make them the limbs of a whore? Never. Or do you not know that he who clings to a whore is one body with her; for, says scripture, the two shall be one flesh. But he who clings to the Lord is one spirit with him. Flee from lechery. Any other sin a man may commit is outside his body, but the lecher sins against his own body. Or do you not know that your body is the temple of the Holy Spirit in you, which you have from God? And you are not your own, since you were bought for a price. Then glorify God in your body.

¶ Concerning the matters you wrote me of, it is a good thing for a man not to touch any woman; but to save you from loose living, let each man have his own wife, and each woman have her own husband. Let the husband give his wife her due, and so likewise the wife to her husband. The wife does not have authority over her own body; her husband does; and so likewise the husband does not have authority over his own body; his wife does. Do not deny each other, except by agreement for a time when you can devote yourselves to prayer, and then be as you were before; for fear Satan may entice you through incontinence. I tell you this as a concession, not as a command. What I should like is for all people to be as I am; but each person has his own endowment from God, some of one kind and some of another.

And I say to the unmarried and the widows, that it is good to remain as I am; but if they cannot control themselves, let them marry, for it is better to marry than to be on fire. And to those who are married, I command; no, not I, but the Lord: that a wife should not separate from her husband; and if she does separate herself, she must remain single or else be reconciled with her husband; and a man should not divorce his wife.

And to the others I, not the Lord, say this: If any brother has a wife who is an unbeliever, and she consents to live with him, he should not divorce her; and a woman who has a husband who is an unbeliever and who consents to live with her should not divorce him. For the unbelieving husband is hallowed by his wife, and the unbelieving wife is hallowed by one who is a brother; since otherwise your children are impure, but this way they are hallowed. But if the unbeliever separates, let him or her be separate; the brother or sister is not bound in such cases; God called you in peace. For how do you know, wife, if you will save your husband? Or how do you know, husband, if you will save your wife?

Unless the Lord has so directed, let everyone go on as he was when God called him; and I so order in all the churches. Was one circumcised when he was called? Let him not try to undo it. Was one uncircumcised when he was called? Let him not be circumcised. Circumcision means nothing and uncircumcision means nothing; only keeping the commandments of God means anything. Let each remain in that condition in which he was called. Were you a slave when called? Let it not trouble you; but even if you can become free, make the best of your condition; for the slave called by the Lord is the Lord's freedman, and so likewise the free man called is the

Lord's slave. You were bought for a price; do not become the slaves of human beings. As each one was when called, brothers, so let him remain before God.

Concerning those who are unmarried I have no mandate from the Lord, but I give you my opinion as one who has been mercifully granted by the Lord to be trustworthy. I think that, because of the impending peril, it is good for a man to remain as he is. Are you bound to a wife? Do not seek freedom. Are you free of a wife? Do not seek a wife. But even if you do marry, you have not sinned. And if an unmarried girl marries, she has not sinned. But such people will have affliction in the flesh. I am trying to spare you. But this I do say, brothers: our time is now short. For the time that remains, let even those who have wives be as if they did not; let those who mourn be as if they did not mourn, and those who rejoice be as if they did not rejoice; and those who buy, as if they kept nothing; and those who use the world, as if they got no use of it. For the form of this world is passing away.

I want you to be free from care. The unmarried man cares about the things of the Lord and how he can please the Lord; but the married man cares about the things of the world and how he can please his wife, and he is of two minds. And the unmarried woman and the virgin care about the things of the Lord, how to be pure in body and spirit; but the married woman cares about the things of the world, and how she can please her husband. I say this for your own good, not to throw a noose around you, but for the sake of propriety, and undistracted devotion to the Lord.

But if a man thinks he is acting shamefully toward his girl if he becomes too impassioned, and it has to be so, let him do what he wants. He is not sinning; let them marry. But the man who stands firm in his heart, and is not constrained, but has control over his will and decides in his own heart to keep his girl a virgin, will be doing well. Thus the one who marries his girl does well, and the one who does not marry does better.

A wife is bound as long as her husband lives. If her husband dies, she is free to marry anyone she wishes, as long as it is marriage in the Lord. But she is happier if she remains as she is, in my opinion; for I think I myself have the spirit of God.

¶ Concerning idol offerings, we are sure that we all have knowledge. Knowledge inflates with pride; love builds. If a man thinks he knows something, he still does not know it as he ought to know it; but if one loves God, he is known by him. Concerning, then, the eating of idol offerings, we know that an idol has no existence in the world, and that there is no god but the one God. For if there are so-called gods, whether in heaven or on earth, as indeed there are many gods and many lords, for us there is one God, the Father, from whom all things are and we are his; and one Lord, Jesus Christ, through whom all things are and we exist through him.

But this knowledge is not in all; and some, through being accustomed hitherto to idols, eat food as if it were idol offerings, and their conscience, being weak, is soiled. But food will not bring us to God; nor, if we do not eat, do we have less; nor, if we do eat, do we have more. But see to it that your freedom does not become a cause of trouble to the weak. For if one sees you, the possessor of understanding, dining in an idol temple, will not his conscience, being weak, be encouraged to eat idol offerings? Then the weak man is undone by your understanding, your brother, for whom Christ died. Thus by sinning against your brothers and battering their weak conscience you are sinning against Christ. Therefore if my eating drives my brother astray, I will never eat meat any more, so as not to drive my brother astray.

¶ Am I not free? Am I not an apostle? Have I not seen Jesus, our Lord? Are you not my handiwork in the Lord? Even if to others I am not an apostle, at least I am to you, since you are the proof of my apostleship in the Lord.

This is my answer to those who call me to account. Do we not have the right to eat and drink? Do we not have the right to take one of our number with us as wife, like the rest of the apostles and the Lord's brothers and Peter? Do only Barnabas and I not have the right not to be laborers? Who ever serves in the army at his own expense? Who plants a vineyard and does not eat its fruit? Who herds a flock and does not drink milk from the flock? Do I speak as an individual or does the law also say this? For in the law of Moses it is written: You shall not muzzle the ox who threshes the grain. Can God be concerned with the oxen, or is he really speaking about us? For it is for us that it is written that the plower must plow in hope, and the thresher must be in hope, of getting his share. If we sowed the things of the spirit among you, is it too much if we reap material benefits from you? If others have this right from you, should we not even more?

But we have not used that right, but we suffer everything so as not to offer any obstruction to the gospel of the Christ. Do you not know that those who perform sacrifices eat some of what has been sacrificed, and those who serve at the altar have their share from the altar? Even so has the Lord instructed those who bring the gospel to live from the gospel. But I have not made use of any of these privileges. I did not write this so that it should be thus for me; for it is better for me to die than that anyone should make my pride an empty thing. For if I preach the gospel, that is no source of pride for me, since the necessity has been laid upon me; woe to me if I do not preach the gospel. For if I do this of my own will, I have my reward; but if I do it not of my own will, I have been entrusted with a duty. What then is my reward? That, as I preach the gospel, I may make the gospel be free of charge, so as not to use up the privilege which the gospel gives me.

For, being free from all, I have enslaved myself to all, so that I may win over the more people. And I have made myself like a Jew to the Jews so as to win over Jews; to those subject to the law like one subject to the law, though I am not myself subject to the law, so as to win over those subject to the law; to those outside the law like one outside the law, though I am not outside the law of God but within the law of Christ, so as to win over those outside the law. To the weak I have made myself weak, to win over the weak. I have made myself all things to all people, so that by some means or other I may save some. And I do all this for the sake of the gospel, so that I may have my share in the gospel.

Do you not know that when they run in the stadium they all run, but only one wins the prize? Run to win. And everyone who competes keeps in training in every way; but they, to win a perishable wreath; we, for an imperishable one. I myself do not race without a goal; I do not box to punish the air; but I batter my own body and enslave it; so that, while calling others to action, I may not myself be disqualified.

¶ Now I do not wish you to be unmindful of the fact, brothers, that our fathers all went under the cloud and all passed through the sea, and were all baptized into Moses under the cloud and in the sea, and all ate the same spiritual food and drank the same spiritual drink, for they drank from the spiritual rock which went with them, and the rock was the Christ. But God was not pleased with most of them; for they died in the desert. These things took place as examples for us, to keep us from desiring evil things as they desired them. Do not become idolaters like some of them; as it is written: The people sat down to eat and drink, and they stood up to play. And let us not be lecherous as some of them were lecherous, and twenty-three thousand fell in a single day. And let us not make trial of the Lord as some of them made trial of him, and they were killed by the snakes. And do not grumble as some of them grumbled, and they were killed by the angel of death. These things made an example of them, and were written of for our instruction, for us with whom the end of the world coincides.

So let him who thinks he is standing see to it that he does not fall. No trial has come upon you which is not human; and God is to be trusted, who will not let you be tried beyond your powers, but with the trial will give you a way out by your being able to endure.

Therefore, my dear friends, flee from idolatry. I speak to you as sensible people; judge for yourselves what I am saying. The cup of blessing which we bless, is that not participation in the blood of the Christ? The loaf which we break, is that not participation in the body of the Christ? Because we many are one loaf, one body, for we all partake of the one loaf. Consider Israel in the matter of the flesh. Do not those who eat the sacrifices share in the altar of sacrifice? What then am I saying? That what is sacrificed to idols amounts to something, or that the idol amounts to something? Rather, that what they sacrifice they sacrifice to demons and not to God, and I would not have you be partners of demons. You cannot drink the cup of the Lord and the cup of demons. You cannot share the table of the Lord and the table of demons. Or are we challenging the Lord? Surely we are not stronger than he?

All things are lawful; but not all things are advantageous. All things are lawful; but not all are helpful. Let no one look for his own good, but for that of the other man.

Eat anything that is sold in the butcher shop without discriminating because of conscience, for the earth with all that fills it belongs to the Lord. If one of the unbelievers invites you and you wish to go, eat everything that is set before you without discriminating because of conscience. But if someone says to you: This is sacrificial meat, do not eat it, for the sake of him who told you, and for conscience; the conscience, I mean, not of oneself but of the other man. For why is my freedom judged by the conscience of another? And if I partake in thankfulness, why am I insulted because of that for which I am thankful?

Then, whether you eat or drink or whatever you do, do it for the glory of God. Be inoffensive toward Jews and

Greeks and the church of God, as I also try to please all in all ways, looking not for my own advantage but for that of the many, so that they may be saved.

¶ Copy me, as I copy Christ.

I have praise for you because you remember everything I say and maintain traditions as I have handed them on to you. But I wish you to know that the head of every man is the Christ, and the head of a wife is her husband, and the head of the Christ is God. Any man who prays or prophesies with his head covered disgraces his head; and any woman who prays or prophesies with her head unveiled disgraces her head; for it is one and the same thing as having a shaven head. If a woman unveils her head, let it be shorn also; but if it is shameful for a woman to have a shorn or shaven head, let her cover it. A man does not need to cover his head, since he is the image and semblance of God; but a woman is the semblance of a man. For man is not from woman, but woman from man; since indeed man was not created for the sake of woman, but woman for the sake of man. Therefore a woman should take care of her head, because of the angels. But, in the Lord, woman does not exist apart from man, nor man apart from woman. For as woman came from man, so man is born of woman; and all is from God.

Judge for yourselves. Is it proper for a woman to pray to God with her head unveiled? Does not nature herself teach you that, if a man has long hair, it is his disgrace, but if a woman has long hair, it is her glory? Since her hair is given to her for a covering. But if I seem to be arbitrary, it is because we do not have that custom, nor do the churches of God.

In giving you my instructions, I have this fault to find with you, that your meetings do more harm than good. For in the first place, I hear that, when you meet together in church, there are dissensions among you; and this in part I believe. For there must be factions among you, so that those who are the true ones may become known among you. Then again, when you meet together, it is not possible to eat the Lord's supper; because each one at dinner seizes his own portion first; and one man goes hungry, another man gets drunk. Do you not have your homes for eating and drinking? Or do you despise the church of God, and put to shame those who are needy? What am I to say to you? Shall I praise you? In this I do not praise you.

For I received from the Lord this tradition which I handed on to you: that the Lord Jesus, on the night when he was betrayed, took a loaf and gave thanks and broke it and said: This is my body, which is for your sake; do this in remembrance of me. So also with the cup after supper, saying: This cup is the new covenant in my blood; do this, whenever you drink, in remembrance of me. For whenever you eat this loaf and drink the cup, you are commemorating the Lord's death; until he comes.

Thus anyone who eats the loaf or drinks the cup of the Lord unworthily is guilty against the body and blood of the Lord. Let a person prove himself worthy, and thus eat from the loaf and drink from the cup. For anyone who eats and drinks is eating and drinking his own damnation if he does not recognize the Body. For that reason many among you are weak and sick, and a good many have even died. If we judged ourselves, we would not be judged; but when we are judged by the Lord, we are being disciplined, so as not to be condemned with the world.

So, my brothers, when you come together to eat, wait for each other. If anyone is hungry, let him eat at home; so your gathering together will not be for your damnation.

I will give you my other instructions when I come.

¶ But concerning matters of the spirit, brothers, I would not have you ignorant. You know that when you were heathens you were led helplessly at random to dumb idols. I make it known to you, therefore, that no one who is speaking in the Spirit says: A curse on Jesus; and no one can say: Jesus is Lord, unless he is speaking in the Holy Spirit.

But there are varieties of gifts; but the same Spirit; and there are varieties of services, and the same Lord; and there are varieties of activities, and the same God, who activates them all among all. To each is given disclosure by the Spirit of what is to his advantage. To one, through the Spirit, it is given to speak with skill; to another, to speak with understanding, through the same Spirit; to another, faith, by the same Spirit; to another, the gifts of healing, by that one Spirit; to another, miraculous powers; to another, prophecy; to another, the power to discern spirits; to another, the varieties of speaking with tongues; and to another, the interpretation of the tongues. One and the same Spirit activates all these things, distributing them separately to each person as it will.

For just as the body is one and has many parts, but all the parts of the body, being many, are one body, so likewise is the Christ; for we were all baptized in one Spirit into one body, whether we were Jews or Greeks, whether slaves or free; and we have all been given one Spirit to drink. For the body is not one part but many. If the foot says: Because I am not a hand, I am not part of the body; it is not for that reason not part of the body. And if the ear says: Because I am not an eye, I am not part of the body; it is not for that reason not part of the body. If all the body were eye, where would our source of hearing be? If all were hearing, where would be our source of smell? But as it is, God has set the parts, each of them, in the body, according to his will. And if all were one part, where would the body be? But as it is, there are many parts, and one body. The eye cannot say to the hand: I have no need of you; nor again can the head say to the feet: I have no need of you. But by so much the more are those parts of the body necessary, which seem to be weak; and those parts of the body which we think are less regarded are those to which we give extra regard; and the unseemly parts of us are treated with more decorum, which our decorous parts do not need. But God has combined the body, giving extra attention to what is inferior, so that there may be no dissension in the body but all parts may be equally concerned for each other. And if one part suffers, all parts suffer with it; and if one part is honored, all parts rejoice with it. You are the body of Christ and its parts, individually.

And those whom God has established in the church are: first, apostles; second, prophets; third, teachers; then, miraculous powers; then, gifts for healing, helpful actions, talents for governing, varieties of tongues. Surely we are not all apostles? Not all prophets? Not all teachers? Not all with miraculous power? Surely not all have gifts for healing? Not all speak with tongues? Not all can interpret these? Aspire to the gifts which are greater.

¶ But now I show you a way that is even better. If I speak with the tongues of men and angels, but have no love, all I am is sounding bronze or a clashing cymbal. And if I have the gift of prophecy and know all mysteries and all understanding, and if I have faith entire so as to move mountains, and have no love, I am nothing. And if I give all I have in alms, and if I give my body to be burned, and have no love, it does me no good. Love is patient, is kind, love has no jealousy, does not swagger, has no pride, is not immodest, does not look for its own advantage, is not stirred to anger, does not keep count of evil done, is not happy over wrongdoing, shares the happiness of the truth; all-sustaining, all-faithful, all-hopeful, all-enduring. Love never fails. If there are prophecies, they will come to nothing; if there are speeches, they will be stopped; if there is understanding, it will come to nothing. For we understand in part and we prophesy in part; but when completeness comes, what is in part will vanish away. When I was a child, I spoke as a child, and thought as a child, and reasoned as a child; now that I am a man, I am through with childish things. For now we see by a mirror, obscurely; but then face to face. Now I know in part; but then I will know in full, as I myself am fully known. And now there remain faith, hope, love; these three; but the greatest of these is love.

¶ Pursue love, aspire to things spiritual, all the more so that you may prophesy. For one who speaks with tongues speaks not to men but to God, since no one understands him, and he talks mysteries by the Spirit; but one who prophesies to men speaks edification and exhortation and consolation. One who speaks with tongues edifies himself; one who prophesies edifies the church. I would like you all to speak with tongues, but would like still more for you to prophesy. He who prophesies is greater than he who speaks with tongues, unless the latter translates it so that the church may be edified. But as it is, brothers, if I come to you speaking with tongues, what good shall I do you; unless I speak to you by way of revelation, or understanding, or prophecy, or teaching? In the same way, if the inanimate things which produce sound, whether flute or lyre, have no distinction in their tones, how will what is played on the flute or lyre be recognized? And again, if the trumpet gives out an unrecognizable call, who will make ready for battle? So too with you, if you do not with your speaking offer orderly discourse, how will what is said by you be understood? You will be talking to the air. Who knows how many kinds of language there are in the world? And none without its own sound. If, then, I do not know the meaning of the sound, I shall be a stupid barbarian to him who speaks it, and he who speaks it will be a stupid barbarian to me. Thus, as for you, since you are eager for the things of the spirit, try to excel in the edification of the church.

So let him who speaks with tongues pray that he may be able to translate it. If I pray speaking with tongues, my spirit prays but my mind adds nothing. What then? I will pray with my spirit, but I will pray also with my mind. I will sing praises with my spirit, but I will sing praises also with my mind. Since if you give thanks and praise in the spirit only, how will one who is in the position of an uninitiate add his amen to your thanksgiving, since he does not know what you are saying? You give thanks very well, but the other man is not edified. I thank God that I speak with tongues more than all the rest of you; but in the church, I would rather say five words rationally and so communicate with others, than ten thousand words with speaking with tongues.

Brothers, do not be children in your thinking; in evil-doing be like little innocents, but in thinking be grown-up. In the law it is written: In strangers' tongues and by the lips of strangers I will speak to this people, and not even so will they listen to me, says the Lord. Thus speaking in tongues is portentous not for believers but only for unbelievers; but prophecy is not for unbelievers, but only for believers. If, then, the whole congregation assembles in one place, and all speak with tongues, and uninstructed persons or unbelievers come in, will they not say you are mad? But if all are prophesying, and an unbeliever or uninstructed person comes in, he is examined by all, and questioned by all, and the secrets of his heart are laid open; and thus he will fling himself down on his face and worship God, announcing: God is really among you.

What then, brothers? When you meet together, each has a song of praise, or a lesson, or a revelation, or speech with tongues, or interpretation. Let all be for edification. If there is speaking with tongues, let it be two at a time or at most three, and in turn, and let one person interpret it. And if there is none who can interpret, let each man be silent in church, and talk to himself and to God. And let two or three speak as prophets, and the rest pass judgment; and if a revelation comes to someone else who is sitting there, let the first speaker be silent. For you can all prophesy, one by one, so that all may learn and all be encouraged; and the spirits of prophets are under the control of the prophets, for God is not the God of disorder but of peace.

As in all the churches of the saints, women must be

silent in church meetings; they are not allowed to speak, so let them submit as the law dictates. If they wish to learn about something, let them ask their own husbands at home; for it is disgraceful for a woman to talk in church.

Did the word of God originate from you? Or did it come to you alone? If any one of you thinks that he is a prophet or gifted with spirit, let him understand that what I write you is the commandment of God; one who disregards this is himself disregarded.

So, my brothers, strive to be prophets, and do not oppose speaking with tongues; but let everything be done properly, in an orderly way.

¶ I remind you, brothers, of the gospel which I brought to you, which you accepted, on which you have stood fast, by which you are saved; what I said when I brought the gospel to you, if you retain it still, if you did not become believers frivolously. To you I handed on what I had been given to believe which was of the highest importance: that Christ died for our sins, as in the scriptures; and that he was buried, and that he rose on the third day, as in the scriptures, and that he was seen by Peter, and then by the twelve. Then he was seen by more than five hundred brothers all at once, and most of them are still with us, but some have died. And then he was seen by James, and then by all the apostles; and last of all, as to an aborted child, he appeared also to me. For I am the least of the apostles, who am not fit to be called an apostle, because I persecuted the church of God. But by grace of God I am what I am, and his gift of grace to me has not been vain, but I, not I but the grace of God which is with me, have worked harder than all of them.

But whether it is I or they, thus we preach and thus you believed.

But if it is preached that Christ rose from the dead, how is it that some among you say that there is no resurrection of the dead? If there is no resurrection of the dead, then neither was Christ raised. But if Christ was not raised, then our preaching is empty, and your belief is empty, and we are found out as false witnesses to God, because we testified against God that he raised up Christ, whom he did not raise up, if, that is, the dead do not rise. For if the dead do not rise, then neither has Christ risen; and if Christ has not risen, your faith is vain, you are still in your sins. And then also those who went to their rest in Christ are lost. If by this life in Christ we are no more than hopeful, then we are the most pitiful of all people.

But in truth, Christ has risen from the dead, the first of the sleepers to rise. For since death came through man, so also resurrection is through man; just as all die in Adam, so in the Christ all will be brought to life. Each in his own appointed place: first Christ, then the Christ's own, at his coming; and then the end, when he hands over his kingdom to his God and Father, when he abolishes every realm and authority and power, for he must be King until he places all his enemies beneath his feet. The last enemy to be abolished is death, for: He has set all things beneath his feet. But when it says that all has been subjected, it means all except the one who subjected all things to him. But when all things are subjected to him, then the son himself will be subjected to him who subjected all things to him, so that God may be all in all.

Otherwise, what will those do who are baptized for

the sake of their dead bodies? If the dead bodies do not rise at all, why are they baptized for their sake? And why do we too go in danger every hour? I die every day; I swear it by the pride I have in you, brothers, through Christ Jesus our Lord. If as a man I fought with beasts in Ephesus, what use is that to me? If the dead do not rise, let us eat and drink, for tomorrow we die. Do not be deceived; bad associations corrupt good characters; be justly sober and sin no more, for there are some who have no knowledge of God. I say this to your shame.

But some one will ask: In what way are the dead raised and with what kind of body do they appear? Foolish man; the seed you sow does not germinate unless it dies. And when you sow it is not the body to come that you are sowing, but the bare seed, whether it be of wheat or any other grain; and God gives it a body according to his will, and to each of the seeds its own body. Not all flesh is the same flesh, but there is one of human beings, and another flesh of beasts, and another flesh of birds, and another of fishes. And there are heavenly bodies and earthly bodies; and the glory of the heavenly bodies is one thing, and the glory of the earthly is another. There is one glory for the sun, and another glory for the moon, and another glory for the stars; star differs from star in glory.

And thus it is also with the resurrection of the dead. The body is sown in corruption and raised in incorruption; it is sown in dishonor and raised in glory; it is sown in weakness and raised in strength. It is sown as a sensual body and raised as a spiritual body. If there is a sensual body, there is also a spiritual body. Thus it is written: The first man, Adam, was created for sensual life; the last Adam is for life-giving spirit. But first comes not the spiritual, but the sensual first, and then the spiritual. The first man is made from earth, the second from heaven. As was the earthly man, so are the earthly ones, and as was the heavenly man, so are the heavenly ones; and as we wore the likeness of the earthly one, so shall we wear the likeness of the heavenly one.

But this I tell you, brothers, that flesh and blood cannot inherit the Kingdom of God, nor shall corruption inherit incorruption. See, I am telling you a mystery. We shall not all die but we shall all be changed, in an instant, in the twinkling of an eye, at the last trumpet; for the trumpet will blow, and the dead will waken uncorrupted, and we shall be changed. For this which is perishable must put on imperishability, and this which is mortal must put on immortality. But when this which is mortal puts on immortality, then will come to pass the word which is written: Death is swallowed up in victory. Where, death, is your victory? Where, death, is your sting? The sting of death is sin, and the power of sin is the law; now thanks be to God who gives us the victory through our Lord Jesus Christ.

So, my beloved brothers, be steadfast, be immovable, surpassing always in the work of the Lord, knowing that your toil is not vain, by reason of the Lord.

¶ Now, regarding the collection for the saints, do you also do as I directed to the churches in Galatia. On every sabbath let each one of you, laying aside money in proportion to his gains, save it, so that there will not have to be collections when I arrive. And when I come to you I will send those whom you have recommended in your letters to convey your charitable gift to Jerusalem; and if it is of any importance for me to go myself, they will travel in my company.

I will come to you when I have passed through Macedonia, for I am going through Macedonia, and perhaps I shall stay with you, or spend the winter, so that you can send me on my way wherever I may be going. For I do not want to see you now only in passing, since I hope to stay for some time with you, if the Lord permits. But I shall stay in Ephesus until Pentecost; for a great and important door has opened for me, and my adversaries are many.

But if Timothy goes to you, see that he has nothing to fear from you, for he does the Lord's work, as I do; let no one treat him with contempt, but send him on his way in peace so that he can come to me, for I am waiting for him with the brothers.

As for our brother Apollos, I have much entreated him to visit you, along with the brothers; but his choice was not to go just now, but he will visit you when the time is right.

Be watchful, be steadfast in your faith, be brave, be strong. Let all be love among you. And I ask this of you, brothers: You know the household of Stephanas, that it was my first conversion in Achaea and that they have given themselves to the service of the saints; I ask you to work under such people, or anyone else who toils and labors with them. And I am happy in the presence here of Stephanas and Fortunatus and Achaicus, because they made up for your absence, since they refreshed my spirit and yours. Give recognition to men like these.

The churches of Asia send you greetings. Aquila and Prisca send many greetings, along with the church at their household. All the brothers send you greetings. Greet each other with the sacred kiss.

This greeting is in the hand of myself, Paul. A curse upon anyone who does not love the Lord. The Lord has come. The grace of the Lord Jesus be with you. My love be with you all, in Christ Jesus.

The Second Letter

to the Corinthians

¶PAUL, APOSTLE OF CHRIST JESUS BY
the will of God; and Timothy our brother; to the church
of God which is in Corinth, together with all the saints
who are in the whole of Achaea: grace and peace to you
from God our Father and the Lord Jesus Christ.

Praised be the God and Father of our Lord Jesus Christ,
the father of the mercies and the God of all consolation,
who comforts us in every affliction of ours, so that we
are able to comfort those who are in every affliction
through the consolation we ourselves received from God.
For as the sufferings of the Christ abound for us, so
through the Christ our consolation abounds. If we are
afflicted, it is for your comfort and salvation; if we are
comforted, it is for your comfort, which works in endurance of those same sufferings which we also undergo;
and our hope for you is firm, since we know that, as you
are sharers in our sufferings, so also you are sharers in
our consolation.

For we do not wish you to be unaware, brothers, of the
affliction which befell us in Asia, how we were burdened
beyond our powers so that we did not know whether we

could survive. For all we could do, we would have got the death sentence; so that our trust had to be not in ourselves but in God, who raises the dead, who rescued us, and will rescue us, from so great a danger of death; in whom we have hope, that he will still protect us, if only you will help with your prayers for us; so that the grace given us because of many persons may be thankfully received by many for our sake.

This is our cause for pride, the testimony of our consciousness that we behaved in the world in the holiness and purity of God, not by fleshly wisdom but by the grace of God, and especially in relation to you. We are not writing you anything except what you can read and understand; and I hope that you will understand us completely, as you have understood us in part; that we are your cause for pride, as you are ours, on the Day of our Lord Jesus.

It was in this spirit of confidence that I wished formerly to visit you, so that you could enjoy me a second time; to visit you on my way to Macedonia, and return from Macedonia to you, so that you could speed me on my way to Judaea. That was what I wished. Then did I turn fickle? Or when I make my plans, do I do it after the way of the flesh, so that I can say both yes yes and no no? Trust God that our message to you is not yes and no. For Christ Jesus the son of God, preached among you by us, myself and Silvanus and Timothy, was never yes and no, but yes is his nature. For all the promises of God through him are yes; and that is why, because of him, the amen is said for the glory of God by us. It is God who confirms us for Christ, along with you; who anointed us, and set his seal upon us, and deposited the first payment of the Spirit in our hearts

And I invoke God as witness, on my life, that it was to spare you that I gave up coming to Corinth; not that we are in charge of your faith; we work with you to bring you joy, since you have stood firm in your faith.

¶ I told myself that I must not visit you again in painful circumstances. For if I cause you pain, who else is there to gladden me, besides you, whom I caused pain? And I wrote this precisely so that I should not, visiting you, be caused pain by those who ought to bring me joy; being sure that, for all of you, my joy is the joy of you all. I wrote to you in great affliction and anguish of heart, with many tears, not so that you should be grieved, but so that you may know the love I have in surpassing degree for you.

But supposing someone really has caused trouble, he has not caused it for me but in part—not to exaggerate— for you all. For such a one, his punishment by the majority has been enough, so that now you should reverse yourselves and forgive and console him, so that the man I mean will not be overwhelmed by excessive suffering. Therefore I implore you to declare your love for him; since that is why I wrote, to learn of your disposition, whether you are in every way obedient. Whom you forgive I too forgive; and if I have forgiven, what I forgave was for your sake, before the face of Christ, so that we may not be taken advantage of by Satan; for we are not ignorant of what he has in mind.

When I reached Troas, for the gospel of the Christ, and when a door was opened for me by the Lord, I got no relief for my spirit because I did not find Titus, my brother; so I took my leave of the people and went on to Macedonia.

Thanks be to God who constantly leads us in triumph through Christ and through us manifests the savor of the knowledge of him in every region; for we are the fragrance of Christ for God among those who go the way of salvation and those who go the way of perdition; to these, the smell of death for death, to those others the smell of life for life. Who is qualified for that? We do not, like most, go about cheapening the word of God, but speak, as it were, out of purity, from God in the presence of God through Christ.

¶ Are we beginning to recommend ourselves to you once again? Or is it that we do not, as some do, need letters of recommendation to you or from you? You are our letter, written on our hearts, known and read by all men; because you are displayed as the letter of Christ administered by us, written not in ink but in the Spirit of the living God, not on tablets of stone but on the heart's tablets of flesh.

Such is the confidence we have in God through the Christ; not that we are qualified in ourselves to reason out anything, as if it came from ourselves, but our qualification is from God, who qualified us to be ministers of the new covenant, not of the letter but of the Spirit; for the letter kills, but the Spirit gives life. For if the ministry of death, engraved in letters on the stone, appeared in such glory that the sons of Israel could not look upon the face of Moses, which was perishable, because of the glory of that face; how can the ministry of the Spirit not be in even greater glory? If the ministry of condemnation is glory, all the more does the ministry of righteousness excel in glory. For what has been glorified is no longer glorious insofar as there is a glory that surpasses it; for if what is perishable has glory, how much greater is glory in what endures.

Having such hope as this, we speak out very plainly, not as when Moses put the veil over his face because the sons of Israel could not gaze upon the end of a glory that was passing away. But their minds were impenetrable. For until this very day the same veil remains when the old covenant is read and is not taken away, because only with Christ does it come to an end; but until this day when Moses is read the veil lies upon their hearts; but when anyone turns to the Lord the veil is taken away. And the Lord is the Spirit, and where the Lord's Spirit is, there is liberty. And all of us, with faces unveiled seeing as in a mirror the glory of the Lord, are transformed into the same image, from glory to glory, as from the Spirit of the Lord.

¶ We therefore, having this ministry bestowed in mercy upon us, do not weaken; but we have renounced acts which are hidden for shame, not going the way of wickedness or falsifying the word of God, but, by making plain the truth, presenting ourselves to the full consciousness of mankind before God. But if our gospel is hidden at all, it is hidden from those who are on their way to perdition. For them the God of this world has blinded the minds of these unbelievers so that the radiance of the gospel of the glory of Christ, who is the image of God, cannot shine upon them. For we do not preach ourselves, but Christ Jesus the Lord, and ourselves as your slaves for Jesus' sake. For the God who said: Out of the darkness light shall shine, has made a light in our hearts for the radiance of the knowledge of the glory of God in the face of Christ.

We keep this treasure in vessels of clay, so that the supremacy of power may be God's, not ours; always afflicted but not crushed, bewildered but not despairing, persecuted but not forsaken, cast down but not destroyed, always carrying the death of Jesus in our bodies so that the life of Jesus also may be made manifest in our bodies; for constantly we the living are handed over to death for Jesus' sake, so that the life of Jesus also may be made manifest in this mortal flesh of ours. So death is at work in us, but life in you.

And having the same spirit of faith as in what is written: I believed, therefore I spoke; we also believe, therefore we also speak, knowing that he who raised up Jesus will also raise us up with Jesus and bring us to him, along with you. For all is for your sake, so that grace increasing through greater numbers may make thanksgiving abound to the glory of God. So we do not weaken, and even if our outer man is destroyed, our inner man is renewed day by day. The light momentary affliction builds in us an ever greater and greater mass of eternal glory, in us who look not on things visible but on things invisible, for visible things are of the moment, but invisible things, eternal.

¶ For we know that if our home in this earthly tabernacle is destroyed, we have from God a home which is a building not made by hands, and eternal, in heaven. For while we are in this one we make complaints, longing to put on above it, like a garment, our habitation in heaven, if we are to be found still in our bodies covered and not naked. For we who are still in this tabernacle groan under our burden, because we wish not to put it off but to put on the other in addition, so that death may be swallowed up by life. And he who brought us to this is God, by granting us a deposit of the Spirit.

Always confident then and knowing that while we live in the body we live away from the Lord, for we go by what we believe, not what we see, we are of good courage and satisfied to leave the body and be at home with the Lord. So we aspire, whether in the body or out of it, to be pleasing to him; for we all must be shown for what we are before the tribunal of the Christ, so that each may receive good or evil according to what he did in the flesh.

Knowing then the fear of the Lord, we try to persuade men. To God we are well known; and I hope that we are also well known to you in your own consciences. We are not recommending ourselves to you again, but offering you some cause for pride in us, so that you may have an answer to those whose pride is in appearance and not in the heart. If we are out of our wits, it is for God; if we are in our right minds, it is for you. For the love of the Christ constrains us as we consider that he, alone, died for all (but really all died); and he died for all so that all who live may live, no longer for themselves, but for him who died for them, and was raised from the dead.

Thus from now on we know no one in the flesh. Even if we did know Christ in the flesh, we now no longer know him thus. So that one who is in Christ is a new creature; the old is gone, behold, the new is here; and all is from God, who reconciled us with himself through Christ, and gave us the ministry of this reconciliation, because when God was in Christ he reconciled the world with himself, not counting their sins against them, and establishing in us the word of reconciliation. So we are ambassadors for Christ, as if God were summoning you through us. For Christ's sake, we implore you, be reconciled with God. He made the one who knew no sin into sin for our sake, so that we, in him, may become the justice of God.

¶ Working with him, we implore you not to let God's grace be given in vain. For he says: At a favorable time I heard you, and on the day for salvation I came to your rescue. Behold, now is the favorable time, now is the day for salvation. We say this, giving no offence in any way, lest our ministry be blamed, but in every way showing ourselves to be ministers of God by enduring much; in afflictions, in duress, in anguish; through beatings, through imprisonments, through riots, through labors, through sleeplessness, through starvation; by purity, by understanding, by forbearance, by goodness, by the Holy Spirit, by undissembling love, by the word of truth, by the power of God; with the weapons of righteousness in the right hand and the left hand; through glory and dishonor, through slander and praise; as false and truthful, as unknown and recognized, as dying, and behold, we live, as punished but not with death, as in pain but always joyful, as poor but making many rich, as having nothing and possessing everything.

Our speech has been open to you, people of Corinth; our hearts are open to you. You are not inhibited by us, your inhibitions are in your own vitals. Give us what we give you; I speak to you as my children; and open your hearts also.

Do not be mismated with unbelievers. For what common ground is there for righteousness and lawlessness, or what fellowship between light and darkness? What agreement is there between Christ and Belial, or what is shared by believer and unbeliever? How can the temple of God make truce with idols? For we are the temple of the living God; as God said: I will live with them and walk among them, and I will be their God and they will be my people. Therefore go forth from among those others, and be apart from them, says the Lord; and do not touch what is unclean; and I will welcome you in; and I will be as a father to you, and you shall be as sons and daughters to me, says the Lord Almighty.

¶ Since we have these promises, dear friends, let us purify ourselves from every pollution of the flesh and spirit, completing our sanctification in the fear of God.

Make room for us. We have injured no one, corrupted no one, taken advantage of no one. I do not say this to fault you; I have told you before that you are in our hearts, to live and die together. I have great confidence in you, I take great pride in you; I am filled with comfort, I am overflowing with joy, through all our affliction.

For when we arrived in Macedonia, our flesh got no relief, but we were afflicted in every way; outward quarrels, inward fears; but God, who comforts the downcast, comforted us through the arrival of Titus; not only by his presence, but in the comfort he had received concerning you; for he told us of your longing, your sorrowing, your enthusiasm for me; so that I rejoiced the more. Even if I did grieve you by that letter, I do not regret it, though I did regret it; I see that that letter did grieve you, if only for a while; but now I rejoice: not because you were grieved but because your grief led to repentance, because you were grieved according to God's will, so that you have lost nothing with us. For grief by God's will causes repentance leading to salvation, not to be regretted; but the world's grief causes death. This very fact of your being grieved by God's will—see what activity it has caused in you: what defensiveness, what indignation, what fear, what longing, what zeal, what vindictiveness. In every way you have established your innocence in this matter. But if I wrote to you, it was not for the sake of the wrongdoer, or of the one who was wronged, but in order to make plain to you, in the sight of God, your own concern for us. Therefore, I have been comforted. And in addition to this, I have been all the more filled with joy over the happiness of Titus, because his spirit was set at rest by all of you. If I have ever boasted of you to him, I have not been put to shame for it; but just as everything I said to you was true, so also our boasting before Titus has proved to be true; and his heart is fully given to you as he remembers the obedient spirit in all of you, how you received him with fear and trembling. I am happy that I have full confidence in you.

¶ We would have you know, brothers, of the grace of God which was granted in the churches of Macedonia; that through a great ordeal of affliction the abundance of their joy, even though their poverty was extreme, overflowed into lavish generosity. I bear you witness that, to the extent of their means, and even beyond their means, of their own free will, they begged us with much entreaty to let them share in our ministering to the saints. And this was not as we had expected, but first they gave themselves, by God's will, to the Lord and to us; so that we asked Titus that, as he had originated this gift of grace, he should go to you to bring it to completion. Then, as you are lavishly endowed with faith and eloquence and understanding and every kind of enthusiasm, and in the love we have inspired in you, be lavish also in this work of grace.

In saying this I am not giving you an order; but by the example of others' eagerness I am trying to prove the genuineness of your own love; for you know the graciousness of our Lord Jesus Christ, and how, when he was rich, he made himself poor so that by his poverty you might become rich. And in this matter, here is my opinion. This is to your advantage. You made a good beginning last year, not only in what you did but in your willingness to do it. Now finish the work, so that your willingness to give may be matched by your actual giving, within your means. For the will is acceptable if one gives what he has, not beyond what he has. It should not be relief for others and hardship for you; but as it is now your surplus should be matched against their deficit, so that when they have a surplus it may meet your deficit, and all be made equal. As it is written: He who got much had no excess, and he who got little did not go short.

Thanks be to God, who granted that the same zealous concern for you should be in the heart of Titus, who accepted our plea and, in an excess of zeal, goes of his own accord to you. With him we are sending the brother whose preaching of the gospel is praised in all the churches; in addition to which he was elected by the churches to journey with us on this mission of grace which is being administered by us, for the glory of the Lord and to satisfy our own urge. We have this in mind, to avoid harsh criticism for the lavishness of this contribution administered by us; for we look for honor, not only in the judgment of God but in that of men. With them we are sending one of our brothers whom we have proved often in many circumstances to be enthusiastic, and who will be all the more so, by far, by reason of his great confidence in you. As for Titus, he is my partner and fellow worker for you; as for our brothers, they are apostles of the churches, the glorification of Christ. Give proof of your love for them, and the truth of the claims we made to them about you, in the presence of the congregations.

¶ It would be superfluous for me to write to you concerning contribution for the saints; for I know your great enthusiasm, a thing about which I have boasted to the Macedonians, saying that Achaea has been ready since last year; and your zeal stirred up most of them. But I am sending the brothers, to keep the boasts I have made about you in this matter from being proved empty; so that you may be ready, as I told them you were; to save us, not to mention you, from being embarrassed by your condition, supposing that some Macedonians were to arrive along with me and find you unprepared. So we thought it necessary to ask the brothers to go on to you before us and arrange for that bounty which has already been promised, so that it will be ready as a bountiful gift, not as something extorted. Consider this: He who sows sparingly will reap sparingly, and he who sows abundantly will reap abundantly. Let each give as he thinks right in his heart, not painfully, not forcibly, since God loves a cheerful giver. God has the power to make every grace abound for you, so that, always having full sufficiency in every way, you may have enough for every good work; as it is written: He scattered his bounty abroad, he gave to the poor; his righteousness abides into eternity. He who provides seed for the sower and bread for food will provide and multiply your store of seed and

increase the products of your righteousness. You will be
rich enough for all that generosity which, through us,
brings about thanksgiving to God; because the ministering of this service not only is the supplying of the saints'
needs, but also overflows into thanksgiving to God by
many. Through the proof of this ministry you will be
glorifying God, in addition to the obedience of your
confession to the gospel of the Christ, and the generosity
of your sharing with them and with all; and to their
prayers for your sakes when they love you for the surpassing grace of God in you. Thanks be to God for his
indescribable gift.

¶ Now I, Paul, appeal to you by the gentleness and cour-
tesy of the Christ, I who am humble when I am face to
face with you, but bold when I am away from you; and
what I ask is that I need not be bold when I am with
you, not with that boldness of confidence in which I believe I can venture against certain people who charge that
we live in the way of the flesh. We do live in the flesh,
but our campaign is not according to the flesh. For the
weapons of our campaign are not of the flesh, but, with
God's help, powerful enough to demolish strongholds. We
demolish arguments and everything raised up in pride
against the knowledge of God, and lead every thought in
captivity to obedience to the Christ, and are ready to
punish every disobedience, when your obedience is made
complete. Look at what is before your eyes. If anyone is
sure in his heart that he belongs to Christ, let him think
again and tell himself that, as he belongs to Christ, so
do we. Even if I do boast rather too much of our authority, which God gave us, to build you up, not to tear you
down, I shall not be put to shame. Let me not be thought

to be trying to frighten you by my letters. His letters, says someone, are weighty and powerful; but when he is here he is weak in body and his discourse is insignificant. Let that person realize that we are the same when we are absent and speaking through letters, and when we are present and acting.

We do not dare to rate ourselves or compare ourselves with certain people who put themselves forward; only they do not realize that they are measuring themselves against themselves and comparing themselves with themselves. We shall not go infinitely far in our pride, but only within the measure of what God gave us as our portion, which reaches as far as to you. We are not overextending our authority, as if it did not reach as far as you, for we were the first to come to you with the gospel of the Christ. We do not spread our proud claims infinitely far, where others have done the work, but rather hope that, as your faith grows, we shall become surpassingly great in our own territory, so that we can bring the gospel to places beyond you, without making proud claims to work already done in someone else's territory. Let him who takes pride take pride in the Lord; for it is not the man who commends himself who is approved, but the man whom the Lord commends.

¶I wish you could put up with a little bit of silliness from me. Please do put up with it; for I am jealous over you as God might be jealous, for I have contracted to bring you like a pure virgin to one bridegroom only: to Christ. But I am afraid that, as the serpent in his knavery seduced Eve, your minds may be corrupted from their innocence and pure devotion to the Christ. For if someone comes along and preaches another Jesus, whom we did not preach, or you receive another spirit which you had not received before, or another gospel which you had not accepted before, you put up with him cheerfully. But I think we do not in any way fall short of the super-apostles; even if I am an amateur in oratory, I am not one in understanding, as we demonstrated to you in each and every way.

Did I make a mistake in lowering myself so that you should be exalted, because we brought you the gospel of God as a free gift? I robbed other churches by accepting stipends from them in order to serve you; when I was with you, and in need, I was never a burden to any one of you, since the brothers who came from Macedonia supplied my needs, and I always kept myself, and shall keep myself, from burdening you. As Christ's truth is in me, I shall not be kept from making this claim in all the region of Achaea. Why? Because I do not love you? God knows I do.

This I do, and this I shall do to cut away the pretexts of those who desire a pretext for boasting that they are found to be our equals. Such people are the false apostles, treacherous workers, disguised as apostles of Christ. And no wonder; even Satan disguises himself as the angel of light, so there is nothing startling if his ministers disguise themselves as ministers of righteousness. Their end will be what their acts have deserved.

I say once again, let no one take me for a fool; but if you do, then accept me as a fool, so that I too can do a little boasting. What I say now has nothing to do with the Lord, but in this state of boastfulness I am speaking, as it were, like a madman. Since many boast about matters of the flesh, I shall boast too. You, being sensible people, cheerfully put up with fools; you put up with anyone who enslaves you, eats you alive, lays hands on you, browbeats you, or hits you in the face. I say to our shame, we are too weak for that; but where one can show his daring, I mean, in madness, I too am daring. Are they Hebrews? So am I. Are they Israelites? So am I. Are they the seed of Abraham? So am I. Are they ministers of Christ? In my madness I say it: I am, more than they. With more labors, more imprisonments, many more beatings, often near the point of death; five times I took the thirty-nine lashes from the Jews, three times I was beaten with rods, once stoned, three times shipwrecked, and spent a day and a night in the water; often on the road, with danger from rivers, danger from brigands, danger from my own people, danger from foreigners, danger in the city, danger in the wilds, danger at sea, danger among false brothers; with toil and hardship, often sleepless, in hunger and thirst, often famished, cold, and naked. Aside from externals, there was the day-by-day pressure on me, my anxious concern for all the churches. Who fails, without my failing with him? Who goes astray, without my burning in sympathy? If I must boast, I will boast about those matters which show my weakness. God, the father of the Lord Jesus, blessed forever and ever, knows that I am not lying. In Damascus the local governor for King Aretas had the city of the Damascenes under guard so as to seize me; but I was lowered in a basket through a window in the wall, and so escaped his hands.

¶ I must make my boast. It does me no good, but I will go on to speak of visions and revelations of the Lord. I know of a Christian man fourteen years ago, who, whether in his body or out of it I do not know, God knows, was caught up into the third heaven. And I know that such a man, whether in his body or out of his body I do not know, God knows, was caught up into paradise and heard secret sayings which it is not lawful for any man to repeat. Of such a man I will boast, but not of myself except in the matter of my weaknesses. If I do choose to boast, I shall not be a fool, because what I say will be true; but I refrain, not wishing anyone to think me better than what he sees and hears, judging me by the greatness of the things revealed to me. Because of these, to keep me from self-conceit, a thorn was stuck into my flesh, an angel of Satan, to hurt me and keep me from self-conceit. Concerning this I called three times upon the Lord to remove it from me; but he said to me: My grace is enough for you; your power is fulfilled in your weakness. Therefore I will boast the more gladly in my weaknesses, so that the power of the Christ may reside in me. So I am well pleased with weaknesses, outrages, duress, pursuit, and hardships, for the sake of Christ; for when I am weak, then I am strong.

I have been a fool. But you forced me to it. I should have been recommended by you. For I have in no way come short of the super-apostles, even though I am nothing; for the signs of the apostle have been demonstrated among you with every kind of patience, by signs and portents and miracles. In what have you been treated worse than the other churches except that I have not been a burden upon you? Pardon me for this injustice.

Here I am ready to visit you for the third time, and I shall not be a burden upon you; for I want you, not your money, since children are not obliged to store up treasures for the parents, but parents for their children. I will most gladly spend and be expended myself for the sake of your lives. If I love you excessively, am I the less beloved? Concede, I did not burden you. But was I really unscrupulous and took you by guile? Could I have taken advantage of you through one of those I sent to you? I asked Titus to go and I sent the brother with him. Surely Titus did not take advantage of you? Do we not go in the same spirit as he? In the same footsteps?

Have you been thinking all this while that we were defending ourselves to you? We are speaking as Christians, before God. And all is for your edification, dear friends, for I am afraid I might arrive and find you not as I would wish you to be, and I myself be found not as you wish me to be; and there will be rivalry, jealousy, rages, ambitions, slanders, whisperings, pretensions, disorderliness. I am afraid God might humiliate me before you once again, and I may have to mourn over many of those who sinned before and did not repent of the viciousness and lechery and unchastity of which they were guilty.

¶ I am coming to you for the third time; and everything said shall be established by the mouths of two, or three, witnesses. As I warned you on my second visit, so I warn you now in my absence, both those who sinned before and all the rest: when I come again I will not spare you, since you demand a proof of the Christ who speaks in me. He is not weak against you but strong among you, since he was crucified because of weakness but lives because of the power of God. We too are weak with him but shall live with him because of the power of God. Test yourselves, whether you are still in the faith, assess yourselves. Do you not know yourselves, and that Jesus Christ is in you? Unless you prove unworthy. I hope you will recognize that we are not unworthy. And we pray to God that you will not do anything wrong, not so that we may appear worthy, but so that you may do what is good and we may be, as it were, the unworthy ones. We cannot do anything against the truth, only on the side of the truth. We rejoice when we are weak and you are strong; that is what we are praying for, your improvement. Therefore I write this while I am still absent from you, so as not to use too sharply, when I am with you, the authority which the Lord gave me (to build you up, not to tear you down).

For the rest, brothers, farewell; improve yourselves, encourage each other, agree, be at peace, and the God of love and peace will be with you. Greet each other with the sacred kiss. All the saints send you greetings. May the grace of our Lord Jesus Christ and the love of God and the fellowship of the Holy Spirit be with you all.

The Letter
to the Galatians

¶PAUL, THE APOSTLE, NOT FROM MEN, nor through man, but through Jesus Christ and God the Father who raised him from the dead; and all the brothers who are with me, to the churches of Galatia: grace to you and peace, from God our Father and the Lord Jesus Christ, who gave himself for our sins, to rescue us from the present age, which is evil; according to the will of our God and Father, whose glory is forever and ever. Amen.

I am amazed that you have so quickly forsaken the man who summoned you by the grace of Christ, for another gospel, which is not another gospel; unless there are some people who are confusing you and trying to upset the gospel of the Christ. But even if anyone, we ourselves or an angel from heaven, announces any gospel that is contrary to the gospel we brought you, let him be damned. I have said it before and I say it again now, if anyone brings you a gospel contrary to the one you have been given, let him be damned.

Am I appealing now to men or to God? Or am I trying to please men? If I were still trying to please men, I should not be the slave of Christ. For I would have you know, brothers, the gospel you received from me is not according to man; nor did I receive it from man, nor was I taught it by man, but by the revelation of Jesus Christ.

For you have heard how I used to act when I was a Judaist, how excessively I persecuted and assailed the church of God, and went further in the Jewish faith than many contemporaries of my own kind, since I was an extreme zealot for the traditions of our fathers. But when he, who had marked me from my mother's womb and summoned me by his grace, was pleased to reveal his son through me, so that I should bring his gospel to the Gentiles, I did not turn at once to any flesh and blood, nor did I go up to Jerusalem to those who were apostles before me, but I went into Arabia and then returned to Damascus. Then after three years I went up to Jerusalem to learn to know Peter, and I stayed with him for fifteen days, but I did not see any other of the apostles except James the brother of the Lord. Behold, before God, what I am writing you is no lie. Then I went to the regions of Syria and Cilicia. But I was not known personally in the churches of Christ in Judaea; they had only heard this: the man who once persecuted us is now preaching the gospel of the faith which he used to assail. And they glorified God for me.

¶ Then after fourteen years I went up to Jerusalem again, with Barnabas, and taking Titus along. I went up in obedience to a vision; and I put before them the gospel which I preach among the Gentiles; but I did it privately, to the men of mark, so that the race I ran should not be run, or have been run, in vain. Even Titus, who was with me and was a Greek, was not forced to be circumcised, but only might have been because of some so-called brothers

who were brought in, who stole in to spy on that freedom which we had in Christ Jesus, and to enslave us.
But we did not for one moment give way and obey them;
so that the truth of the gospel might be preserved for
you. But of those who were thought to have some standing—which ones they were does not matter to me, God
is no respecter of persons—those who were thought to
have some standing did not make any additions to my
gospel. On the contrary, they saw that I had been entrusted with the gospel for the uncircumcised just as Peter had been with the circumcised; for he who had moved
Peter to his mission to the circumcised had moved me
to go to the Gentiles. And realizing the grace that had
been granted to me, James and Peter and John, who are
held to be the pillars of the church, gave Barnabas and
me the right hand of fellowship, that we should go to
the Gentiles and they to the circumcised; only we should
remember their poor, which I have taken pains to do.

Then when Peter came to Antioch, I stood up to him
face to face because he was plainly at fault. Before the
arrival of certain people from James he had been eating
with the Gentiles; but when these came he flinched and
removed himself from them, fearing the representatives
of the circumcised. And the other Jews were hypocrites
along with him, so that even Barnabas followed them in
their hypocrisy, but when I saw that they were deviating
from the truth of the gospel, I said to Peter before them
all: If you, a Jew, live like a Gentile and not like a Jew,
how can you make the Gentiles be like Jews?

We, Jews by birth, not sinners from among the Gentiles, knowing that a man is not justified by doing what
is in the law unless it is through belief in Christ Jesus,
believe, we too, in Christ Jesus, so that we may be jus-

tified by faith in Christ and not by doing what is in the law. It is not from the law that all flesh shall be justified. But if while seeking to be justified in Christ we ourselves are found to be also sinners, then is Christ the minister of sin? Never! But if I rebuild what I tore down, I make myself a transgressor. Because of the law I died in the law to live for God. I have been crucified with Christ. It is no longer I who live, but Christ lives in me. But I who now live in the flesh live in faith in the son of God who loved me and gave himself for me. I do not reject the grace of God. For if righteousness comes through the law, then Christ died in vain.

¶ O foolish Galatians, who bewitched you, before whose eyes Christ was displayed on the cross? I should like to learn this one thing from you: Did you receive the Spirit from doing what is in the law or from listening to faith? Are you so foolish? Did you begin with the spirit and now end with the flesh? Did you undergo all this in vain? If it really is in vain. Does he who provides you with the Spirit and works wonders among you do this because you are doing what is in the law or listening to faith? It is like Abraham, who believed God and it was counted as righteousness in him.

You know that it is those who believe who are the sons of Abraham. For the scripture, foreseeing that God would justify the nations by faith, brought this gospel first to Abraham, saying: In you all the nations shall be blessed. So that those who are of the faith are blessed along with the faithful Abraham. All whose conduct is controlled by the law are subject to a curse; for it is written: Anyone is accursed who does not abide by all things written in the book of the law, that he must do them.

That no one is justified with God by the law is evident, because: The righteous man shall live by faith. But the law is not a matter of faith; rather it says: He who does these things shall live by them. Christ ransomed us from the curse of the law by becoming the thing accursed, for our sake, since it is written: Accursed is everyone who hangs upon the tree; so that, by Jesus Christ, the blessing of Abraham might come to the nations, so that we may receive the promise of the Spirit through our faith.

Brothers, I am speaking in human terms. No one can nullify or add to the testament of a human being when it has been ratified. The promises were spoken to Abraham and his descendant. It does not say, and to his descendants, as for many; but as for one, and to your descendant, that is, Christ. This is what I am saying; that law, which came four hundred and thirty years later, does not disqualify so as to make void the promise, a testament that was ratified before by God. For if the inheritance came from the law, it would not come from the promise; but to Abraham God gave it as a grace through the promise.

What, then, of the law? It was added because of transgressions, until the coming of the descendant to whom the promise was made. It was ordained by angels through the hand of a mediator. But what is one does not have a mediator; and God is one. Then is the law against the promises of God? Never. For if a law which could create life had been given, righteousness would have been in the law. But scripture had everything confined in sin so that the promise could be given, by faith in Jesus Christ, to those who believe.

For before faith came we were in the custody of the law, confined until the coming revelation of faith. Thus the law was our tutor until Christ, so that we could be justified by faith; but since faith came we are no longer under a tutor. For you are all sons of God through your faith in Christ Jesus. All of you who have been baptized in Christ have armed yourselves in Christ. There is neither Jew nor Greek, slave nor free, male nor female; for you are all one in Christ Jesus. And if you are Christ's, then you are the seed of Abraham, heirs by the promise.

¶ But I am saying, that as long as the heir is a child, even if he is head of the whole household he is no better than a slave; he is under guardians and caretakers until the time, set by his father, when he comes of age. So we too when we were children were enslaved to the elements of the world; but in the fullness of time God sent his son, born of a woman, born under the law, to ransom those who were under the law so that we may be given our adoption. Because you are sons, God sent the Spirit of his son to our hearts crying Abba, Father. So you are no longer a slave but a son; and if a son, then heir, because of God.

Now at that time you did not know God and were enslaved to beings which are not by nature gods; but now, when you do know God, or rather are known by God, how is it that you turn back to the weak and beggarly elements, and want to be their slaves once more? You keep count of days and months and seasons and years. I am afraid I may have labored on you in vain.

Be as I am, brothers, I pray you, because I am as you are. You did me no wrong. You know that I was sick in body when I brought you the gospel before; and when I was a trial to you, because of my physical state, you did not despise or reject me, but received me as if I were an angel of God, as if I were Christ Jesus. Where then is your delight in me gone? For I testify to you that if you could have, you would have dug out your eyes and given them to me. Then have I turned into your enemy by telling the truth? They are zealous for your favor, not fairly, but they wish to keep you in seclusion, so that you may be zealous for their favor. To be honorably favored, not only when I am there with you, is always good, my children, whom I am laboring to give birth to once more until Christ takes shape in you. But I wish I could be with you now, and change my way of speaking; because I do not know what to do about you.

Tell me, you who wish to be under the law, do you not listen to the law? It is written that Abraham had two sons, one by the slave girl and one by the free woman. But the one by the slave girl was begotten in the flesh, and the one by the free woman through the promise. These are allegories. For the women are the two covenants: one is from Mount Sinai, breeding for slavery; this is Hagar, and Hagar is Mount Sinai in Arabia, but she corresponds to the present Jerusalem, for she is enslaved along with her children. But the Jerusalem which is above is free, and she is the mother of us. Since it is written: Rejoice, barren woman who bore no child; break forth and shout aloud, woman who had no labor pains; for the children of the deserted one shall be far more than hers who kept the husband.

Now we, brothers, are children by the promise, like Isaac. But just as then the one born in the flesh persecuted the one born in the spirit, so it is now. But what does the scripture say? Cast out the slave girl and her son, for the son of the slave girl shall never inherit with the son of the free woman. Thus, brothers, we are the children not of the slave girl but of the free woman.

¶ Christ liberated us to freedom. Stand fast, then, and do not be caught again under the yoke of slavery.

Behold, I, Paul, tell you that if you become circumcised Christ will do you no good. And I testify once more to every man who is circumcised that he is under obligation to perform all the law. All of you who justify yourselves by the law are lost to Christ; you have fallen from grace. For we are given hope of righteousness by the Spirit, from faith. For in Christ neither circumcision nor uncircumcision has force, but only faith working through love.

You were running well. Who broke your stride, so as to keep you from believing the truth? The temptation was not from him who called you. A little leavening raises the whole mass of dough. I believe in you, that, the Lord helping, you will not take the wrong view; but the one who is confusing you shall bear the blame, whoever he may be. If I, brothers, am still preaching circumcision, why am I still persecuted? Then the difficulty of the cross has been made void. I wish that those who are unsettling you would also castrate themselves.

You were called to freedom, brothers; only not freedom for the impulse of the flesh. Rather be enslaved to each other by love. For the entire law is fulfilled in one saying, that is: You shall love your neighbor as yourself. But if you bite and try to devour each other, beware of being destroyed by each other. But I tell you, follow the spirit and do not fulfill the desire of the flesh. For the flesh has its desires, which oppose the spirit, and the spirit opposes the flesh; for these two are set as opposites to each other, to keep you from doing what you wish to do. But if you are led by the spirit, you are not subject to the law. And the works of the flesh are plain to see. They are lechery, viciousness, unchastity, idolatry, sorcery, hatreds, rivalry, jealousy, rages, ambitions, dissensions, partisanships, envy, drinking bouts, orgies, and that sort of thing. And I warn you, as I warned you before, that those who practice that sort of thing shall not inherit the Kingdom of God. But the harvest of the spirit is love, joy, peace, patience, kindness, goodness, faithfulness, gentleness, temperance. The law is not against such things. But those who belong to Jesus crucify their flesh with its passions and desires. If we live by the spirit, let us also follow the spirit. Let us not be vain-minded, challenging each other, envying each other.

¶ Brothers, if a person is caught in some transgression, you, who are spiritual, must set him right in a spirit of gentleness; examining yourself, for fear you also may be tempted. Take up each other's burdens, and thus fulfill the law of the Christ. For if a man thinks he amounts to something and does not, he is deceiving himself; let each one evaluate his own actions, and then he will have cause for pride in himself alone and not in any other; for each one will carry his own burden.

And let the one who is being instructed in the word share in all good things with his instructor.

Do not be deceived: God is not made light of. For what a man sows, that he will also reap; because if he sows for his own flesh, he will reap, from the flesh, destruction; but he who sows for the spirit will reap, from the spirit, life everlasting. Let us not weaken in doing good, for at our proper time we shall reap, if we do not give out. So then, while we have time, let us do good to all, but especially to those who are of the family of the faith.

See with what big letters I have written in my own hand.

Those who wish to look well in the flesh are the ones who are trying to make you be circumcised, only so that they may not be persecuted for the cross of Christ. For those who are circumcised do not themselves keep the law; but they want you to be circumcised so that they can take pride in your bodies. But for us, let there be no pride except in the cross of our Lord Jesus Christ, through whom the world is crucified for me, and I for the world. For neither circumcision nor uncircumcision means anything; only to be created anew does. And for all who follow this rule, peace and mercy to them, and to God's Israel.

Henceforth, let no one give me trouble; for I carry the stigmata of Jesus on my body.

May the grace of the Lord Jesus be with your spirit, brothers. Amen.

The Letter
to the Ephesians

¶PAUL, APOSTLE OF CHRIST JESUS BY
the will of God, to the saints who are in Ephesus and
who believe in Christ Jesus: grace to you and peace from
God our father and the Lord Jesus Christ.

Blessed be the God and father of our Lord Jesus Christ,
who blessed us in Christ with every spiritual blessing in
heaven, as he chose us in Christ, before the foundation
of the world, to be pure and blameless in love in his presence; preordaining us for adoption to himself as sons
through Jesus Christ, by the favor of his will, for the
praise of the glory of his grace he bestowed on us through
his beloved son. We have our redemption through his
blood, the remission of our sins, by the wealth of the
grace which he made abundant for us, by complete wisdom and intelligence making known to us the mystery
of his will; by the favor which he set forth in him, for
his scheme for the fulfillment of the ages, that everything in heaven and on earth should be summed up in
the Christ. It was he by whom we, preordained, received
our inheritance by the plan of him who works all things
according to the purpose of his will, so that we, the first
to hope in Christ, must praise his glory. You too are with

him; having heard the word of truth, the gospel of your salvation, and believing, you have been sealed by the Holy Spirit of the promise. This is the first installment of our inheritance, for our redemption as his property, and the praise of his glory.

I also, therefore, hearing of your faith in the Lord Jesus and the love you have for all the saints, never cease to give thanks for you; and I remember you in my prayers, praying that the God of our Lord Jesus Christ, the Father of glory, may grant you the spirit of wisdom and revelation in the recognition of him; that the eyes of your hearts may be filled with light, so that you may know what is the hope he calls you to, what is the wealth of glory in the inheritance he grants you among the saints, and what is the surpassing greatness of his power for us who believe, by the working of the supremacy of his strength which he has realized in the Christ. This he did by raising him from the dead, and seating him by his right hand in the heavens, above every realm and authority and power and lordship, and every name that is named not only in this age but in the age to come. And he put everything beneath his feet, and gave him headship entire over the church, which is his body, the fulfillment of him who fulfills all things in all.

¶ You were dead men by reason of your transgressions and sins in which you once walked, following the Presence of this world, the lord of the dominion of the air, the spirit which is now at work in the sons of disobedience. And with you we too, all of us, once followed the desires of our flesh, doing the bidding of our flesh and our senses, and we were natural children of the wrath, like all the rest. But God, being rich in mercy through the great love he has for us, though we were dead by our transgressions, brought us to life along with Christ; you have been saved by grace; and he revived us, along with Christ Jesus, and seated us beside him in the heavens, to show to ages to come the surpassing abundance of his grace in his kindness to us through Christ Jesus. You have been saved by grace through faith. This does not come from you; God's is the gift; not from anything you have done; let no one be proud. We are his handiwork, made in Christ Jesus for the good works for which God readied us so that we should be active in them.

Remember, then, that once you, the Gentiles in the flesh, called uncircumcision by what is called circumcision, a thing done in the flesh by human hands; that at that time you were without Christ, shut out from the community of Israel and strangers to the covenants of the promise, without hope and godless in the world. But now through Christ Jesus you, who were once far off, are now near by the blood of the Christ. He himself is the peace between us. He made the two things one, who broke down the middle partitioning wall, the hatred, with his own body, who abolished the law of the commandments given in ordinances; to make the two men in him into one new man by establishing peace, and reconcile both, in one body, with God, killing the hatred in his own person by the cross. With his coming he announced the gospel of peace to you, who were far off, and peace to those who were near; because through him we have, both alike, access to the Father in a single Spirit.

You are, therefore, no longer foreigners and resident aliens, but you are fellow citizens of the saints and members of the household of God; built upon the foundation of the apostles and prophets, whose capstone is

Christ Jesus himself. By him all construction is made harmonious and grows into a temple sacred in the Lord; into which you also are built as a dwelling place of God in the spirit.

¶Because of this, I, Paul, prisoner of Christ Jesus for the sake of you, the Gentiles, say this to you. You must have heard of the stewardship of grace which was granted to me to bring to you. Through revelation a mystery was made known to me, as I have already written to you in a brief account; reading which, you can understand my insight into the mystery of the Christ. This was not made known to other generations of the sons of man as it has now been revealed in the Spirit to his holy apostles and prophets; namely, that the Gentiles are co-heirs, incorporate, fellow sharers in the promise by Jesus Christ through his gospel. Of this I became a minister by God's gift of grace granted to me by the working of his power; to me, the least of all the saints, this grace was given, to bring to the Gentiles the gospel of the incalculable bounty of the Christ, and to bring to light the nature of the scheme of the mystery, which was hidden from the ages in God, who created all things; so that now the intricate wisdom of God may be made known, through the church, to all the realms and authorities in heaven. All this is according to the eternal plan which he brought about in Christ Jesus our Lord, in whom we have our confidence and access in trust because of our faith in him.

Therefore I ask you not to lose heart because of my sufferings for your sake. This is your glory.

Because of this, I bend my knees before the father from whom every family in heaven and on earth is named, praying that in the abundance of his glory he may grant that you be confirmed in strength, of the inward man, through his spirit, and that by your faith you make the Christ dwell in love in your hearts; that, rooted and founded, you may, with all the saints, have strength to understand the breadth and length and height and depth of the love of Christ and know it, though it surpasses knowledge; so that you may be filled with all the fullness of God.

To him who can bring to pass all things far beyond what we ask or think of through the power which is at work in us, to him be the glory in the church and in Christ Jesus for all the generations forever and ever. Amen.

¶ I, then, prisoner for the Lord, call upon you to proceed in a way worthy of the calling you received; with all humility and gentleness, with patience, bearing with each other in love, striving to preserve your singleness of spirit by the bond of peace: one body and one spirit, as your calling involved one hope; one Lord, one faith, one baptism; one God and Father of all, who is over all and through all and in all. But to each one of us was given a gift of grace in accordance with the measure of the Christ's giving.

Therefore scripture says: He went up to the height, and took many captives; and he gave gifts to men. But what does: He went up mean, unless he had also gone down to the nether parts of the earth? He who went down is the same as he who went up above all the heavens, to make all things complete. And the same one granted to some to be apostles, some to be prophets, some to be evangelists, some to be pastors and teachers; all these for the training of the saints for the work of ministry, for

the building of the body of the Christ, until we all attain
to singleness of faith and knowledge of the son of God,
to complete manhood and the measure of full maturity
of the Christ. Thus we shall no longer be children storm-
tossed and swept along by every wind of doctrine, at the
mercy of people unscrupulous in contriving our misdirection; but truthfully and with love grow in all ways
toward him who is our head, Christ; dependent on whom
the whole body, harmonized with itself and joined together by every connective sinew, through the measured
activity of every part, brings about the body's development toward its own completeness by love.

I tell you, then, and charge you by the Lord, to live no
longer as the heathens do in the vanity of their minds,
darkened as they are in their perceptions, alienated from
the life of God through the ignorance that is in them
because of the impenetrability of their hearts. In their
insensibility they have given themselves up to debauchery for the practice of every kind of vice, insatiably. This
is not how you learned the Christ, if indeed you did hear
him and were taught in him how the truth is in Jesus:
namely, that you must put off, with your former way of
life, your old person, the one corrupted by desire for pleasure, and be remade anew in the spirit of your minds,
and put on the new person, the one created by God's will
in true righteousness and piety.

Put aside falsehood, therefore, and each of you speak
the truth with your neighbor, because we are members
of each other. Are you angry? Even so, do no wrong. Do
not let the sun set on your anger; do not give the devil
room. Let the thief steal no longer, but rather work hard
with his hands to produce some good, so that he will
have enough to share with one who is in need. Let no

corrupt speech proceed from your mouth, but only what will help where it is needed, to bestow grace on those who hear you. And do not exasperate the Holy Spirit of God by which you have been sealed for the day of redemption. Let all bitterness and anger and rage and loudness and abuse be gone from you, with every kind of malice. Be kind and compassionate toward each other, forgiving each other as God through Christ forgave you.

¶ Make yourselves imitators of God as beloved children, and act in love; as Christ loved you and gave himself as a fragrant sacrificial offering to God for your sake.

Let lechery and every kind of immorality or greed be, as befits saints, not even mentioned among you; avoid also indecent silly facile talk, which is unbecoming. You should rather be giving thanks. For you know well that any lecherous or vicious or greedy person, an idol worshipper, that is, has no share in the Kingdom of the Christ and God.

Let no one deceive you with empty talk. Through this, the anger of God comes against the sons of disobedience. Have nothing to do with these. Once you were darkness, now you are light, through the Lord. Conduct yourselves as children of light, for what issues from light is always goodness and righteousness, and truth. Try to determine what is well pleasing to the Lord; and have no part in the barren works of darkness, but rather expose them, for the things that are done in secret by those people are shameful even to speak of; but everything that is exposed by the light is illuminated, for everything that is illuminated is light. Therefore scripture says: Sleeper, awake, and rise from the dead, and the Christ will give you light.

So watch your behavior carefully, like wise people, not foolish ones, making the most of your time, because these are evil days. Therefore do not be thoughtless but study to know the Lord's will; and do not get drunk on wine, which means dissipation, but fill yourselves with the Spirit, talking to each other in psalms and hymns and spiritual songs, singing and making music for the Lord in your hearts, always giving thanks for all things to God the Father in the name of our Lord Jesus Christ, and subordinating yourselves to each other in awe of Christ. Wives should subordinate themselves to their own husbands as to the Lord, because the husband is the head of the wife as the Christ is the head of the church, the very savior of the body. But as the church is subordinate to the Christ, so wives should be subordinate to their husbands in everything.

Husbands, love your wives as Christ loved the church and gave himself up for her sake, to sanctify her by washing her clean with water in the word, so as to set the church next to himself in glory, with no spot or wrinkle or anything of the sort upon her, but to be holy and without flaw. Thus also husbands ought to love their wives as they love their own bodies. One who loves his wife loves himself, for no one ever hated his own flesh, but one nourishes it and cherishes it, as the Christ does with the church, because we are parts of his own body. For this reason a man will leave his father and mother and cling to his wife and the two of them will be one flesh. This is a great mystery; I am speaking of Christ and the church; but you also should each one of you love his own wife as he does himself, and the wife should be in awe of her husband.

¶ Children, be obedient to your parents; it is right to do so. Honor your father and mother, for this is the first commandment, with the promise: That so it may be well with you, and you will live long upon the earth. And you, fathers, do not try your children's patience, but raise them in the training and precepts of the Lord.

And you, slaves, obey your human masters as you obey the Christ, with fear and trembling and in simplicity of heart, not with service to catch the eye and please people, but as slaves of Christ doing the will of God, doing slave work with good will from the heart, as for the Lord and not for men, knowing that everyone who does what is good will receive good from the Lord, whether he be slave or free. And you, masters, do likewise toward them, sparing your threats, knowing that their master and yours also is in heaven, and that there is no discrimination with him.

Lastly, strengthen yourselves in the Lord and in the supremacy of his might. Put on the full armor of God so that you can stand against the treacherous attacks of the devil; because ours is no struggle against flesh and blood, but against the realms, against the authorities, against the world rulers of this darkness, against the spirits of evil in heaven. Therefore assume the full armor of God so that you can oppose them on this evil day and, overcoming all, stand firm. Take your stand then, belted around the waist with truth, wearing the breastplate of righteousness, and your feet shod with the boots of the gospel of peace, over all holding up the shield of faith with which you will be able to put out all the burning arrows of the Evil One. And take the helmet of salvation, and the sword of the Spirit, which is the word of God. Do this with all prayer and entreaty, praying in the spirit on every occasion. To this end be wakeful with full endurance, and with prayers for all the saints. And pray for me, that the words may come when I open my mouth, to make known boldly the mystery of the gospel whose ambassador, in chains, I am; that I may be able to speak boldly, as I ought to do.

And so that you also will know about me, and how I am faring, Tychicus will tell you everything; my beloved brother and trusted helper in the Lord, whom I send you for this very purpose, so that you may learn about us, and so that he may comfort your hearts.

Peace to the brothers, and love, with faith, from God the Father and the Lord Jesus Christ. Grace be with all who love our Lord Jesus Christ in his immortality.

The Letter
to the Philippians

¶PAUL AND TIMOTHY, SLAVES OF
Christ Jesus, to all the saints of Christ Jesus who are
in Philippi, together with their bishops and deacons:
grace to you and peace from God our Father and the Lord
Jesus Christ.

I thank my God for you every time I mention you in
my prayers, in every one of my prayers for all of you. I
make my prayer with joy, because of your sharing in the
gospel from the first day until now; being confident that
he who began the good work among you will go on per-
fecting it until the Day of Jesus Christ. So it is right for
me to feel thus about all of you, because you hold me in
your hearts, and during my imprisonment and my defense of myself and confirmation of the gospel you have
shared in grace with me, all of you. As God is my witness, I long for you with the love of Christ Jesus. And
this is my prayer, that your love may grow more and
more in understanding and all perception, so that you
can determine what is right and wrong; so that you may
be pure and blameless for the Day of Christ, fulfilling
the harvest of righteousness that comes through Jesus
Christ for the glory and praise of God.

I wish you to know, brothers, that what has happened to me has gone toward the advancement of the gospel; so my imprisonment for Christ has become well known in the whole praetorian camp and to everyone else; and most of our brothers, trusting in the Lord, begin to preach the word of God the more fearlessly because of my imprisonment. Some preach the Christ in a spirit of envy and contentiousness, others in good will; these with love, knowing that I lie in prison because of my defense of the gospel; but the others proclaim the Christ out of spite, not sincerely, thinking to cause trouble through my bondage. But what of that? In one way or another, whether in pretense or in truth, Christ is being proclaimed, and in that I rejoice. And I shall continue to rejoice, for I know that this will turn out to be salvation for me, through your prayers and the support of the spirit of Jesus Christ; all this as I hope and eagerly expect that I shall not be put to shame in any way, but that with full freedom of speech, as now and always, Christ will be exalted in this body of mine, whether in life or death.

For me, Christ is life, and to die is a gain. But what if living in the flesh brings some good from the effort? I do not know which to choose. I am caught between the two. My desire is to depart this life and be with Christ, for that is much better; but my staying in the flesh is more useful, because of you. And this I confidently know, that I will stay and stand by all of you for the advancement of your faith and your joy in it, so that your pride in me may abound in Christ Jesus when I am with you once again.

Only live lives worthy of the gospel of the Christ, so that whether I come and see you or hear about you in my absence, I shall know that you are enduring in a sin-

gle spirit, in a single feeling striving to help the belief in
the gospel, in no way frightened by your adversaries. This
is the proof of destruction for them and salvation for you,
and it comes from God: that with respect to Christ you
were given the privilege not only of believing in him but
of suffering for him. Your contest is the same one that
you have seen as mine, and now hear of as mine.

¶ If, then, there is any encouragement in Christ, any consolation in love, any community of spirit, any compassion and feelings of pity, make my joy complete by being
unanimous, sharing the same love, harmonious, one in
purpose; without emulation or vanity but in your modesty always thinking that others among you are better
than yourselves; not looking each for his own interest
but every one for the rest. Keep this purpose in yourselves, one which is also in Christ Jesus. He was in the
form of God, but did not think to seize on the right to
be equal to God, but he stripped himself by taking the
form of a slave, being born in the likeness of a human
being; and being found in the guise of a human being,
he humiliated himself and was obedient to the death,
death on the cross. Therefore God exalted him and graced
him with the name which is above every name, so that
at the name of Jesus every knee shall bend, of those in
heaven and on earth and under the earth, and every
tongue shall confess, to the glory of God the Father, that
the Lord is Jesus Christ.

So, my beloved people, as you have always been obedient, continue to work out your own salvation in fear
and trembling, not only when I am with you but now all
the more by far in my absence. For it is God who causes
you to wish and to act for the sake of his good will. Do

everything without mutterings and disputations, so that you may be blameless and pure, flawless children of God in the midst of a crooked and perverse generation, among whom you shine in the world like stars by holding to the word of life, to make me proud on the Day of Christ because I did not run my course in vain or labor in vain. But even if I am being offered up to the sacrificial service of your faith, I rejoice and share my joy with all of you. Do you likewise rejoice, and share your joy with me.

I hope, if the Lord Jesus is willing, to send Timothy to you soon, so that I myself may learn how things are with you, and take heart. I have here not one with a spirit like his, who would be honestly concerned about you; they are all after their own interests, not those of Christ Jesus. You know how Timothy has proved himself, you know how like a son with his father he has toiled with me for the gospel. So I hope to send him as soon as I can find out what my own future is; and I trust in the Lord that I myself shall come to you soon.

I also thought it necessary to send Epaphroditus to you; my brother and helper and fellow soldier sent by you as an emissary to minister to my needs; since he has been longing to see you and was concerned because you heard that he had been sick. And indeed he was sick, almost to the point of death, but God took pity on him; not only on him, but also on me, so that I should not have one grief on top of another. Thus I send him the more urgently, so that you may see him and be happy again, and I too may be the less troubled. Welcome him, then, with all joy, in the Lord's name, and prize people like him, because in doing the Lord's work he came very close to death, risking his life in order to fill the need you felt to have someone helping me.

¶ For the rest, my brothers, rejoice in the Lord. But I have no hesitation in writing you the same thing once again, and it is safe, as regards you.

Beware of the dogs, beware of evil practitioners, beware of mutilation. It is we who are the circumcised, we who serve the spirit of God and take pride in Christ Jesus and do not put our confidence in the flesh —although I myself do have reason for confidence in the flesh also. Even if another man may think he has reason for confidence in the flesh, yet I have more: circumcised on the eighth day, of the race of Israel, of the tribe of Benjamin, a Hebrew of Hebrews; in law a Pharisee, in zeal, a persecutor of the church, in righteousness according to the law, without fault. But all those things which had been gains for me I now count as loss, because of the Christ. I do then count everything else as loss because of the greater value of knowing of Christ Jesus, my Lord, for whose sake I was deprived of everything; and I count it all as garbage if so I may gain Christ and be found in him, not keeping my righteousness which came from the law but that which came through faith in Christ, the righteousness from God which rests on faith; from knowing him and the power of his resurrection and the sharing of his sufferings, conforming myself to his death, so as somehow to arrive at the resurrection of the dead. Not that I have already got it or am already made perfect, but I pursue it, trying to overtake it, as I was overtaken by Christ. My brothers, I do not count myself as one who has caught it yet, but I do only one thing: forgetting what is behind me and straining on toward what is ahead of me, I pursue my objective, the prize, which is to be summoned aloft by God with Christ Jesus. Let those of us who are mature be so minded; and if you think otherwise on any point, God will make that also clear to you; only let us stand fast at the place we have already reached.

Join in following my example, brothers, and since you have us for a model, observe those who conduct themselves as I do. For there are many people about, of whom I have spoken to you often and now, tearfully, speak of them again: the enemies of the cross of the Christ, whose end is destruction, whose god is their belly and whose glory is in their shamefulness, whose minds are on earthly things. But we have our city in heaven, from which we also await our savior the Lord Jesus Christ, who will transfigure the body of our lowliness to conform to the body of his glory, through the activity of his power and because all things are subject to him.

¶ So, my brothers, longed for, my joy and my crown, be thus steadfast in the Lord, my dear ones. I implore Euodia and I implore Syntyche to agree in the Lord. Yes, and I ask you, my true yoke-fellow, come to their aid; in my evangelism they strove along with me, together with Clement and the rest of my helpers, whose names are in the book of life. Rejoice in the Lord always; I say it again, rejoice. May your goodness be made known to all men. The Lord is near; never be anxious, but in every prayer and entreaty let your requests be communicated with thanksgiving to God; and the peace of God which passes all understanding will keep your hearts and your thoughts in Christ Jesus.

Finally, brothers, all things that are true, that are honorable, that are just, that are pure, that are lovely, that are admirable; if there is any virtue, if there is anything praiseworthy; think upon these things. And all that you have ever learned and taken over and heard and seen in me, so do; and the God of peace will be with you.

I rejoiced greatly in the Lord that your concern for me has flowered once again; after the time when you were concerned, but had no opportunity to help. I do not speak about needing help, since I have learned how to be self-sufficient in whatever circumstances I may be. I know how to do without and how to have plenty; anywhere and in anything I have been initiated into how to be full, how to be hungry, to have more than enough and to have not enough. I have strength for everything through him who fortifies me.

Still you did well to share my suffering with me. And, Philippians, you yourselves know that, in the early time of my mission when I had left Macedonia, not one other church shared in my gains and losses: only you; and that even when I was in Thessalonica once and then again you sent me what I needed. Not that I ask for the gift but what I do ask is that the excess profit be credited to you. I am paid in full, and more; I am fully rewarded in receiving from Epaphroditus the gift from you, a fragrant offering, an acceptable sacrifice, well pleasing to God. And my God will fill every need that you have through his glorious riches in Christ Jesus. Glory be to our God and Father forever and ever. Amen.

Greet every saint in Christ Jesus. The brothers who are with me send you greetings. All the saints send you greetings, especially those of Caesar's household.

The grace of the Lord Jesus Christ be with your spirit.

The Letter
to the Colossians

¶PAUL, THE APOSTLE OF CHRIST JESUS
by the will of God, with Timothy our brother; to the
saints and faithful brothers in Christ who are in Colos-
sae: grace to you and peace, from God our Father.

In all our prayers to God the Father of our Lord Jesus
we give thanks for you, since we have heard of your faith
in Christ Jesus and your love for all the saints, because
of the hope which is laid up for you in heaven, hope of
which you heard before in the word of truth in the gospel which is present among you; the gospel which grows
and bears fruit in all the world, as it does among you,
since the day when you heard it and truly acknowledged
the grace of God; as you learned it from Epaphras our
beloved fellow slave, who acts for us as a trusted minister of the Christ, and who told us of the love you have
in the Spirit. Therefore we also, since the day when we
heard about you, never cease from praying for you. We
pray that you may be fulfilled in your understanding of
his will, in full wisdom and spiritual comprehension; so
as to act in a manner worthy of the Lord and always
pleasing to him, productive in every good work and increasing in your understanding of God; empowered with

every power, by the supremacy of his glory, to be always steadfast and joyfully enduring, thankful to the father who made you fit for your share in the fortune of the saints, in the light. It was he who rescued us from the power of darkness, and removed us to the Kingdom of the son of his love, where we find our redemption, the remission of sins.

He is the image of the invisible God, first-born of all creation, because in him were created all things in heaven and on earth, the visible and the invisible, whether thrones or lordships or realms or authorities. All things have been created through him and for him. And he is before all things and all things come together in him, and he is the head of the body, the church. He is the beginning, first-born from the dead, to be first himself in all things, because all fulfillment has been well pleased to reside in him and through him to reconcile all things to him, establishing peace by the blood of his cross; whether it be the things on earth or the things in heaven. And as for you, who were once estranged and hostile in your minds with your wicked doings, he has now reconciled you in his physical body by his death, so as to bring you, holy and blameless and unimpeachable, into his presence; provided that you remain firm-founded and steady in your faith, not shaken from your hope in the gospel you have heard, the gospel preached in all creation under heaven, the gospel of which I, Paul, have been made the minister.

Now I am happy in my sufferings for your sake; and in my own flesh I am filling out what is still lacking in the sufferings of the Christ, for his body, which is the church. Of this I have been made a minister through the dispensation of God granted to me, to bring to completion among you the word of God, the mystery which has been hidden away for ages and for generations. But now it has been revealed to his saints, since God wished to make known to them how rich is the glory of this mystery among the Gentiles. This is Christ in you, your hope for glory. It is he whom we proclaim, admonishing every person and teaching every person by every kind of wisdom, so as to present every person as one complete in Christ. I toil to bring this about, struggling in obedience to his activity, which is powerfully at work in me.

¶ For I wish you to know what a struggle I maintain for the sake of you and the people in Laodicea and all those who have never seen me in the flesh. I do it so that their hearts may be comforted, so that they may be brought together in love and to all the resources of fulfilled comprehension, to the recognition of the mystery of God: Christ, in whom are hidden all the treasures of wisdom and understanding. I say this so that none may mislead you by persuasive argument. For even if I am absent in person, yet in the spirit I am with you, rejoicing as I observe the good order and solidity of your faith in Christ.

So, as you have accepted the Christ, Jesus the Lord, go by him, rooted in him and built upon him, confirmed in your faith as you were taught it and abounding in gratitude. See to it that there shall be no one to steal you away by philosophy and by empty deception according to the tradition of men, according to the fundamentals of the world, and not according to Christ. Because in him resides, physically, all the fulfillment of the divine, and you have been fulfilled in him. He is the head of every realm and authority; in him also you were circumcised with a circumcision not done by human hands, in the putting off of the body of the flesh, in the circumcision of the Christ. You were buried with him in your baptism, and with him you were raised again, through your faith in the working of God, who raised him from the dead. When you were dead because of your sins and the uncircumcision of your flesh, he brought you to life along with himself. He forgave us all our sins, obliterating the unfavorable bond, with its decisions, that went against us, and removed it from our midst by nailing it to his cross; disarming authorities and powers, he made a spectacle of them by leading them captive in his train.

Do not, then, let anyone pass judgment on you over any matter of food or drink or detail of a festival or new moon or sabbath. These are the shadows of things to come; the body belongs to the Christ. Let no one willingly condemn you by excessive humility and adoration of angels, basing himself on his visions. Such a one is irrationally puffed up by the mind in his own body; he does not hold fast to the head, dependent on which the whole body, supported and held together by its joints and sinews, increases as God makes it increase.

If with Christ you are dead to the fundamentals of the world, why are you to be regulated as if you were still living in the world, with *do not handle, do not taste, do not touch?* These prohibitions concern what perishes with use; they accord with the commandments and teachings of man. They have some show of reason through the will to be religious, and humility, and the mortification of the flesh, but they are of no use for preventing carnal indulgence.

¶ If, then, with Christ you were wakened from the dead, look for what is above, where the Christ is, seated by the right hand of God. Think upon the things above, not the things on earth, for you died, and your life has been hidden away in God, with the Christ; when the Christ appears, then so will our life, and you too will appear in glory along with him.

Then put to death those elements in you which are of the earth: lechery, impurity, passion, base desire, and that greed which is idolatry. These are what bring on the anger of God. Once you went the way of these feelings, when you lived by them. Put them off now, all of them, anger, rage, baseness, blasphemy, foul language from your mouths. Do not lie to each other. Strip off the old person with all his doings and put on the new one, renewed in understanding after the likeness of him who created him: where there is no room for Greek or Jew, circumcision or uncircumcision, barbarian, Scythian, slave, free man, but Christ is all in all. As the chosen of God, holy and beloved, take on the feelings of compassion, kindness, humility, gentleness, patience, putting up with each other and forgiving each other when anyone has some fault to find with anyone else. As the Lord has forgiven you, so do likewise. Above all is love, which is what holds perfection together. And let the peace of the Christ, into which you were called in one body, rule in your hearts; and be thankful. Let the word of the Christ live within you abundantly in all wisdom, as you teach and admonish yourselves with psalms, hymns, spiritual songs, with thanks, singing to God in your hearts. And whatever you do, in word or act, do all in the name of the Lord Jesus, giving thanks for him to God the Father.

Wives, subordinate yourselves to your husbands, as is your duty in the Lord. Husbands, love your wives and do not be sharp with them. Children, be obedient to your parents in everything, for this is pleasing to the Lord. Fathers, do not try your children's patience, for fear they may lose heart. Slaves, obey your human masters in all things, not with service to catch the eye and please people, but in simplicity of heart and fearing the Lord. Whatever you do, do it from the heart, as for the Lord and not for men, knowing that you will receive your share of the inheritance as a reward. You are serving Christ the Lord. The wrongdoer will be requited for the wrong he did, and there is no discrimination.

¶ Masters, be just and fair with your slaves, knowing that you also have a master in heaven.

Be constant in your prayers, with wakefulness and thanksgiving; and at the same time pray also for us, that God may open the door of the word to us, to speak of the mystery of the Christ, for which I am in prison; so that I may reveal it in the language I ought to use.

Conduct yourselves wisely toward outsiders, making the most of your time. Let your speech be always gracious, seasoned with salt, so that you know how to talk to each particular person.

Tychicus, my beloved brother and trusted helper and fellow slave in the Lord, will tell you all the news about me. I send him to you for this very purpose, so that you may know about me and so that he may comfort your hearts. He is with Onesimus, my trusted and beloved brother, who is one of you. They will tell you about everything here.

Aristarchus, my fellow prisoner, sends you greetings, as does Mark, the cousin of Barnabas, concerning whom you have received instructions from me; if he comes to you, welcome him. So too Jesus, who is called Justus.

These, of the circumcised, are the only ones who have worked with me for the Kingdom of God, and have been a comfort to me. Epaphras sends you greetings; he is one of you, a slave of Christ Jesus, forever striving for you in his prayers so that you may stand complete and fulfilled in every way God wishes. For I bear him witness that he works very hard for you and for those in Laodicea and Hierapolis. Luke the beloved physician sends greetings, as does Demas. Give greetings to the brothers in Laodicea and to Nympha and the church which is in her house. And when this letter is read before you, arrange to have it read also in the church of the Laodiceans, and see that you also read the one from Laodicea. And say to Archippus: Be sure to carry out the ministry you received from the Lord.

The greeting is written in the hand of myself, Paul. Remember my chains. Grace be with you.

The First Letter
to the Thessalonians

¶PAUL AND SILVANUS AND TIMOTHY
to the church of the Thessalonians, in God the Father
and the Lord Jesus Christ. Grace to you and peace.

We thank God at all times for all of you, as we make
mention of you in our prayers and constantly remember
the work of your faith and the labor of your love and the
endurance of your hope in our Lord Jesus Christ before
our God and Father; knowing, God-beloved brothers, of
your election, because our gospel came to you not in word
alone, but also with power, and the Holy Spirit, and great
assurance; just as you know what we were when we came
to you for your sake. And you followed the example of
us and of the Lord, and received the word, in great affliction, with joy in the Holy Spirit, so that you became
a model for all believers in Macedonia and Achaea.
From you the word of the Lord has re-echoed not only
in Macedonia and Achaea, but your faith in God has gone
forth to every region, so that there is no need for us to
say anything. For they themselves report our visit to you,
what it was like, and how you turned from idols to God,
to serve the true and living God, and to await his son

from the heavens, the son whom he raised, Jesus, our protector from the anger to come.

¶ For you yourselves know, brothers, how our visit to you was not in vain; but after first suffering and being outrageously treated in Philippi we were bold in God to tell you the gospel of God, under great strain. For our appeal to you comes not from error, nor from impurity, nor in deceitfulness, but as we had had God's approval to have the gospel entrusted to us, thus we speak, not trying to please men but God, the examiner of our hearts. For we said nothing by way of flattery, as you know; nor as a pretext for profit, God is our witness; nor looking for honor from men, neither you nor others; though we could have put pressure upon you, as apostles of Christ. But we were innocents among you, as when a mother cherishes her children; so longing for you that we thought it right to share with you not only the gospel of God but also our own lives, because you had become dear to us. You remember, brothers, our toil and labor; how we worked with our hands night and day so as not to lay any burden on you as we preached to you the gospel of God. You and God are our witnesses how piously and justly and blamelessly we acted toward you who are believers, just as you know how, like a father with his children, we urged and advised and reasoned with each one of you, to make you walk in a way worthy of the God who summons you to his Kingdom and his glory.

Therefore we also thank God at all times, that when you received the word of God which you heard from us, you accepted it not as the word of men but the word of God as it really is, which works also in you who believe.

For you, my brothers, followed the example of the churches of God which are with Christ Jesus in Judaea, in that you have suffered the same treatment from your own fellow countrymen as they have from the Jews; who killed the Lord Jesus and the prophets and chased us out; unpleasing to God, against all men; trying to prevent us from speaking to the Gentiles, to save them, and filling up the measure of their own sins, always; and the wrath has overtaken them in the end.

But we, brothers, who have been bereft of you for a space of time, in actual presence not in the heart, have been the more eager and in great longing to see you face to face. Thus we have wished to go to you, I, Paul, again and again, but Satan blocked our way. For what is our hope or joy or crown of exultation, if not you, before our Lord Jesus and at his coming? You are our pride and joy.

¶ Therefore when we could no longer endure it, we decided to stay behind in Athens by ourselves, and we sent Timothy, our brother and the servant of God in the gospel of Christ, to strengthen you and encourage you on behalf of your faith, so that none should weaken in these present sufferings. For you know yourselves that sufferings are our lot; since, when we were with you, we warned you that we must suffer, as has happened and as you know. Therefore when I could no longer endure it, I sent him to find out about your faith, fearing that the tempter might have tempted you and all our labor gone for nothing. But Timothy came back to us from you a little while ago and brought us the good news of your faith and your love for us, and told us that you have a good memory of us and long to see us as we long to see you; and for this, brothers, we have taken comfort in you through all our hardship and suffering, because of your faith, since if you are steadfast in the Lord now, we live. For what thanks can we render to God for you, for all the joy we have in you before our God, as night and day we pray most urgently to see you face to face and to mend any shortcomings in faith? May God our Father himself and our Lord Jesus direct our way to you; and may our Lord multiply and increase your love for each other and for all, as we also love you, to strengthen your hearts so that they are blameless in holiness before our God and Father at the coming of our Lord Jesus with all his saints.

¶ Finally, brothers, we ask you this and urge you, by the Lord Jesus. You were told by us how you should live your lives in a way that would be pleasing to God, and so indeed you are doing. But improve even more. For you know what instructions we gave you, through the Lord Jesus. This, your sanctification, is the will of God; that you should abstain from lechery, and each one know how to keep his own body in sanctity and honor, not in subjection to desire like the heathens who do not know God; not to trespass against any brother and take advantage of him in this matter; since the Lord punishes these things, as we have warned you and attested. For God did not call us to unchastity but to sanctity. Therefore he who refuses this refuses not man but God, who gave us his Holy Spirit.

As for brotherly love, you have no need for me to write you, for you yourselves have been taught by God to love each other; and this you do to all the brothers in all of Macedonia. But we urge you, brothers, to improve further, and to rival each other in keeping the peace, to pursue your own business, to work with your hands, as I have advised you, so that you may be respected by those outside our number and need nothing from anyone else.

Also, we do not wish you to be ignorant, brothers, concerning those who are asleep, nor to be grieved like the rest of mankind, who have no hope. For if we believe that Jesus died and rose again, so also God, through Jesus, will bring back the sleepers along with him. For this we say, by the word of the Lord, that we the living, the survivors, will not join the coming of the Lord before the sleepers do. For at the signal, at the cry of the archangel and the trumpet of God, the Lord himself will come down from heaven, and first those who are dead in Christ will rise up, and then we the living, the survivors, will be caught up with them into the clouds to meet the Lord in the air. And thus we shall be with the Lord forever. So comfort each other by saying this.

¶ Concerning the times and occasions, brothers, you have no need for anyone to write you, for you yourselves know well that the day of the Lord will come like a thief in the night. When they say: Peace and safety, that is when doom will come suddenly upon them, like birth pangs to a pregnant woman, and they cannot escape. But you, brothers, are not in darkness, for the day to catch you like thieves, since all of you are sons of light and sons of day. We are not of the night or the dark; then let us not sleep, as the others do, but be wakeful and sober. For the sleepers sleep at night, and the drunkards are drunk at night; but we who are of the day should be sober, putting on the breastplate of faith and love, with hope of salvation our helmet. For God did not destine us to the anger but to the winning of salvation through our Lord Jesus, who died for us so that, whether we wake or sleep, we shall live with him. Therefore, comfort each other and strengthen one another; as indeed you are doing.

Let us then, brothers, ask you to recognize those who are working for you and acting for you with the Lord and giving you counsel, and hold them in special love because of their work. Be at peace among yourselves. And we implore you, brothers, admonish the disorderly, comfort the faint-hearted, protect the weak, be patient with all. See to it that no one returns evil for evil, but always pursue the good, toward each other and toward all. Be always joyful, pray constantly, be thankful on every occasion; for this is God's will for you, through Christ Jesus. Do not quench the Spirit, do not ignore prophecies. Examine everything, hold fast to the good, keep away from every kind of wickedness.

May the very God of power sanctify you completely, and may your entire spirit and soul and body be kept safe without fault at the coming of our Lord Jesus Christ. Faithful is he who summons you, who will act accordingly.

Brothers, pray for us.

Greet all the brothers with a sacred kiss. I charge you by the Lord to have this letter read to all the brothers.

May the grace of our Lord Jesus Christ be with you.

The Second Letter to the Thessalonians

¶PAUL AND SILVANUS AND TIMOTHY to the church of the Thessalonians, in God our Father and the Lord Jesus Christ. Grace to you and peace from God the Father and the Lord Jesus Christ.

We must be thankful to God at all times on your account, brothers, as is only right, because your faith increases, and the love of all of you for each other is growing; so that we also can take pride in you in the churches of God, because of your endurance and faith in all the persecutions and sufferings you endure. This is a demonstration of the just judgment of God, for you to be counted worthy of the Kingdom of God, for whose sake you suffer; if indeed it is God's justice to repay with affliction those who afflicted you, and to grant to you, the afflicted, relief with us at the revelation of the Lord Jesus from heaven with the angels of his power, in flame of fire; who will bestow punishment on those who do not know God and do not obey the gospel of our Lord Jesus. These will pay the penalty of everlasting destruction, far from the face of the Lord and the glory of his power, when he comes to be glorified among his saints and admired among all believers, on the great Day, because our testimony to you was believed. Until then we pray constantly for you, that our God may consider you worthy of election, and fulfill all your desire for goodness, and the work of your faith by his power, so that the name of our Lord Jesus may be glorified in you, and you in him, by the grace of our God and the Lord Jesus Christ.

¶ But let us ask you, brothers, in the matter of the coming of the Lord Jesus Christ and our meeting with him, not to be lightly driven out of your minds or terrified by any spirit or report, or letter that seems to come from us saying that the Day of the Lord has arrived. Let no one deceive you in any way; since first must come the rebellion and the revelation of the man of iniquity, the son of perdition, who opposes and sets himself above whatever is called divine and worshipful, so that he seats himself in the temple of God, displaying himself still as God. Do you not remember that I told you this when I was with you? And you know what now restrains him, until he will be revealed in his own time; for the mystery of iniquity is now at work, only there is one who prevents it until he is gone from our midst. And then the iniquitous one will be revealed, but the Lord will kill him by the breath of his mouth and annihilate him by the manifestation of his coming. But this one's appearance will come by the working of Satan with all his power, with the signs and portents of falsehood, with full deception of wrong for those who perish because they did not accept the love of truth for their salvation. Therefore God visits them with the force that makes them go astray, to believe in the lie; so that all who did not believe in the truth, but favored unrighteousness, may be condemned.

But we owe constant thanks to God for your sake,

brothers beloved by the Lord, because from the beginning he chose you for salvation by sanctification of the spirit and belief in the truth. He summoned you to this through our gospel, to a share in the glory of our Lord Jesus Christ. Therefore, brothers, be steadfast, and preserve the traditions you were taught by us whether by word of mouth or by letter. May our Lord himself, Jesus Christ, and God our Father, who loves us and gave us everlasting comfort and good hope through grace, comfort your hearts and strengthen you in every good action and word.

¶ For the rest, pray for us, brothers, that the word of the Lord may go forward and gain in glory, as with you, and that we may be kept safe from the wrong and wicked people. For faith is not for all. But the Lord is to be trusted, who will strengthen you and protect you from evil. And we trust in the Lord concerning you, because you do and will do what we tell you. And may the Lord direct your hearts to the love of God and endurance to await the Christ.

And we charge you, brothers, in the name of the Lord Jesus Christ, to keep yourselves from every brother who follows a course that is idle and not in accordance with the tradition you received from us. For you yourselves know how you should copy us, in that we were not idle when we were among you and did not eat food supplied as a gift by anyone else, but plied our trade with hard labor night and day so as not to be a burden on any of you; not that we did not have that right, but so as to present ourselves as a model for you to copy. For when we were with you we taught you that anyone who would not work should not eat. Since we hear that some among you follow an idle course, and do not work but mind the business of others. And these, by the Lord Jesus Christ, we direct and urge to ply their trade in peace and earn their own living. But you, brothers, do not weaken in your good works. And if anyone disobeys our instructions in this letter, mark him and have nothing to do with him, to make him ashamed. But do not count him as an enemy, but counsel him as a brother. And may the very Lord of peace give you peace of every kind, always. The Lord be with you all.

The greeting is by the hand of myself, Paul. This is my signature to every letter. This is my writing. May the grace of our Lord Jesus Christ be with you all.

The First Letter
to Timothy

¶PAUL, APOSTLE OF CHRIST JESUS BY
the order of God our savior and Christ Jesus our hope, to
Timothy, my own true child in faith: grace, mercy, peace,
from God the Father and Christ Jesus our Lord.

As I asked you, when I was setting out for Macedonia,
to stay on in Ephesus, it was so that you could tell certain people not to teach heretical doctrines, not to put
their minds on myths and interminable genealogies
which lead to speculations rather than the plan of God,
which is through faith. The aim of my instruction is love,
from a pure heart and a good conscience and unfeigned
faith, qualities which certain people have missed and
turned to talking nonsense, wanting to be teachers of the
law without either knowing what they are saying or what
those things are about which they are so firm. We know
that the law is a fine thing if one uses it lawfully, in the
knowledge that the law is not established for the just
man, but for the lawless and disobedient, the impious
and sinful, the unholy and profane, the parricides and
matricides, murderers, lechers, pederasts, kidnappers,
liars, oath breakers, or anything else that is opposed to

healthy teaching according to the gospel of the glory of the blessed God in whom I believe.

I am grateful to him who gave me power, to Christ Jesus our Lord, because he thought me trustworthy when he established me in my ministry, though before I had been a blasphemer and persecutor and a violent man. But I was given mercy, because I had been acting ignorantly in unbelief, and the grace of our Lord overabounded in love and faith, which is in Christ Jesus. This word is to be believed and worthy of full acceptance, that Christ Jesus came into the world to save sinners; of whom I am the foremost, but for this reason I was given mercy, so that in me, foremost of all, Christ Jesus might display his complete patience, for an example of those to come who will believe in him for everlasting life. To the king of the ages, imperishable, invisible, single God, honor and glory forever and ever. Amen.

I entrust this charge to you, Timothy my child, in accordance with those prophecies which pointed to you before, so that in their spirit you may serve in the good campaign, keeping faith and good conscience. This certain people have rejected and come to grief in the matter of faith. Among them are Hymenaeus and Alexander, whom I consign to Satan to be taught not to blaspheme.

¶So I ask you first of all to make your prayers, entreaties, intercessions, thanksgivings, for all people, for kings and all who are of high degree, so that we may live a quiet and peaceful life in all piety and dignity. This is good and acceptable in the sight of God our savior, who wishes all people to be saved, and to come to the recognition of the truth. For there is one God, and also one mediator between God and men, a man, Christ Jesus, who gave himself as ransom for all, a testimonial to his own times. To which fact I was appointed herald and apostle —I am speaking the truth, I do not lie—the teacher of the Gentiles in faith and truth.

I wish, therefore, that men in every place should pray, uplifting reverent hands, without anger or disputations. So too I wish women to dress in decorous style with modesty and good taste, not in hairstyles and gold or pearls or expensive fabrics, but as becomes women who profess piety through good works. Let a woman be a learner, quietly and in all obedience; I do not permit a woman to teach, nor to have authority over her husband. She should hold her peace. For Adam was made first, then Eve; and Adam was not deceived but the woman was deceived and went astray; but she will be saved through motherhood, if women are steadfast in faith and love and sanctity, with good behavior.

¶ This word is to be believed. If anyone desires to be a bishop, it is an honorable wish. But then a bishop must be irreproachable, married to one wife, sober, discreet, orderly, hospitable, good at teaching, not given to wine, no brawler, but forbearing, peaceable, not avaricious, a good head of his own household, keeping his children under control in full respectability. If a man does not know how to be head of his own house, how shall he take charge of the church of God? And he should not be a new convert who might become conceited and fall into the devil's damnation. And he must be well spoken of by those who are outside our church, so as not to fall into disrepute and the entrapment of the devil.

So also deacons must be dignified, not two-tongued,

not given to heavy drinking, not shamefully grasping, keeping to the mystery of the faith with a clear conscience. And they must first be examined, and then serve as deacons when they are found to be unimpeachable. So also their wives should be dignified, not gossips, sober, faithful in every way. Let deacons be married to one wife, exercising good authority over their children and their own households. For those who serve well as deacons provide themselves with a good standing and much confidence in faith in Christ Jesus.

I write you these things hoping to come to you speedily, but, in case I am slow in coming, so that you may know how you should conduct yourself in the house of God, which is the church of the living God, which is the pillar and foundation of truth. And, admittedly, great is the mystery of religion. He appeared in the flesh; he was justified in the spirit; he was seen by angels; he was preached among the nations; he was believed in the world; he was taken up to heaven in glory.

¶ The Spirit expressly says that in times to come some will forsake the faith, giving themselves to deceitful spirits and the teachings of demons through the hypocrisy of liars, branded in their own conscience, opposers of marriage, telling us to abstain from food which God created to be partaken of with thanksgiving by believers and those who recognize the truth. Because everything created by God is good, and nothing is to be thrown away which is received with thanksgiving, for it is hallowed by the word of God and prayer.

If you teach these things to the brothers you will be a fine deacon of Christ Jesus, trained in the words of faith and good teaching which you have followed; but reject the profane old wives' tales. And exercise yourself toward piety. Exercise of the body is good for only a little, but piety is good for everything, containing the promise of life now and to come. This that I say is to be believed and is worthy of full acceptance, for this is what we toil and struggle for; because our hopes are in the living God, who is the savior of all people, but most of all of the believers.

Teach and promote these beliefs. Let no one belittle you because of your youth, but make yourself a model of the faithful in speech, in behavior, in love, in faith, in chastity. Until I come, devote yourself to reading, to exhortation, to teaching. Do not neglect the gift of grace that is in you, which was given to you through prophecy by the laying of the council's hands upon you. Give your mind to these matters, occupy yourself with them, so that your progress may be visible to all. Attend to yourself and your teaching; keep on with it; for by doing so you will save yourself and those who hear you.

¶Do not reprove a man older than yourself, but exhort him as a father, and the younger men as brothers, older women as mothers, and younger ones as sisters in complete chastity. Revere widows who are really widows. And if a widow has children or grandchildren, let these learn first of all to respect their own household and return to their forebears what they owe them, for this is acceptable in the sight of God. She who is really a widow and lives alone has put her hope in God and is constant in her prayers and entreaties night and day. She who indulges in pleasure is one of the living dead. Impress these ideas on people so that they may be above reproach. But if anyone does not take care of his own people, and particularly his own family, that one has denied his faith and is worse than one who never believed.

Let one who is registered as a widow be not under sixty years of age, widow of one husband, attested for good works: whether she cared for children, was hospitable to strangers, washed the feet of the saints, rescued the oppressed, or gave herself to whatever good work. But refuse the younger widows, since when their lusts take them away from the Christ, they want to marry, being open to the charge of breaking their original pledge. And at the same time they learn how to be shiftless, going about from house to house; and not only shiftless but silly and meddlesome and improper in their talk. So I desire that the younger widows marry, have children, run their own houses, thus giving the Adversary no occasion for slander; for already some of them have turned back to follow Satan. If any woman believer has widows in her family, let her take care of them and not let the church be burdened, so that the church may take care of those who are really widowed.

The elders who have been good leaders should be accorded twice as much honor, especially those who work hard at speaking and teaching. For scripture says: You shall not muzzle the ox who treads the grain; and: The laborer is worthy of his hire. Do not accept a charge made against an elder unless it was before two or three witnesses; but convict those who do wrong openly before all, so that the others may be afraid. I charge you before God and Christ Jesus and the chosen angels to keep these commandments without prejudice, doing nothing in partiality. Do not lay hands hastily on anyone or have anything to do with the sins of others. Keep yourself chaste. Do not go on being a water drinker, but take a little wine because of your stomach and your frequent illnesses.

The sins of some men are obvious and lead the way to judgment, but those of others lag behind: so also some good deeds are evident, and those that are otherwise can not remain hidden.

¶ Those who are slaves under the yoke should consider their own masters worthy of full honor, so that the name and teaching of God may not be ill spoken of. Those who have masters who are believers should not therefore treat them with disrespect because they are brothers, but work all the harder as their slaves, because those who have the benefit of their good work are believers, and are beloved.

Teach and urge these principles. If anyone deviates from them in his teaching and does not adhere to wholesome doctrines, those of our Lord Jesus Christ, and teaching that accords with piety, he is conceited, understands nothing, but is sick over controversies and battles of words; from which grow spite, rivalry, blasphemies, base suspicions, the frictions of men who are corrupted in mind and deprived of the truth, who think that piety is gain. And piety, with self-sufficiency, is a great gain; for we brought nothing into the world, and because we can take nothing out of it, and while we have food and covering we shall be satisfied with them. Those who want to be rich fall into temptation and entrapment and many senseless and harmful desires which sink people into ruin and destruction. For the root of all evils is the love of money, in longing for which some have strayed from their faith and transfixed themselves with many pains.

But you, man of God, avoid all this. Pursue righteousness, piety, faith, love, endurance, gentleness. Strive in the good contest of faith, lay hold on everlasting life, to which you were summoned and confessed to the good confession before many witnesses. I charge you before God, who gives life to all things, and Christ Jesus, who testified to the good confession in the time of Pontius Pilate, to keep this commandment stainless and irreproachable until the appearance of our Lord Jesus Christ, which in his own time the blessed and single ruler will display; the King of Kings and Lord of Lords, sole holder of immortality, dwelling in unapproachable light, whom no man has seen or can see: to whom be glory and power everlasting. Amen.

Charge those who are rich in the present time not to be haughty and not to put their hopes in the uncertainty of riches, but in God, who provides us richly with all means for enjoyment, to do good, to be rich in good deeds, to be liberal, sharing, laying away for ourselves a good foundation for the future so that all may partake of what is really life.

Oh, Timothy, guard this which has been entrusted to you, putting aside the profane babblings and antitheses of what is falsely called knowledge; which some have professed, and thus failed in their faith.

Grace be with you.

The Second Letter

to Timothy

¶PAUL, APOSTLE OF CHRIST JESUS, BY
the will of God through the promise of life in Christ Jesus; to Timothy, his beloved son: grace, mercy, peace
from God the Father and Christ Jesus our Lord.

I give thanks to God, whom I serve with the clear conscience which is from my ancestors, as I mention you
continually in my prayers. I long to see you, night and
day, remembering your tears; to make my joy complete
as I am reminded again of the unfeigned faith that is in
you. First it dwelt in Lois your grandmother, and Eunice
your mother; and I believe that it is also in you. For
which reason I am reminding you to rekindle the gift of
God which is in you through the laying on of my hands;
for God did not give us any spirit of cowardice, but of
power and love and discretion.

Do not then be ashamed of your testimony to our Lord,
nor of me his prisoner, but take your share of suffering
for the gospel, with strength from God: God who saved
us and summoned us with a holy summons, not because
of what we had done but according to his own purpose
and his grace, grace in Christ Jesus granted to us countless ages ago, but made evident now through the appear-

ance of our savior Christ Jesus, who abolished death and spread the light of life and imperishability through his gospel. Of this I have been appointed the herald and apostle and teacher; and that is the cause for which I suffer as I do. But I am not ashamed, but I know whom I trust, and I am persuaded that he can guard my trust until the great Day. Preserve the standard of wholesome precepts which you have heard from me in faith and love and in Christ Jesus; guard the good which has been entrusted to you through the Holy Spirit which lives in us.

You know this, that all the people in Asia turned away from me; among them are Phygelus and Hermogenes. But may the Lord grant mercy to the house of Onesiphorus, because many times he refreshed me, and was not ashamed of my chains; rather, when he arrived in Rome he eagerly sought me out, and found me; may the Lord grant that he find mercy from the Lord on the great Day; and you know better than I all the services he did in Ephesus.

¶ But you, my child, be strong in the grace which is in Christ Jesus; and what you have heard from me before many witnesses, pass this on to trustworthy men who will be able to teach it to others as well. Take your share of sufferings like a good soldier of Christ Jesus. No soldier in service involves himself in the business of ordinary life, if he is to please the man who enlisted him. And if an athlete competes, he wins no wreath unless he competes by the rules. The farmer who does the work must be first to have his share of the crops. Think upon what I say, for the Lord will grant you understanding in all things.

Remember Jesus Christ, of the seed of David, who rose

from the dead, according to the gospel I preach; the gospel for which I am mistreated to the point of chains, like a criminal. But the word of God is not in chains; and through this I endure all for the sake of the elect, so that they also may attain the salvation which is in Christ Jesus with glory everlasting. This word is to be believed: If we die with him, we shall live with him; if we endure, we shall be kings with him; if we disown him, he will disown us; if we lose our belief, he is still to be believed, for he cannot disown himself.

Keep reminding people of this, charging them before God not to fight verbal battles, which are of no use for anything except for the subversion of those who listen to them. Strive to present yourself to God as one who is worthy, a worker with nothing to be ashamed of, drawing a straight line of argument for the truth. But avoid profane and empty words, for they will advance people in impiety and their speaking will spread like gangrene. Among such people are Hymenaeus and Philetus, who have strayed from the truth in saying that the resurrection has already taken place; and so they are upsetting the faith of some. But the foundation of God stands firm, with this seal upon it: The Lord knows those who are his; and: Let everyone who names the name of the Lord abstain from wrongdoing. In a great house there are vessels not only of gold and silver but also of wood and clay; and some are to be prized and others to be despised. If, then, a person purges himself from what I have been speaking of, he will be a vessel to be prized, hallowed, useful to his master, made ready for every good work. But avoid the desires of youth, and pursue righteousness, faith, love, peace, with those who call upon the Lord from a pure heart. Put aside stupid uninstructed speculations, knowing that they breed quarrels. A slave of the Lord must not quarrel but be mild toward all, instructive, patient, gentle, enlightening his opponents; on the chance that God may grant them to repent and recognize the truth, and they come to their senses and escape the entrapment of the devil, though they had been captured by him for his own will.

¶ Know this, that in the final days hard times will set in. For men will be lovers of themselves and lovers of money, pretentious, proud, blasphemous, disobedient to their parents, ungrateful, impious, loveless, implacable, troublemakers, intemperate, wild, with no love for good, treacherous, rash, conceited, lovers of pleasure rather than God, keeping the form of piety but denying its force.

Have nothing to do with these people. For from their number come those who get into houses and captivate women who are overcome by sins, who are seduced by fantastic desires, always learning something but never able to come to the recognition of the truth. As Jannes and Jambres stood up against Moses, so these men will stand up against the truth, being corrupt in mind and unworthy in the matter of faith. But they will progress no further, for their madness will be made evident to all, as was that of those others.

But as for you, you have followed my teaching, my behavior, my devotion, my faith, my patience, my love, my steadfastness; my persecutions, my sufferings, the sort of thing that happened to me in Antioch, in Iconium, in Lystra; such persecutions have I borne, but the Lord rescued me from all of them. And all who desire to live piously in Christ Jesus will be persecuted; bad men and wizards will make progress, for the worse, leading men astray and led astray themselves. But as for you, abide by what you learned and what you came to believe, realizing from what people you learned it, and that even when you were a child you knew sacred scriptures, which have power to make you wise for your salvation through faith in Christ Jesus. Every writing that is divinely inspired is also useful for teaching, for argument, for correction, for education in righteousness, so that the man of God may be complete and equipped for every good work.

¶ I charge you before God and Christ Jesus, who will judge the living and the dead, and by his coming appearance and his Kingdom: preach the word, insist on it in season and out of season; confute, reprove, exhort, with complete patience, with every kind of instruction. For the time will come when people will no longer put up with healthy doctrine, but will get themselves masses of teachers who accord with their own desires; their ears will be flattered, and they will turn their ears from the truth, and go over to myths. But as for you, keep your head at all times, endure your suffering, do your evangelist's work, fulfill your ministry.

For I am now being offered up as a sacrifice, and the hour for my departure is upon me. I have run the good race, I have finished the course, I have kept the faith; for the rest, the wreath for righteousness is set aside for me. The Lord, the just umpire, will award it to me on the great Day; and not to me alone, but to all who have loved his appearing.

Try hard to come to me soon. For Demas has forsaken me, being in love with the present age, and gone to Thessalonica. Crescens went to Galatia and Titus to Dalmatia. Only Luke is with me. Bring Mark along with you; he is helpful in my service. I sent Tychicus back to Ephesus. Bring with you when you come the cloak which I left behind with Carpus at Troas; also the book rolls, especially the parchments.

Alexander the bronzesmith did me a great deal of harm. The Lord will repay him according to his acts. Beware of him, you also, for he has been all too much opposed to our speaking.

In my first defense, no one stood by me but all forsook me. May it not be counted against them. But the Lord was with me and gave me strength, so that through me the message should be completed and all the nations should hear it; and I was rescued out of the lion's mouth. And the Lord will rescue me from every bad action and will save me for his heavenly Kingdom. To him be glory forever and ever. Amen.

Give greetings to Prisca and Aquila and the household of Onesiphorus. Erastus remained in Corinth; I left Trophimus sick in Miletus.

Try hard to come before winter.

Eubulus and Pudens and Linus and Claudia, and all the brothers, send you their greetings.

May the Lord be with your spirit. Grace be with you.

The Letter
to Titus

¶PAUL, THE SLAVE OF GOD, AND APOS-
tle of Jesus Christ in the faith of the chosen of God and
the recognition of the truth which comes by piety in the
hope for life everlasting, which God, who cannot lie,
promised countless ages ago and, in his own time, revealed in the annunciation with which I have been entrusted at the bidding of God our savior; to Titus, my
true child through shared faith; grace and peace from God
the Father and Christ Jesus our savior.

This is the reason that I left you in Crete, so that you
could set right what remains to be done, and institute
elders in every city, as I have instructed you to do. Such
an elder must be unimpeachable, married to one wife,
with children who are believers, not open to the charge
of dissipation, not disobedient. For the bishop, as God's
steward, must be unimpeachable, not self-willed, not
choleric, not given to drinking, no brawler, not shamefully grasping; but hospitable, lover of the good, discreet,
just, pious, temperate, holding fast to the word of faith,
according to doctrine, so that he can have power to exhort men by healthy teaching and confute those who oppose it.

For there are many who are disobedient, speakers of vanities and deceivers of the mind. They come mostly from among the circumcised. One must stop their mouths; for they overturn whole households by teaching as they should not, out of love for shameful gain.

For one of their number, their own prophet, has said: Cretans are always liars, foul beasts, lazy gluttons. That testimony is true. For this reason, confute them sharply, to make them grow healthy in faith, no longer giving their minds to Jewish myths and the commandments of people who reject the truth. To the pure all things are pure; but to the defiled and unbelieving nothing is pure, but their mind and conscience are defiled. They confess that they know God, but in their acts they deny him, being abominable, and disobedient, and unfit for any good work.

¶ Go on telling them, in the way that befits healthy doctrine, that older men should be sober, dignified, discreet, sound in faith, in love, in endurance. So also older women should be, in their behavior, reverent, not troublemakers or enslaved to excessive wine drinking, and teachers of the good; so as to set the young women right and make them love their husbands and their children, be discreet, chaste, housewifely, good, obedient to their own husbands, so that the word of God may not be ill spoken of. So also exhort the younger men to behave themselves. In every case present yourself as an example of good works: in your teaching, integrity, dignity, discourse that is irreproachably sound, so that anyone who opposes you may be put to shame, unable to say anything bad about us. Slaves should be obedient to their own masters in everything, pleasant, not talking back to them, not misappropriating anything, but showing completely good faith, to improve the image of the teaching of God our savior among people in general.

For the saving grace of God was shown forth to all people. It educates us, so that disowning impiety and worldly desires we may live discreetly and righteously and piously in this present age, looking forward to the blessed hope and the appearing of the glory of the great God and our savior Christ Jesus; who gave himself for our sakes, to set us free from all lawlessness and purify for himself a chosen people, making them eager for good works. Keep on speaking thus and exhorting and confuting. Let no one despise you.

¶ Remind them to be submissive and obedient to powers and authorities, ready for every good work, to speak ill of no one, be peaceable and reasonable, showing complete gentleness toward all men. For once we too were thoughtless, disobedient, led astray, enslaved to desires and fantastic pleasures, spending our lives in vice and spite, hateful, hating each other. But when the kindness of God our savior was revealed, and his love for mankind, not because of any things we had done righteously, but through his own mercy, he saved us by the washing of regeneration and the renewal of the Holy Spirit, which he poured abundantly upon us through Jesus Christ our savior, so that, justified by his grace, we may become heirs in the hope of life everlasting. This word is to be believed, and I want you to insist on these principles so that those who believe in God may concern themselves with good works. These are honorable and useful for mankind; but avoid silly speculations and genealogizing and contention and controversies about the law, since these are useless and vain. Banish a heretic after one, and then a second, warning; knowing that such a man is perverted and sinful, since he has condemned himself.

When I send Artemas or Tychicus to you, make haste to come to me at Nicopolis, since that is where I have decided to spend the winter. Send Zenas the lawyer and Apollos on their way, trying to see that they lack for nothing. And let our own people also learn to follow honorable trades, for their essential needs. They must not be unproductive.

All who are with me send you greetings. Greet all who are our friends in the faith.

The grace of God be with you all.

The Letter
to Philemon

¶PAUL, THE PRISONER OF CHRIST JE-
sus, and Timothy our brother; to Philemon, our beloved fellow worker, and Apphia, our sister, and Archippus, our fellow soldier, and to the church which is in
your house: grace to you and peace from God our Father
and the Lord Jesus Christ.

I thank my God at all times as I make mention of you
in my prayers, when I hear of the love and faith you have
for the Lord Jesus and for all the saints. I pray that your
sharing in the faith may work toward understanding all
the good we have in Christ; since I took much joy and
comfort in your love, because, brother, the hearts of the
saints were refreshed through you.

I, therefore, though I have full authority in Christ to
order you to do your duty, because of our love prefer to
entreat you to it, though I am what I am, Paul, ambassador, and now prisoner, of Christ Jesus. My entreaty
concerns my child, Onesimus, whose father I have become while in my chains; who once was worthless to
you, but now is of great worth to you and to me. Now I
send him, the child of my heart, to you. I would have
wanted to keep him with me, to serve me for your sake

in my bondage for the gospel; but I did not wish to do anything without your will, so that your good deed would be done not by constraint but voluntarily. Perhaps this is why he was taken away for a while, so that you could have him back for always, no longer as a slave but more than a slave, a brother greatly beloved by me but so much the more by you, both in the flesh and in the Lord. If, then, you hold me to be your partner, welcome him as you would me. If he did you any injury or owes you anything, charge it to me. I, Paul, write it in my own hand: I will pay. Not to mention that you owe me your very self. Yes, brother, let me have some good of you in the Lord; refresh my heart in Christ.

Confident in your obedience, I write you this, knowing that you will do even more than I ask. At the same time, make ready a guest room for me, since I hope that, because of your prayers, you will be granted a visit from me.

Epaphras, my fellow prisoner, greets you in Christ Jesus, as do Mark, Aristarchus, Demas, and Luke, my fellow workers.

May the grace of the Lord Jesus Christ be with your spirits.

The Letter
to the Hebrews

¶GOD, WHO IN ANCIENT TIME SPOKE
to our fathers in many and various ways through the
prophets, has now in these last days spoken to us through
his son, whom he made the heir to all things and through
whom he also created the ages. He is the gleam of his
glory and the representation of his nature, he carries all
things by his word of power; and when he had caused
purification from sins, he took his seat on the right hand
of the majesty, in the highest; thus proving to be greater
than the angels by as much as the name he inherited is
more exalted than theirs.

For to which of the angels did God ever say: You are
my son, this day I begot you? And again: I will be a father to him, and he will be a son to me?

And when, once more, he introduces his firstborn to
the world, he says: And let all the angels of God fall down
and worship him; and as to the angels he says: He who
makes his angels into winds, and his servants into flame
of fire. But to the son he says: Your throne, O God, is
forever and ever, and the scepter of your uprightness is
the scepter of his Kingdom. You love righteousness and
hate lawlessness; because of which, God, your God,

anointed you with the oil of exultation, beyond your companions. And: In the beginning, Lord, you laid the foundations of the earth, and the works of your hands are the heavens. They will perish, but you endure. And they all will be outworn like a garment, and like a mantle you will roll them up, and like a garment they will be changed; but you are the same, and your years will not give out.

But to which of the angels did he ever say: Sit on my right, so that I may make your enemies a footstool for your feet? Are they not all ministering spirits sent forth into service for the sake of those who are to inherit salvation?

¶ Because of this, we must all the more strongly hold to what we have heard, lest we slip away from it. For if the word spoken by the angels proved certain, and every transgression and disobedience got its just punishment, how shall we escape if we neglect so great a salvation? This began by being proclaimed by the Lord, and was confirmed for us by those who heard it, with God adding his testimony by signs and portents and miracles and apportionments of the Holy Spirit, according to his will.

For he did not make the world to come, of which we are speaking, subject to angels. To this someone bore testimony at one point, saying: What is man, that you are mindful of him, or the son of man, that you consider him? You have made him a little lower than the angels; you have crowned him with glory and honor. And you set him over the works of your hands. You have subjected all things beneath his feet. In subjecting everything he left nothing that was not to be subjected. But now we do not yet see everything subjected to him; but we do see him who was a little below the angels, Jesus, through the suffering of death crowned with glory and honor, that by the grace of God he should taste of death for the sake of all. For it was right for him, by whom and for whom all things are, to lead many sons to glory and make perfect the author of their salvation through suffering. For the consecrator and the consecrated are from a single source; for which reason he is not ashamed to call them brothers, saying: I will announce your name to my brothers; in the midst of the congregation I will hymn you. And again: I will put my trust in him. And again: Here am I and my children, whom God gave me.

Since, then, his children share his flesh and blood, so likewise he too partakes of theirs, so as by his death to abolish the one who has power over death, that is, the devil; and set free those who through fear of death had been condemned to slavery all their lives. For he is not, surely, concerned with angels, but with the seed of Abraham. Hence he needed to be made like his brothers in every way, to be merciful and the faithful high priest for all that concerns God, to expiate the sins of the people; for by the fact that he himself suffered through trial, he can help those who undergo trial.

¶ Therefore, sacred brothers, sharers of a heavenly summons, think upon the apostle and high priest of our belief, Jesus, faithful to him who made him as Moses also was faithful in the house of God. He is worthy of greater glory than Moses, inasmuch as he who made the house has more honor than the house; since every house is made by someone, and he who made all things is God. And Moses was faithful in all the house of God as a servant to witness to things that are to be spoken, but Christ as the son in his own house. We are his house, if we keep our courage and the pride of our hope.

Thus, as the Holy Spirit says: Today, if you hear his voice, do not close your hearts as in the time of rebellion, on the day of trial in the desert, when your fathers made trial of me in a test of me, and they had looked on my works for forty years. And therefore I was enraged with that generation, and said: They always go astray in their hearts, and they do not understand my ways. So I swore in my anger that they shall not come into my rest.

See to it, brothers, that there can never be in any of you a heart evil and faithless in forsaking the living God, but keep encouraging each other every day, while it is still called today, so that no one of you may be hardened by the beguilement of sin; for we are partners of the Christ, if only we can keep our original condition firm to the end.

In the saying: Today, if you hear his voice, do not close your hearts as in the time of rebellion, who heard and rebelled? Was it not all who went out of Egypt led by Moses? And with whom was God enraged for forty years? Was it not with the sinners, whose bodies collapsed in the desert? Against whom, if not the unbelievers, did he swear that they should never come into his rest? And we see that they did not come into his rest, through unbelief.

¶ We should be afraid, then, that, while his promise that we shall come into his rest still remains open, some one of you might be judged to have come short. For we also have received the gospel as those others did, but the word they had heard did them no good, since they had no admixture of faith in what they had heard. For we who do

believe are going into his rest; but as he said: So I swore
in my anger, that they shall not come into my rest. And
yet his works had been done since the beginning of the
world; for scripture says at one point concerning the seventh day: And on the seventh day God rested from all
his works; and again, in this place: They shall never come
into my rest. Since, then, it remains for some to come
into it, and those who formerly received the gospel did
not come in because of their unbelief, once more he sets
a certain day, today; as he says through David after all
that time, as has been said here before: Today, if you
hear his voice, do not close your hearts.

For if Joshua had given them rest, he would not have
spoken about another day after that. But there remains a
sabbath for the people of God; since one who comes into
God's rest also rests from his works, as God rested from
his own works.

Let us then strive to enter into that rest, so that none
may fall through the same example of unbelief. For the
word of God is alive and active, and sharper than any
two-edged sword, and cuts through to the division of soul
and spirit, of joints and marrows, and it can judge the
thoughts and purposes of the heart; and there is no creature that is hidden from his sight, but all things are naked and helpless before the eyes of him with whom we
have to do.

Since, then, we have a great high priest, Jesus the son
of God, who has passed through the heavens, let us hold
fast to our belief; for the high priest we have is not one
who cannot sympathize with our weaknesses, since he
has suffered all the trials we have, except that he did not
sin. So let us confidently approach the throne of grace,

so that we may receive mercy and find grace to rescue us in our time of need.

¶ For every high priest is selected from among men and appointed to perform, on behalf of men, duties before God, to offer gifts and sacrifice for sins committed. He can be moderate with those who are ignorant and go astray because he himself is submerged in weakness, and because of it he is bound to make offerings for sins on his own account also, as well as for the people. And the priest does not take the office upon himself but is called by God, like Aaron. So even the Christ did not do himself the honor of becoming high priest, but rather he who said to him: You are my son, this day I begot you; as he also said in another place: You are priest forever in the order of Melchizedek. And in his days of the flesh he addressed entreaties and supplications to him who could save him from death, with strong outcry and tears; and after being heard because of piety, even though he was the son, he learned obedience from his sufferings; and, made perfect, he became for all who obey him the cause of everlasting salvation, being called by God high priest in the order of Melchizedek.

About him we have much to say which is difficult to explain to you, since you have become dull listeners. For by this time you ought to be teachers, but you need to have someone teach you again the elementary first principles of the oracles of God, and you have come to need milk, not solid food. For anyone who takes milk is ignorant of the study of righteousness, since he is an infant; solid food is for the mature who have their faculties trained through practice to distinguish good from bad.

¶ Let us therefore pass over the elementary study of the Christ and go on to mature study; not once again laying down the foundations of repentance for dead acts, and belief in God, teaching about baptisms and the laying on of hands, the resurrection of the dead and the everlasting judgment. This we shall do, if God permits. For when once men have been enlightened, when they have tasted the gift of heaven and been participators in the Holy Spirit, and known the beautiful language of God and the powers of the age to come, and then fallen away, it is impossible for them to come into a new repentance, since they are crucifying the son of God for themselves and making a spectacle of him. For when the earth drinks the rain constantly falling upon it, and produces an acceptable plant for those by whom it is cultivated, it wins praise from God; but when it bears thorns and thistles it is despised and close to being accursed, and the end is burning.

But concerning you, dear friends, even though we speak as we do, we are convinced of better things, which go with salvation. For God is not unfair, so that he could forget your work and the love you have shown for his name, serving the saints in the past and serving them still. But we desire that each one of you should show the same enthusiasm, to the last, toward the fulfilment of your hope; not to be dull, but to imitate those who, by faith and patience, are given a share in the promise.

For when God made his promise to Abraham, since he had no one greater to swear by, he swore by himself, saying: In my blessing I will surely bless you, and in my multiplying I will multiply you. And thus, after waiting patiently, Abraham gained the promise. For human people swear by one greater than themselves, and the oath is final confirmation in any dispute. God, therefore, wishing to make even plainer to the heirs of his promise how unchangeable was his will, guaranteed it with an oath; so that, by means of two acts in which it is impossible for God to deceive us, we who have taken refuge with him may have strong assurance that we shall grasp the hope that lies before us. This hope we have as an anchor for our life, steady and secure and reaching to the innermost place behind the curtain, where Jesus entered as our forerunner, made high priest forever in the order of Melchizedek.

¶ This Melchizedek, King of Salem, priest of God the all-highest, is the one who met Abraham as he returned from the slaughter of the Kings, and blessed him, the one to whom Abraham allotted a tenth of all the spoils; meaning, when translated, first, King of Righteousness, then King of Salem, that is, King of Peace, fatherless, motherless, without genealogy, with neither a beginning of his days nor an end of his life, in the likeness of the son of God, he remains as priest for all time.

Consider how great was this one to whom Abraham the patriarch gave a tenth of his spoils. And those from among the sons of Levi who assume the priesthood are commanded by the law to collect a tenth from the people, that is, from their brothers, even though these are the issue of the loins of Abraham; but the one with no genealogy took a tenth from Abraham, and blessed the holder of the promises. Beyond any argument, it is the lesser who receives the blessing of the greater. And here, it is men who perish who take the tenth; but there, it is he of whom it is testified that he lives. And, so to speak, Levi also, who received the tenths, paid his tenth also, through Abraham, being still in the loins of his fore-father when Melchizedek encountered him.

If, then, there could be perfection through the Leviti-cal priesthood, through which the people received the law, what use would there be in having another priest raised up in the order of Melchizedek rather than his being called in the order of Aaron? For when the priest-hood is changed, of necessity there comes a change of the law. He of whom these things are said belonged to a different tribe, no member of which approached the al-tar; for it is evident that our Lord originated from the tribe of Judah, which Moses never mentioned in connec-tion with priests. And the case is still clearer when an-other priest is raised up in the order of Melchizedek, and has become priest not by decree of human law but through the power of imperishable life; for it is attested: You are priest forever in the order of Melchizedek. The former commandment is canceled because of its weak-ness and uselessness, since the law brought nothing to perfection; but a better hope is introduced by which we draw near to God. And inasmuch as it was not without an oath sworn; for these others became priests without an oath sworn, but he with an oath sworn by the one who said to him: The Lord swore, and he will not change his word, you are priest forever; by so much the more is Jesus the guarantee of a greater covenant. Those priests were many because death prevented any one of them from enduring; but he, because he endures forever, holds a priesthood in which none can succeed him. He can, therefore, forever save those who through him come be-fore God, since he lives forever to intercede for them.

It was fitting that our high priest should be such a one, holy, without evil, without stain, removed from sinners and made higher than the heavens. He has no day-by-day need, as the high priests do, to offer sacrifices first for his own sins and then for those of the people. For he did this once for all in offering up himself. For the law appoints as high priests human beings who have their weaknesses; but the word of the oath sworn since the law appoints the son, perfect forever.

¶ To summarize what has been said, such is the high priest we have, one who sits at the right of the throne of greatness in the heavens, minister of the sanctuary and of the true tabernacle which the Lord, not man, set in place. Now every high priest is appointed to offer gifts and sacrifices; so he too would have to have something to offer. If he were on earth, he would not even be a priest, since there are those who offer gifts according to the law. These serve the imitation and the shadow of the things in heaven, as Moses was directed to do when he was about to complete the tabernacle; for see to it, God said, that you make everything on the model of what was shown you on the mountain. But Christ has been given a higher ministry, inasmuch as he is mediator of a greater covenant, which is made law on the strength of greater promises. For if that first covenant had been without fault, no place would have been needed for a second; but he does find fault with them when he says: Behold, the days are coming, says the Lord, when I will compact a new covenant with the house of Israel and the house of Judah, not like the covenant which I made with their fathers on the day when I took them by the hand to lead them out of the land of Egypt. Because they did not keep to my covenant, and I have put them out of my mind, says the Lord. For this is the covenant which I will make with the house of Israel after those days, says the Lord, giving them my laws for their understanding, and I will inscribe them on their hearts; and I will be their God, and they shall be my people. And they must not instruct each other, each man saying to his fellow citizen or his brother: Know the Lord; because all of them, from small to great, will know me; because I shall be merciful to their wrongdoings, and I shall no longer remember their sins.

In speaking of a new covenant he has made the old one antiquated; but what is antiquated and grows old is close to disappearing.

¶ The first covenant did have its rules for service and a sanctuary on earth. A tabernacle was set up, the first one, in which were the lampstand and the table and the display of the showbread; this is called the Holy. And beyond the next curtain is the tabernacle which is called the Holy of Holies, containing a golden altar of incense and the ark of the covenant, entirely overlaid with gold; and there is a golden jar containing the manna, and Aaron's rod which budded and the tablets of the covenant, and above it the cherubim of glory overshadowing the seat of mercy; concerning which things it is not now possible to speak in detail. Such being their arrangement, the priests enter the first tabernacle constantly in the performance of their duties; but only the high priest enters the second, once a year, not without blood offering which he brings for his own errors and those of the people. And this is what the Holy Spirit shows us: that while the first tabernacle is still in place the way to the sanctuaries is not revealed. It is a symbol for our present time, when gifts and sacrifices are brought which cannot make the worshipper conscious of perfection, but it is only a matter of things eaten and drunk and various washings, regulations for the flesh applied until the time of the new order.

But Christ arrived as high priest of all the good things which have come about through the greater and more final tabernacle not made by human hands, that is, not of this world; and not by the blood of goats and calves but by his own blood he entered once for all into the holy place, having found everlasting redemption. For if the blood of goats and bulls and the sprinkled ashes of a heifer can hallow those who are defiled for the lustration of their flesh, how much more will the blood of the Christ, who through his everlasting spirit offered himself without fault to God, purify our conscience, away from dead acts to the service of the living God. And for this reason he is the mediator of a new testament, so that, with his death coming for absolution from their sins under the first covenant, those who are called may receive the promise of an everlasting inheritance. For in the case of a testament, the death of the testator must be involved; since a testament has force after death has occurred, but it has no force while the testator is still living.

Even the first covenant, therefore, was not established without blood; for when the whole commandment had been declared by Moses to all the people, according to the law, he took the blood of calves and goats, with water and scarlet wool and hyssop, and sprinkled the book itself and all the people, saying: This is the blood of the covenant which God decreed for you. And in the same way he sprinkled the tabernacle and all the articles of service. And, by the law, practically everything is purified by blood, and without bloodshed there is no remission.

It must be, then, that while the copies of things in heaven are purified by these means, the actual things in heaven must be purified by sacrifices greater than these. For Christ did not enter a sanctuary made by human hands which was a copy of the real thing, but he entered heaven itself, to appear before the face of God for our sake. Not to offer himself again and again, as the high priest enters the sanctuary once every year with blood that is not his own, since then he must have suffered again and again since the beginning of the world; but now, once for all at the conclusion of the ages, he has appeared, to abolish sin by the sacrifice of himself. And as it is the lot of man to die once, with the judgment coming after that, so the Christ was offered once for the taking away of the sins of many, and will appear a second time, without relation to sin, to those who look for his coming, for their salvation.

¶ The law, possessing the shadow of the good things to come, not the actual form of the things, cannot, by the same sacrifices which they offer, continually year by year, ever bring to perfection those who come to God. Otherwise, would not these have ceased to be offered? Since, once absolved, the worshippers would no longer have any consciousness of sin. But in these sacrifices is the yearly remembrance of sins, for it is impossible for the blood of bulls and goats to take sins away.

So, coming into the world, Christ says: You did not want sacrifice and offering, but you prepared a body for me. In whole burnt offerings even for sin, you took no delight. Then I said: Behold, I come; in the scroll of a book it is written concerning me; to do, O God, your will. And, while he said above that you did not want sacrifices and offerings and whole burnt offerings even for sin, which are offered according to the law, nor take delight in them, then he said: Behold, I come to do your will. He takes away the first so that the second may stand. By which will we are sanctified by the offering of the body of Jesus Christ, once for all.

And every priest stands day by day performing services and again and again offering the same sacrifices, which can never take away sins. But he, after offering for sins one sacrifice for all time, sat down on the right hand of God, waiting henceforth for his enemies to be made a footstool for his feet; for with one offering he has made those who are consecrated perfect for all time. And our witness to this is the Holy Spirit; for after saying: This is the covenant I will make with them after those days, says the Lord, giving them my laws for their hearts, and I will inscribe them upon their understanding. And I shall no longer remember their sins and their transgressions. But where there is remission of these, there is no longer any offering for sins.

Having therefore confidence, brothers, for entrance into the sanctuary by the blood of Jesus, the new and living way he has made for us through the curtain, that is, his flesh, and having a great priest set over the house of God, let us approach with true heart in abundance of faith, our hearts purged of bad conscience, our bodies washed in pure water. Let us hold fast to our belief in the hope, for he who gave us the promise is to be trusted. And let us study each other to stimulate love and good works, not failing to attend our own meetings, as is the way of some, but encouraging each other, all the more so inasmuch as you see the Day coming nearer.

For when we willingly sin after having received perception of the truth, there is no longer left any sacrifice for sin, only the terrible expectation of judgment, and of fire eager to devour its opponents. If one has broken the law of Moses he dies without pity on the word of two or three witnesses; how much worse do you suppose will be the punishment accorded to one who has trampled down the son of God, and called unclean the blood of the covenant by which he was sanctified, and outraged the spirit of grace? We know who it was who said: Mine is the vengeance, I will repay. And again: The Lord will judge his people. It is a terrible thing to fall into the hands of the living God.

Remember the days that have been, when you, the enlightened ones, underwent a hard struggle with sufferings, both when you were publicly exposed to revilements and afflictions, and when you shared them with those who were so treated; for you suffered along with those who were imprisoned, and you accepted the seizure of your property with joy, knowing that you have a greater possession and one that endures. Do not lose your courage, which brings a great reward, for you have need of endurance in order to do the will of God and win the promise. For (it is written): In a very little time he who is coming will come, and he will not delay; the one who is righteous will live by faith and if anyone falters, my soul is not well pleased with him. We do not belong to faltering, for destruction, but to faith, for the saving of the soul.

¶ Faith is the substance of things hoped for, the proof of things unseen; for by it our forebears were attested. By faith we understand that the ages were formed by the word of God, so that what is seen did not come from things that appear. By faith Abel brought to God a better offering than Cain, and by this he was proved righteous, with God himself bearing witness to his gifts; and by faith, though he died, he still speaks. By faith Enoch was taken up aloft, so as not to look on death, and he was never found because God had taken him; since it is attested that before his taking up he was pleasing to God, and without faith it is impossible to please him; for one who approaches God must believe that he exists and that he is the rewarder of those who seek him out. By faith Noah, divinely warned of things not yet apparent, took careful thought and built the ark for the salvation of his household; and by this he refuted the world, and became heir to that righteousness that comes through faith. By faith Abraham obeyed when he was called to go forth into that region which he was to receive as his inheritance, and he went forth not knowing where he was going. By faith he moved to the land of the promise as to a foreign land, living in tents as did also Isaac and Jacob, who shared with him the inheritance of the same promise; for he was waiting for the city with foundations, of which the architect and designer is God. By faith also Sarah herself found strength to give birth, though past her time of life, since she thought the giver of the promise was to be believed; so that from one man, even from one far gone, there came a number like the stars in the sky, or like the innumerable sands at the edge of the sea.

All of these died in faith without winning the promise,

but seeing it from far off and hailing it, and confessing that they were strangers and visitors on earth. They who say such things make it clear that they are searching for their own country. If they had been remembering the country from which they came, they would have had occasion to turn back; but as it is they long for a better one, that is, the one in heaven. Therefore God is not ashamed to be called their God, for he has made ready a city for them.

By faith Abraham offered up Isaac when he was put to the test, and accepting the promise, offered up his only son, the one of whom it had been said: Your seed shall be called after Isaac; reasoning that God can even raise men from the dead; therefore symbolically he did recover him. By faith even in things to come Isaac blessed Jacob and Esau. By faith Jacob, dying, blessed each of the sons of Joseph and prayed for them over the end of his staff. By faith Joseph, dying, remembered the exodus of the sons of Israel and gave instructions concerning his bones. By faith when Moses was born he was hidden for three months by his parents, because they saw that the baby was a fine one, and they were not frightened by the edict of the King. By faith Moses, grown big, refused to be called the son of Pharaoh's daughter, choosing to suffer with the people of God rather than have the temporary enjoyment of sinfulness, considering the despised estate of the Christ a richer thing than the treasures of Egypt, since he looked forward to his reward. By faith he left Egypt, not fearing the anger of the King, for he endured as if he saw him who cannot be seen. By faith he established the Passover and the sprinkling of blood so that the destroyer of the firstborn might not strike them. By faith they walked across the Red Sea as if on dry land, which the Egyptians tried to do and were engulfed. By faith the walls of Jericho fell down when they were circled for seven days. By faith Rahab the harlot did not perish with the unbelievers, because she had received the spies in peace.

Why should I say more? My time will run out as I tell about Gideon, Barak, Samson, Jephthah, David and Samuel and the prophets. By faith they overthrew kingdoms, did works of righteousness, won promises, stopped the mouths of lions, quenched the force of fire, escaped the edge of the sword, grew strong out of weakness, proved mighty in battle, routed the lines of their opponents. Wives recovered their resurrected dead. But others were tortured, refusing release so as to win a greater resurrection; others again accepted the ordeal of mockery and whippings and even of chains and prison. They were stoned, tortured, sawn in two, slaughtered by the sword. They went about in the skins of sheep and goats, in want and affliction and abuse. The world was not worthy of them as they wandered in deserts and mountains and caves and holes in the ground.

Yet all of these, though proved through their faith, did not achieve the promise, since God for our sake contemplated something better: that they should not be perfected apart from us.

¶ Let us also, therefore, surrounded by such a cloud of witnesses, putting aside every obstacle and the sin that easily besets us, run with tenacity the course that lies before us, looking to the originator and perfecter of faith, Jesus; who, instead of the joy that lay ready before him, endured the cross, despising the shame of it, and has sat down to the right of the throne of God. Consider him who endured so great a rebellion by sinners against himself; so that you may not falter, weakening in your spirits. You have not yet gone to the point of bloodshed in your struggle against sinfulness, and you have forgotten that appeal that speaks to you as sons: My son, do not think lightly of the Lord's discipline, and do not lose heart when you are punished by him; for whom the Lord loves he disciplines, and he whips every son whom he acknowledges. Put up with discipline. God treats you as sons. Where is there a son whose father does not discipline him? If you go without the discipline which all are born to share, you are bastards, not sons.

Also, we had the fathers of our flesh to discipline us, and we have let them; should we not far rather submit to the father of our spirits, and live? For they disciplined us for a few days, as it seemed right to them, but he does it for our good so that we can participate in his sanctity. All discipline, for the moment, seems to belong not with pleasure but with pain; but later, to those who have been through it, it yields a peaceful harvest of righteousness. So straighten up the slack arms and the tottering knees, and take straight steps with your feet, so that your lameness may not put you off, but rather be set right.

Seek to be at peace with all, and seek sanctification, without which no one will see the Lord; taking care that no one of you who lacks the grace of God, some root of bitterness pushing up among you, cause you trouble so that all are polluted by it; someone lewd or profane, like Esau, who sold his birthright for a single meal. You know that afterward he wished to inherit the blessing but was rejected, for he found no place for repentance, though he begged for it in tears.

You have not come to the place that is felt, which

burns with fire, to the gloom and darkness and storm and the clamor of the trumpet and voice speaking, which those who heard it begged not to have to hear it again; for they could not bear the commandment: If even a beast touches the mountain, it shall be stoned to death. And so frightful was the apparition that Moses said: I am terrified and shaking.

But you have come to Mount Zion and the city of the living God, heavenly Jerusalem, to myriads of angels, the festal gathering and assembly of the firstborn whose names are written down in heaven, and to God the judge of all, and the souls of the just made perfect, and Jesus the mediator of the new covenant, and his blood sprinkled which speaks louder than the blood of Abel. See to it that you do not ask not to hear him who speaks to you; for if those others who asked not to hear did not escape him who warned them on earth, even less shall we escape if we turn from him who speaks from heaven. At that time his voice shook the earth; now he has given a promise, saying: One more time I will shake not only the earth but also heaven. The words: One more time, mean the abolition of the shaken things as things that had been made, so that what was not shaken may remain. So, taking over a kingdom unshaken, let us keep our gratitude and in it serve God with piety and fear so that he may be well pleased; for our God is a consuming fire.

¶ Let brotherly love abide. Do not forget your hospitality, for through this some have entertained angels without knowing it. Remember the prisoners as if you were in prison with them, the abused as if you were so in body. Honorable is marriage among all, and the undefiled bed, for God condemns lechers and adulterers. Let your living be without avarice, making do with what is on hand; for he himself said: I will never let you go, I will never forsake you. So that we can be confident and say: The Lord is my aid, I shall not fear. What can man do to me?

Remember your leaders, who spoke the word of God to you, and as you consider the end of their life, imitate their faith. Jesus Christ is the same yesterday and today and forever. Do not be carried away by strange and complex teachings; it is good to strengthen the heart with grace, not foods, by which those who followed that way have not been helped. We have an altar from which those who serve the tabernacle are not allowed to eat. For the beasts whose blood is offered at the sanctuary for sin by the high priests, their bodies are burned outside the camp. Jesus, therefore, to sanctify the people by his own blood, suffered outside the gate. Let us therefore go to him outside the camp and bear the abuse he bore, since we have no enduring city here but are looking for the one to come. For him let us offer a sacrifice of praise to God continually, that is, the product of lips which confess to his name. And do not forget to do good, and to share, for with such sacrifices God is well pleased.

Obey your leaders and give way to them, for they go sleepless for the sake of your souls, since they will be accountable for them; so that they may do this with joy and not grieving, for that would be unprofitable for you.

Pray for us, for we believe that we have a good conscience, trying always to conduct ourselves well. And I ask you to do this all the more so that I may be restored to you the sooner. May the God of peace who brought back from the dead the great shepherd of the flock through the blood of the everlasting covenant, that is,

our Lord Jesus, confirm you in all good for the doing of
his will; working in us what is pleasing in his sight,
through Jesus Christ, to whom be the glory forever and
ever. Amen.

And I ask you, brothers, to be patient with my message of exhortation, for I have written to you in only a
few words.

Know that our brother Timothy has been released, and
if he arrives soon, I will see you in his company.

Give greeting to all your leaders and all the saints.
Those from Italy send you greetings. May grace be with
you all.

The General Letter
of James

¶JAMES, SLAVE OF GOD AND THE LORD
Jesus Christ, to the twelve tribes in their dispersion.
Greetings.

Count it all as cause for joy, my brothers, when you
are forced into various trials, knowing that the proved
quality of your faith engenders fortitude; but let your
fortitude have complete scope, so that you may be complete and blameless, lacking in nothing. But if any one
of you does lack in wisdom, let him ask for it from God
who gives to all simply and without reproach, and it will
be given to him. But let him ask with faith and without
any doubt, since one who doubts is like the sea waves
blown and tossed; let such a one not suppose that a man
who is of two minds and uncertain in all his ways will
receive anything from the Lord.

Let the humble brother glory in his exaltation and the
rich brother in his humiliation, because he will be gone
like the flower of the grass. The sun rises with its burning heat and shrivels the grass, and the flower falls to
the ground and the beauty of its face is destroyed. Just
so the rich man in his comings and goings will wither
away.

Blessed is the man who endures trial, because when he passes the test he will win the wreath of life which the Lord promised to those who love him. Let no man who is tempted say: I am being tempted by God. For God is not tempted by evil things, and he himself tempts no one. Each man is tempted when he is attracted and seduced by his own desire. Then the desire conceives and gives birth to sin, and the sin when it is full-grown brings forth death. Do not be deceived, my beloved brothers. Every good giving and every perfect gift comes from above, descending from the father of lights, in whom there is no change, nor any shadow of variation. He willed it and brought us forth by the word of truth, for us to be a kind of first fruits of his creatures.

Know this, my beloved brothers: every man should be quick to listen, slow to speak, slow to anger, for the anger of a man does not effect the righteousness of God. Putting aside, therefore, all filthiness and any excess of baseness, meekly accept the implanted word which can save your souls. Be practitioners of the word, not mere self-deceiving listeners. Since if one listens to the word but does not practice it, he is like a man who looks at his natural face in a mirror; for he looks at himself and then goes on his way and forgets what he looked like. But one who gazes into the perfect law of freedom and abides by it; not a listener to something to be forgotten, but one who performs an act; that man will be blessed in his activity. If one believes that he is religious, but does not curb his tongue, and if he deceives himself, his religion counts for nothing. This is the pure and undefiled worship before our God and Father: to care for orphans and widows in their affliction, and to keep oneself untarnished by the world.

¶ My brothers, surely the faith you have in the glory of our Lord Jesus Christ does not go with discrimination among persons? If a man wearing golden rings and shining clothes comes into your synagogue, and there also comes in a poor man in filthy clothes, and you look at the man wearing shining clothes and say: Sit here, in a place of honor, but say to the poor man: Stand, or else sit down there below my footstool, are you not discriminating among yourselves and being judges who give vicious opinions? Listen, my beloved brothers. Did not God choose out those who are poor in the things of the world but rich in faith and heirs to the kingdom which he promised to those who love him? But you despised the poor man. Are not the rich lords over you, and is it not they who drag you into the law courts? Is it not they who insult the noble name which has been bestowed upon you? If you fulfill the kingly law accordingly as scripture says: You shall love your neighbor as yourself; you are acting well. But if you discriminate among persons, you are committing a sin, and are convicted by the law as transgressors. For anyone who obeys all the rest of the law but fails in one respect is guilty in all respects. He who said: You shall not commit adultery; also said: You shall not murder. But if you do not commit adultery but do murder, you are breaking the law. Speak and act as if you were about to be tried by the law of freedom. For him who acts without mercy, judgment is merciless. Mercy triumphs over judgment.

What good does it do, my brothers, if someone says that he has faith but does not have the acts of faith? Surely his faith will not save him? If a brother or a sister is naked and short of daily nourishment, and one of you says to them: Go in peace, keep warm and eat, but you do not give them what they need for their bodies, what good does it do? So even faith, if it does not have the acts of faith, is a dead thing in itself. But someone will say: You have faith, but I have actions. Show me your faith apart from your actions, and I will show my faith from my actions. You believe that there is one God? You do well to do so. Demons also believe this, and they shudder. But are you willing to understand, O empty man, that faith without acts is idle? Was not Abraham our father justified by his actions, when he offered up Isaac, his son, on the sacrificial altar? You see that his faith worked with his actions and through his actions his faith was made a thing complete, and so the scripture was fulfilled which says: Abraham believed God, and it was counted as righteousness in him, and he was called the friend of God. You see that a person is justified by his acts and not by faith alone. So likewise was not even Rahab the harlot justified by her action when she received the messengers and sent them off by the wrong way? As the body without spirit is a dead thing, so also faith without acts is a dead thing.

¶ My brothers, not many of you should become teachers. We know that we teachers shall be given a stricter trial; for we all make many mistakes. But if a man makes no mistakes in what he says, he is a complete man and able also to control his entire body. If we put bits in the mouths of horses to make them obey us, we can also control the entire body. Consider also ships, which, big as they are and driven by severe winds, are directed by a very small rudder wherever the impulse of the steersman chooses. So also the tongue is a small part of the body but makes a big noise. Consider how small a fire ignites how great a forest. The tongue too is a fire; the tongue is appointed among the parts of our bodies as a whole world of wickedness, which stains the entire body and sets fire to the wheel of creation, and which itself is burned by Gehenna. For the whole world of beasts and birds and reptiles and sea creatures is subjected, and has been made subject, to the world of men. But no man can make a subject of the tongue. It is an evil that is never still, full of deadly poison. With it we praise the Lord and Father, and with it we curse men, who were born in the likeness of God; out of the same mouth come praise and cursing. This, my brothers, should not be so. Surely the spring does not run sweet and bitter from the same opening? Surely, my brothers, a fig tree cannot grow olives, nor a grape vine figs? Neither can a salt spring give sweet water.

Who among you is wise and knowledgeable? Let him show, with the gentleness that comes from wisdom, the actions of his good disposition. But if you have bitter envy and ambition in your hearts, do not be boastful, do not lie about the truth. That is not the wisdom which comes from above, but it is earthly, sensual, demonic; for where there is envy and ambition, there there is disorder and everything that is bad. But the wisdom which comes from above is, first of all, pure; it is also peaceful, forbearing, open to persuasion, filled with mercy and a good harvest, impartial, not hypocritical; the harvest of righteousness is sown in peace by those who make peace.

¶ Where do these hostilities come from, where do these quarrels, which take place among you? Is it not from here, from the pleasures that go to war inside your bodies? You want, and do not have. You covet and murder, and cannot get; you quarrel and are at war. You do not have, because you do not ask; you do ask and do not receive, because you ask badly: for means to spend on your pleasures. Adulterous people, do you not know that love of the world is hatred of God? He who wishes to be a friend of the world becomes an enemy of God. Or do you think it is meaningless when the scripture says: He has jealous longings over the spirit which he lodged in us? But the grace he gives is stronger than that. Therefore scripture says: God is set against the proud but gives favor to the humble.

Submit, then, to God; stand up against the devil and he will run away from you. Come to God and he will come to you. Wash your hands clean, you sinners, and purify your hearts, you doubters. Be miserable and mourn and lament; let your laughter turn to sorrow and your joy to dejection. Humble yourselves before the Lord, and he will exalt you.

Brothers, do not speak against each other. The man who speaks against his brother or judges his brother is speaking against the law and judging the law. But if you judge the law you are not one who carries out the law, but its judge. But there is one lawgiver and judge, the one who can save you and who can destroy you. Who are you to judge your neighbor?

Come now, you who say: Today or tomorrow we shall go to a certain city and spend a year there and do business and make money. But you do not know about tomorrow or what your life will be like then. For you are a mist that appears for a little while and then disappears. You should rather have said: If the Lord wills it and we are alive we shall also do this or that. But as it is, you are boasting in your arrogance. All such boasting is bad.

If one knows how to do right and does not do it, that is a sin in him.

¶ Come now, you rich men: Lament, bewailing the miseries that are advancing upon you. Your wealth has rotted away and your clothes are eaten by moths, your gold and silver have rusted and their rust will testify against you and feed on your flesh. You have stored away treasures for the fire in the final days. Behold, the unpaid wages of the laborers who mowed your fields cry out against you, and the cries of the harvesters have reached the ears of the Lord of the hosts. You reveled and luxuriated upon the earth, you fed your hearts on the day of slaughter. You condemned and murdered the righteous man. Is he not against you?

Be patient then, brothers, until the coming of the Lord. Behold, the farmer looks for the precious harvest of his land when he watches patiently over it until it gets the early and the late rain. Be patient, you also, strengthen your hearts, because the coming of the Lord is near.

Do not complain, brothers, against each other, for fear you may be judged; behold, the judge stands before your doors. As your example of suffering and patience, brothers, take the prophets who spoke in the name of the Lord. Behold, we call blessed those who have endured. You have heard of the endurance of Job, and you know what the Lord did in the end, because the Lord is generous and takes pity.

Before all else, my brothers, do not swear, neither by heaven nor earth, nor any other oath. Let your yes be yes and your no, no, for fear you may be brought to judgment.

Is one of you in distress? Let him pray. Is anyone

happy? Let him sing praises. Is one of you sick? Let him call in the elders of the church, and let them pray over him, anointing him with oil in the name of the Lord; and the prayer of faith will save the sufferer, and the Lord will restore him; and if he has committed sins, they will be forgiven him. So confess your sins to each other and pray for each other, that you may be healed. The prayer of a righteous person at work has great strength. Elijah was human, with the same nature as ours; and he asked in his prayer that it should not rain, and it did not rain on the land for three years and six months; and again he prayed, and the sky gave its rain, and the land grew a flourishing harvest.

My brothers, if one among you is led astray from the truth, and someone else brings him back to it, be sure that the man who brought back the sinner from the error of his ways will save his own soul from death, and cover up a multitude of sins.

The First General Letter

of Peter

¶PETER, APOSTLE OF JESUS CHRIST, TO the chosen exiles in their dispersion through Pontus, Galatia, Cappadocia, Asia, and Bithynia, according to the predestination of God the Father, by the consecration of the Spirit to the service of Jesus Christ and through the sprinkling of his blood. May grace and peace be multiplied for you.

Blessed is the God and Father of our Lord Jesus Christ. Through his great mercy he granted us to be born again into living hope through the resurrection of Jesus Christ from the dead, and into an inheritance which is imperishable and stainless and cannot fade, which has been kept in heaven for you who are held safe in the power of God through your faith in the salvation which is ready to be revealed in the final time. Rejoice over this, even if for a little while, when it had to be, you have been hurt by all kinds of trials; this was so that the quality of your faith might be found far more precious than gold—which, though perishable, is proved by fire—for praise and glory and honor at the revelation of Jesus Christ. You have not seen him but you love him, and now, not seeing him but believing in him, rejoice, with a joy which is inexpressible and glorious, as you win what is the end of faith, the salvation of your souls. Concerning this salvation, the prophets, who prophesied about the grace that would be yours, studied and sought for answers, trying to determine the time for which the spirit of Christ within them foretold the sufferings of Christ and his glory thereafter; and it was revealed to them that they were serving not themselves but you in these matters which have now been announced to you by those who have brought you the gospel through the Holy Spirit sent from heaven; secrets into which angels long to look.

Accordingly, gird up the loins of your mind, in complete sobriety, and put your hopes in the grace which is brought to you in the revelation of Jesus Christ. As children of obedience, do not conform to the desires you had before in your ignorance, but, like the holy one who summoned you, be yourselves holy in all your behavior; because it is written: You shall be holy, because I am holy. And if you invoke as Father the one who judges without prejudice according to what each has done, then spend the time of your exile here in fear; knowing that it was not by perishable things, silver or gold, that you were ransomed from the vain way of life you inherited from your fathers, but by precious blood, as of a blameless unblemished lamb, Christ. He was foreknown before the establishment of the world but revealed at the end of the ages, for you, who because of him believe in God who raised him from the dead and gave him glory, so that your faith and hope is in God.

Sanctifying your souls in obedience to the truth toward unfeigned brotherly affection, love each other from the heart, constantly, since you have been reborn not from a perished seed but from one that is imperishable, through the word of God which lives and endures. Thus: All flesh is like grass, and all its glory is like the flower of the grass. The grass withers and its flower falls to the ground, but the word of the Lord endures forever.

¶ This is the word which was brought to you as gospel. Putting aside, therefore, all malice and all treachery and hypocrisy and envious thoughts and calumnies, crave, like newborn babies, the guileless milk of reason, so that by it you may grow to salvation, if you have tasted and know that the Lord is good. Come to him, a living stone, rejected by men but selected for honor by God; and yourselves, like living stones, be built into a spiritual house for sacred priestly service, to offer up through Jesus Christ spiritual sacrifices which are well pleasing to God. As it says in scripture: Behold, I lay down on Zion a stone that is select and prized at the uttermost corner; and he who believes in it shall not be put to shame. It is a thing prized by those who believe; but for those who do not believe, it is: The stone which the builders rejected has come to be at the head of the corner, and a stone to stumble on and a rock of catastrophe. On which they stumble, by disbelieving in the word; to which end they were appointed. But you are a race elect, a royal priesthood, a sacred nation, a people to be preserved, so that you may proclaim the virtues of him who summoned you from darkness into his own wonderful light; who once were no people but now are the people of God, who received no mercy but now have been granted mercy.

I call upon you then, dear friends, as resident aliens and transients in this world to refrain from carnal desires, which take up arms against the soul. And keep your behavior among the heathens good, so that, whereas they now speak against you as evildoers, they may learn from your good works and glorify God on the Day of Visitation.

Be obedient to all human authority for the sake of the Lord; to a king, as one who is above you; to governors, because they are sent by him to punish the evildoers and to praise the doers of good; since this is the will of God, that by doing right you should suppress the unwisdom of thoughtless men; as free men, having your freedom not as a covering up of baseness, but as slaves of God. Give honor to all; love the brotherhood; fear God; honor the King.

Servants should be obedient with all respect to their masters, not only when they are good and kind, but also when they are unjust. For it is grace when, through consciousness of God, one endures pain when suffering unfairly; but what honor is there when you endure punishment for doing wrong? But when you do good and suffer and endure it, there is grace with God. It was to this that you were called, because Christ also suffered, for your sake, leaving you his example so that you might follow in his footsteps. He did no wrong, nor was any treachery found in his utterance; he was reviled and did not revile in answer; he suffered and spoke no threats but gave himself up to him who judges justly; he took up our sins in his own body onto the cross, so that, dying for sins, we might live for righteousness. You were healed by his wound. For you were like sheep gone astray, but now you have turned to your shepherd and the guardian of your souls.

¶ So likewise you wives should be submissive to your husbands, so that, even if some husbands do not believe in the word, they may, even without the word, be won over by their wives' way of life as they observe how chastely you live out of respect for them. Your beauty should not be the outward kind, in the arrangement of your hair or addition of gold ornaments or the clothes you wear, but the person hidden in the heart, in the incorruptibility of a peaceful and gentle spirit, which is greatly prized in the sight of God. It was thus that, long ago in the old days, the sainted women whose hopes were in God made themselves beautiful, by subordinating themselves to their husbands, as Sarah was submissive to Abraham. She called him lord; and you are her daughters, so long as you do good works and fear no threat. So likewise, you husbands, live with them understandingly, giving them due honor as to the weaker feminine vessel, and as heirs together to the grace of life, so that your prayers may not be stopped.

Finally, be, all of you, as one in your thoughts and feelings, full of brotherly love, compassionate, humble. Do not repay evil with evil or insult with insult but, on the contrary, give a blessing, because it was to this that you were called, to be the inheritors of a blessing. For if one desires to love life and look upon good days, let him keep his tongue from evil and his lips from uttering treachery; and let him turn aside from evil and do good, and seek out peace and pursue it. Because the eyes of the Lord are on the righteous, and his ears are for their prayer. But the face of the Lord is set against the doers of evil.

And who will do you harm if you are zealous for good? Yet even if you suffer for righteousness, you are blessed. Do not fear their terror and do not be shaken, but hallow the Lord Christ in your hearts, always ready to answer anyone who demands that you give a reason for the hope that is in you; but with gentleness and respect, with good conscience, so that those who attack your good life in Christ may be shamed in their slander. For if it is God's will that you suffer, it is better to suffer for doing good than for doing evil. Since even Christ once died for sins, the just for the unjust, to bring you to God. He was put to death in the flesh and brought to life in the spirit; in which he went even to the spirits in prison and preached to them. They had been disobedient once when the patience of God waited for them, in the days of Noah when the ark was being built and in it few souls, eight that is, were saved in the flood. This flood as baptism, its antitype, saves you now. This is not a riddance from the filth of the body, but a plea to God for good conscience, through the resurrection of Jesus Christ, who went to heaven and is at the right hand of God with angels and authorities and powers subjected to him.

¶ Since Christ suffered in the flesh, arm yourselves also with the same understanding, since he who suffers is relieved of his sinfulness, to live out his time in the flesh no longer by the desires of mankind but by the will of God. The time that has gone by has been enough to do the will of heathens, going the way of unchastity, desire, wine tippling, revelries, drinking parties, and disgraceful idolatry. Herein they are surprised if you do not rush to join them in the same excess of dissipation, and speak ill of you. They will have to answer for it to him who will presently judge the living and the dead. Since it was for this that the gospel was brought even to the dead, that they must be judged in the flesh like men but live in the spirit according to God.

The end of all things is at hand. Be temperate, then,

and sober for your prayers. Above all, be constant in your love for each other, since love covers up a multitude of sins. Be hospitable to each other without grumbling; as you have individually been given a gift of grace, dispense it to each other like good stewards of the complex grace of God. If anyone speaks, let it be as if he were quoting the sayings of God; if he serves, as if from the strength which God assigns; so that God may be glorified among all, through Jesus Christ, to whom be the glory and the power forever and ever. Amen.

Dear friends, do not be surprised at the trial by fire which comes to you as if it were some strange thing that happened to you, but as you share in the sufferings of the Christ, rejoice so that in the revelation of his glory you may rejoice and be glad. If you are blamed in the name of Christ, you are blessed, because the spirit of glory and of God comes to rest on you. None of you must suffer punishment for being a murderer or thief or malefactor, or as a troublemaker; but if he suffers for being a Christian, let him take no shame, but glorify God for this name. For it is time for the beginning of the judgment with the household of God; and if it begins with us, what will the end be for those who refuse to believe in the gospel of God? And if the righteous man is barely saved, where will the impious and sinful man be found? Thus even those who suffer by the will of God should, by doing good, entrust their souls to God, their good creator who is to be trusted.

¶ To the elders among you, I, your fellow elder and witness to the sufferings of the Christ and sharer in the glory which is to be revealed, send this appeal: Be shepherds to God's flock that is with you, not under constraint but

willingly, not for shameful greed but freely; not as over-
lords of your charges but making yourselves models for
the flock; and when the chief shepherd appears, you will
win the unfading wreath of glory. In the same way, you
younger men, be obedient to your elders. And all, gird
yourselves with humility, because God is set against the
proud and gives favor to the humble.

Humble yourselves, therefore, to the mighty hand of
God, so that in time he may exalt you. Cast all your
trouble upon him, because he cares for you. Be sober, be
watchful. Your adversary, the devil, prowls like a lion,
roaring and looking for what he may devour. Stand up
against him, firm in your faith, knowing that the same
sufferings are befalling your brothers in the world. But
the God of all grace, who called you to his everlasting
glory in Christ, will, after you have suffered a little while,
himself make you whole and firm and strong. To him be
the power forever. Amen.

Through Silvanus, a faithful brother as I believe, I have
written you thus briefly, appealing to you and testifying
that this is the true grace of God. Stand fast by it.

My fellows among the chosen in Babylon send you
greetings, as does Mark my son. Greet each other with
the kiss of love.

Peace to all of you who are in Christ.

The Second General Letter of Peter

¶SIMON PETER, SLAVE AND APOSTLE
of Jesus Christ, to those who have been granted faith like
ours in the righteousness of our God and savior Jesus
Christ: may grace and peace be multiplied for you in the
recognition of God and Jesus our Lord. His divine power
has bestowed upon us everything that leads to life and
piety through the knowledge of him who called us in
glory and virtue. By this the greatest and most precious
promises have been given to us; so that you may become
sharers in the divine nature, escaping the world's corruption that comes through lust. For this very reason, bringing all your energy to bear, provide, by your faith, virtue;
and by virtue understanding, by understanding continence, by continence steadfastness, by steadfastness piety,
by piety brotherliness, by brotherliness love. All these
qualities, being yours and in abundance, will cause you
to be not useless or unproductive toward the knowledge
of our Lord Jesus Christ; but one who does not have them
is myopic and blind, forgetful of how he has been purified from his former sins. For this reason, brothers, try
the more strenuously to make sure of your calling and
your election. By so doing you cannot ever fail, for thus

your entrance into the everlasting Kingdom of our Lord and savior Jesus Christ will be generously provided for you.

So I shall constantly remind you of these matters, even though you know and are firm in the truth that is with you. For I think it is right, as long as I am still in this tabernacle of the flesh, to keep you wakeful by reminding you, knowing as I do that the putting off of this tabernacle of mine will come soon, as our Lord Jesus Christ has made clear to me; and I shall try to see to it that you will always remember these things after my departure. For it is not by following artfully constructed myths that we have made known to you the power and the presence of our Lord Jesus Christ, but because we were eyewitnesses to his greatness. For when he received honor and glory from God the Father, a voice like this came to him from the magnificent glory: This is my son, whom I love, in whom I am well pleased. And we heard this voice coming to him from heaven while we were with him on the holy mountain. We have the prophetic word, which is certain; you do well to hold to it, as to a lamp shining in a dingy place, until the day dawns in light and the morning star rises in your hearts. But first, know this, that no prophecy in scripture is subject to personal interpretation; for prophecy did not ever come by the will of man, but men, carried along by the Holy Spirit, have spoken from God.

¶ There were also false prophets among the people, as among you also there will be false teachers, who will bring in destructive heresies, even disowning the master who bought their freedom and bringing swift destruction upon themselves. But many will follow their vicious practices, and because of them the way of truth will be blasphemed; and in their greed they will exploit you with made-up stories; but, long since, the judgment against them has not been inactive, and their destruction has not been sleeping.

For if God did not spare the angels who sinned but consigned them to the lower depths of darkness where they are kept for judgment; and if he did not spare the ancient world, but did protect Noah, the herald of righteousness, with seven others, while he let loose the flood on the world of the impious; and if he doomed the cities of Sodom and Gomorrah to ashes, making them an example of what is in store for the impious; and if he rescued the righteous Lot, who was afflicted by the vicious behavior of these lawless people (for, righteous as he was and living among them, by what he saw and heard day after day he was tormented in his righteous soul by their lawless behavior); then the Lord knows how to rescue the pious from their ordeal and to keep the unrighteous under punishment until the Day of Judgment; especially those who follow the flesh in lust for corruption, and who despise high authority. Daring, headstrong, they do not tremble before glorious creatures, but insult them; whereas angels, who are greater in strength and power than they, do not insult them as they demand judgment against them.

But these men, like unreasoning beasts, creatures of nature bred to be caught and slaughtered, insulting what they do not understand, will be slaughtered as such beasts are slaughtered, damaged for the damage they have done. They think of happiness as the luxury of the day, they are blots and blemishes who revel in their own beguilements as they share your feasts. They have eyes that are full of adultery, insatiable in sinning, and they seduce unstable souls since their hearts are well practiced in serving their greed. Children of the curse, they left the straight road and went astray, following the course of Balaam the son of Beor, who longed for the wages of wickedness but was reproved for this transgression; a dumb beast spoke in a human voice and stopped the madness of the prophet.

These men are waterless springs, clouds before the whirlwind; the dark of hell is in store for them. For speaking loud in their lewdness they seduce, through the lusts of the flesh, through depravity, some who are barely escaping from the wrong way of life. They promise them freedom, being themselves the slaves of corruption; for anyone is the slave of one to whom he has lost. If they once escaped from the defilements of the world by recognizing the Lord and savior Jesus Christ, and then once more are involved in these and overcome, what happened to them last is worse than what happened first. For it would have been better for them not to have known the way of righteousness than, having known it, to turn back from the holy commandment that was handed down to them. What has happened to them is what is in the true proverb: The dog returns to his vomit; and: The sow washed clean goes back to roll in the mud.

¶ This, dear friends, is the second letter I have written you, to quicken the pure purpose in you by reminding you: that you should remember the words spoken of old by the holy prophets, and the commandment of the Lord and savior from your apostles. But first understand this, that in these final days mockers will come with their mockery, people who go the way of their own desires, who will say: Where is the promise of his coming? For since our fathers were laid to rest, all things remain as they have been since the original creation. But they are unaware, as they wish to be, that the skies existed from of old, and the earth formed from water and standing in the water, by the word of God; and through these waters the earth was flooded with water and perished. And by the same word the skies that are now and the earth that is now are stored away for the fire, kept for the Day of Judgment and the destruction of impious people.

Do not forget this one thing, dear friends; that with the Lord one day is like a thousand years, and a thousand years like one day. The Lord is not slow with his promise, as some think it is slowness; but he is patient with you, because he does not want any to be destroyed, but all to come to repentance. But the day of the Lord will come like a thief, and on it the heavens will disappear with a sizzling noise, and the heavenly bodies will fall apart in flames, and the earth and the things inside it will be laid open. When all these things break up, how great is the need for you to keep to the saintly and pious life, expecting and urging on the coming of the day of God, when the heavens will fall apart in fire and the heavenly bodies melt in the flames. Then, according to his promise, let us look for new heavens and a new earth, in which righteousness resides.

So, dear friends, in this expectation, strive to be found spotless and blameless in his peace, and believe that your salvation is the patience of our Lord; as our beloved brother Paul has also written to you in the wisdom that has been granted to him, even as he speaks of these matters in all his letters; but places in them are hard to understand, and these the ignorant and unstable distort, as they do the other scriptures; but to their own destruction. But for your part, dear friends, being forewarned, keep yourselves from being carried along in the deviation of the iniquitous, and from falling away from your own firm position; but grow in grace and the knowledge of our Lord Jesus Christ. To him be the glory now and to the day of eternity.

The First General Letter

of John

¶WHAT WAS FROM THE BEGINNING, what we have heard, what we have seen with our eyes, what we have watched and our hands have felt, concerning the word of life; and the life was revealed, and we have seen and attest and announce to you the life everlasting which was with the Father and was revealed to us; what we have seen and heard we announce to you also, so that you also may share it with us; and our sharing is with the Father and with his son Jesus Christ. And we write you this so that your joy may be complete.

And this is the message which we heard from him and announce to you, that God is light and there is not any darkness in him. If we say that we have a share in him, and yet walk in darkness, we are lying and not enacting the truth; but if we walk in the light, as he is in the light, we share with each other, and the blood of Jesus his son washes us clean of all sin. If we say that we have no sin, we are deceiving ourselves and the truth is not in us. If we confess our sins, he is righteous and to be trusted to forgive us our sins and wash us clean of all guilt. If we say that we have not sinned, we are making him a liar and his word is not in us.

¶ My little children, I write you this so that you will not sin. And even if one does sin, we have a just advocate before the Father, Jesus Christ; and he himself is an expiation for our sins, and not for ours alone but for those of all the world. And by this we know that we have come to know him, if we keep his commandments. The man who says: I know him, and does not keep his commandments, is a liar, and the truth is not in him. But if a man obeys his word, truly in that man the love of God is fulfilled. By this we know that we are with him; the man who says that he abides with him must walk in the ways in which he walks.

Dear friends, I am not writing you any new commandment, but the old one which you have had from the beginning. The old commandment is the word to which you listened. Yet, again, I am writing you a new commandment, which is the truth in him and in you, that the darkness is passing away and the true light is now shining. The man who says he is in the light and hates his brother is in the dark even now. The man who loves his brother remains in the light, and there is no offense in him; but the man who hates his brother is in the dark and walks in the darkness, and does not know where he is going, because the darkness has blinded his eyes.

I am writing to you, little children, because your sins are forgiven through his name. I am writing to you, fathers, because you know him who was from the beginning. I am writing to you, young men, because you have overcome the evil one. I wrote to you, children, because you know the Father. I wrote to you, fathers, because you know him who was from the beginning. I wrote to you, young men, because you are strong and the word abides in you and you have overcome the evil one.

Do not love the world, nor the things in the world. If one loves the world, love of the Father is not in him; because all that is in the world, the lust of the flesh and the lust of the eyes and the vainglory of life, is not from the Father but from the world. And the world and its lust are passing away, but he who does the will of God endures forever.

Children, this is the final hour; and as you have heard that antichrist is coming, even so there are now many antichrists. From this we know that it is the final hour. They went forth from us, but they were not of our number (for if they had been of our number they would have remained with us); they went forth from us so that it might be made clear that they are not of our number. And you have been anointed by the holy one; and all of you have knowledge. I do not write to you because you do not know the truth, but because you do know it, and because no lie comes from the truth.

Who is the liar, if not the man who denies that Jesus is the Christ? This is the antichrist, the one who denies the Father and the Son. Anyone who denies the Son also fails to have the Father. He who acknowledges the Son has the Father also. Let that which you have heard from the beginning abide in you; and if that which you have heard from the beginning abides in you, you also will abide in the Son and the Father. And this is the promise which he promised us, the life that is everlasting.

I write you this concerning those who are trying to lead you astray. As for you, the anointing which you received from him abides in you, and you have no need for anyone to teach you; but as his anointing teaches you concerning all things, and is the truth and no lie, and as he himself taught you, abide in him. And now, little children, abide in him, so that if he is revealed to us we may feel confident and not be shamed by him at his coming. If you know that he is righteous, realize that every one who acts righteously is sprung from him.

¶ See what love the Father has bestowed on us, that we should be called God's children; and we are. This is why the world does not know us; because it did not know him. Dear friends, we are God's children now; what we shall be has not yet been revealed. We know that when he is revealed we shall be like him, because we shall see him as he is. And everyone who has this hope in him makes himself pure, as God is pure.

Everyone who commits sin commits lawlessness, and sin is lawlessness. And you know that he was revealed to take sins away, and there is no sin in him. Anyone who abides in him does not sin; anyone who sins has not seen him and does not know him. My little children, let no one deceive you. Everyone who acts righteously is righteous, as the Lord is righteous. Everyone who acts sinfully is from the devil, because the devil is a sinner from the beginning. This is why the Son of God was revealed, to undo the work of the devil.

Anyone sprung from God does not sin, because God's seed endures in him, and he is unable to sin, because he is sprung from God. By this it is clear which are the children of God and which the children of the devil; anyone who does not act righteously is not from God, nor is the one who does not love his brother. Since this is the message we have heard from the beginning, that we should love each other. We should not be like Cain, who came from the evil one and murdered his brother. And why did he murder him? Because his own actions had been evil, and his brother's had been righteous.

Brothers, do not be surprised if the world hates you. We know that we have crossed over from death to life, because we love our brothers. He who does not love remains in death. Anyone who hates his brother is a manslayer, and you know that no manslayer has life everlasting lodged within him.

We know of the Lord's love by this, that he laid down his life for us; and we have a duty to lay down our lives for our brothers. But when a man has worldly means and sees his brother in need and closes his heart against him, how can the love of God be in that man? Little children, let us love, not with talk and the tongue, but in action and truth.

By this we shall know that we are on the side of the truth, and in his presence persuade our hearts that, if our heart condemns us, God is greater than our heart, and knows all. Dear friends, if our heart does not condemn us, we have confidence before God, and what we ask for we receive from him, because we keep his commandments and do what is pleasing in his sight. And this is his commandment, to believe in the name of his son Jesus Christ, and love each other, as he commanded us to do. And he who keeps his commandments abides in him and he abides in that man. And we know that he abides in us from the Spirit which he gave us.

¶ Dear friends, do not believe every spirit, but test the spirits to see if they are from God, because many false prophets have gone out into the world. The spirit of God is known by this: every spirit which acknowledges that

Jesus Christ has come in the flesh is from God, and every spirit which does not acknowledge Jesus is not from God. And this is the spirit of the antichrist. You have heard that he was coming, and now he is already in the world.

But you are of God, little children, and you have over-come these false prophets, because he who is in you is greater than he who is in the world. They are of the world; they speak, therefore, from the world and the world listens to them. But we are of God; the man who knows God listens to us, the one who is not of God does not listen to us. From this we know the spirit of truth and the spirit of error.

Dear friends, let us love each other, because love is from God, and everyone who loves is sprung from God and knows God. One who does not love does not know God, because God is love. The love of God was revealed among us by this, that God sent his only-begotten son into the world so that we might live through him. Love is in this, not in that we have loved God, but in that he loved us and sent his son as propitiation for our sins. Dear friends, if God so loved us we also have a duty to love each other. No one has ever seen God; if we love each other, God abides in us and his love is made perfect in us. We know that we abide in him, and he in us, by this fact, that he has given to us from his spirit. And we have seen and we testify that the Father sent his Son to be the savior of the world. If one acknowledges that Jesus is the Son of God, God abides in him and he in God. And we know and believe the love that God has for us.

God is love, and he who abides in love abides in God, and God in him. By this love is made perfect in us, so that we may have confidence on the Day of Judgment, because as he is in this world so also are we. There is no fear in love, but love that is perfect casts out fear; because fear involves punishment, but one who is afraid is not made perfect in love. We love, because he loved us first. If a man says: I love God, and hates his brother, he is a liar. For one who does not love his brother, whom he has seen, cannot love God, whom he has not seen. And we have this commandment from him, that he who loves God should also love his brother.

¶ Everyone who believes that Jesus is the Christ is begotten from God; and everyone who loves the begetter loves the one begotten from him. By this we know that we love the children of God, when we love God and carry out his commandments. For this is the love of God, to keep his commandments; and his commandments are not burdensome, because everything which is sprung from God overcomes the world. And this, our faith, is the victory that overcomes the world. Who is it who overcomes the world if not he who believes that Jesus is the Son of God? This is he who came through water and blood, Jesus Christ; not in water alone but in water and blood. And the Spirit is what testifies, because the Spirit is the truth. Since there are three who testify, the Spirit and the water and the blood, and the three are at one. If we accept the testimony of men, the testimony of God is stronger, because it is God's testimony where he testified concerning his son. He who believes in the Son of God has the testimony within him; one who does not believe God makes him a liar, because he has not believed in the testimony of God concerning his son. And this is the testimony, that God gave us life everlasting, and that life is in his son. He who has the son has the life; he who does not have the Son of God does not have the life.

I write you this so that you may know that you have life everlasting, you who believe in the name of the Son of God. And this is the confidence we have in his presence, that if we ask him for something that accords with his will he listens to us. And if we know that he listens to us, whatever we ask, we know that we are given what we ask him for. If one sees his brother committing a sin which is not a deadly sin, he shall ask, and God will grant him his life. This is for those whose sin is not deadly. There is a sin which is deadly. I am not saying that he should pray for that kind. Every wrong is a sin, but there is sin which is not deadly.

We know that anyone born of God does no sin, but one who is born of God obeys him, and the evil one does not touch him. We know that we are from God, and our whole world lies in the power of the evil one. We know that the Son of God has come, and he has given us the wit to know who is the true one. And we are under the true one, under his son Jesus Christ. He is the true God and life everlasting.

Little children, keep yourselves from idols.

The Second General Letter
of John

¶THE ELDER TO THE CHOSEN LADY and her children, whom I love in truth, and not I alone, but so also do all who know the truth, through the truth which abides in us and will be with us forever. Grace, mercy, and peace will be with us from God the Father, and from Jesus Christ the Son of the Father, in truth and love.

I was overjoyed to find that some of your children were going the way of truth as we have been commanded by the Father to do. And now I ask you, lady, as one who writes you no new commandment but the one we have had from the beginning, that we should love each other. And this is love, to go according to his commandments; this is the commandment, as you have heard from the beginning, to follow love. For many deceivers have come forth into the world, who do not acknowledge the coming of Jesus Christ in the flesh; such is the deceiver and the antichrist. Look to yourselves, so as not to lose what we have done but receive your full reward. Whoever breaks forward and does not abide by the teaching of the Christ does not have God; the one who abides by his teaching has the Father and the Son. If anyone comes to you and does not bring this doctrine, do not take him into your house and do not give him any greeting; for anyone who gives him a greeting shares in his evil deeds.

Though I have much to write you about, I would rather not do it with paper and ink, but hope to be with you and speak to you face to face, so that our joy may be complete. The children of your chosen sister send you greetings.

The Third General Letter

of John

¶THE ELDER TO HIS BELOVED GAIUS, whom I love in truth. I pray, dear friend, that you are in good health and that all your condition is as good as is the condition of your soul. For I was overjoyed when some brothers arrived and testified to your true life, as you do indeed follow the truth. I have no greater joy than this, to hear that my children are following the truth. Dear friend, you are acting faithfully in what you are doing for our brothers, even those who are foreigners. They have testified to your love before the congregation. You will do well to help them on their way as God would wish you to; since they set out for the sake of his name, without taking any funds from pagans. So we have a duty to support such people so that we can all work together for the truth.

I wrote something to the church; but Diotrephes, their would-be leader, does not accept us. For that reason, if I come, I shall speak of the things he has been doing, talking wicked nonsense about us; and not content with that, he refuses to welcome brothers himself, and prevents those who wish to do so and drives them out of the church.

Dear friend, do not imitate evil but good. He who does good is from God; he who does evil has not seen God. Demetrius has testimonials from all and from the truth itself; and we also testify to him, and you know that our testimony is true.

I had much to write you about, but I do not want to write it out for you with pen and ink. But I hope to see you soon, and we shall talk face to face. Peace be with you. Our friends send you greetings. Greet our friends each by name.

The General Letter
of Jude

¶JUDE, SLAVE OF JESUS CHRIST AND brother of James, to those who are loved by God the Father and kept safe for Jesus Christ, the chosen ones. May mercy, peace, and love be multiplied for you.

While making all haste to write to you, dear friends, concerning our common salvation, I found it necessary to write to you entreating you to fight for the faith which was, once for all, handed down to the saints. For some persons have slipped in among us who had been marked out long in advance for this judgment, impious men, who turn the grace of our God into licentiousness, and deny our sole master and Lord, Jesus Christ. And I wish to remind you, although you once knew it all, that the Lord, after rescuing his people out of Egypt, then later destroyed those who did not believe; and those angels who did not obey their government but forsook their proper dwelling place he stored away in everlasting chains deep in the darkness to await judgment on the great Day. Just so Sodom and Gomorrah and the cities around them, who like those angels debauched themselves and strayed after unnatural sex, lie before us as an example, submitting to the punishment of everlasting fire.

Like them, these people also in their dreaming defile the flesh, deny high authority, and insult glorious creatures. And yet the archangel Michael, when he was matched against the devil and disputing for the body of Moses, did not have the audacity to pronounce an insulting judgment, but said: May the Lord punish you. But these people insult what they do not understand; and what they do understand, in a physical way like dumb beasts, is what destroys them. Woe to them, because they have gone the way of Cain, and given in, for a price, to the error of Balaam, and perished in the rebellion of Corah. It is these who are blemishes on your love feasts when they join you in them, shamelessly looking after themselves: rainless clouds driven by on the gales, autumn trees without fruit uprooted and dying twice, wild sea waves foaming their own shame, wandering stars with the dark of hell in store for them.

Enoch, seventh from Adam, prophesied about these, saying: Behold, the Lord comes with his sainted tens of thousands, to pass judgment upon all, and to convict all the impious for all the acts of impiety they have committed, and for all the harsh things the impious sinners have said about him. These people are grumblers, complainers, going the way of their desires, and their mouths talk loud, flattering personages to do themselves good.

But as for you, dear friends, remember the words of prophecy spoken by the apostles of our Lord, Jesus Christ. Because they told you: In the final time there will be mockers, impious men going the way of their desires. These are the causers of divisions, sensual men without spirit. But as for you, dear friends, building yourselves up on your most holy faith and praying in the Holy Spirit, keep yourselves in the love of God, looking forward to the mercy of our Lord Jesus Christ for everlasting life. And pity some who are in doubt and save them by snatching them out of the fire; but pity others with fear, hating even the garment stained by their flesh.

To him who has the power to keep you from stumbling and set you blameless in exultation in the presence of his glory; to the only God our savior through Jesus Christ our Lord; glory, greatness, power, and authority before all time, and now, and through all the ages forever. Amen.

THE
REVELATION
OF JOHN

It is now widely believed that the *Revelation* was written not by the author of the gospel, but by another John, of whom tradition speaks as living in Ephesus toward the end of the first and the beginning of the second century.

¶ THE REVELATION OF JESUS CHRIST, which God gave him, to show to his slaves what must happen soon, and he indicated it by sending it through his angel to John, his slave, who bore witness to the word of God and the testimony of Jesus Christ, the things that he saw. Blessed is he who reads and blessed are they who listen to the words of the prophecy and who keep what is written in it. For the time is near.

John to the seven churches which are in Asia: grace be with you, and peace, from him who is, and who was, and who is to come, and from the seven spirits which are in the presence of his throne, and from Jesus Christ, the witness who is to be believed, the first-born among the dead and the leader of the Kings of the earth. To him who loves us and by his own blood set us free from our sins, who made us a Kingdom and made us priests to his God and father, to him the glory and the power forever and ever. Amen. Behold, he will come with the clouds, and every eye shall see him, even they who transfixed him, and all the tribes of the earth shall beat their breasts at the sight of him. Yes. Amen.

I am alpha and omega, says the Lord God, who is, who was, who is to come, the almighty.

I, John, your brother and companion in affliction and in the kingdom and in the endurance which is in Jesus, I was in the island which is called Patmos because of the word of God and the witnessing to Jesus. I was in the spirit on the Lord's day, and I heard behind me a great voice as of a trumpet, saying: Write down what you see into a book and send it to the seven churches, to Ephesus and to Smyrna and to Pergamum and to Thyatira and to Sardis and to Philadelphia and to Laodicea. And I turned to see what voice was speaking with me, and when I turned I saw seven lamps of gold, and in the midst of the lamps one who was like the son of man, wearing a robe that came to his feet and girt beneath the arms with a belt of gold. His head and his hair were white as white wool, as snow, and his eyes were like the flame of fire, and his feet were like fine bronze, as if fired in the furnace, and his voice was like the voice of many waters, and he held in his right hand seven stars, and from his mouth projected a sword, two-edged and sharp, and the sight of him was as the sun shines in its power. When I saw him I fell at his feet like a dead man; and he set his hand upon me and said:

Do not fear. I am the first and the last, I am he who lives, I have been dead, and see, I am alive forever and ever, and I hold the keys of death and Hades. Write, then, what you have seen, and what is and what is to be after this. The mystery of the seven stars which you saw in my right hand, and the seven lamps of gold: the seven stars are the angels of the seven churches, and the seven lamps are the seven churches.

¶ To the angel of the church in Ephesus, write: Thus speaks he who holds the seven stars in his right hand, who walks in the midst of the lamps of gold: I know your works, and your toil and your endurance, and that you are not able to endure evil men, and that you have tried those who call themselves apostles and are not, and found them false; you have endurance, and have borne a burden for the sake of my name, and have not grown weary. But I hold it against you that you have lost the love you had at first. Remember whence you have fallen, and repent, and do the works which you did at first; if not, I shall come to you and remove your lamp from its place; unless you repent. But this you have in your favor, that you hate the works of the followers of Nicolaus, which I also hate. He who has ears, let him listen to what the Spirit says to the churches. To the victor, I shall give to eat of the tree of life, which is in the garden of God.

And to the angel of the church in Smyrna, write:

Thus speaks he who is the first and the last, who was dead and came to life: I know your affliction and your poverty, yet you are rich, and I know the blasphemy of those who call themselves Jews and are not, but a congregation of Satan. Do not fear what you are to suffer. See, the devil will throw some of you into prison so that you may be tested, and you will be afflicted for ten days. Be faithful even to the point of death, and I will give you the crown of life. He who has ears, let him listen to what the Spirit says to the churches. The victor shall not be hurt by the second death.

And to the angel of the church in Pergamum, write:

Thus speaks he who holds the sharp two-edged sword: I know where you live. It is where the throne of Satan is. And you keep my name and did not deny your faith in me even in the days of Antipas, who testified to me and was faithful and was put to death in the place where you are and where Satan dwells. But I hold against you a few things; that you have there some who hold with the teaching of Balaam, who taught Balak to set a trap in the way of the sons of Israel so they should eat what was sacrificed to idols, and commit fornication. So too you have those who hold with the teaching of the followers of Nicolaus. Repent then, or else I shall come to you speedily and fight with them with the sword of my mouth. He who has ears, let him listen to what the Spirit says to the churches. To the victor I will give of the manna that is hidden, and I will give him a white stone, and upon the stone will be written his new name, which no one knows, only he who receives it.

And to the angel of the church in Thyatira, write:

Thus speaks he who is the son of God, who has eyes like the flame of fire and his feet are like bronze: I know your works, your love and faith and service and endurance, and that your last works are more than your first. But I hold it against you that you have forgiven the woman Jezebel, who calls herself a prophetess, and teaches my slaves and leads them astray into fornication and the eating of what was sacrificed to idols. And I have given her time in which to repent, and she will not repent of her fornication. Behold, I will cast her upon a bed, and will cast her adulterers into great affliction, if they do not repent of their acts, and I will strike down her children in death; and all the churches shall learn that I am he who examines the vitals and the hearts, and I will give to each of you according to his acts. I say to the rest of you in Thyatira, who do not hold this teaching, who have not known the depths of Satan, as they say: I shall not put another burden upon you, but that which you have, keep it until I come. And the victor and he who keeps my works to the end, I shall give him power over the nations, and he shall shepherd them with a staff of iron, breaking them as pottery is broken, as I too have been given by my father; and I will give him the morning star. He who has ears, let him listen to what the Spirit says to the churches.

¶ And to the angel of the church in Sardis, write:

Thus speaks he who holds the seven Spirits of God and the seven stars: I know your works, that you have the name of being alive, and are dead. Be wakeful, and strengthen what is left, which was on the point of death; for I have not found that your tasks were carried out in the sight of my God. Remember then what you have been given to do, and have been told, and observe this, and repent. If you are not wakeful, I shall come to you like a thief, and you cannot tell at what hour I shall come to you. But you have the names of a few in Sardis who have not soiled their clothes, and they shall walk with me in white, because they are worthy. And he who is thus victorious shall be clothed in robes of white, and I shall not obliterate his name from the book of life, and I shall acknowledge his name in the presence of my father and in the presence of the angels. He who has ears, let him listen to what the Spirit says to the churches.

And to the angel of the church in Philadelphia, write:

Thus speaks he who is holy, who is true, who holds the key to David, who opens and none shall close, who closes and none shall open: I know your works. See, I have given you an open door which is before you, and none shall be able to close it; because you have little power, and you have kept my word and have not denied my name. Behold, I deliver to you those of the congregation of Satan, those who call themselves Jews, and they are not, but are lying; behold, I shall make them come and worship before your feet, and know that I have given you my love. Because you have kept the word, which was that you should wait for me, I too shall keep you from the time of trial which will come upon the whole inhabited world, to try those who live on earth. I shall come soon. Keep what you have, so that none may take away your crown. The victor, I shall make him a pillar in the temple of my God, and he shall never go forth from it again, and I shall write upon him the name of my God and the name of the city of my God, the new Jerusalem which will come down from heaven from my God; and also my new name. He who has ears, let him listen to what the Spirit says to the churches.

And to the angel of the church in Laodicea, write:

Thus speaks he who is Amen, the faithful and true witness, the beginning of the creation of God: I know your works, that you are neither cold nor hot. You should be cold or hot. Thus because you are lukewarm and neither cold nor hot, I will spew you out of my mouth. Because you say, I am rich, and have grown rich, and have no need; and you do not know that you are the wretched one, the pitiful, the poor, the blind, the naked; I advise you to buy of me gold that has been refined in the fire, so that you may be rich; and white clothes to put upon you so that the shame of your nakedness may not be seen; and collyrium to salve your eyes with so that you may see. And those I love, I reprove and admonish. Be eager, then, and repent. See, I stand at the door and knock. If one hears my voice and opens the door, I shall come in to him, and dine with him, and he with me. The victor, I will grant him to sit with me on my throne, as I too have been victorious and sat with my father on his throne. He who has ears, let him listen to what the Spirit says to the churches.

¶ After that, I looked, and behold, a door opened in the sky, and the first voice I heard as the voice of a trumpet talking to me, saying: Come up here, and I will show you what must happen after this. And at once I was possessed by the Spirit; and behold, a throne was set in the sky, and there was one sitting upon the throne, and he who was sitting was like stone of jasper and cornelian to see, and a rainbow in a circle around the throne, like emerald to see. And in a circle about the throne were twenty-four thrones, and on the thrones were twenty-four elders seated, in white clothing, and crowns of gold upon their heads. And from the throne issue lightning flashes and voices and thunders; and seven lamps of fire burn before the throne, which are the seven spirits of God; and before the throne it is like a sea of glass, like crystal; and in the presence of the throne and in a circle about the throne are four animals, teeming with eyes, both before and behind. And the first animal is like a lion, and the second animal is like a calf, and the third animal has a face like a man's, and the fourth animal is like an eagle flying. And the four animals, each by each of them, have six wings, and round about and within they are full of eyes; and they take no rest, day and night, from saying: Holy holy holy, the Lord God, the almighty, who was and is and is to come. And when the animals give glory and honor and thanks to him who sits upon the throne, who lives forever and ever, the twenty-four elders shall fall down before him who sits upon the throne, and shall worship him who lives forever and ever, and they shall cast down their crowns before the throne, saying: You are worthy, our lord and our God, to receive the glory and the honor and the power, because you created all things, and through your will they were, and were created.

¶ And I saw, in the right hand of him who was sitting on the throne, a book-roll written on the inside and on the back, sealed with seven seals. And I saw a strong angel who cried in a great voice: Who is worthy to open the book and break the seals on it? And no one in heaven or on the earth or below the earth was able to open the book, or to look at it. And I wept much, because no one was found worthy to open the book and look at it. And one of the elders said to me: Weep no more. See, the lion from the tribe of Judah, the scion of David, has prevailed to open the book and the seven seals upon it. And I saw, in the space between the throne and the four animals and the elders, in their midst, a Lamb standing, like one that has been slaughtered, with seven horns and seven eyes, which are the seven Spirits of God sent about to all the earth. And he came and took it from the right hand of him who sat upon the throne. And when he had taken the book, the four animals and the twenty-four elders fell down before the Lamb, having each one a harp and golden bowls filled with incense, which are the prayers of the saints. And they sang a new song, saying: You are worthy to take the book and open the seals upon it, because you were sacrificed and you bought for God by your own blood people from every tribe and tongue and people and nation, and for our God you made them be a kingdom, and priests, and they shall be kings upon the earth.

And I looked, and I heard the voice of many angels in a circle about the throne and the animals and the elders, and the number of them was myriads of myriads and thousands of thousands, saying in a great voice: The Lamb who has been sacrificed is worthy to receive the power and the riches and the wisdom and the strength and the honor and the glory and the blessing.

And I heard all creation, whatever is in the sky and on the earth and beneath the earth and in the sea, and everything which is within these, I heard them saying: To him who sits upon the throne, and to the Lamb, blessing and honor and glory and power forever and ever.

And the four animals said: Amen; and the elders fell down and worshipped.

◀ And I saw when the Lamb opened one of the seven seals, and I heard one of the four animals saying in a voice as of thunder: Come. And I looked, and behold, a white horse, and the rider upon it holding a bow, and he was given a crown, and he came forth a conqueror and to conquer. And when he opened the second seal, I heard the second animal saying: Come. And there came forth another horse, red, and to the rider upon him it was granted to take peace out of the world, so that they shall kill each other, and he was given a great sword. And when he opened the third seal, I heard the third animal saying: Come. And I looked, and behold, a black horse, and the rider upon him holding a balance in his hand. And I heard as it were a voice in the midst of the four animals, saying:

A measure of grain for a denarius, and three measures of barley for a denarius, and do not damage the oil and the wine. And when he opened the fourth seal, I heard the voice of the fourth animal saying: Come. And I looked, and behold, a pale horse, and the rider upon it, his name is Death, and Hades came following him, and he was given power over one quarter of the earth to kill by the sword and hunger and death, and by the wild beasts of the earth.

And when he opened the fifth seal, I saw beneath the altar the souls of those who have been slaughtered because of the word of God and the testimony they maintained. And they cried out in a great voice, saying: How long, O Lord holy and true, will you wait to judge and to avenge our blood from those who live upon the earth? And each of them was given a white robe, and it was said to them that they must rest yet a little time until the number is filled of their fellow slaves and their brothers who are to be killed as they were. And I looked when he opened the sixth seal, and there came a great earthquake, and the sun turned black like cloth of hair, and all the moon became as blood, and the stars of the sky dropped upon the earth as the fig tree casts its unripe figs shaken by a great wind, and the sky shrank upon itself like a scroll curling, and every mountain and island was shaken from its place. And the kings of the earth and the great men and the commanders of thousands and the rich and the strong, all, slave and free, hid themselves in the caves and the rocks of the mountains, and said to the mountains and the rocks: Fall upon us and hide us from the face of him who sits upon the throne and the anger of the Lamb, because the great day of their anger has come, and who can stand?

❡ After that I saw four angels standing upon the four corners of the earth, holding the four winds of the world, so that no wind might blow upon the earth or upon the sea or upon any tree. And I saw another angel going up from the rising place of the sun, carrying the seal of the living God, and he cried in a great voice to the four angels, to whom it was granted that they should devastate the earth and the sea, saying: Do not devastate the earth, or the sea, or the trees, until we mark with the seal the slaves of our God, upon their foreheads. And I heard the number of those who were marked, a hundred and forty-four thousand were marked, from every tribe of the sons of Israel:

From the tribe of Judah twelve thousand marked with the seal;

from the tribe of Reuben, twelve thousand;

from the tribe of Gad, twelve thousand;

from the tribe of Asher, twelve thousand;

from the tribe of Naphthali, twelve thousand;

from the tribe of Manassah, twelve thousand;

from the tribe of Simeon, twelve thousand;

from the tribe of Levi, twelve thousand;

from the tribe of Issachar, twelve thousand;

from the tribe of Zebulon, twelve thousand;

from the tribe of Joseph, twelve thousand;

from the tribe of Benjamin, twelve thousand marked with the seal.

After that I looked, and behold, a great multitude whose number none could count, from every nation and tribe and people and language, standing before the throne and before the Lamb, wearing white clothing, and palms in their hands; and they cry out in a great voice, saying: Salvation to our God who sits upon the throne, and to the Lamb. And all the angels stood in a circle about the throne and the elders and the four animals, and threw themselves down on their faces before the throne and worshipped God, saying: Amen, blessing and glory and wisdom and thanksgiving and honor and power and strength to our God forever and ever. Amen.

Then one of the elders spoke to me and said: Who are these who have white robes put upon them, and where have they come from? And I said to him: My Lord, you know. And he said to me: These are they who have come out of the great persecution, and washed their robes and made them white in the blood of the Lamb. Therefore these are before the throne of God, and they serve him day and night in his temple, and he who sits upon the throne will spread his tabernacle over them. They will not be hungry or thirsty any more, nor shall the sun strike upon them, nor any burning heat, because the Lamb who is in the place before the throne will be their shepherd and guide them to the springs of the waters of life; and God shall wipe every tear from their eyes.

◖ And when he opened the seventh seal there was silence in heaven for about half an hour. And I saw the seven angels who stood before God, and there were given to them seven trumpets. And another angel came and stood at the altar holding a golden censer, and there was given to him much incense, for him to place it with the prayers of all the saints in the golden censer which is before the throne. And the smoke went up from the incense, by the prayers of the saints, from the hand of the angel before God. And the angel took the censer and filled it with fire from the altar and cast it upon the earth, and there came thunders and voices and lightnings and earthquake; and the seven angels who held the seven trumpets made themselves ready to blow.

The first angel blew his trumpet; and there came hail and fire mixed with blood and it was cast upon the earth, and a third of the earth burned up, and a third of the trees burned up, and all the green grass burned up. And the second angel blew his trumpet; and something like a great mountain burning with fire was cast into the sea, and a third of the sea was turned to blood, and there died a third of the creatures of the sea, those which were alive, and a third of the boats were destroyed. And the third angel blew his trumpet: and there fell from the sky a great star burning like a torch, and it dropped upon a third of the rivers and upon the springs of the waters. The name of this star is called Wormwood. And a third of the waters became wormwood, and many of the people died from the waters because they were made bitter. And the fourth angel blew his trumpet; and a third of the sun was struck, and a third of the moon, and a third of the stars, so that a third of them was darkened, and the day lost a third of its shining, and the night likewise.

And I looked, and I heard an eagle flying in the middle of the sky, saying in a great voice: Woe woe woe to those who live upon the earth from the voices of the trumpet still to come, from the three angels who will blow their trumpets.

◀ And the fifth angel blew his trumpet; and I saw a star fallen from the sky upon the earth, and there was given to him the key to the well of the bottomless pit. And he opened the well of the bottomless pit; and there came up smoke from the well like the smoke of a great furnace, and the sun was darkened and the air was darkened from the smoke of the well. And out of the smoke came locusts upon the earth, and power was given them, such power as the scorpions of the earth have. And it was said to them that they must not hurt the grass of the land, or any green thing, or any tree, but only those people who do not wear the mark of the seal of God upon their foreheads. And it was granted to them not that they should kill them but that they should torture them five months; and their torture is like the torture of the scorpion, when he strikes a man. And in those days men shall look for death but not find it, and they shall desire death but death shall escape them. And the appearance of the locusts was like that of horses armed for battle, and upon their heads crowns like gold, and their faces like the faces of men, and they had hair like the hair of women, and their teeth were like those of lions, and they had breastplates like breastplates of iron, and the noise of their wings was as the noise of the chariots of many horses galloping into battle. And they have tails like scorpions, and stings, and in their tails is the power to hurt men for five months. They have as king over them the angel of the bottomless pit, whose name in Hebrew is Abaddon, and in Greek he has the name Apollyon. One woe has come and gone; see, there are still two more woes to come after this.

The sixth angel blew his trumpet; and I heard a single voice from the horns of the altar of gold which is before God, saying to the sixth angel, who held the trumpet: Set free the four angels who are bound, by the great river Euphrates. And the four angels were set free, they who were made ready for the hour and the day and the month and the year, to kill a third part of mankind. And the number of the cavalry of their armies is twenty thousand ten thousands; I heard their number. And thus I saw the horses in my vision and the riders upon them, wearing breastplates colored as fire and hyacinth and sulphur, and the heads of the horses are like the heads of lions, and from their mouths issue fire and smoke and sulphur. From these three afflictions a third of the people were killed, from the fire and smoke and sulphur that came out of their mouths. For the power of the horses is in their mouths and in their tails; for their tails are like snakes with heads, and with these they do harm. And the rest of the people, who had not been killed in these afflictions, did not repent of the works of their hands, so as to stop their worshipping of demons and idols of gold and silver and bronze and stone and wood, which can neither see nor hear nor walk; nor did they repent of their murders or their magic-making or their fornication or their thieving.

◀ I saw another strong angel coming down from the sky, clothed in cloud, and the rainbow was on his head, and his face was like the sun, and his feet like pillars of fire, holding in his hand an opened book-roll. He planted his right foot upon the sea, and his left foot upon the land, and cried out in a great voice, as a lion roars. And when he cried, the seven thunders spoke in their own voices. And when the seven thunders spoke, I was about to write, and I heard a voice out of the sky, saying: Seal up what the seven thunders have spoken, and do not write it down. Then the angel whom I saw standing on the sea and the land lifted his right hand into the sky, and swore by him who lives forever and ever, who created the sky and what is in it, and the earth and what is in it, and the sea and what is in it, that there shall be no more time; but in the days of the voice of the seventh angel, when he shall blow his trumpet, the mystery of God shall be accomplished, as he announced to his slaves the prophets. The voice which I heard out of the sky, I heard it again speaking to me, saying: Go, take the open book-roll in the hand of the angel who stands upon the sea and the land. I went toward the angel, bidding him give me the book. And he said to me: Take it, and eat it, and it will make your stomach bitter, but in your mouth it will be sweet as honey. And I took the book from the hand of the angel, and ate it, and in my mouth it was like sweet honey; and when I had eaten it, my stomach was bitter. Then they said to me: You must prophesy again concerning the peoples and the nations and the languages, and many kings.

❡ He gave me a reed that was like a staff, saying: Rise up, and measure the temple of God and the altar and those who are worshipping there. But leave out the courtyard which is outside the temple and do not measure it, for it has been given to the Gentiles, and they shall walk the holy city forty-two months. I shall give power to my two witnesses, and they shall prophesy for a thousand two hundred and sixty days, wearing sackcloth.

These are the two olive trees and the two lamps that stand before the Lord of the world. And if anyone tries to injure them, fire comes out of their mouth and eats up their enemies; and if anyone tries to injure them, so must he be killed. These have the power to close the sky, so that no rain may drench the days of their prophesying, and they have power over the waters to turn them into blood, and to strike the earth with every plague, as many times as they wish.

And when they finish their testimony, the beast that comes up from the bottomless pit will do battle with them and defeat them and kill them. Their bodies will lie in the square of the great city, which is called in the way of the spirit Sodom and Egypt, where also their Lord was crucified. Those of the peoples and the tribes and the tongues and the nations shall look upon their bodies three days and a half, and they shall not give up their bodies to be laid away in the tomb. And those who dwell on the earth shall rejoice over them and be happy, and send each other gifts, because these two prophets tormented the dwellers upon the earth.

But after three days and a half the breath of life from God went into them, and they stood upon their feet, and great fear fell upon those who were watching them. And they heard a great voice out of heaven saying: Come up here. And they went up into heaven in the cloud, and their enemies beheld them. In that hour there was a great earthquake, and a tenth part of the city fell down, and in the earthquake seven thousand names of men were killed, and the rest were full of fear and gave glory to the God of heaven. The second woe has come and gone; behold, the third woe comes soon.

The seventh angel blew his trumpet, and there were great voices in the sky, saying: The kingdom of the world has become the kingdom of our Lord, and of his Christ, and he shall be king forever and ever. Then the twenty-four elders who were seated before God on their thrones fell down upon their faces and worshipped God, saying: We thank you, Lord God almighty, who are and who were, because you have taken your great power and become King. The nations were angry, and your anger came, and the time for the judging of the dead, and for the giving of their wages to your slaves, the prophets and the saints and those who fear your name, the small and the great; and the time to destroy the destroyers of the earth.

Then the temple of God in the sky was opened, and the ark of his covenant was seen in his temple, and there came lightning flashes and voices and thunders and earthquake and much hail.

❡ Then there was seen a great portent in the sky, a woman clothed in the sun, and the moon beneath her feet, and upon her head a crown of twelve stars, and she was great with child, and cried out in her travail and the pain of birth. And there was seen another portent in the sky, behold, a dragon ruddy and great, with seven heads and ten horns, and upon his heads seven diadems, and his tail swept a third of the stars from the sky and threw them upon the earth. The dragon stood before the woman who was about to give birth, so that when she bore her child he might devour it. And she bore a son, a male, who will shepherd all the nations with a staff of iron; and her child was snatched away to God and to his throne. Then the woman fled away into the desert, where she has her place made ready for her from God, to be nourished there for a thousand two hundred and sixty days. And there was a battle in the sky, Michael and his angels fighting with the dragon. The dragon and his angels fought, but they did not have the power, and there was no more place found for them in heaven, but he was thrown out, the great dragon, the ancient snake, who is called the Devil and Satan, who leads astray the whole inhabited earth, he was flung to the earth and his angels were flung with him. Then I heard a great voice in the sky, saying: Now is come the salvation and the power and the kingdom of our God and the authority of his Christ, because the prosecutor of our brothers has been cast down, who accused them before our God, day and night. And they defeated him through the blood of the Lamb and the word to which they testified, and they did not love their life; even to the point of death. Therefore, be glad, heavens and those who pitch their tents there. Woe to you, earth and the sea, because the devil has gone down to you, in great anger, knowing that he has little time.

After the dragon saw that he had been flung down upon the earth, he pursued the woman who had borne the male child. There were given to the woman the two wings of the great eagle, so that she might fly into the desert to her place, where she is kept time and times and half a time away from the face of the snake. But the snake cast from his mouth behind the woman water like a river, so that he might have her swept away on the river. But earth helped the woman, and earth opened her mouth and drank down the river which the dragon had cast out of his mouth. Then the dragon was angry because of the woman, and went away to do battle with the rest of her seed, those who keep the commands of God and hold the testimony of Jesus. And he stood on the sand of the sea.

❡ Then I saw a beast coming up from the sea, with ten horns and seven heads, and upon his horns ten diadems, and upon his heads the names of blasphemy. The beast I saw was like a leopard, and his feet as those of a bear, and his mouth as the mouth of a lion. And the dragon gave him his power and his throne and great authority. And one of his heads was as if stricken to death, and his death blow had been healed. Then the whole earth went in wonder after the beast, and they worshipped the dragon because he had given authority to the beast, and they worshipped the beast, saying: Who is like the beast, and who can fight with him? And there was given to him a mouth to speak great things and blasphemies, and he was given authority to act for forty-two months. Then he opened his mouth to blasphemies against God, blaspheming his name and his habitation, those who inhabit the sky. [And it was given to him to do battle against the saints, and defeat them,] and he was given authority over every tribe and people and language and nation.

And all who dwell upon the earth shall worship him, each one whose name is not written in the book of life of the slaughtered Lamb from the establishment of the world. He who has ears, let him listen. He who leads into captivity, into captivity he goes. He who kills with the sword must himself be killed by the sword. Such is the endurance and the faith of the saints.

Then I saw another beast coming up out of the ground, and he had two horns like a lamb, and spoke like a dragon. He exercises all the authority of the first beast in the sight of the first beast; and he causes the earth and all who dwell upon it to worship the first beast, whose death blow was healed. He makes great portents, so that he even makes fire come down from the sky to the earth in the sight of men. And he leads astray the inhabitants of the earth, because of the portents it has been given him to make before the beast, telling the inhabitants of the earth to make an image to the beast, who took the blow of the sword and lived. And it was granted to him to give life to the image of the beast, so that the image of the beast may even speak, and cause those who will not worship the image of the beast to be killed. And he causes all, the small and the great, the rich and the poor, the free and the slaves, he causes the giving of his mark to them upon their right hand or upon their forehead, so that none can buy or sell unless he has the mark, the name of the beast or the number of his name. The secret meaning is read thus. He who has a mind, let him compute the number of the beast; for it is the number of a man. And his number is six hundred and sixty-six.

❡ Then I looked, and behold, the Lamb standing on Mount Zion, and with him a hundred and forty-four thousand with his name and the name of his father written on their foreheads. And I heard a voice out of the sky like the voice of many waters and like the voice of great thunder, and the voice which I heard was like the voice of lyre players who play upon their lyres. They sing a new song before the throne and before the four animals and the elders; and none could understand the song except only the hundred and forty-four thousand who have been bought from the earth. These are they who have not been soiled with women; for they are virgin. These are they who follow the Lamb wherever he leads. These were bought from men as a first fruit for God and the Lamb, and in their mouth was found no lie. They are blameless.

Then I saw another angel flying in the middle of the sky, with an everlasting message of good news to announce to those who sit upon the earth and to every nation and tribe and language and people, saying in a great voice: Fear God, and give glory to him, because the hour of his judgment is come, and worship him who made the sky and the earth and the sea and the springs of waters.

And another second angel followed him saying: Babylon
the great is fallen, is fallen, she who from the wine of the
fury of her lust has drunk up all the nations. And another
third angel followed them saying in a great voice: If anyone worships the beast and his image, and takes the mark
upon his forehead or his hand, he himself also shall drink
of the wine of the fury of God, which has been poured of
unmixed wine in the cup of his anger, and he shall be
tortured with fire and sulphur before the holy angels and
before the Lamb. And the smoke of their torture shall go
up forever and ever, and they shall not rest, day and night,
they who worship the beast and his image, and any who
takes the mark of his name.

Such is the endurance of the saints, who keep the
commands of God and the faith of Jesus.

And I heard a voice out of the sky saying: Write. Blessed
are the dead who die in the Lord henceforth. Yes, says the
Spirit, so that they may rest from their labors; for what
they have done goes with them.

Then I looked, and behold, a white cloud, and sitting
upon the cloud one who was like the son of man, wearing
upon his head a crown of gold and in his hand a sharp
sickle. And another angel came out of the temple, crying
in a great voice to him who sat upon the cloud: Put forth
your sickle and reap, for the time to reap has come, because the harvest of the earth is ripe. And he who was
sitting upon the cloud put forth his sickle upon the earth,
and the earth was harvested. And another angel came out
of the temple in the sky, he also having a sharp sickle.
And another angel came from the altar, he who has charge
of the fire, and spoke in a great voice to the holder of the
sharp sickle, saying: Put forth your sharp sickle and cut

the clusters on the vine of the earth, because its grapes are ripe. And the angel put forth his sickle on the earth, and gathered from the vine of the earth and put the grapes in the great press of the anger of God. And the press was trampled outside the city, and the blood from the press came up to the bridles of the horses, for sixteen hundred furlongs.

❡ Then I saw another portent in the sky, great and wonderful, seven angels who have seven plagues which are the last, because the anger of God is fulfilled in them. And I saw what was like a sea of glass mixed with fire, and those who had come triumphant from the beast and his image and the number of his name standing by the sea of glass, with the lyres of God. They sang the song of Moses the slave of God and the song of the Lamb, saying: Great and wonderful are your works, Lord God almighty; just and true your ways, King of the nations; who shall not fear you, Lord, and glorify your name? Because you alone are holy, because all the nations will come and worship before you, because your judgments are made manifest.

After this I looked, and the temple of the pavilion of testimony was opened in heaven, and the seven angels with the seven plagues came out of the temple wearing clean bright linen and girt beneath the arms with belts of gold. And one of the four animals gave to the seven angels seven bowls full of the anger of the God who lives forever and ever. And the temple was full of the smoke of the glory of God, and of his power, and no one was able to go into the temple, until the seven plagues of the seven angels are done with.

❡ Then I heard a great voice from the temple saying to the seven angels: Go and pour out the seven bowls of the anger of God upon the earth. And the first went forth and poured out his bowl upon the earth, and there was a sad sore wound inflicted upon the men who have the mark of the beast and worship his image. Then the second poured out his bowl upon the sea; and there was blood as from a dead man, and every living thing died which was in the sea. And the third poured out his bowl into the rivers and the springs of the waters; and they turned to blood. I heard the angel of the waters saying: You are just, you who are and were, the holy one, because you made these judgments, because they poured out the blood of the saints and the prophets, and you have given them blood to drink. They are worthy of this. And I heard from the altar a voice saying: Yes, Lord God almighty, true and just are your judgments. Then the fourth poured out his bowl upon the sun; and it was granted to it to burn men in fire. And men were burned in a great blaze, and they blasphemed the name of God who holds authority over these plagues, and did not repent so as to give him glory. The fifth poured out his bowl upon the throne of the beast; and his kingdom turned dark, and they chewed their tongues from pain, and blasphemed the God of heaven because of their pain and their wounds, and did not repent of their works. And the sixth poured out his bowl upon the great river Euphrates; and its water was dried, so as to make ready the way of the kings from the rising of the sun. And I saw from the mouth of the dragon and from the mouth of the beast and from the mouth of the false prophet three unclean breaths, like frogs; for these are breaths of spirits, making portents, which go out to the kings of all the world, to gather them for the battle of the great day of almighty God.

Behold, I come like a thief; blessed is he who is watchful and keeps care of his clothes, so that he does not walk about naked and people see his disorderliness.

And he brought them together in the place which is called in Hebrew Armageddon.

Then the seventh poured out his bowl upon the air; and a great voice came out of the temple from the throne, saying: It is done. And there were lightning flashes and voices and thunders, and there was a great earthquake, such as there has not been since man has been upon the earth, so great was this earthquake. And the great city was made into three parts, and the cities of the nations fell down. Then Babylon the great was remembered before God, to give her the cup of the wine of the fury of his anger. And every island fled, and the mountains were not found. And hail heavy as talents' weight came down from the sky upon men; and the men blasphemed God from the affliction of the hail, for its affliction is very great.

❡ Then there came one of the seven angels who held the bowls and talked with me, saying: Come here, I will show you the judgment upon the great harlot who sits upon many waters, with whom the kings of the earth have made free, and the inhabitants of the earth have been made drunk on the wine of her lechery. He took me away in the spirit to a deserted place. And I saw a woman sitting on a scarlet beast, full of the names of blasphemy, with seven heads and ten horns. The woman was wearing purple and scarlet, and gilded with gold and precious stone and pearls, with a golden cup in her hand, full of the abomination and filthiness of her harlotry, and on her forehead a name written, a mystery, Babylon the Great, the Mother of Harlots and of the Abominations of the Earth. And I saw the woman drunk from the blood of the saints and the blood of the martyrs of Jesus. And I wondered, seeing her, with a great wonder. Then the angel said to me: Why did you wonder? I will tell you the mystery of the woman and of the beast who carries her, who has the seven heads and the ten horns. The beast you saw was and is not, and will come up out of the bottomless pit and go to destruction; and the inhabitants of the earth will admire him, they whose names have not been written in the book of life from the establishment of the world, when they see the beast and that he was and is not and is to be. Thus interprets the mind which has wisdom. The seven heads are seven hills, where the woman sits, upon them. And there are seven kings. Five have fallen, one is, the other has not come yet, and when he comes, short is the time he is to stay. And the beast who was and is not, he too is the eighth and comes from the seven, and he goes to destruction. And the ten horns you saw are ten kings, who have not yet taken their kingdom, but take their authority as kings for one season together with the beast. These have a single will, and they give their power and authority to the beast. These shall fight with the Lamb and the Lamb shall defeat them, because he is the Lord of Lords and the King of Kings, and those on his side are called and chosen and faithful. Then he said to me: The waters you saw, on whom the harlot is sitting, are peoples and multitudes and nations and tongues. And the ten horns you saw, and the beast, they shall hate the harlot and make her desolate and naked, and eat her flesh, and burn her with fire; for God has given it into their hearts to do his will, and make one purpose and give their kingship to the beast, until the words of God are fulfilled. And the woman you saw is the great city who holds kingship over the kings of the earth.

❡ After that I saw another angel coming down from the sky, having great authority, and the earth was lit with his glory. And he cried out in a strong voice, saying: Babylon the great is fallen, is fallen, and has become the habitation of demons and the prison of every unclean spirit and the prison of every bird that is unclean and detested, because all the nations have drunk of the wine of the fury of her lechery, and the kings of the earth have made free with her, and the merchants of the earth have become rich from the power of her luxury.

And I heard another voice out of the sky saying: Come out of her, my people, so that you may not have any part in her sins, and may not share any of her afflictions; because her sins are stuck fast, and reach the sky, and God has remembered her wrongdoings. Give to her duly as she has given, and double what is double according to her acts; in the cup where she has mixed mix double for her; as much as she has glorified herself and taken her delight, give her in like measure torment and sorrow; since in her heart she says: I sit as a queen, and I am not widowed, and I cannot look upon sorrow. Because of this in one day her afflictions will come, death and sorrow and hunger, and she shall be burned in the fire; because God who has judged her is a strong master. And the kings of the earth, who reveled with her and took their delight with her, shall weep and beat themselves over her when they see the smoke of her burning, standing far off for fear of her torment, saying: Woe woe for you, the great city, Babylon the city, the strong city, because in a single hour your judgment came. And the merchants of the earth shall weep and mourn over her, because no one buys their cargo any more, their cargo of gold and silver and precious stone and pearls and linen and purple and silk and scarlet, and every aromatic wood and every article of ivory and every article of most precious wood and bronze and iron and marble, and cinnamon and cardamon and incense and perfume and frankincense and wine and oil and fine flour and wheat and cattle and sheep, their cargo of horses and chariots and bodies, and the souls of men. And the harvest of the desire of your soul is gone from you, and all that was fat and bright is perished from you, and they shall never find it again. The dealers in these things, who grew rich from her, shall stand far off for fear of her torment weeping and mourning, saying: Woe woe for the great city, who was clothed in linen and purple and scarlet, and gilded in gold and precious stone and pearl, because in a single hour all these riches were made desolate.

And every shipmaster and every navigator of the coast and the sailors and they who work on the sea stood far off and cried out as they saw the smoke of her burning, saying: Who is like the great city? And they threw dust on their heads and cried out in tears and lamentations: Woe woe for the city, the great city, from whom all who have ships on the sea grew rich, from her prosperity; because in a single hour she is made desolate.

Rejoice over her, heaven and saints and apostles and prophets, because God has judged her with your judgment.

Then one strong angel lifted up a stone like a great

millstone and threw it into the sea, saying: With such a stroke Babylon the great city shall be stricken and shall not be found any more. And the voice of lyre players and singers and flute players and trumpeters shall not be heard in you any more, and every craftsman of every craft shall not be found in you any more, and the voice of the mill shall not be heard in you any more, and the light of the lamp shall not shine in you any more, and the voice of the groom and the bride shall not be heard in you any more; because your merchants were the great men of the earth, because in your witchery all the nations wandered astray. And in her was found the blood of the prophets and the saints and all who were slaughtered upon the earth.

¶ After this I heard a great voice as of a great multitude in heaven, saying: Alleluia: the salvation and the glory and the power of our God, because his judgments are true and just; because he judged the great harlot who spoiled the earth with her harlotry, and he avenged the blood of his slaves shed by her hand. And they said again: Alleluia. And the smoke of her goes up forever and ever. Then the twenty-four elders fell down, and the four animals, and worshipped the God who sits upon the throne, saying: Amen, alleluia. And a voice came from the throne, saying: Praise our God, all you his slaves, who fear him, the small and the great. And I heard a voice as of a great multitude and as the voice of many waters and as the voice of strong thunders, saying: Alleluia: because the Lord our God the almighty is king. Let us rejoice and be glad, and we shall give glory to him, because the marriage of the Lamb has come, and his wife has made herself ready, and it has been given to her to clothe herself in bright clean linen; for the linen is the righteousness of the saints. And he said to me: Write: Blessed are they who have been called to the feast of the marriage of the Lamb. And he said to me: These are the true words of God. And I fell down before his feet to worship him. But he said to me: See that you do not. I am your fellow slave and the fellow slave of your brothers who keep the testimony of Jesus. Give your worship to God. For the testimony of Jesus is the spirit of prophecy.

Then I saw the sky open, and behold, a white horse, and the rider upon him called faithful and true, and in righteousness he judges and does battle. His eyes are flame of fire, and on his head are many diadems, inscribed with the name which no one knows except himself, and he wears a mantle dyed in blood, and his name is called the Word of God. And the armies which are in heaven followed him on white horses, wearing linen white and clean. And from his mouth projects a sharp sword, so that he may strike the nations; he will shepherd them with a staff of iron; and he will trample the press of the wine of the fury of the anger of God almighty. He wears upon his mantle and upon his thigh the name written: King of Kings and Lord of Lords.

Then I saw an angel standing in the sun, and he cried out in a great voice saying to all the birds that fly in the middle air: Come, gather here to the great feast of God, so that you may eat the flesh of kings and the flesh of captains of thousands and the flesh of the strong and the flesh of horses and of their riders, and the flesh of all the free and the slaves and the small and the great. And I saw the beast and the kings of the earth and their armies gathered to do battle with him who sits upon the horse and with his army. Then the beast was captured, and with him the false prophet, who made the portents in his presence, by which he led astray those who took the mark of the beast and worshipped his image. The two of them were cast alive into the lake of the fire that burns with sulphur. And the rest were killed by the sword of the rider on the horse, the sword which projects from his mouth, and all the birds fed upon their flesh.

◀ Then I saw an angel coming down from the sky, holding the key to the bottomless pit and a great chain in his hand. And he seized the dragon, the ancient snake, who is the Devil and the Satan, and bound him for a thousand years, and cast him into the bottomless pit, and locked it and sealed it over him, so that he may lead the nations astray no longer, not until the thousand years are ended. After that he must be set free for a little time.

And I saw thrones, and there were some seated upon them, and judgment was given by them; and I saw the souls of those killed with the ax for the testimony of Jesus and the word of God, and who did not worship the beast or his image or take his mark upon their forehead and their hand. And they came to life and were kings with Christ for a thousand years. The rest of the dead did not come to life until the thousand years were ended.

This is the first resurrection. Blessed and holy is any of those who have part in the first resurrection. Over them the second death has no power, but they shall be priests of God and Christ, and be kings with him for the thousand years.

And when the thousand years are ended, Satan shall be set free from his prison, and will go out to lead astray the nations also who are in the four corners of the earth, Gog and Magog, to lead them into battle, and their number is as the sand of the sea.

And they went up across the width of the earth, and encircled the encampment of the saints and the beloved city; and fire came down from heaven and ate them up; and the devil, who led them astray, was cast into the lake of fire and sulphur, where is also the beast, and the false prophet, and they shall be tortured day and night forever and ever.

And I saw a throne, great, white, and sitting upon it was he from whose face the earth and the sky fled, and no place was found for them. And I saw the dead, the great and the small, standing before the throne, and books were opened. And another book was opened, which is the book of life. And the dead were judged from what was written in the books, each according to his works. And the sea gave up the dead that were in her, and Death and Hades gave up the dead that were in them, and each was judged according to his works. And Death and Hades were cast into the lake of fire. This is the second death, the lake of fire. And if anyone was not found written in the book of life, he was cast into the lake of fire.

❡ I saw a new heaven and a new earth; for the first heaven and the first earth are gone, and the sea is no more. And I saw the holy city, the new Jerusalem, coming down out of heaven from God, and made ready as a bride is arrayed for her husband. And I heard a great voice from the throne saying: Behold, the tabernacle of God among men, and he shall dwell with them, and they shall be his people, and God himself shall be among them and shall wipe every tear from their eyes, and death shall not be any more, nor shall sorrow nor lamentation nor pain be any more, because the first things have gone. And he who sat upon the throne said: Behold, I make all new. And he said: Write, because these words are trustworthy and true. And he said to me: They have come to pass. I am alpha and omega, the beginning and the end. I shall give to him who is thirsty from the spring of the water of life, a free gift. The victor will inherit these things, and I shall be his God, and he will be my son. To the cowards and the unbelievers and the corrupt and the murderers and the fornicators and the wizards and the idolaters and all who are false, their portion shall be in the lake that burns with fire and sulphur, which is the second death.

Then there came one of the seven angels who held the seven bowls full of the seven last plagues, and he talked with me, saying: Come here, I will show you the bride, the wife of the Lamb. And he took me away, in the spirit, to a mountain great and high, and showed me the holy city Jerusalem coming down out of heaven from God, wearing the glory of God. Her radiance is like most precious stone, like stone of jasper that shines as crystal. She has a wall great and high, with twelve gates, and on the gates twelve angels, and names inscribed, which are of the twelve tribes of the sons of Israel. On the east three gates, and on the north three gates, and on the south three gates, and on the west three gates. And the wall of the city has twelve lower courses, and on them the twelve names of the twelve apostles of the Lamb.

And he who was talking with me had a measuring rod of gold, to measure the city and its gates and its wall. The city is set foursquare and its length is as much as its width. And he measured the city with his rod at twelve thousand furlongs; the length and the width and the height of it are equal. And he measured the wall at a hundred and forty-four cubits, according to the measurement of man, which is that of an angel. The material of the wall is jasper, and the city is gold clear like clear glass. The lower courses of the wall of the city are adorned with every precious stone. The first course is jasper; the second sapphire; the third chalcedony; the fourth emerald; the fifth sardonyx; the sixth cornelian; the seventh chrysolite; the eighth beryl; the ninth topaz; the tenth chrysoprase; the eleventh hyacinth; the twelfth amethyst. And the twelve gates were twelve pearls; gate by gate each was a single pearl. The great street of the city is gold clear as translucent glass. I saw no temple in it; for the Lord God almighty is its temple; and the Lamb. And the city has no need of the sun or the moon, to shine on it, for the glory of God illuminates it, and its lamp is the Lamb. And the nations shall walk about through its light, and the kings of the earth bring their glory into it; and its gates shall never be closed for the day, for there will be no night there; and they shall bring the glory and honor of the nations into it. Nor shall anything that is profane enter into it, nor anyone who practices foulness and lying, but only they who are written in the book of life of the Lamb.

◀ And he showed me the river of the water of life shining like crystal and issuing from the throne of God and the Lamb. Between the great street of the city and the river which were on one side and the other was the tree of life, bearing twelve fruits, yielding its fruit month by month, and the leaves of the tree for the healing of the nations. Everything accursed shall be gone henceforth. And the throne of God and the Lamb shall be in it, and his slaves shall serve him, and they shall see his face, and his name shall be upon their foreheads. And there will be no night any more, nor shall they have any need of the light of the lamp and the light of the sun, because the Lord God will illuminate them, and they shall be kings forever and ever.

Then he said to me: These words are trustworthy and true, and the Lord God of the spirits of the prophets sent his angel to show his slaves what must happen soon. Behold, I shall come soon. Blessed is he who keeps the words of the prophecy of this book.

And I, John, am he who heard and saw these things. And when I heard and saw, I fell down to worship before the feet of the angel who showed me these things. But he said to me: See that you do not. I am your fellow slave and the fellow slave of your brothers the prophets and those who keep the words of this book. Give your worship to God.

And he said to me: Do not seal up the words of the prophecy of this book, for the time is near. Let the wrongdoer do wrong still, let the foul man be foul still, let the righteous man do right still, let the saint be saintly still. Behold, I shall come soon, and my repayment comes with me, to give to each according to his work. I am alpha and omega, the first and the last, the beginning and the end. Blessed are they who wash their robes, so that they shall have access to the tree of life and may enter by the gates into the city. Outside shall be the dogs and the wizards and the fornicators and the idolaters and all who love and do falsehood.

I Jesus sent my angel to bear witness to these things for you to the churches. I am the scion and generation of David, the shining star, the morning star.

And the Spirit and the bride say: Come. Let him who hears say: Come. Let him who is thirsty come, let him who wishes take the water of life, a free gift.

For all who hear, I bear witness to the words of the prophecy of this book. If anyone adds to them, God will inflict upon him the punishments that have been written in this book; and if anyone takes away from the words of the book of this prophecy, God will take away his share of the tree of life and the holy city, which have been written in this book.

And he who bears witness to these things says: Yes, I come soon. Amen, come, Lord Jesus.

May the grace of the Lord Jesus be with all.

Notes

Notes

1.14   "After John was betrayed." John was turned in or handed over (*paradidōmi*) to the authorities, but the word frequently implies treachery, as in Judas's betrayal, 3.19, 14.18, etc.

3.12   "not to divulge what he was doing." Literally, "not to make him known."

3.18   "Cananaean." Or "the zealot," see Matthew 10.4 and Luke 6.15. Cananaean does not refer to a place.

6.3   "made it difficult for him." *Eskandalizonto*. See the note on Matthew 5.29. Here we are to understand that the disbelief of his own people actually impeded Jesus in the exercise of his powers. In Matthew 13.58 it merely made him unwilling.

6.22   "the daughter of Herodias." Some manuscripts would make this girl "his daughter Herodias."

6.52   "their hearts had become impenetrable." More literally, "their hearts were hardened" (perfect passive participle of *pōreō*); but the sense is not that that they were hardhearted or pitiless, but that meaning and message did not get through to them. Compare Matthew 13.15.

7.3   "elders"; or "ancestors."

8.24   Here, as in 16.4, the word is *anablepō*. In neither place does the usual sense, "look up," seem to have any point. Here, possibly, the meaning is that the man recovered some sight.

The prefix *ana* frequently indicates that something is done again.

9.43   "Gehenna." Here I cannot do better than quote Nineham's note in full: "*hell*: A word with so many irrelevant associations that it is probably better to keep to the original word, *Gehenna*. This was a valley west of Jerusalem where at one time children were sacrificed to the god Moloch (2 Kings 23.10, Jer. 7.31, 19.5f., 32.35); after being desecrated by Josiah it came to be used as a refuse dump for Jerusalem, a fact which explains the imagery of worm and fire borrowed from Isaiah 66.24 in v. 48. The suggestion is of maggots preying on offal and fires perpetually smoldering for the destruction of refuse. Because of all its bad associations, the Jewish imagination had come to picture *Gehenna* as the place of future torment for the wicked cf. e.g. 2 Esdras 7.36."

10.30   "now in this time . . . persecutions." I follow Nineham in thinking these words are probably spurious.

14.3   "Simon the leper." In Matthew 26.6, this scene of anointing also takes place in the house of Simon the leper. But it remains inconceivable that in this time and place any leper could have had his own house and entertained guests at dinner. This Simon remains a mystery. Note, however, that in John 12.1–3, the anointing takes place in the house of Lazarus; and though this Lazarus was surely no leper, his name has in later times been constantly associated with leprosy in such terms as "lazaretto" and "lazar-house." This may be through confusion with Lazarus the beggar of Luke 16.20–21, who, though not described as a leper, was covered with sores. But there is no explanation of how the confusion could have existed *before* Mark's composition.

14.34   "keep watch." Or "stay awake." So too in 14.37.

14.46   "bound him." A little free, perhaps, but the normal sense of the word *krateō*, "seized him," as in 49 below, would be tautologous here. "Overpowered" would imply a struggle. What the verb really means is that they prevailed over him, got him into their power or under their control.

14.72 "threw himself down." Meaning uncertain, variously translated.

16.4 "looking again." See 8.24 and note.

16.8 In many manuscripts the Gospel of Mark ends here.

16.20 The following two sentences constitute an alternative ending to follow on 16.8.

MATTHEW

1.1 "origin" is *genesis*, that is, "birth," but also "genealogy." "son," that is, "descendant."

1.2 "was the father of." Literally (throughout 2–16) "begot."

1.16 "the Christ." Greek *christos*, "the anointed," "the Messiah."

1.18 "engaged." The engagement is regarded as a marriage except that it has not been consummated. So Joseph is called her husband, Mary is called his wife, and the word translated "put away" is the same as that used elsewhere for "divorce."

2.1 "Magians." *Magoi*. In Classical Greek, *Magos* denotes: 1. a member of one of the tribes of the Medes; 2. a priest or seer, within the Medo-Persian empire, who must belong to this tribe. This may be the sense here, but it is not certain, and I have thought it best to leave the term as a proper name. Though *Magos* gives us "magic," these Magi were not necessarily magicians, and though they may well have been astrologers, to translate "astrologers" is to say more (despite the star) than the Greek does.

2.13 "Awake." Or, "when you awake." So also in verse 20.

3.1 "preaching." Here and elsewhere the word *kēryssō* has been translated, according to convention, "preach." Literally, it denotes the activity of a herald (*kēryx*), the announcing or proclamation of a message; in this case, the gospel or the good news. It is thus to be distinguished from "teaching" (*didaskō*), for which see 4.23 and note.

4.1 "tested." The word *peirazō* may be translated "test" or "make trial of" (the basic meaning) or "tempt." In this case the testing is done by means of temptation.

4.12 "betrayed." See the note on Mark 1.14.

4.15 "Gentiles." The plural of *ethnos*, which means a nation or tribe. In the Gospels, this plural usually, but not always, signifies all who are not Jews.

4.23 "teaching." The word is *didaskō*, to be clearly distinguished from *kēryssō*, "preach," see note on 3.1. "Teaching" covers not only such extended discourses as the "Sermon on the Mount" but also the expounding of the scriptures, the parables, and other sayings of Jesus, and answers to questions and challenges.

5.22 "fool." Greek *raka*; but the exact meaning is not known.

"sinner." Greek *mōros*, regularly "fool." But this second insult is obviously worse than the other, and I think it may not here mean "fool" but denote immorality or lewdness, a sense found several times in Euripides.

"Gehenna." See Mark 9.43 and note.

5.29 "makes you go amiss." The Greek verb is *skandalizō*. The basic concept is that of a physical block (*skandalon*) which impedes right progress or understanding and causes diversion into wrong courses, sin, or error, or at least causes difficulty. There is no one English word which will translate *skandalon* or *skandalizō*. For other notes on the term, see on Matthew 13.21, 15.12, 16.23, 17.27, 26.31; Mark 6.3.

5.47 "pagans." *Ethnikoi*, found here and at 6.7 and 18.17, is perhaps to be distinguished from *ethnē* (see note on 4.15) as being more a term of reproach.

6.2   "hypocrites." *Hypokritēs* means "actor." The people in question are here not so much dissemblers as those who put on an act, or make a big production of their good works.

6.11   "sufficient." A guess. *Epiousios* is rare and of uncertain meaning. Enough for the day, day by day? See below, 34.

6.13   "temptation." Or "do not bring us to the time of trial." *Peirasmos*, from *peirazō*; see on 4.1, and see Luke 22.40.
       "from evil." Or "from the evil one."

6.24   "mammōn." That is, money.

8.6   "son." Greek *pais*. This means "child" but, like Latin *puer*, can also mean "servant," here and elsewhere. Luke (7.2), telling the same story, definitely calls the sufferer a slave (*doulos*), whereas John (4.46) calls him the man's son.

9.18   "official." *Archōn*. This may mean no more here than "leading citizen" or "important man." Mark (5.22) calls him Jairus, one of the leaders of the synagogue.

10.2   "apostles." The noun *apostolos* is formed from the verb *apostellō*, "send forth," which appears below (5).

11.5   "are told good news." Or "have the gospel preached to them." These phrases, in fact, mean the same thing. See above, 3.1, and note.

13.15 "stiffened." Matthew uses the word *pachynō* in much the same sense as Mark's *pōreō*, see Mark 6.52 and note.

13.21 "does not stand fast." Or "is driven from his course"; *skandalizetai*, see on 5.29.

14.1   "children." Or "servants." Plural of *pais*. See 8.6 and note.

15.2   "elders." Or "ancestors," see note on Mark 7.3.

15.12 "objected." The Greek is *skandalizō*, on which see 5.29 and note. The sense here is unusual. One is tempted to translate "were scandalized," which would fit the sense, and "scandal," like "slander," does derive from *skandalon*. But in view of the basic sense, it is more likely that the Pharisees were "put off."

16.19   "close . . . open." Perhaps, more literally, "bind . . . loose."

16.23   "you would put me off." Literally, "you are my *skandalon*," that is, my misleader, thus like the arch-misleader, Satan.

17.27   "cause . . . trouble." *Skandalizō* again. The use of the term here introduces a commentary on it in chapter 18, where it appears as "leads astray" (6), "troubles which shall be caused" (7), "makes you go amiss" (8, 9).

           "stater." This coin was worth four drachmas, that is, twice two.

18.24   "ten thousand talents." A fantastic sum, amounting to millions. The denarius, mentioned below (28), is a day's wage for a laborer, 20.2.

19.12   "sexless men." The Greek word used here is *eunouchos*, but I have refrained from "eunuch" because only those "made sexless by other men" are commonly so called in English (I do not believe that "have made themselves sexless" denotes self-castration). *Eunouchos* means "bed-keeper." It first appears in Herodotus and applies particularly to the King of Persia's castrated harem guards, who also, as the only males admitted to the bedchamber, were his trusted confidential agents.

21.3   "their master." Or "the Lord."

21.35   "one they stoned." I think the sense intended may well be: "One they beat to death, and one they killed with weapons, and one they stoned to death."

23.12   "He who is greater than you." So I read it. But the meaning may be "he who is greatest (the greater) among you."

25.21   "come in and share your master's festivities." Literally, "enter into the joy [*chara*] of your master." But as the word *euphrosynē* can mean either a state of happiness or a joyous occasion, a banquet, so I think *chara* is here similarly extended. Here and in other passages, the chosen come inside (enter) to the feast, and those not chosen are shut out in the dark.

26.7   "reclined." The custom at dinner was to recline, not sit, at table. See note on Luke 7.38.

26.31   "made to fail me." From *skandalizō* again.

26.38   "keep watch." That is, or implies, "stay awake."

26.50   See note on Mark 14.46.

27.16   In a number of manuscripts of Matthew the man is called *Jesus* Barabbas. Bar-Abbas means simply the son of the father.

28.2   In view of the Greek preference for the simple past tense (aorist) where a pluperfect is really meant, I believe it is possible to translate the first part of this sentence: "And behold, there *had been* a great earthquake, for the angel of the Lord *had come* down."

LUKE

1.35   "man." Or "husband."

2.14   Or (variant reading) "good will to men."

2.26   "Anointed." That is, the Christ, or Messiah.

2.37   Or possibly "a widow eighty-four years old."

3.14   "no extortion." The word practically translates into "shakedown."

3.16   "spoke forth." The word *apokrinomai* is usually translated "answer," but in the Gospels is frequently used where no question is indicated; but in this particular case "answer" would be acceptable.

3.23–38 For this list, as for that in Matthew 1.2–16, I have done my best to be reasonably consistent. No two translations that I have consulted agree exactly on spellings. Also, some names appear in both Greek and Hebrew forms. For "Old Testament characters" I have generally preferred the Hebrew forms (written for our texts, of course, in Greek letters). But Judah of the

Old Testament really has the same name as Judas of the New, and Jacob is the same as James; and Jesus is the Greek form of Joshua.

4.43 "bring the good news." That is, preach the gospel.

7.38 "stood behind by his feet." Jesus, in accordance with the custom of the time and place, was not sitting at a table, but reclining on a couch with his head toward the table and his feet away from it.

11.3 "sufficient." See Matthew 6.11 and note.

11.51 "the temple." Strictly, "the house," but where the stoning of Zachariah is mentioned in 2 Chronicles 24 it is "the house of God."

12.20 "that soul." That is, "that life," since *psychē* means both "soul" and "life."

16.22 "to recline close by Abraham." Literally, "to Abraham's bosom," but what this seems to mean is reclining close by him at a feast. See also John 13.23, and for feasting with Abraham, Isaac and Jacob, Matthew 8.11.

21.19 "possess your own souls." Or "win your lives."

21.25 "nations." Or "Gentiles."

22.19–20 The words enclosed in square brackets are not found in all manuscripts, and are thought by many, if not most, scholars to be a later addition.

23.16 "teach him a lesson." The word *paideuō* properly means "educate," but in Biblical Greek it seems to have the special sense "chastise," that is, have someone whipped.

JOHN

1.1 "the word was God." Or, more literally, "God was the word."

1.15 "he cried out, saying." Or "saying: This is he of whom I said."

1.38 "master." That is, "teacher."

1.41   "Messiah." See Matthew 1.16 and note.

1.42   "Cephas" and "Peter" both mean "rock." See Matthew 16.18.

2.4   "madam." Greek *gynai*, that is, the form of direct address, or vocative, of *gyne*. *Gyne* translates into "woman," "lady," and "wife." Here "woman" in English is merely rude, and in tragedy *gynai* is, or may be, a term of respect, used by messengers and slaves in addressing queens and great ladies. For the vocative there is *no* good English equivalent, and in translating I have used various words. Here, perhaps, "mother"?

3.3   "from above." Or "again."

3.5   "spirit." The word *pneuma* means both "spirit" and "wind" as in verse 8 below.

4.9   "Jew." John uses the term Jew, usually in the plural, *Ioudaioi*, far more frequently than the other three evangelists put together. Here the use seems to be straightforward and clear. Elsewhere, as in 5.10, 16, 18, "Jews" means the religious authorities who appear in the other Gospels, and sometimes in John, as any or all of "high priests, scribes and Pharisees." Still another usage is exemplified in 11.19 where, from the sequence of thought, "Jews" plainly means "the people of Jerusalem."

        "have no dealings with." Greek *ou gar synchrōntai*, more literally, "do not share what they use," that is, do not eat and drink from the same vessels. See Marsh, p. 210.

5.2   For the Sheep Gate, see Nehemiah 3.1. The pool is evidently a swimming pool. The better-known form for the name Bethzatha is Bethesda.

5.3–4   The bracketed words are missing from many manuscripts and are deleted by many editors and translators; but without context the reply of the paralytic to Jesus is incomprehensible.

5.41   I have translated *doxa* as "glory" because that is its regular meaning in the New Testament. But in Classical Greek *doxa* also means "opinion," and it goes with the verb *dokeō*, "think," "suppose," which appears in this very passage: "because you *think* they have life everlasting" (verse 39 just above; so also verse 45 below). So verse 41 could also read either "I do not derive my opinion from men" or "I do not accept the opinion of men." Contrast verse 42, "I know" (*egnōka*). Then in verse 44 the opinion, not glory, which men take from each other is contrasted with the true thought which comes from God alone. See 12.43 and note.

6.26 "signs." The word is *sēmeia*, sometimes translated "miracles" or "portents."

6.66 "because of this." Or "from this time on," but then "thenceforth" would be repetitious.

6.70 "an enemy." The Greek is *diabolos*: "a devil"? I prefer "an enemy" or "my enemy."

7.53–8.11 The material here enclosed in square brackets is missing entirely from some manuscripts, and placed elsewhere in others. Most modern editors and commentators reject it as spurious.

8.28 "when you raise the son of man aloft." The allusion is probably to his crucifixion, but may also hint at his ultimate exaltation.

8.45 "and so is his father." Or "and the father of it (that is, the lie, or falsehood)."

10.24 "agitating our spirits." Or "keeping us in suspense."

11.19 "Jews." In the context, this plainly means "the people of Jerusalem." See the note on 4.9.

11.33 "raged at his own spirit." Very difficult. The word *embrimaomai* seems to mean, originally, "be angry with" (Mark 14.5) or "enjoin sternly" (Matthew 9.30; Mark 1.43). Here the object of the verb is plainly his own spirit; the idiom in verse 38 below shows inward disturbance. I had thought at first that the meaning would be that Jesus was angry with himself, and the words could easily bear that meaning. And he had been told twice that he has failed his friend. But self-reproach is not to the point; self-incitement is. I take it that not in anger but something close to it, furious urgency, Jesus is nerving himself to

an extraordinary act. "Sternly enjoined" is not strong enough;
therefore, "raged at."

12.11   "going away." That is, leaving the flock, deserting, defecting.

12.34   "remains." That is, here or *with us*.

"must be lifted aloft." That is, taken away *from us*. See also
8.28.

12.43   "glory of God." The word *doxa*, used here twice, can mean
both "opinion" and "glory." See the note on 5.41.

13.2   "betray him." This I take to be the meaning of the Greek, rather
than "the devil had already put it into the heart of Judas . . .
to betray him."

13.19   "I am I." Or, simply, "I am."

15.27   "Do you also bear witness." Or "You also are my witnesses."

16.2   "will be thought to be doing a service to God." Or "will think
he is doing a service to God."

17.15   "evil." Or "the evil one."

19.20   "Jews." That is, the people of Jerusalem, see the notes on 4.9
and 11.19.

ACTS

6.1   "Hellenists." These would be Greek or Greek-speaking Jews,
not Hebrews but converted to Judaism or descended from such
converts, and now converted to Christianity. They are to be
sharply distinguished from the Gentiles, who do not accept
Judaism.

7.2–53   This is *all* a continuous speech of Stephen's.

7.60   "he fell asleep." That is, he died; but the choice of this expres-
sion for a death in such violent circumstances is surely
deliberate.

8.36–38   "baptized? . . . So he ordered." Omitting the suspect verse
37, which reads: "Philip said to him: If you believe with all

your heart, it is permitted. He answered and said: I believe that Jesus Christ is the son of God." Even here there are variations.

9.36   "which translated means Dorcas." Dorcas means "gazelle."

12.17   "James." The reference is to James the brother of Jesus Christ. See Galatians 1.19.

13.9   "Saul, who is also Paul." After this point, "Paul" is regularly used in Acts, as elsewhere.

14.19   "from Antioch and Iconium." The Antioch meant here is the city in Pisidia previously visited by Paul, not the great city in Syria.

15.14   "Simon," Properly, "Symeon." The reference is to Saint Peter.

15.33–35   "sent them . . . But Paul." Omitting verse 34, which is doubtful and uncertain.

16.6   "Asia." This signifies, not the whole continent or even the whole of what we call Asia Minor, but the Roman province of Asia.

16.10   "We." This first person plural, which comes in so abruptly, will reappear from time to time in *Acts*, ostensibly indicating that the author himself was present during some of Paul's travels.

17.19   "Areopagus." "The Hill of Ares" in Athens, and the court or council located on top of it.

19.9   "Way of God." The Greek has simply "the Way."

19.31   "Asiarchs." This apparently means members of the governing council of the Province of Asia.

20.28   "guardians." Or "bishops" (*episkopoi*).

23.8   "and neither angel nor spirit." The probability is that the Sadducees disbelieved in resurrection either *as* (in the form of) angel or as spirit.

25.13   "King Agrippa and Bernice." This is Herod Agrippa II, son of the Herod whose death is recorded in 12.23. Bernice (it should really be Berenice) was his sister, also his mistress.

25.25   The terms "Augustus," "our master" (26), and "Caesar" (11, 21) all refer to the Emperor Nero.

28.28–30   "listen . . . He remained." Omitting verse 29, which reads: "When he said this, the Jews went away with much discussion among themselves."

ROMANS

2.12   "outside the law." Paul here continues the contrast of Greeks, or Gentiles (outside the law), and Jews (inside the law).

9.16   "But that is not a matter of wish or effort but of God's mercy." Literally: "But that does not belong to him who wishes or him who runs, but to God, who has mercy."

10.14   "preach." Literally: "announce," "proclaim."

12.6–8   "We have . . . graciousness." The original is one long sentence which has no main verb or any independent clause at all. The translator has to fabricate some structure.

15.11   "All nations, praise the Lord." The word *ethne*, usually translated as "Gentiles," here seems to indicate *all* the nations of the world.

1 CORINTHIANS

1.12   "Christ is partitioned!" Or "Is Christ partitioned?"

2.14   "sensual." The sensual man is contrasted to the spiritual, as being alive, but animated by the earthly *psyche* rather than the unearthly *pneuma*, which is the word used for the Holy Spirit.

7.25   "unmarried." The word is *parthenoi*, generally used of girls, but what follows is obviously directed to the unmarried of both sexes.

10.11   "end of the world." Or "the ends of the ages."

11.4   "prophesies." This is not here introduced as if it were an activity requiring extraordinary gifts, and presumably may mean nothing more than reading, quoting, or interpreting scripture. See also 14.1ff. and note.

11.10   "Therefore a woman should take care of her head, because of the angels." Translation and exact bearing are uncertain.

12.7   "to his advantage." Or "for the common good."

14.1   In what follows, "prophesying" is contrasted with "speaking with tongues." The latter describes an attested phenomenon, "the broken speech of persons in religious ecstasy." By contrast, prophecy is reasoned, comprehensible utterance. See 11.4 and note.

15.19   "If by this life in Christ we are no more than hopeful." Or "If our hopes in Christ are for this life only."

2 CORINTHIANS

2.5   "supposing someone really has caused trouble." A particular case is obviously being referred to.

5.3   "Still in our bodies covered and not naked." The reference may possibly be to those who are found still alive on the Day of Judgment.

12.7   "a thorn." The Greek is *skolops*, a stake or spike.

GALATIANS

1.18   "Peter." Here, as always except for Galatians 2.7, Paul uses the Hebrew form, "Cephas." See John 1.42 and note.

2.4   "but only might have been" is not in the text. I have supplied it, provisionally, for the sake of sense and syntax. An occasional unconstructed sentence is characteristic of Saint Paul.

4.13   "You know that I was sick in body when I brought you the gospel before." Or "You know that it was because of bodily sickness that I brought you the gospel before." This is better (Greek) grammar but poorer sense.

5.20   "envy" (Greek *phthonoi*). But the Latin has *homicidia* (Greek *phonoi*), that is, murder.

EPHESIANS

3.1   "say this to you." Conjecturally supplied; there is no main verb, or any independent clause at all.

4.11   "pastors." Literally, "shepherds."

4.26   "Are you angry? Even so, do no wrong." The simplest literal translation would be: "Be angry and do not sin."

PHILIPPIANS

3.5   "a Hebrew of Hebrews." Or "a Hebrew with Hebrew parents."

4.12   "do without." The word here usually means "be humble," but we seem to need something that will contrast with having plenty.

1 THESSALONIANS

4.13   "those who are asleep." These sleepers are, of course, the Christian dead or "those who are dead in Christ" (16).

5.5   "catch you like thieves." Or "come upon you like a thief" (alternate readings).

2 THESSALONIANS

1.10   "because our testimony to you was believed." If the text is sound, as it probably is not, "because" must refer back to the just reward of the Thessalonians, because they believed.

1.12   "our God and the Lord Jesus Christ." Or "our God and Lord Jesus Christ."

1 TIMOTHY

5.5   "lives alone." Or "has been left desolate."

5.16   Text and sense uncertain.

2 TIMOTHY

3.3   "troublemakers." The word is *diaboloi*.

TITUS

1.10   "from among the circumcised." From Jews, that is, rather than Gentiles.

1.12   "their own prophet." The allusion is not to any contemporary but to the almost mythical Epimenides of Crete (sixth century B.C.).

2.10   "among people in general." Or "in every way."

2.13   "the great God and our savior." Or "our great God and savior."

3.10   "heretic." Or perhaps merely a factious man, a causer of dissensions.

HEBREWS

2.7 "a little lower than the angels." Or "for a little while lower than the angels."

3.11 "rest." Or "resting place."

JAMES

1.9 "Let the humble . . . humiliation." A variation on the familiar theme that God can easily bring down the rich and powerful and exalt the poor and weak.

1.12–13 "trial," "tempted." We pass from one to the other sense of the Greek *peirazō, peirasmos.*

3.6 "wheel of creation." Or "round of existence."

5.6 "Is he not against you?" Or, without the question mark: "He does not resist you."

1 PETER

3.1 "even without the word." The hope is that they may be influenced to act like Christians without being actually converted. But the sense may be "without a word being spoken."

5.13 "Babylon." That is, Rome.

2 PETER

1.13 "of the flesh" is not in the text. Supplied for the sake of clarity.

2.14 "full of adultery." The Greek *moichalis* properly means, however, an adulterous woman, but this is hard to construe with "full of." The phrase might be wrested into meaning "on the lookout for an adulterous woman."

1 JOHN

3.7 "the Lord." Greek: "he." So also in 3.16.
4.2 "The Spirit of God is known." Or "you know the Spirit of God."
5.8 "the three are at one." Or "the three agree."

2 JOHN

1 "lady." She is surely not a person; this is a letter from the elder (leader) of one church to another church.

THE REVELATION OF JOHN

22.21 Or "with his saints."